D1808053

WILLING ACCOMPLICES

WILLING ACCOMPLICES

How KGB Covert Influence Agents
Created Political Correctness,
Obama's Hate-America-First Political Platform,
And Destroyed America

Kent Clizbe

For those who care to see, and those who dare to see.

Ashburn, Virginia, USA
www.kentclizbe.com
kent@kentclizbe.com

10 9 8 7 6 5 4 3 2

TABLE OF CONTENTS

Preface

In Willing Accomplices, using counter-intelligence analytical techniques honed while serving as an espionage officer in the CIA, I will demonstrate that the emergence of Political Correctness (PC) in America was as intentionally orchestrated as Coca-Cola's advertising is carefully planned and implemented.

Perhaps it should come as no surprise that the roots of the strategy to implant PC in the American ethos came from an old and familiar adversary: the former Soviet Union's Committee for State Security (Russian acronym—*KGB*).

My thesis is that the KGB, beginning soon after the Communist takeover of Russia in 1917, implemented massive covert influence operations. Their goal was to destroy the core moral fabric of American society. Taking advantage of the intellectual and philosophical climate of the early 1900s, the Soviet intelligence apparatus began what would now be called in intelligence circles, "a preparation of the battle space" to move the world towards the inevitable dictatorship of the proletariat. Covert operatives realized that America's greatest strengths were its proud exceptionalism and belief that freedom and liberty were part of man's divine destiny. Our free society also made us vulnerable to covert operations. KGB case officers and their agents had easy access to a wide range of American society.

Prior to and during the Russian Revolution, Bolshevik head Vladimir Lenin and his cronies learned the value of conspiratorial practices and the value of disinformation, propaganda, agents of influence, and other covert influence techniques. Russian society and culture were uniquely suited for these practices of secrecy and espionage. Trotsky described his first experience in Communist agitation, saying "[w]e knew...contacts with workers demanded secret, highly 'conspiratorial' methods. And we pronounced the word solemnly, with a reverence that was almost mystic."

The Bolsheviks employed these tactics first during the many years of preparation for the October Revolution but then more ambitiously as part of a long term project that was designed to soften their capitalist enemies for their imagined global Communist revolution.

A target of energetic covert influence operations was the Soviet Union's "Main Adversary"—the United States. The covert operations, in which KGB officers recruited and ran agents, were aimed at influencing "Innocents," which is the term Soviet covert operatives used to describe Westerners who could be manipulated into doing the Communists' bidding.

The KGB identified and focused on the three areas of a free society that pass on its cultural heritage: the media, academia and education, and entertainment. In addition, they focused their efforts on vulnerable governmental policy-makers, particularly in the State Department.

Using experienced operatives and highly compartmented operations, the KGB sought to insert covert influence "payloads" designed to call into question the fundamental bases on which American society and culture had been built. Many American Progressives eagerly carried out these covert operations for the Communists. Others not involved in the operations received the covert messages and accepted them as gospel.

The messengers denigrated American patriotism, capitalism, and individualism, and called into question American foreign policy. The critical view of America seemed to form the philosophical basis of an elite anti-American attitude. The attitude coalesced during the Great Depression. It was nurtured and strengthened by the

American transmitters of the KGB's covert influence operations: journalists, screenwriters, and professors, among others.

Willing Accomplices

I call these Americans "Willing Accomplices." They were witting, and unwitting, agents of influence. They were Willing to imbibe the superior attitude conferred by the high-minded ideals of the fronts. And they were Accomplices to the communists' goal of destroying their country—the greatest cultural destruction operation in the history of mankind.

The Willing Accomplices in the KGB's efforts to destroy American culture may, or may not, have known exactly who they were dealing with. They may, or may not, have known that the KGB was helping them. They may, or may not, have known that they were receiving special treatment and favors for being a conduit for the "America is a hateful place" message.

Whether they were witting or unwitting of KGB or Comintern involvement by their friends does not matter. Whether they actively spread the influence payload of the Soviets, of hate-America-first, out of good intentions, or because of true belief in normal America's inferiority and their own, and Soviet, superiority, does not matter. Whether they received a bundle of cash, or a check, or any money at all does not matter. As we'll see in the counterintelligence analysis chapter, each of the Willing Accomplices put themselves in the control of the Russians, and their situations favorably changed.

Recent writers have used the term *Dupes* for the fellow travelers and others who fell within the communist sphere of influence. This is too kind, and at the same time misunderstands the true nature of most communist operations. The targets, the Willing Accomplices, may have appeared to be duped, but as we'll see, this appearance was a fig leaf, provided by the Soviets to their Accomplices, so they could appear innocent, if their conscience or reputation required that appearance.

The communist master of feel-good America hating, Willi Muenzenberg perfected the "Popular Front" operational concept. He and his agents set up multiple organizations with high-minded names and reasons for existence—for example the International Congress Against Fascism and War, and the Hollywood Anti-Nazi League. These fronts gave intellectuals, journalists, artists, and educators a higher calling—while serving as cover to insert covert influence payloads into the targeted cultures.

The perceived moral superiority of the Soviet's covert influence messages provided Popular Front members a chance to show "you were a decent human being," in fact, a better human being. Muenzenberg despised these Popular Front members, and called them "Innocents."

A Willing Accomplice in Hollywood, in the 1950s, commented that by participating in anti-anti-communist groups, "I would be spared the agony of thinking my way through difficult issues: all the thinking would be done for me by an elite core of trained [thinkers]..."

The goal of the operations was to make Americans feel that their country was bad. The KGB utilized Willing Accomplices to spread the message that America was an evil, racist, imperialist war-monger and that Communism was a benign, noble experiment designed to rid the world of corruption, oppression and injustice.

Covert Influence Payload

Babette Gross, wife of KGB agent Willi Muenzenberg, explained the content of the Soviet payload to Stephen Koch:

> You claim to be an independent-minded idealist.
>
> You don't really understand politics, but you think the little guy is getting a lousy break.
>
> You believe in open-mindedness.
>
> You are shocked, frightened by what is going on right here in our own country.
>
> You're frightened by the racism, by the oppression of the workingman.
>
> You think the Russians are trying a great human experiment, and you hope it works.
>
> You believe in peace.
>
> You yearn for international understanding.
>
> You hate fascism.
>
> You think the capitalist system is corrupt.

This payload exactly matches today's PC-Progressive message. The message that Soviet covert operators propagated through American Willing Accomplices. The Willing Accomplices, wittingly or unwittingly, spread the anti-American message. And this message bloomed and grew into the pernicious set of taboos and strictures that we call PC today.

It is important to note that Soviet espionage simply planted the seeds of PC. The seedlings did not need continued communist cultivation. The Soviets' American Willing Accomplices nurtured the anti-American message in universities, newsrooms, and in Hollywood.

After the payloads were planted, the vast majority of the communist intelligence operatives met the fate of most stooges of totalitarian thugs—violent death at the hands of their comrades.

Communist dictators demand absolute obedience. Nimble, smart, and crafty, covert influence operators did not make good slaves. Stalin feared their abilities. One by one, they were called back to Moscow. An economical one-bullet execution, a 7.62x38mm slug from the KGB's favorite revolver, the Nagant M1895, ended the lives of the fathers of American PC.

The attitude of wise superiority to the American masses, disdain for the racist, sexist, homophobic, foreigner-hating, dead-white-male-worshipping ignoramuses spread quickly throughout the three domains of cultural transmission. First academia rejected traditional America, her people, her founders, and her foundations. The press was next, closely followed by Hollywood.

The most stunning aspect of Muenzenberg's message was its ability to self-propagate. Like a fertile flower, once planted and growing, it spread its seeds far and wide, with no need for a gardener to nurture it. The payload, so powerful and seductive, once planted in the American intelligentsia, grew and metastasized, like a political cancer, until it burst forth in full flower as PC in the 1980s.

Muenzenberg's skillful covert influence operations, aiming to destroy American Exceptionalism, are still bearing fruit today. Willi's influence operations outlived every one of the Comintern officers that recruited the Willing Accomplices, the American agents who carried the influence messages into the heart of our culture. The effects of Willi's operations outlived the USSR, and communism as a practical political platform.

PC 2011: Reflexive Loathing of the United States

It is not likely that any of the Comintern covert influence operators realized that they were creating a monster that would grow for decades. They likely believed that after a few years their ops would have sown enough confusion to cause the global communist revolution they knew was coming. Even though the revolution never came in their lifetimes, the "hate America first" attitude slowly caught on. The Elites spread their anti-American message. It had to go underground from the late 1940s to the early 1960s. But after the late 1960s, the Elite Vanguard emerged in full flower.

A more concise description of PC cannot be found than Babette Gross's formulation of Muenzenberg's covert influence payload. Look inside any PC ideas, speech codes, or requirements, and you'll find a "reflexive loathing" of traditional America, our values, history, and morals.

By the late 1980s, full-blown PC infected academia, education, the media, Hollywood, and American society in general. Americans were constantly bombarded with reminders of their hatefulness, bigotry, racism, sexism, and imperialism. Confused by the message of hate and disgust, while their daily lives were filled with positive energy, normal Americans became wracked with guilt. They were reminded daily that they were guilty of slavery, bigotry, killing babies in Vietnam, oppressing minorities and women around the globe, stealing the continent from the Indians, being arrogant in dealing with foreigners, killing the Earth with their hairspray, and various other sins.

In 2008, PC blossomed into full flower. In a spasm of PC-induced guilt, America elected our first anti-American president, who did not hide his disgust for normal Americans. Obama is the first president to apologize repeatedly for America's sins against foreign countries, and to speak disparagingly against the country that elected him. Obama's cool, detached Elite attitude, loathing the "bitter clingers" of the heartland, is a living testament to the power and success of Muenzenberg's covert influence operations.

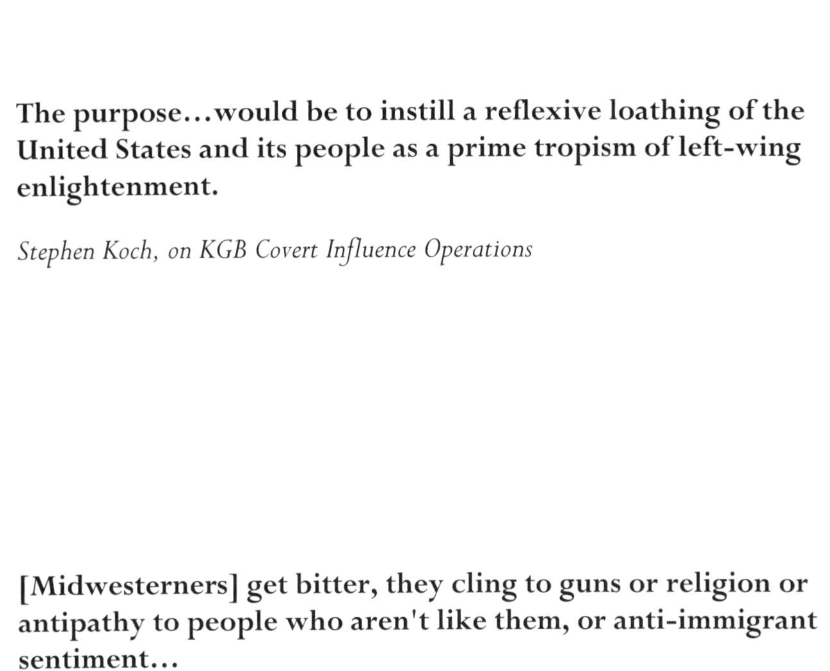

The purpose...would be to instill a reflexive loathing of the United States and its people as a prime tropism of left-wing enlightenment.

Stephen Koch, on KGB Covert Influence Operations

[Midwesterners] get bitter, they cling to guns or religion or antipathy to people who aren't like them, or anti-immigrant sentiment...

Barack Obama, Reflexive loathing on display, San Francisco, April 2008

Admit nothing. Deny everything. Make counter-accusations.

Covert Operations Motto

PART ONE

LENIN'S OP

Chapter 1

Unique qualifications

I was fed the milk of "racist, sexist, imperialist American warmongers" through the nipple of my baby bottle. My familiarity with both the messages and the methods of the anti-American left sensitized me as I began to search for the covert influence that produced these attitudes.

Red Diaper Baby

Although it took me the better part of my adult life to figure it out, I was raised, in effect, as a red diaper baby. My father grew up adrift in the post-war generation, born in 1930, too young to fight in World War II, and at an impressionable age during the post-war so-called "Red Scare" years. Possibly influenced by a distant relative, who was a Wobbly (member of the communist International Workers of the World), and definitely influenced by hatred of his own father, who he disrespectfully referred to as "Moose", he was fair game for the leftist propaganda washing over the country during those years. He fell for it hook, line and sinker.

My Dad rejected his familial birthright of our ancestors' Puritanism, Methodist-Episcopalianism or Congregationalism, and dabbled in Unitarianism, subjecting me and my siblings to several years of organized atheism. Working for the federal government, in the Bureau of Indian affairs, he saw poverty on Indian reservations first hand. A transfer to a civilian job with the Air Force in Puerto Rico led to his being involved with Puerto Rican laborers with grievances against their Federal employers. A true believer, who put workers' Solidarity over the well-being of his family, my father took up the fight for the downtrodden workers, at the expense of his own job, his marriage, his family, his health, and ultimately his sanity.

Unfortunately, he took the propaganda seriously, and attempted to live his life by the leftist code. He left his wife and family, took a Colombian wife, who used him to secure a green card, and then quickly dumped him. He ended up bankrupt after a starry eyed business failure (a water-powered grist mill in the swamps of upstate New York, just as the demand for local milling died out). He joined various bands of itinerant hippies, migrant workers, and a circus until his Volkswagen bus finally died, and he lost mobility.

Leeching off his step-mother, who he plied with a passive-aggressive guilt trip, the last 20 years of his life were a pitiful slide down a steep slope. At the bottom of that slope was a dumpster in San Diego near the storage lockers where he lived. He dived in the dumpster, searching for rotten meat to feed his only companion, a dog. His over-exerted, swollen heart had enough. He suffered a massive heart attack and stroke in the dumpster. He never made it back to his storage lockers, where he kept his flea market junk, which he was sure would be valuable someday.

I made the trip out to California and cleaned the junk out of his storage lockers. The vain search for some hints to help me understand this pitifully failed life provided a satisfactory closure to my relationship with my Dad.

Only after his death did I really analyze his life. I came to realize that instead of being the villain of the piece, as I, the abandoned child, in my self-centered universe had considered him; my Dad was actually the victim. A smart and sensitive young man, headstrong and willful, he clashed with his father during his teenage years. Apparently, this led him to reject anything that smacked of paternalism, or authority, and to embrace attitudes that seemed rebellious. This set him up, during the 50s and 60s, as an almost perfect convert to the leftist cause. And convert to the leftist cause he did indeed.

Growing up, I can remember our home being filled with leftist literature, even though at the time I had no idea what it was, and socialist messages, activities, and propaganda: *Ramparts* magazine, *New Republic* magazine, evenings around the campfire singing communist hymns like "Joe Hill", listening to endless repetitions of folk song recordings by Pete Seeger and other communists pounded the socialist message into my little skull-full-of-mush, attending a Unitarian congregation and participating in their Christmas pageant by reciting that well-known religious nursery rhyme, "Little Jack Horner," being inundated with leftist political slogans, like "it's the smell of Goldwater," when passing a stinking chemical refinery. Such are the memories of the infant son of a socialist.

I guess the only lucky thing is that he was out of my life by the time I was ten. Even so, it took me the better part of two decades to overcome my brainwashing as a child and emerge with a clear mind able to differentiate reality from utopian dreams.

My socialist childhood, prepared me well for this undertaking. I was nursed on the covert influence messages fed into the American Socialist brotherhood. I ate, slept and breathed loathing of America. I was fed the milk of "racist, sexist, imperialist American warmongers" through the nipple of my baby bottle. My familiarity with both the messages and the methods of the anti-American left sensitized me as I began to search for the covert influence that produced these messages.

Development of the Case Officer Skill-set

An adolescence spent in blissful ignorance of international affairs provided me with a valuable skill set which I later put to use in intelligence operations—street smarts. After my parents' divorce, my mother returned to her rural Southern roots. Growing up in a small town in rural North Carolina in the 1970s, experimenting with illegal substances, under-age drinking, fighting, and cruising for action every night, beer in hand, through the two county area—Halifax and Northampton counties, North Carolina. Constantly on the lookout for police, friends being arrested killed and maimed in accidents—that semi-underground life developed a valuable point of view. Being "the hunted" was perfect training for intelligence operations.

One night Johnny and I were out with two high school girls, experimenting with mixing marijuana and cheap wine. When we stopped, to let the girls pee, at a motel that was closed for the night, around midnight, a highway patrolman noticed us. When the cop did a u-turn a quarter mile down the road, to follow us, I quickly turned off at the next side street. Pulling into a driveway a couple hundred yards down the street, I hid the car in the dense bushes surrounding the dark house. The patrolman sped by, and we all breathed a sigh of relief—until he slammed on his brakes and reversed back to the driveway.

After the patrolman pulled me from the car, he shone his light inside. This was another test of my skills in dealing with hostile authorities. I passed with flying colors. Explaining that we were taking the girls home, I assured the patrolman that we were heading home before we saw his car. The patrolman confiscated the open bottle of wine, ignored the bag of marijuana and counseled me to drive directly to the girls' homes, and then directly to my home. After thanking him and apologizing, I drove away. I also learned not to step on the brake pedal, when you're trying to hide from the police in a dark driveway.

Multiple run-ins with the law like this during the course of my late teenage and college years, although they never led to an arrest, were unparalleled real-world training for intelligence operations. Suffering through a couple of muggings, a near-by shooting, witnessing several drunken assaults, all were tucked away in my growing bag of experiences.

My brief college career out of high school was doomed from the start. In the summer of 1978, the year I graduated, two events came together that ensured I could not finish my degree. First, Playboy magazine named East Carolina University the number one "party school" in the country. And second, *National Lampoon's Animal House* was released. Non-stop keg parties, toga parties, foosball in downtown bars, art parties, football parties, party parties, road trips, beach trips, mountain trips, and every imaginable and unimaginable frivolity fully engaged my attention. While my academic career suffered, with a final GPA of 0.25 after two years of "study," my social skills were dramatically improved. I could approach anyone, anywhere, at any time and talk about any subject for any length of time.

I met and got to know foreigners for the first time (I'll never forget chatting for an hour with a stoned Ethiopian with a huge floppy afro, while he sat outside the Attic bar and hallucinated.) This two year hiatus came to an end when I hit bottom while working as the screen maker in a t-shirt factory for five dollars an hour. While the job allowed me to remain in the party town, the paycheck was not enough to pay for a six-pack every night, and rent, gas for my motorcycle, and food. It only took me six months to realize there was no future in this. After a visit to the Air Force recruiter, I began the rest of my life.

Foreign Cultures

Operating in a foreign culture became second nature after joining the Air Force. Military aptitude tests revealed my affinity for foreign languages. After a one year course in Vietnamese at the Defense Language Institute in Monterey, California, I found myself deployed for three years at Clark Air Base, in the Philippines. The local bars were like a cross-cultural laboratory. I enthusiastically threw myself into a practical study of this Southeast Asian culture. Being arrested by the Air Police for "grave oral defamation" (cursing is a crime in the Philippines), let me see the inside of a military jail.

After the military, I earned a BA in Southeast Asian studies, and worked in Vietnamese refugee programs in America and abroad, supervising teachers of cross-cultural training and English as a Second Language (ESL) for refugees. ESL brought me to a university in the middle of the al-Qaeda recruitment grounds in Saudi Arabia. Marriage to a Malaysian fellow student in Illinois required my conversion to Islam. This status opened the doors for an in-depth orientation to the inner workings of Islamic extremism in Saudi Arabia.

As the only westerner in the province, I was invited to desert picnics, which in retrospect were likely recruiting events for the jihad that was going on, in the late 80s, against the Soviets in Afghanistan. In the Wahabi heartland, I learned several lessons. One was that the Saudi-dominated religion was cruel and morally bankrupt. I quickly identified the problems inherent in the dysfunctional twisting of medieval Saudi culture, the Arabic language, and the Muslim religion. But, immersed daily in the extremist culture, I also developed a deep understanding of these people who despised my culture.

Trips to Mecca and Medina, in the company of my faculty colleagues—all of them were Arabs, from Egypt, Palestine, Jordan, Iraq, Libya, Tunisia, Algeria, Sudan, and other countries—added to my stock of experience. Saudi security forces stopped our bus at the entrance to Mecca. Singling out the only American, they confiscated my iqama, internal passport, and kept the bus waiting for nearly an hour before releasing us.

Arrested by the Saudi provincial police, after my car's license plate fell off during a tire blow-out, I had to make my case, with the help of an Egyptian driver, in the majlis (open court) of the local potentate. These and other experiences taught me lessons about the absolute power of minor minions in a totalitarian regime. I learned how to scrape and bow with the rest of the subjects.

Later, I took part in the hajj in Mecca and Medina, with Muslim Americans and Canadians. Living cheek-by-jowl with several million Muslims, moving in unison through the rites, I developed insights into the complex inner workings of the Islamic community. My companions provided case studies of America jihadis. The Black Muslim from the Bronx, a wandering sad-sack, who went from training camps in Pakistan, to a mosque in Mauritania, to the hajj, constantly moaning about his need for a wife.

Watching the Iranians arrive in their buses with the tops sheared off; the Dagestanis selling animal skins and Russian optics by the side of the road. African children, hobbled and blinded for sympathy, put on display by their owners, collecting donations. The gang of huge Africans, pumped up as if on amphetamines, jumping up and down like kangaroos, forcing their way through the crowd at the stoning of the devil rites. These and more added to my store of understanding.

Working for, and with and in, British, Italian, Malaysian, Filipino, and various other foreign cultures, in foreign companies, taught me how to maneuver in these cultures. These lessons could never come from a school. They were life lessons, only available to those willing to live outside the comfort zone.

Applications in Espionage

My career in the CIA began when I was nearly 35. After returning from my ESL work overseas, during and after graduate school, I worked a variety of menial jobs. These included a stint at the National Sexually Transmitted Diseases (STD) Hotline. Answering the concerns of up to a hundred sexually active callers a day provided another lesson in patiently dealing with the dregs of the earth.

Then after leaving the Agency, I put my recruiting skills to work in the dot.com boom. I established myself as the world's premier headhunter for Computational Linguistics. I used my skills to analyze my client's talent needs, create a position description, and then to find the proper candidate to fill that position. I left this lucrative business after 9/11 to serve as a contractor in multiple counter-terrorism deployments around the globe.

During my career in the CIA, operational training covered all aspects of human intelligence collection. I trained in both official cover and nonofficial cover operations. By that time I was a natural salesman, and the development and recruiting exercises during training were no problem at all.

However, operational writing and research was a challenge. I had been spoiled by two different bureaucratic systems. The military writing style is more like telegraphy, straight and to the point, with no wasted words, thoughts, feelings, or emotions needed or wanted. On the other hand, graduate school writing style was all third person passive voice, convoluted, with extra points for lack of clarity.

Once the old alcoholic NOC who was my primary instructor got through to me that we were paid for our judgments and assessments, my operational writing opened up and became a better chronicle of my operational activities.

My abilities in the fundamental tasks of an intelligence operative were quickly confirmed, during my first assignments. Unfortunately, I also discovered the bureaucratic sclerosis that is choking off the flow of blood to the Agency's brain. I arrived in time to be in the first sexual harassment training sessions, and to see the initial affirmative action based assignments and promotions. While the "good old boys" network was hobbled, at the same time an affirmative action network—the estrogen crowd—was created.

The dreaded part of operational training was time spent in Headquarters, "riding a desk." But I soon learned that this was not as dreadful as my colleagues made it out to be, at least not for me. For a student of human psychology, fascinated by human motivations, delving into operational records was better than reading novels. A case file, from the case officer's first meeting the target at a reception, through the developmental meetings on the golf course or in sleazy bars, through the eventual recruitment, provided hours of interesting diversion.

Extensive Ops Research

As a CIA case officer, my experience included thousands of hours conducting operational research in the CIA's records system. Each meeting with a contact that occurs anywhere in the world creates a request for a search to be conducted in the CIA's operational records system. The search, if it results in no records found, may take only a few minutes. Depending on the individual's name, the search can result in scores of records being uncovered. Wading through the "hits," weighing and evaluating each of these documents, can take hours and days for just one case. And this is just for a simple trace.

When a case becomes complex, with an interlocking network of people, operations, organizations, governments, technical equipment, training, travel, trade craft, and CI issues, reading and analyzing a file can become a time sink. An effective headquarters operations officer, providing support to operations in the field from headquarters, needs to be able to perform this research quickly and accurately.

It's a function that is best done by an experienced field officer. However, a paradox of the espionage profession is that experienced field operations officers generally have absolutely no interest in performing operations support from headquarters. While I am at heart and personality a field ops officer, due to my personal and family situation, as well as bureaucratic issues, I have spent more than my fair share of time performing support operations from headquarters.

The personality of a successful operations officer is comparable to that of a salesman. However, an operations officer's job is sales in reverse. That is the case officer, when developing a target, and when eventually pitching the target, instead of asking his "customer" to pay money for a product or service, actually offers money to his "customer" in return for provision of a product or service. This sales-turned-upside-down still requires the personality and skills of a sales expert, the ability to earn that customer's trust and to appear to be friends with the customer—to share that customer's interests, and the ability to make that customer believe that you truly care about him.

What a case officer offers in return for treason is the solution of his agent's problems. Identification of his agent's problems/issues is what the "developmental" process is all about. During this process the case officer "befriends" his target. The case officer delves deeply into the developmental agent's psyche, identifying potential motivations and vulnerabilities. The case officer accompanies the developmental agent on recreational and social outings. The case officer may involve his own family in this process. When done correctly, the target doesn't realize what's going on, viewing the whole process as just a normal social relationship.

Each and every step, during this developmental process is documented in official agency channels. One two-hour meeting can result in a written message to Headquarters, exceeding 15 or 20 pages. The case officer must document, in addition to the motivations and vulnerabilities of the developmental, his access, or potential access, to targeted information, or other intelligence objectives.

Back home, ops support officers read each message "with interest." Counterintelligence officials attempt to remain up-to-date on each of the developments occurring in their areas of responsibility. Their job is to advise and assist the operations officers in the process of validating each of the targets being considered for recruitment, in addition to those already recruited.

While I'm more at home and comfortable working in a foreign environment, I have also spent many years working with operational records. In researching Soviet covert influence operations, my operational point of view and experience, both in the field and in headquarters, provides an advantage over other researchers and writers who have considered Soviet espionage operations in the United States, but have never written, filed, or delved into operational records.

Demand Operational Results

In fact, my point of view as an espionage operator is also unique among most intelligence officers. Because I had long experience in the private sector, I brought a unique perspective to my intelligence operations. My commercially-influenced operational style was to demand results from my operations. That is, I looked at intelligence operations much like a commercial investment, or business transaction. While that may seem intuitive to those who have never been in the government service, it is actually quite unusual for a bureaucrat to think this way.

Application of Experience

The *Willing Accomplices* research project involved examining 100 year old diaries, memoirs, biographies, and other sources, delving into personalities, motivations, connections, and beliefs of suspected agents. This process is almost exactly like doing a counter-intelligence review of an intelligence case file. My instincts, street sense, knowledge of intelligence recruiting and human motivations, and experience evaluating such cases, along with careful analysis of the cases result in diagnoses and opinions that add exponential knowledge to the uninformed, amateur points of view of the historians who have considered these cases to date.

When comparing my ability to spot counter-intelligence issues in the historical record to the historians who have been studied and written about these cases in the past, a good analogy might be an annoying noise in your Ford Focus. You could drive your car for years with the noise. You hear it constantly, but you have absolutely no idea what it signifies. To you, it is a clunking squeak that seems to be coming from the backseat.

But when a Ford mechanic, a professional who has taken apart and put back together more than 5,000 Fords in the last twenty years, drives your car, he immediately diagnoses the problem, with one listen, "Your u-joint's needle bearings are going." Twenty years of experience and hands-on work go into that 10 second diagnosis.

You could drive your car for the next twenty years, and you would never have understood what was making the noise. Historians have studied and written about most of the Willing Accomplices that I reveal here. There are biographies and memoirs, articles and reports, on most of the subjects. Some of the biographers and writers report on the squeaks coming from their subjects, but none of them have had the skills necessary to diagnose the source of the squeaking.

In *Willing Accomplices*, I will diagnose the squeaks, and walk you through the analysis.

Shocking Conclusion

There is traditionally not a lot of accountability for operational results in any intelligence bureaucracy. However, linking operations and results was what led me to research the results of communist covert influence operations against the United States.

I knew that the Communists had run intelligence *collection* operations against America; and I knew that Progressive-PC had emerged in the 1980s. The questions that have never before been answered are:

> Did the KGB run covert influence operations against the U.S.?
>
> If so, how effective were those operations?
>
> What were the KGB's covert influence payloads?
>
> Did those payloads give birth to PC?

I believe that you will come to the same shocking conclusion I did, after you study the evidence I've compiled in *Willing Accomplices*.

Chapter 2

Field already plowed?

A tantalizing lure has trapped most researchers and historians who specialize in Soviet intelligence operations against the USA. That is the Communist Party of the USA (CPUSA).

A close reading of the work of cultural commentators, from the late 1990s up to today, will show that conservative commentators consistently express puzzlement at the Politically Correct attitudes and actions of Progressives. At times, conservatives lash out at Progressives as "Marxists." Listening to one of these commentators, in late 2007, it dawned on me that although today's Progressives are not card-carrying Marxists, their message surely has much in common with Marxism, in many ways.

This started me thinking about how this connection came to be. As an intelligence professional, I eventually came around to considering espionage as a potential connection. Reviewing the Venona files, and the Mitrokhin files, led me to deeper and deeper study of Communist espionage operations. Eventually, I discovered in-depth documentation of the KGB covert influence operations, although no operational files.

The research has been a long and sometimes tedious road to follow. However, I've uncovered a treasure trove of original documents, and much secondary material. Traveling around the country visiting archives and libraries, online searches, telephone interviews, all contributed to this search.

I left the government service during the dot.com boom in the 1990s to open an executive recruiting agency. I had not given a second thought to government intelligence operations after that, until that sunny September morning in 2001. After the plane hit the Pentagon, fighting traffic down the Dulles Toll Road to my kids' school, ditching my car in a parking lot, and walking the last half-mile because of the backed up traffic, reports were that one more plane was heading towards Washington DC.

As for thinking about communism, even when I had been a CIA operations officer, the Berlin Wall had just fallen, the USSR had just crumbled, and beyond running into KGB case officers on the circuit, I had paid little attention to communism. The last time I had seriously considered communism was during my study of the Vietnamese language, and the extensive vocabulary I picked up at that time. Working against the Vietnamese Communists, listening to their radio transmissions, had led me to study both the Vietnam War and Communism in depth. But that was more than 20 years ago.

I did a brief review of Marxism-Leninism and its goals and objectives, as well as a review of the Soviet leadership's policies towards the United States. The more I learned, the clearer the link became between the Soviets' ancient policies, international Communism's goals, the KGB's covert influence operations designed to achieve those goals and policies, and today's PC.

Interestingly, I uncovered U.S. Congressional hearings into what they called at the time, "subversive activities" against the U.S. Looking more deeply into these investigations, I found several contemporary (1917-1950) publications, by civilians and U.S. government officials, that indicated a general understanding of influence operations, and the danger the communist influence posed to American culture and society. These publications, and their authors, seem to have faded down the memory-hole.

Generally speaking, the authors and analysts who saw the influence happening, during its early days, were criticized and denounced as “Red baiters,” “racists,” and other derogatory terms. This too, as we’ll see later, is a manifestation of Soviet Active Measures operations. If the influence message is exposed, the tactics shift to making counter-accusations. This tactic is quite familiar to conservative politicians and commentators today, who face the wrath of the Progressives, heirs of the Soviet Active Measure strategies and tactics.

Although many former CIA case officers have written memoirs, autobiographies, and fiction, generally speaking these works have not included research into the questions I consider here. While interesting and relevant, the former CIA officers’ works have not considered the effects of Soviet covert influence operations on modern day American culture, politics, or society. Generally speaking, works by former CIA officers have either been “I was there,” or “this was my life in espionage,” or political science examinations of the Cold War, and the KGB vs. CIA competition during the Cold War.

At the same time, many former KGB case officers have written about their experiences. These books illuminate the subject, and show the importance of Active Measures and covert influence operations. However, they are limited to the operations that these officers ran themselves, or heard about. None of the Comintern intelligence operatives survived much past World War II. Those that did never published their stories.

In addition there are quite a few books by former FBI agents, who worked against the KGB’s espionage operations inside the United States. These accounts, while interesting, do not provide an insider’s view, or an insider’s understanding of espionage operations. The FBI’s main role, at which it is very competent, is counter-espionage, not espionage. The FBI is a law enforcement organization, working within its own country, tracking law breakers. Its agents generally do not excel in work outside of the United States.

Thoroughly researched books by historians of communism and Soviet intelligence operations have confirmed the facts of the massive espionage penetrations of American government. The Radoshes, Haynes and Klehr, Romerstein, Christopher Andrew, Mitrokhin, Weinstein and Vassiliev, Joe Goulden, and many others delved deep into the Soviet archives, interviewed intelligence officers and agents, and documented the facts of the traitorous actions of the American left, so long denied by the covert actors of the media and Hollywood.

A tantalizing lure has trapped most researchers and historians who specialize in Soviet intelligence operations against the USA. That is the Communist Party of the USA (CPUSA). The KGB did make use of the CPUSA in many ways. Spotting and assessing potential agents. Recruiting agents directly out of the ranks of the CPUSA and its myriad affiliated organizations (Young Communists, labor unions, front organizations). CPUSA spotters would turnover a promising candidate to the KGB before the candidate joined the Party. The CPUSA was covertly supported by the Soviet government, including the KGB, with funding, and other logistical, administrative and talent support.

This obvious and inviting target has attracted the attention and energy of many, if not most, historians and researchers of Soviet espionage in the U.S.A. Each historian I've been in touch with during this research returns to the CPUSA time and again. The abundance of files, in Russia and in America, and primary sources, even old American communists, and their memoirs makes the CPUSA attractive and relatively easy to research.

However, as the case of the ten Russian espionage agents arrested and quickly returned to Russia in 2010 showed, the Russians are and were experts in operating non-official cover, or "illegal" operations.

While these historians deserve great credit for their discoveries, analysis, and continued research revelations, none of them have experience as operations officers, intelligence collectors, case officers, recruiting spies, running covert influence operations, or other hands-on experience.

There is absolutely no reason to focus on ties to the CPUSA as the definitive indicator of an American working as an agent for the KGB. This would be as counter-productive in actually identifying espionage agents as if Russian counterintelligence only suspected members of the Russian-American Chamber of Commerce as potential agents for American intelligence.

In fact, in this research I developed a screening method for identifying suspected Comintern covert influence agents, which will be described in detail in a later chapter. The key indicators are travel to the Soviet Union, expression of a point of view congruent with the line of the communist party of the Soviet Union, and an improvement in living circumstances.

A careful CI analysis, even separated from the espionage by eight decades, using my technique, provides a very powerful method to identify those who carried out influence operations against the USA for the communists. Lacking this unique combination of experience, skills, methodology, and research, other researchers or counterintelligence investigators, have been unable to put together the jumbled pieces of the communist covert action operations, and their ultimate effects on America.

Running human intelligence operations is one of the most nuanced and subtle of professions. In teaching new operators the trade, I find it useful to make an analogy to courtship to help them understand how complicated their new profession is. The process of meeting, developing a relationship with, assessing, and ultimately recruiting an espionage agent is fraught with all the complications and nuances of meeting a potential mate, becoming engaged, and then marrying.

The bureaucratic methods of managing, funding, and controlling human recruitment operations are nearly identical across cultures. The need for secrecy, compartmentation, documentation, maintaining files, security, personnel selection and control, is the same whether you are a case officer in a Russian service, a Chinese service, a British service, or an American.

For an experienced ops officer, studying a Russian recruitment in 1925 is no different from working on a recruitment in 2010. The same principles apply, and the operational instincts guide one's analysis as if it was happening now, not 85 years ago.

Studying, researching, and writing about human intelligence operations without having actually run an operation would be like studying courtship, and love-making without ever having dated, been engaged, slept with the opposite sex, been married, or divorced. The researcher can come close to an understanding, and find and reveal many relevant issues, but a non-practitioner will always leave some issues unexplored, and will miss nuances that an experienced operations officer simply feels.

My experience in counter-intelligence (CI) operations and analysis is a unique point of view that few, if any, researchers of communist history have shared. The tasks of reading the primary and secondary sources about the communist covert influence agents during preparation of this book was virtually identical to the task of reviewing intelligence files for counter-intelligence and asset validation purposes. Without experience reviewing files for CI issues, or asset validation, a researcher is unlikely to feel the CI nuances.

Thus, my efforts, informed by my experience in espionage, are complementary to, and bring a current and previously unseen point of view to professional researchers' efforts.

So, while it may seem that the subject of KGB intelligence operations against the United States has been sufficiently covered, with numerous articles, books, movies, scholarly research, and memoirs, addressing the subject, I believe that this book is the first to address what is arguably the most important issue regarding communist intelligence operations against the United States: the ultimate effect that these operations had on our country, the 21st century United States of America.

Chapter 3

Destroy children's patriotism

Leftists are more comfortable with the words of Marx than the Constitution.
Rush Limbaugh, *Dec 5, 2007*

Who We Were—1916

The preface of a 1916 children's history of the United States, salvaged from the collection of a rural high school library in Aurelian Springs, North Carolina, reflected the proud view that the US was a country of great good and was a guiding light to the world, in freedom, and education. Its author, R.D.W. Connor wrote:

> The United States has taken the lead of all the nations of the world in inventions, in agriculture, in public education, and in bringing about peace and liberty on earth. When you have read this book, you will be a poor American indeed, if

> you do not love your country more and become more willing to serve it and make sacrifices for its welfare.

Connor's unabashed pride in achievement and leadership sings from the pages, urging young Americans to revel in their country's progress, and at the same time to prepare to join their fellow citizens in service to the country.

Who We Are—21st Century

The preface of a children's history of the United States, written in 2006, by Howard Zinn, reflects the PC view of the U.S. as irredeemably racist, imperialist, and in need of correction and exposure to its young citizens as a fraud:

> I am not worried about disillusioning young people by pointing to the flaws in the traditional heroes. We should be able to tell the truth about people whom we have been taught to look upon as heroes, but who really don't deserve that admiration. Why should we think it is heroic to do as Columbus did...? Why should we think it heroic for Andrew Jackson to drive Indians out of their land? Why should we think of Theodore Roosevelt as a hero because he fought in the Spanish-American war...paving the way for the United States to take control of Cuba? ... My point of view, which is critical of war, racism, and economic injustice, carries over to the situation we face in the United States today.

Contempt for dead white males drips from each page of this two volume history of America. Zinn, a PC stalwart and hero to the forces of anti-American revisionism, seems to feel a moral responsibility to knock all the heroes of American history off their pedestals. He strives to point out the failings and short-comings of Americans. At the same time he hails as true heroes the victims of the disgraced heroes of the past. Indigenous people who greeted Columbus, Indians killed by Andrew Jackson, Cubans ground under the heels of the reprehensible Teddy Roosevelt.

Reading the 1916 text followed by an immediate reading of Zinn's 2007 text, it is almost impossible to believe that these were written by citizens of the same country. But they were; and separated by less than 90 years. What could have happened in the intervening time? Had the country gone mad? Had the world's guiding light, American freedom and capitalism, been smashed and set the world afire?

PC Removal of Patriotic Pride

The implicit goal of Zinn's textbook is to steal the sense of pride in their country from children. By focusing on mistakes, errors, and cruelty, at the expense of the beauty, truth and successes, Zinn aims to make his readers *ashamed* of America.

In the words of the country song, "I'm proud to be an American, 'cause at least I know I'm free." But Zinn's PC history, foisted on unsuspecting parents and children, discounts our freedom and focuses on negatives.

As one of Hollywood's PC purveyors, Oliver Stone, said, "Nationalism and patriotism are the two most evil forces that I know of..."

Children exposed to this insidious self-hate are programmed to hate themselves, their ancestors and predecessors, their country's founders and leaders, past and present. The final result is as if Zinn planted a guided missile, with a time-delayed fuse, aimed at the heart of our nation. His goal: program the children to destroy their own country.

During the November 2010 Wikileaks release of thousands of classified documents, commentators wondered why America was vulnerable to such an attack. Tunku Varadarajan, writing on the liberal website, The Daily Beast, noted that American children used to be brought up, in school and at home, with the belief that we have a "shared sense of purpose and destiny." But Varadarajan seems at a loss for an explanation when he wistfully continues, "Alas, we no longer do. Many in our midst see their own country as 'imperialist and 'evil'—...beyond redemption."

Varadarajan, evidently unwittingly, defined PC for us. And it's worthwhile to restate his definition, more clearly: *America is imperialist and evil, beyond redemption*. This is how "many in our midst" see their own country.

Attempt to Define PC

PC is easier to identify than it is to define. It is an attitude more than it is a philosophy. The attitude is easy to adopt. No thinking is necessary. No introspection or reflection is required. The attitude is handed down to PC believers fully formed.

A Hollywood insider, quoted in the Radoshes' *Red Star Over Hollywood* could have been describing PC Hollywood, when he described his relationship with the communist party [my substitution of "PC" for communist party]: "when I joined [PC] I was handed ready-made friends, a cause, a faith and a viewpoint on all phenomena.... I learned the [PC] view... on everything under the sun. An airtight, ready-made worldview came along with [being PC]."

That's the essence of PC—it's so easy to be PC. No thinking required. No need to deal with messy evidence and conflict, debate and discussion. The PC powers have spoken, case closed. Debate is over, time to act.

Do you think that Leonardo Vicario is really a climate scientist? Or does he just accept the PC "the science is settled"? Is Sean Penn really a social worker? Or is he just channeling the PC point of view? Is Michael Moore really an expert on health care? Or is he just spouting the ready-made, America-sucks, PC point of view?

PC, at his heart, is a hatred of all things traditionally American. Its credo, if it had an overt credo, might be: "America sucks. Living straight white American men suck. Dead straight white American men suck. America is bad. America is imperialist. America is racist. America is homophobic. America hates foreigners. Rich people suck (see special dispensations below). American tradition sucks. American history sucks. American morality sucks. American taboos suck. Rich white American males suck really hard."

Implicit in the attitude/definition is the requirement that PC believers must be dedicated to "changing" America. So for each of the "...sucks" credos above, there is a corresponding "change" that PC-Progressives seem to believe is required.

Note that "American" is inserted in most of the credo's beliefs. It may be better to substitute "traditional American" instead of American, because some American straight white males are okay. For example, Al Gore is PC-approved, so is Bill Ayers. John F. Kennedy is PC-approved. John Kerry is PC-approved. Eminem is PC-approved.

Straight white non-Americans are more likely to be PC-approved than not, but it's a bit tricky. If they have a cute accent, like an Aussie or a Brit, they're probably okay—see Julian Assange, for example. Italian, French, Dutch, German, and most Russian, straight men are probably okay. This is a tricky business for the PC doyens, so it's best to check with an expert—like any American student under 21. They instinctively know who's okay, and who isn't.

At the same time, some minority Americans are deemed to be PC-traitors, or maybe "honorary straight white males" for the purposes of PC-hate targeting. Thus, Clarence Thomas is considered a straight white male. Condoleezza Rice is considered the same as a straight white male. Sarah Palin *is* a straight white male.

Rich people can get a special dispensation from the PC arbiters. If they are not white, that is an automatic PC pass. If they are scummy, rich minority rap stars (or white rap stars who act ghetto) with lots of tattoos and felony convictions, they have a permanent pass into the upper echelons of PC society. If they are scummy, rich minority athletes (or white athletes who act ghetto) with lots of tattoos and felony convictions, they too have a permanent pass to PC society.

If they are straight white males, they can be given a PC pass if they give a lot of money to PC causes (AIDS, hunger in Africa, Democrats, global warming, recycling, and abortion) and/or if they publicly denounce Republicans, straight white men, or anything related to traditional America.

An ethnological study of PC society is long overdue. I invite anthropologists to begin such a study so that the next edition of this book can include a more scholarly treatment of the question, "What is PC?"

Not PC

To end this attempt at defining PC, it would be best to provide a few examples of things that are *not* PC:

The Boy Scouts of America Oath:

> *On my honor I will do my best to do my duty to God and my country and to obey the Scout Law; to help other people at all times; to keep myself physically strong, mentally awake, and morally straight.*

Christian wedding vows:

> *In the name of Jesus, I____ take you, ____, to be my (husband/wife), to have and to hold, from this day forward, for better, for worse, for richer, for poorer, in sickness and in health, to love and to cherish, for as long as we both shall live. This is my solemn vow.*

American patriotism—God bless America!

Believing that life begins at conception and that killing a pre-born human is murder.

Using firearms to protect yourself.

Using firearms to hunt cute bunnies and other furry creatures.

Using firearms for anything except rounding up haters.

The Republican Party.

The Tea Party.

American conservatives.

Anyone or anything that indicates belief in traditional America or traditional American values.

Anyone who is in favor of enforcing immigration laws, or enhancing the legal protection of America with more strict immigration laws or enforcement.

You can likely add more examples to this list. PC is a silent censor of our public and private discourse, and even thoughts. The PC Thought Police are nearly here.

PC Ignorance of Common Cultural and Historical References

In February 2008, *USA Today* noted that American teenagers had lost touch with what used to be considered common American cultural heritage. Less than half of 1,200 17 year-old American students surveyed could place the American Civil War in the correct 50 year time span—1850 to 1900.

In 2010, the Tonight Show's Jay Leno did a segment of his "Jaywalking," in which he asks Americans on the street relatively simple questions. For this segment, with questions focused on the upcoming 4th of July, he was apparently in a Southern California amusement park. His questions were simple, related to America's Independence Day celebrations. They were:

> *What do we celebrate on July 4th?*
> *In what year did we achieve it?*
> *From what country did we get it?*
> *Name the General who led our troops.*
> *Who sewed (needle and thread) the first American Flag?*
> *What did Paul Revere shout when the British were coming?*
> *Who were the Minutemen?*
> *What is the name of our National Anthem?*

How many original Colonies were there?
From what country did we get the Statue of Liberty?

The answers, at least those that the producers chose to air, demonstrated the incredible disaster that our education system has wrought.

In a video that went viral (interestingly enough, it has now, in early 2011, been scrubbed from the internet), clueless Americans, including a "professor" at a California college, took uneducated guesses at the questions that any 5th grader in 1916 could have answered.

The most telling segment involved a three-generation family. A child, about 10 to 12 years old, his parents, in their 30s, and his grandfather, in his 60s or 70s, tackled the questions, in turn.

The kid and the 30-something parents, all victims of the PC education system in place since the 1980s, struggled with even the most simple of the questions.

Finally, the grandfather stepped up for his turn. He rattled off the correct answers. As quickly as Leno asked, Grandpa answered.

This devastating video is probably the most damning evidence against both the PC education system and PC in general, that I came across in my research.

America and Europe—Presidential Views—1916 vs. 2009

In 1916 the American President, Woodrow Wilson, addressed the Europeans, convulsed in a bloody continental war, on America's global role and his vision of that role:

> [George Washington and the leaders of the American Revolution] spoke and acted, not for a single people only, but for all mankind. They were thinking not of themselves...They entertained no private purpose, desired to peculiar privilege. They were consciously planning that men of every class should be free and America a place to which men of every nation might resort who wished to share with them the rights and privileges of free men...We here in America believe our participation in [World War I] to be only the fruitage of what [George Washington and the Founding Fathers] planted. (NY Times, July 5, 1916)

Wilson believed that America was a special place, and Americans were special people. He believed that the Founding Fathers sacrificed for a higher purpose; that the result was a free nation which people all over the world aspired to emulate, or even to join.

In contrast, the American President, Barack Obama, on his first visit abroad after his inauguration, addressed an assembly of young Europeans in Strasbourg, France in April, 2009: "America has shown arrogance and been dismissive, even derisive [towards Europe]." (London Telegraph, April 3, 2009) The palpable disdain for America drips from the words, no matter how smoothly delivered.

Again, one must assume that the President's attitude is a snapshot in time of the accepted attitude. In his speech, Obama revealed the Politically Correct view of America. Again, what had changed since Wilson's speech in 1916? Had the USA subjugated, raped, pillaged, and plundered throughout the globe, specifically in Europe, the target of both Wilson and Obama's rhetoric? Far from it. The US had sacrificed vats of American blood, and tons of American gold in two World Wars, the Cold War, and two regional wars, rebuilding from the wars, all in Europe between the day of Wilson's speech and Obama's speech. What happened between 1916 and 2009 that created a President so derisive of America's unique historical role in the world, and seemingly bent on destroying the possibility that America would ever again play such a role?

Tropical Asian Island

March 2002

In the arrival area at the airport, the former Special Forces sergeant grabbed my leather carry-on over my objection. "Don't worry about it, man. I got it," Ron said.

The shabby arrival area was packed with a polyglot mixture. Conversations swirled around us. He and I were the only whites in the crowd. The ceiling fans turned slowly, with no noticeable lessening effect on the sticky heat.

Baggage handlers emptied the belly cargo hold of the plane from the capital and piled the contents on the terminal floor—a makeshift baggage carousel. Cardboard boxes, carefully taped and tied with neon-colored plastic cord, were piled on the floor, the treasures of returning overseas workers, and were picked over by the arriving passengers. Spying my small soft-side suitcase in the melee, I grabbed it, and told Ron, "Let's go."

The crowd parted for us, gawking at the foreigners in their midst. We towered over them. Though neither one of us was over six feet, the average islander is less than five feet five inches, and the women much shorter. Ron was driving an old armored pick-up truck. It was parked along the approach to the terminal. The open-air terminal was small, and he'd left the truck where he could see it as he waited for my plane to arrive.

9/11 Jolt

Being back on the island was what I'd worked toward since September 12, 2001. Now, five months later, I had finally arrived. I'd closed my successful executive recruiting business the day after the terrorist attacks on the World Trade Center and the Pentagon.

Living in Northern Virginia, the attacks were close to home. The plane that hit the Pentagon took off from Dulles, five miles from my house. I watched arriving planes in the Dulles approach pattern from my home office window.

The beautiful morning on 9/11, 2001, I'd ditched my car a mile from my kids' school because traffic was so backed-up. I walked the last mile, and hurried hand-in-hand with my two sons down the grassy shoulder of Sunrise Valley Drive back to the car. Eleven and five years old, neither of them realized the gravity of the attacks. I didn't hide the facts from them, but I also didn't sensationalize the issue.

After calling my wife, and talking her into leaving the office, likely the target for the plane that went down in Pennsylvania, I started working the phones.

The next morning at nine, I walked into the CIA's New Headquarters Building, in Langley. The human resources lady, whose husband I had worked with before I'd resigned three years previously, took me in for a quick round of interviews.

Within a month, I badged in at the CIA as a staff officer. My expertise in Southeast Asia, unfortunately, was not recognized. Like any bureaucracy, the CIA only cared, even at its most desperate hour, about putting out bureaucratic fires.

Counter-terrorism Ops

Matching expertise with needs wasn't a priority. I bided my time in an office dealing with a Middle Eastern terrorist group that had not attacked us on 9/11. I rebuilt my network of contacts and operational colleagues. Within a couple months, I'd maneuvered my way into the tropical island assignment.

This was the beginning of a solid four years of shuttling around the world working counter-terrorism.

Long months in hardship conditions, in the desert and in the jungle, were filled with seven day weeks of working ten or twelve hour days. Not a lot of time for introspection. Always focused on whatever mission was at hand, my post-9/11 operations were intense and exhausting.

Family Pressures

My oldest son started high school. My youngest son moved up through elementary school to middle school. We contracted to move into a house under construction. My wife, working full-time, shouldered the responsibilities of both mother and father. She went to back-to-school nights, school plays, teacher conferences, soccer games, birthday parties.

I called home nearly every night, but the trans-Pacific and trans-Atlantic conversations were perfunctory at best. Behavior issues cropped up with the high schooler. He needed his Dad at home and rebelled without my strong hand. We did the best we could.

My operations were all intimately involved with foreigners. My ability to immerse myself in the foreign cultures made my operations fruitful and very effective counter-terrorism.

Reverse Culture Shock

Arriving back at Dulles about every three or four months, I'd go through reverse culture shock. Readapting to driving on the right side of the road. Getting used to the cold weather. Adjusting to a different pace of life. Patting my waistband and not feeling a handgun. Waking up in a panic, sure that I'd missed an operational meeting. It wasn't easy for me to readjust. But it sure wasn't easy for my family either.

These rapid-fire, intense trips out of, and back into, my native culture tripped a thought process. I'd long ago rejected PC, years before recognizing it for the mindless, anti-American set of principles that it was. We'd put our kids in private schools, to avoid the PC proselytizing against normal America in public schools.

But I hadn't really thought about PC in years. My culture shock readjustment into my home culture each time I came back from an operational immersion forced me to re-consider again America's PC disease.

Vietnamese Linguist

The first time I'd gone overseas to work, in 1982, I had realized how wrong the emerging PC line about America was. Even before I ever left the States, while studying Vietnamese at the Defense Language Institute (DLI) in California, seeds of doubt were planted and nurtured. Busy with rebuilding the structure of a normal life, however, I didn't give it much thought.

To practice my Vietnamese, I helped Vietnamese refugees in the southern Bay area, from San Jose down to Monterey. I went to Vietnamese festivals. At one, the sponsors had me make an announcement in my new language. I tutored older Vietnamese housewives. The Northern Vietnamese women had black teeth, from years of chewing betel nut.

There was an amazing diversity in the refugees. Sophisticated urban Southerners, who spoke native French, drank café au lait, ate baguettes, and had a degree from a French university. Northern farmers. Catholics, Buddhists. Muslims. They were all united in their disgust with the communists who had seized their native country and ruled with an iron fist. They were also united in their love for their adopted country, and appreciation for Americans' sacrifices and hospitality.

The bitter, anti-American rants that I'd heard my whole life (as a pre-schooler, I became aware of radio and TV news in 1964, during America's military expansion in Vietnam) were suddenly suspect.

DLI

But at DLI, I was struggling to prove myself, and didn't have time to delve into cultural criticism. I was terrified of failing again, and was totally focused on getting good grades in Vietnamese class.

I had flunked out of the nation's number one party school, East Carolina University, and joined the military as a last resort, hoping to stay alive and out of jail. Less than a year after leaving North Carolina, I was on the stage at a ceremony in Callifornia, led by former South Vietnamese soldiers, marking the day their country fell to the communists.

Seeing America's involvement in Vietnam through the eyes of these people who had lost everything—generations of family history, homes, careers—and traveled thousands of miles to resettle in America choked me up nearly every day.

Every refugee's family had suffered death or loss at the hands of the communists—nearly incomprehensible stories of whole families slaughtered or imprisoned. Many had fled by boat after the communist victory. Many had fled as the communists poured south in the spring of 1975.

Communism had been for me a topic of dorm-room rap sessions, pungent marijuana smoke filling the room while a long-haired sophomore philosopher quoted something he'd heard Dan Rather say about baby-killing American soldiers.

But now, listening to an elderly Vietnamese grandmother tell me in her own language how the communists had destroyed everything that was her life, obliterated the memories of those sophomoric bull sessions.

Again, small seeds of doubt were planted, but I wasn't even aware of PC in the early 80s. I had no idea what it was, much less any idea where it came from. I did have the tenets of PC deep within my poorly functioning, alcohol-addled brain, though. I knew that America was racist, sexist and imperialistic. And our misadventure in Vietnam was because of that dastardly Republican evil-doer, Tricky Dick Nixon, who was also responsible for the Red Scare, and had played some role in the McCarthy witch hunts.

PC in My Face

In 2005, landing at Dulles after four long months working against terrorists in Asia, I browsed the Washington Post. PC was thrust into my face. Already the PC anti-Americans in the Post were attacking President Bush for his robust and measured actions against terrorists around the world.

Echoing the media attacks against the Republican president during Vietnam, they called Bush a baby killer, a torturer, an imperialist. As I landed on American soil, the anti-American message struck me as more than a little ironic.

The irony stoked my creative fires. With years of experience as an intelligence operator behind me now, and with years of experience studying communism, a theory was formulating in my mind while I rode the People Mover shuttle from terminal B to the customs and immigration arrival gate. Where did PC come from? How had it infected our once proud country? Why were Americans more anti-America than most of the rest of the world? Why did the media in America interpret American actions in the worst possible way?

PC from Outside America?

Waiting in line, passport in hand, I didn't even notice that the line was moving. The PC received wisdom that America was nastiness defined was ludicrous. Could it have come from outside?

Islamic extremists were now spouting the PC point of view almost verbatim. Osama bin Laden's video-taped rants could have been taped in almost any American university's faculty lounge.

Suddenly, it hit me. I knew the communists had worked long and hard against the free world, led by the U.S. They had strong and successful espionage operations. But the Cold War had been over for nearly 20 years. I had stopped paying attention to the Russians and the communists after the Wall fell. But could their operations have been so successful that they simply took root and grew, even without active nurturing?

Russian Professionals

The KGB, and its successors, were actively working against the U.S., I knew. An instructor during my CIA operations training, Jim Nicholson, was in prison, serving a long sentence as a Russian spy.

After an advanced training course, I'd come back to Headquarters, looking for an assignment. Working my network of contacts, I discovered Jim sitting in a warren of offices off an Old Headquarters Building stairwell, managing a small counter-terrorism group. I popped in one day to see if Jim might have a job for an aggressive ops officer who knew the Middle East, like me.

Jim was open and friendly, and made vaguely positive noises about potential work with his group, but when I left his office, I knew he didn't really have a job. I never saw him again. The next time I heard his name was a few weeks later when the media announced his arrest at Dulles, on his way to a rendezvous with his Russian handlers.

Knowing the professionalism of the Russians, and their success against the CIA, probably the hardest target in their objective list, I wondered how successful they must have been during the early days of the Soviet Union, before they were our enemies.

The Hypothesis

With a light understanding of the early 20th century, World War I, the Russian Revolution, American counter-intelligence and counter-espionage, the KGB's operations at the time, I decided to undertake intensive research to understand the communists' operations.

At the same time, I formulated a hypothesis:

> American PC in 2005 is an artifact of Russian communist covert influence operations carried out in the years after the Russian Revolution.

My next challenge was to prove it.

Passing through the huge automatic doors into the international terminal, I didn't see my wife. She was at work, and couldn't get away to pick me up. On the cab ride home, I resolved to take up this theory, to research it, and pursue it to its end.

Research

For the next three years, I studied part-time, and worked full-time. My family needed me at home, so I stopped traveling. Taking on administrative and training contracts, I had a bit of free time (every night and weekend) to study and research.

The research took me around the country, physically and electronically. I delved into archives at Stanford and Princeton, and at the CIA. I talked to some of the CIA's oldest living Russia hands. I met former KGB case officers. I read everything I could find on the subject, both by contemporaries of Lenin and Stalin, and by today's experts.

I focused on the KGB, the Russian Revolution, and the KGB's operations in America, the American communist party, World War I, and the time before World War II. I met, emailed, or interviewed many of the experts.

Ironically, defending my country from foreign terrorists, working with refugees, and living immersed in foreign cultures was the impetus for awakening me to both the greatness of my own country, and the threat to America from within.

Just as I could not avoid participating in the Global War on Terror, the results of my research must be shared with the country, and the world.

Need to Share

My unique understanding of the operations, the operators, the American Willing Accomplices from academia and education, the media and Hollywood, my skills in vetting and counter-intelligence analysis, and my research skills drove me to find the truth. My exertion and the shocking conclusions compel me to complete and publish this project.

Once I had the smoking guns linking today's PC to Soviet and Comintern covert influence ops, I realized that Americans needed to know.

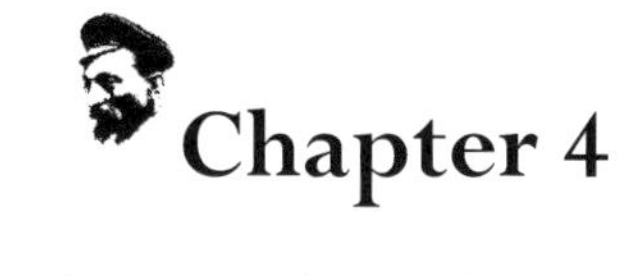

Chapter 4

New taboos—the cult of PC

What is capitalism? Well, I'm a PhD in Sociology, so I can give you the Marxist definition.

***Laura Clawson**, contributing editor at PC-Progressive website Daily Kos*

In the mid-20th century, "conscious and enlightened people" in America were expected to go against the current, to be counter-culture, to be part of the "adversary culture." But inside the communist utopia of the Soviet Union, the "duty of the intelligent was to go *with*, not against, the current. Because the adversary culture had triumphed in Russia, opposition no longer had any place. See? Simple." (Koch, *Double Lives*).

So strikingly parallel to today's America. In 2004, "conscious and enlightened people" chained themselves to gas pumps and chanted "No blood for oil!" and "Bush lied people died!"

In 2011, Obama conducted covert action in Libya, an Arab country with huge oil reserves, and conducted drone strikes that killed hundreds in Pakistan. Now "the conscious and enlightened" elite are silent. Because the adversary culture has triumphed, opposition is no longer proper. See? Simple.

Americans from all sides of the political spectrum can appreciate that America's culture in 2010 is very different from the America of just thirty years ago. The PC thought code now pervades our culture.

The PC code, reduced to its essence, is the belief that America is an irredeemably bad country: a racist, sexist, homophobic, xenophobic, unfair, and cruel nation.

Implicit in PC attitude is required action. America must be "changed." The assumption is that the "change" will achieve some ill-defined utopian vision of a perfect society, culture, government and citizens.

PC is the credo of the Progressive American left (Note: I'll use a capitalized "Progressive" to refer to the left-wing movement in America. The movement constantly changes the way it refers to itself, making it hard to pin down. It has gone through Socialist, Communist, Liberal, Left, New Left, and other names. But it has returned to Progressive with Obama. Progressive seems to have some sort of special cache for the left.)

PC-Progressives believe that traditional, fundamental American values are somehow wrong. Progressive politics and policy prescriptions are based on exacting retribution for our country's mistakes and errors. Progressives strive to "change" America's errant ways and to create absolute fairness, justice, and a level playing field.

The policy manifestations of PC-Progressivism are numerous. Redistribution of wealth. Attacking traditional Christian organized religion. Critiquing American industries and their role in causing "global warming." Lambasting America's "imperialist" foreign policy. Deriding the accomplishments of America's Founding Fathers, white Christian males.

Social researchers have extensively documented the shift to PC in America. Dinesh D'Souza has explored PC in several books. Jonah Goldberg's *Liberal Fascists* laid out a compelling case. Bernard Goldberg, in *Bias* documented the Progressive media's rampant PC.

But no one has been able to answer certain fundamental questions. What are the origins of PC? What motivates American Progressives to hold the negative views of America that are at the heart of PC? Was the change to PC as an accepted national attitude a natural evolution of our culture, or was there some other manipulating influence?

Occasionally the questions manifest themselves in more indirect ways. Critics sometimes ask why the media, Hollywood, and academia are so liberal. These three sections of our society have been called the "transmission belts of culture."

Recently, Rush Limbaugh, on his radio show, said "People have been told by the media and government to hate big retail, big pharma. Business is out to screw them." (April 2, 2008) Rush's sharp powers of observation captured the essence of PC. American capitalism is the enemy.

Various theories are advanced to explain the Progressive imbalance in the transmission belts of American culture. The right-brain versus left-brain theory hypothesizes that people drawn to certain fields are more artistic and social-science oriented.

But these theories, at best, only explain trends that may be evident in contemporary society and provide little insight into the true source of PC Progressivism in America.

Multiculturalism and Diversity

During one of my graduate programs, an M.A. in Linguistics, Teaching English as a Second Language (ESL), I took a class on cross-cultural issues in teaching English. The visiting professor, a woman from Arizona, began the class with a lecture on the need for ESL teachers to understand the culture of their students. Her experience was in teaching immigrant students in elementary school in Arizona. In her fevered PC imagination, it was more important for her to understand the Mexican, Honduran, Salvadorian, and Guatemalan cultures than it was for her students to understand the culture of their new home.

After an hour of her PC proselytizing, I finally had to speak up. I proposed that it would be counter-productive to our goal—teaching American culture and language—for us to spend time trying to understand the nuances of the cultures of our students. Of course, that unleashed the PC furies. It was the only graduate class in which I earned a C grade. PC harridans are mistresses of the intricacies of inflicting bureaucratic revenge. Ensconced in their academic lairs, they have no compunctions about damaging those who dare to challenge their PC diatribes.

The Melting Pot visualization of American society helped immigrants assimilate and become Americans. Immigrants brought their culture to their new country, and were free to practice their religions, speak their languages, and wear their clothes, or any other cultural practice, as long as it didn't scare the horses in the street. Of course, there were exceptions, but the exceptions prove the rule. There is no infallibility in this world.

In the late 19th century, Irish immigrants flooded into the country, and were despised by their White Anglo-Saxon Protestant predecessors. Italians and Eastern Europeans followed. A wave of Jewish immigrants crashed onto American shores. A polyglot mass of Europeans flooded the east. Asians, while inhibited by discriminatory laws, still poured into the west.

Each successive wave of immigrants burrowed into ethnic enclaves. Poles in Chicago. Jews in Manhattan. Slavs in Cleveland. Germans in Pennsylvania. In these enclaves, they could speak their own languages, cook their native delicacies, pursue their trades, study, marry, raise children, and live in freedom. They saw that the key to real success in their new country was assimilation. Their children were eligible for free, English language education.

The schools served as the cultural orientation centers for new generations of Americans. The schools did not just teach language. Language is culture. The schools inculcated the immigrants with traditional American culture. Work hard, study hard, pray to God, follow the rules, George-Washington-chopped-down-the-cherry-tree-and-couldn't-tell-a-lie, the Pilgrims, Manifest Destiny, freedom, liberty, and opportunity. Students left school with American attitudes, American names, and American accents.

Kids who spoke Hebrew, Russian, Polish, Lithuanian, and German at home went to school and emerged after a decade of English-only classes, as Americans. These new Americans became leaders and successes in their new home. An Irish Catholic became President. Polish and Russians achieved high positions in government and industry. Jews served as Supreme Court justices. A black man is our president. Truly the land of opportunity, American kids really can be anything they want to be.

But now, after two centuries of assimilation-based immigrants succeeding, PC demands that American culture be sacrificed so that Limited English Proficiency (LEP) students are coddled and cuddled in counter-productive classes designed to create permanent dependents. Instead of teaching American culture and language, the PC solution to educating immigrants is to fake interest in their native culture, and ignore America. The victims of this PC madness go on to form such groups as MEChA—the Chicano Student Movement of Aztlan.

Aztlan is a mythical extended Mexican state that includes all or parts of California, Arizona, Texas, Utah, New Mexico, Oregon and Washington. In some American schools, Chicano Studies classes advocate seizing Aztlan from the U.S. Various groups that believe in Aztlan advocate revolution against American rule. How's that for understanding your students' culture?

In 1992, the historian, Arthur Schlesinger, Jr. wrote *The Disuniting of America*. Before multiculturalism had peaked in its PC efforts to destroy American exceptionalism, Schlesinger saw the damage already wrought, and declared it dangerous. In his chapter, *The Decomposition of America*, he wrung his hands over the effects of PC. He saw the day coming when, in the name of that PC god Diversity, "...*only* blacks can teach and write black history...leads...to...blacks can teach and write *only* black history...Chinese must be restricted to Chinese history, women to women's history, and so on.

Schlesinger, a self-described "liberal Harvard professor," notes with horror that, by 1991 more than a hundred colleges had in force "speech codes," ostensibly to protect women and racial and ethnic minorities from offensive speech. He relates a case involving a "diversity education committee" at the University of Pennsylvania. A student mentioned, in a note to the committee, her "deep regard for the individual." The diversity czars, offended by the mention of the word "individual," told the student that, "This is a *red flag* phrase today, considered by many to be *racist*. Arguments that champion the individual over the group ultimately privileges [*sic*] the 'individuals' belonging to the largest or dominant group."

PC in Education and Academia

Today elite schools of Education, led by Columbia University's Teachers College, constantly harp on the need to fundamentally change America. Their research and teaching focus on "social justice." Most articles in the self-proclaimed "Voice of Scholarship in Education," the *Teachers College Record* have titles like these:

Academic Engagement and Achievement among Newcomer Immigrant Youth

Teaching Ethnic Identity

Ethnic Advocacy on California School Boards

Building Relationships between Immigrant and Long-time Resident Youths

Hip Hop, the "Obama Effect" and Urban Science Education

Toward a Praxis of Recognition for Latina/o Students in U.S. Schools

En La Lucha: The Struggles and Triumphs of Latino/a Preservice Teachers

Miseducating Teachers about the Poor: A Critical Analysis of Ruby Payne's Claims about Poverty.

Who Really Cares? The Disenfranchisement of African American Males in PreK-12 Schools: A Critical Race Theory Perspective

The Joint Enterprise of Social Justice Teacher Education

Imagine that you came from another planet, and all you knew about American education in 2010 was what you learned from the Teachers College Record. You would believe that American students were literate in English, science and math. You would believe that the most important need in American education was to help immigrant and minority students deal with pervasive racism, sexism, and homophobia.

The University of Virginia's Curry School of Education is a typical American institution, in a state university, for training kindergarten through 12th grade teachers. The School touts its focus on "Research" and "Diversity." One of the School's sections is a graduate program in "Social Foundations." A teacher at Curry can get a Masters degree in Social Foundations.

The program proudly states on its website that it was founded in

> ...1970, but we are linked to a broader field of inquiry pioneered at Teachers College, Columbia University in the 1930's and now encompassing most major universities in the United States. Like John Dewey, George S. Counts, and Harold Rugg, we insist that educational activities must be

> evaluated in terms of their social as well as their pedagogical outcomes. Like our colleagues in Social Foundations across the country, we maintain that there is much more to education than schooling and that there is much more to schooling than the technology of educational practice.

In a later volume of this series, I'll examine in depth the roots of this "Social Foundations" movement in education. Dr. George Counts was a professor at Columbia's Teachers College for nearly thirty years. But for now, let's note that this prestigious school for training teachers rejects "schooling" in education. They call for "social outcomes" in American schools.

In a Trends in International Mathematics and Science Study (TIMSS) in 2007, American fourth graders were in 11th place in math. American 8th graders did a bit better, coming in 9th in math.

In science tests, American students placed about the same—fourth graders were 9th, and eighth graders placed 11th. And in both math and science, by 12th grade American students were only two or three places from the bottom of the table.

The latest measurement of American mediocrity came in December 2010. The Organization for Economic Cooperation and Development's (OECD) Program for International Student Assessment (PISA) released results of math and science tests administered in 2009. Once again, U.S. students placed in the middle of the pack of 60 countries. 15 year-old Americans placed 31st out of 60 in the math test. Our teenagers placed 23rd out of 60 in science.

Chinese students were on the top of the lists for both math and science.

The Obama administration's Secretary of Education, the architect of a failed education system in Chicago, but a basketball buddy of the President, professed shock, "For me, it's a massive wake-up call," he said.

You'd think that such poor results relative to the rest of the world would have galvanized American universities that train our children's teachers, if not the teachers themselves. How can we be satisfied with being 10th in the world? Or 31st? Or 23rd? With the resources thrown at education (Washington D.C. spends more than $12,000 per student each year), you'd think we would have world class results ("U.S.A.! We're number 31!").

Maybe our results have something to do with the Curry School's Social Foundations approach to educating our kids. They're focused on "social outcomes," not how well the students know academic subjects. Maybe if there was an International Trends in Social Outcomes survey our children could finish first.

SRH Replaced the Three R's

My wife and I took our kids out of Fairfax, Virginia public schools when our oldest was in 5th grade. He was in a Gifted and Talented program. At the back to school night, a week after classes started, his math teacher, an earnest young Vietnamese girl, a recent graduate of the University of Virginia, said, "The right answer is not important. What is important is how the kids feel working on the problem."

Observing the school, I learned that the three R's--Reading, 'Riting, and 'Rithmetic—had been replaced. The new triumvirate of American education was Self-esteem, Recycling, and *Heather has Two Mommies*.

Bill Ayers

Teachers College seems to focus its massive resources on the PC task of rejecting American exceptionalism, and emphasizing negatives. Some of Teachers College's famous graduates include the terrorist William "Bill" Ayers, President Obama's close friend. Ayers earned his doctorate from Columbia with a dissertation titled: *The Discerning 'I': Accounts of Teacher Self-Construction Through the Use of Co-Biography, Metaphor, and Image*. What?

Ayers went on to become a Distinguished Professor of Education at the University of Chicago, where he spread his particular brand of America-hating PC. Most of his classes required students to read Ayers' own books. Most of his writing is revolutionary ("off the pigs") sort of rabble-rousing.

Laura Clawson

C-Span's Washington Journal questioned (Nov. 28, 2010) Laura Clawson, a contributing editor to the Progressive website Daily Kos. The interviewer asked, "What is capitalism?" Her voice dripping with amused contempt, as if she was speaking to a slightly retarded child, said, "Well, I'm a PhD in Sociology, so I can give you the Marxist definition."

Clawson's two-fer, illustrates PC in both Academia and the media. She (inadvertently?) shows the audacity of the PC Progressive movement. Her one sentence answer reveals that, in American universities of 2010, PC has infected the academy so thoroughly that she considers it a given that a Sociology PhD will be versed in anti-American, anti-capitalist Marxist philosophy.

Clawson's tone of voice told an even larger story. The PC elite, like Clawson, take it for granted that the great unwashed masses in flyover land are simpletons, clinging to their guns and religion, and patriotism, in need of her enlightened guidance.

Speech Codes

Nearly every American university today has a speech code. Ostensibly created to protect the weak and vulnerable (apparently females, ethnic/racial minorities, and homosexuals are assumed to be weak and vulnerable), these codes punish anyone for saying or writing "offensive, demeaning, or threatening" words.

The broad scope of these speech codes, and the subjective interpretations of offensive and demeaning, has led to a virtual reign of terror on many campuses.

Newly enrolled freshman usually have to undergo an orientation to the campus. These orientations can involve elaborate role playing or other exercises in which "culturally dominant" students are called to task for their privilege.

Ethnic Enclaves

Across the country, universities have established "Latino Student Cultural Centers," and "African-American Cultural Centers." Graduation ceremonies are racially segregated, with a "Black Graduation," an "Asian Graduation," or a "Hispanic Graduation."

The goal of pre-PC civil rights movements of a color blind society has been rejected for a fully race-conscious rejection of traditional America.

PC Case Study—Lynching of Duke Lacrosse Players

The convergence of PC forces in the 2006 case of Duke University lacrosse players accused of raping a stripper during a private performance was almost comical—unless you were in the cross-hairs of the PC firing squad.

The combined forces of the PC media and PC academia aligned against the demonized straight white males were nearly fatal to the young men wrongly accused by a criminal stripper. All that was missing was a quickie made-for-TV movie about the poor young minority mother brutalized by the savage straight white males. Who knows, maybe there actually was a movie.

Progressive Fatwa

The PC media lynching of the accused, assumed by PC-Progressives to be guilty, were swift, public and savage. A group of Duke University faculty members, led by Houston A. Baker, Jr., the George D. and Susan Fox Beischer Professor of English and the Editor of American Literature (a journal?), took the university to task for not punishing the young men before they had a chance to defend themselves in a trial. Two weeks after the allegations surfaced, the professors were so enraged that their employer had yet to punish the students that they broadcast what is best described as a Progressive Fatwa.

The PC-Progressives, led by Professor Baker, were enraged that the university was subjected to national embarrassment due to a "culture of silence" that he said "seeks to protect white, male athletic violence."

Baker's letter dripped with disgust. He was shocked, I say shocked to learn that, in university-controlled property, there was "underage drinking and out-of-control bacchanalia." He and his colleagues were outraged at the "the harms to body and soul allegedly perpetrated by white males."

The PC lynch mob demanded immediate dismissal, evidently for anyone white and male who had ever had anything to do with the lacrosse team: "Surely the answer ... must come in the form of immediate dismissals of those principally responsible for the horrors....Coaches of the lacrosse team, the team itself and its players, and any other agents who silenced or lied about the real nature of...the evening of March 13, 2006.

The PC demons, howling for blood, went on to brand the day the drug-addled stripper made her false accusations as, "A day that, not even in a clichéd sense, will, indeed, always live in infamy for this university."

These normal-America-hating academics were disgusted that the falsely accused Duke students were allowed to "feel they can claim innocence and sport their disgraced jerseys on campus, safe under the cover of silent whiteness."

Their disdain and disgust for the victims of the street trash stripper, the falsely accused students, knew no bounds. The PC-power-brokers were only concerned for the perpetrator of the false police report, "But where is the black woman who their violence and raucous witness injured for life? Will she ever sleep well again? Young, white, violent, drunken men among us - implicitly boasted by our athletic directors and administrators - have injured lives."

Not sure where she was on March 28, 2008, but, according to WRAL.com, on February 18, 2010, she was in jail. Charged with attempted first-degree murder, five counts of arson, assault and battery, communicating threats, three counts of child abuse, injury to personal property, identity theft, and resisting a public officer.

The PC pack, screaming in their missive over and over about how horrible white males are, asked, "How many more people of color must fall victim to violent, white, male, athletic privilege ... coaches who make Chevrolet and American Express commercials...?" This quote allowed them to slip in a bit of anti-capitalism too, another two-fer.

Professor Baker ended his screed by tying together all the loose ends of PC in one neat package:

> How soon will confidence be restored to our university as a place where minds, souls, and bodies can feel safe from agents, perpetrators, and abettors of white privilege, irresponsibility, debauchery and violence?...Today I polled my class whose enrollment is predominantly women and white. All said that nothing had happened in terms of this university's response that had left them anything but afraid. The shame of this is unconscionable. Still, these women will surely sleep better this evening than the black woman injured at 610 Buchanan Boulevard by the white lacrosse team's out-of-control violent partying will ever again rest in her life."

White privilege, agents, abettors, minds, souls and bodies, scared white women, sleepless black woman, violent white men, shame...it's all there. PC-Progressives in a nutshell.

In case you didn't follow the Duke case, the alleged rape victim concocted the story, maybe to get even for being stiffed a tip, maybe to cover up something else, maybe because she was so wasted she didn't know what was happening. In fact, the lacrosse players were tried and convicted in the PC-media court of public opinion before they had a chance to bring the case to trial in court. Clearly, as the Duke faculty made clear, their crime had nothing to do with rape or sexual assault. Their crime was that they were white, and male. Being athletes didn't help much either, but their overt whiteness, and their unapologetic masculinity enraged the PC-mavens.

The local prosecutor, basking in the PC-media's spotlight, thinking he was making a name for himself, and would ride the gravy train to PC nirvana, was nailed for misconduct, lost his law license, and eventually spent a night in jail for lying to a judge.

Destruction of Normal American Pride and Patriotism

The Duke lacrosse rape case and the PC-media and PC-academia response was textbook. Unfortunately, it is a symptom of the problem, not the problem itself. The nasty, hateful attitudes and ideas expressed by Professor Baker and his cohorts are not only common, but almost mandatory in academia, education, the media, and in Hollywood today.

Another example of the anti-normal-American PC insanity comes from the University of Minnesota's College of Education and Human Resources' training program for educating new teachers, its Teacher Education Redesign Initiative (TERI). Submitted for consideration in July, 2009, the "Race, Culture, Class, and Gender Task Group," suggested a detailed program of ways to suppress the whiteness of new Minnesota teachers.

Their goal was made clear, in accord with good education practice, up front. They listed the desired outcome of their portion of the program as: "Our future teachers will be able to discuss their own histories and current thinking drawing on notions of white privilege, hegemonic masculinity, heteronormativity, and internalized oppression." Pity a straight white male lacrosse player who happened into that classroom!

It must be difficult to be PC in Minnesota, though. The U.S. census in 2009 found that 88.6% of the population was white. But forget those pesky facts. TERI's PC-troopers start their report quoting a report on students of color in American schools. They conclude that "our educational institutions must wrestle with issues of multicultural education and the development of bilingual programs....The diversity index of the United States stands at 49, indicating that there is approximately one in two chances that two people selected at random are racially or ethnically different."

Of course that's somewhere else, California specifically. Their own schools racial make-up is immaterial. PC demands that multiculturalism be worshiped. And this worship does not end with admiring those who are not white. It requires aspiring teachers to loathe their own American whiteness:

> As an Anglo teacher, I struggle to quiet voices from my own farm family, echoing as always from some unstated standard...How can we untangle our own deeply entrenched assumptions?

They share the story of a pitiful American teacher, who marks her students' papers with a red pen. Her ethnic Korean students take offense. She is called to the office and counseled by the principal that seeing their child's name written in red ink terrified the Korean parents. Silly American! She should know and be aware of every culture's every taboo—who would ever think that those of foreign cultures should adapt to American ways?

The activities the TERI designers have planned for their victim/teacher trainees have much in common with communist "self-criticism" sessions. These sessions usually began with the victim being forced to write his auto-biography, focusing on his "class privileges." Then the victim would be forced to read the story to a group. The group would then berate the victim; the victim would also be forced to join in the fun.

The TERI PC-teacher-training lesson plan objectives gets down to dealing with those (apparently really bad) things—"white privilege, hegemonic masculinity, heteronormativity, and internalized oppression."

This objective will be met by forcing the trainees to write a "reflection and self-discovery paper [that] requires students to: (a) define 'culture;' (b) describe their own ethno-cultural background, (c) identify three of their personal motives (desires, needs) that are potentially beneficial and three that are potentially harmful..."

Other TERI outcomes include:

> Future teachers are able to explain how institutional racism works in schools
>
> Future teachers will recognize & demonstrate understanding of white privilege.
>
> Future teachers create & fight for social justice...

> Our future teachers will be able to construct and articulate a sophisticated and nuanced critical analysis of this story of America, for what it illuminates and what it hides or distorts. In pursuing this analysis, students will make use of, among other concepts and theories, the following:
> -myth of meritocracy in the United States
> -historical connections between scientific racism, intelligence testing, and
>
> -assumptions of fixed mental capacity
> -alternative explanations for mobility (and lack of it)
> -history of demands for assimilation to white, middle-class, Christian meanings and values
> -history of white racism, with special focus on current colorblind ideology

The poor teacher-trainees, forced to endure this grueling marathon of PC-mind-washing. Is it any wonder that American students linger in the middle of the pack in every international measure of academic success?

Successfully Neutralize Opposition

Progressives' PC accusations successfully neutralize opposition and place dissenters on the defensive. Progressive success with PC attacks has been adopted beyond the American Progressive movement as well. Even radical Islam has recognized that PC represents America's great vulnerability. They accuse America of treating enemy combatants unjustly. They too speak of the U.S. as an imperialist nation that denies Muslims basic human rights.

American Exceptionalism

In the face of constant PC accusations against America, it is easy to forget that America is, in fact, the most tolerant, just, and compassionate nation in the history of the world. With few exceptions, our nation was founded upon and has always embodied those ideals. Yet, at some point, an alternative view—the PC view—developed and infected our culture.

Young American adults, their entire short lives stewed in PC, are the supreme victims of PC. They suffer from PC's warped version of American history. Living in the greatest, most free and prosperous country in the history of the world, PC tells them that they are guilty oppressors.

Before my work, there have been few answers as to exactly why or how our children are abused like this. PC efforts to undermine the culture of America were done covertly, but deliberately. It is no surprise that the full explanation has eluded Americans until now. With the exposures in *Willing Accomplices,* we can begin to recognize the origins of Progressives' blunt PC weapon against America. With a solid understanding of PC's origins, we can begin the struggle to reclaim American values and start pushing back against PC's hate-America-first.

PC in Hollywood

A staple of Hollywood throughout the early 2000s was the Bush-bashing, Iraq-War-no-blood-for-oil, 9/11-was-an-inside-job, capitalism-is-killing-us, help-we-need-Socialism hysterical rant movie.

Michael Moore

Michael Moore is the master of the form, but he is not the only practitioner. It is clear that Moore represents the Hollywood received wisdom about America, capitalism, Republicans, American health-care, and every other PC criticism of America. His movies include:

Fahrenheit 9/11

Sicko

Capitalism: A Love Story

Bowling for Colombine

Roger & Me

In *Sicko* the morbidly obese Moore reviles the best healthcare system in the world, and holds up as a model Cuba's communist healthcare debacle. While Moore's medical records are not public, it doesn't take a medical degree to figure out that someone as fat as he is has multiple medical problems. It would seem that Moore would publicize his trips to visit his Cuban doctors. I'm still searching for that evidence.

In *Capitalism* Moore excoriates the system that has made him fabulously wealthy. American capitalism, starting with protection of intellectual property, and continuing through capital formation, banking, marketing, advertising, retailing, supply, and more. All these combine to provide Moore with untold millions of dollars.

Oliver Stone

Oliver Stone, another Hollywood stalwart, has produced a non-stop parade of anti-American, PC movies since the early 1970s. As American educators abdicated their roles in teaching American history, many young Americans have learned "history" from Stone's movies.

His mainstream career began with a critical view of American foreign policy in *Platoon*, based on his own experiences as a low-level soldier in Vietnam.

He took on another PC target in *Wall Street*, which eviscerates the "greed is good" ethic that Stone imagines drives capitalists.

In *Talk Radio* Stone lets loose on the neo-Nazis that he imagines populate fly-over country.

Dripping with disgust for America, he returned to the subject of the Vietnam War to eviscerate his country with *Born on the Fourth of July*.

Once he had arrived with Oscar recognition, his rage was unleashed. Stone's anti-American PC rants spiraled into rage. *JFK* became a conspiracy theorists' guide to conspiracies. Stone's paranoid delusions proliferate throughout this attempt to simulate a documentary.

Stone's overtly PC polemics also include another fake documentary, *Nixon*. His love affair with Latin American dictators apparently began when he did two television documentaries on the brutal Cuban, Fidel Castro.

Looking for Fidel and *Comandante* slobber and drool over the Spanish-speaking Stalin-wannabe. Stone continued exploring his fascination with Latin American leftists in *South of the Border*, a cinematic love letter to the leftist strong man in Venezuela, Hugo Chavez.

Stone's PC point of view, strongly anti-American, pro-communist, and conspiracy driven permeates Hollywood. According to the website IMDB, Stone is currently working on another PC conspiracy movie, about "an attempted assassination plot by the Republican Party against President Franklin Delano Roosevelt."

IMDB also quotes Stone, "Nationalism and patriotism are the two most evil forces that I know of..." Of course, Stone here is talking about American nationalism and patriotism, not Venezuelan or Cuban nationalism or patriotism.

PC in Media

The view of America (when Republicans are in power) one gets from reading America's dying newspapers and listening to its dying TV news is unremitting social injustice. Relentless coverage of starving homeless thrown on the street by heartless Republicans, pitiful AIDS-stricken homosexuals deprived of medications, children deprived of nutrition and education, poor people denied their welfare entitlements, elderly eating pet food to survive, lonely orphans kidnapped off foreign streets and imprisoned indefinitely while suffering torture at the hands of the dastardly CIA, and on and on.

The in-bred, hot-house, buddy-buddy atmosphere of traditional news media in America leaves no room for dissenting views. The Progressive PC point of view gets precedence and legitimacy. Any other point of view, if presented at all, is characterized as a little whacky, if not outright insane. Coverage of Sarah Palin, from the time she was nominated, until today, is a perfect case study.

Tea Party in 2009

The emergence of the Tea Party movement in 2009 was a watershed. Normal Americans from across the country spontaneously formed grass-roots groups to protest out-of-control government interference in their lives, over-taxation, and outrageous spending.

At first the media studiously ignored the movement. On September 12, 2009, hundreds of thousands gathered on the mall in Washington D.C., blocks from the White House. The media pretended the rally was not happening. And Obama, interviewed just after the gathering, pretended he didn't know there had been a rally of citizens on his front steps.

And then, thirteen months later in the elections of 2010, the Tea Party movement destroyed the Progressive strangle-hold on Congress. The conservative tide swept in a record number of new Congressmen. The results were a shock to the media.

During the run-up to the election, the media went into a frenzy. The New York Times, the Washington Post, CNN, ABC, CBS, NBC, MSNBC, Comedy Central, John Stewart, the chosen news reader to the slacker generation, all worked to marginalize the normals in the Tea Party. The media used PC terminology in attempts to delegitimize them: racist, lily-white, haters, Ku Klux Klan, rich, out-of-touch, and more.

Dan Rather

The poster boy for media's PC anti-Americanism is Dan Rather. Almost a caricature of KGB covert influence Rather ran his own disinformation operation, complete with counterfeit documents. During President George W. Bush's re-election campaign in 2004, Rather conspired to create fake letters from Bush's military career. His reporting was intended to denigrate President Bush's military record. When his plot was uncovered, like covert operators, he never revealed the truth.

Prior to his final PC disinformation operation, Rather hosted a CBS special in 1988. The program, *The Wall Within*, could have been produced by the KGB's disinformation division. Rather interviewed six "former American soldiers, veterans of Vietnam." They told harrowing stories of atrocities they'd participated in during their combat tours of Vietnam.

Rather somberly and seriously listened to their stories, damning America's involvement in the anti-communist war in Southeast Asia. But, Rather's carefully chosen interviewees were telling stories that were not true.

Later research revealed that only one of Rather's six interviewees had actually been in Vietnam. And that one had been an equipment repairman, and did not serve in combat. Rather's tactics were revealed for all to see.

The difference between Rather's Progressive disinformation operation in 1988, and his operation in 2005, was the internet. In 2005, immediately upon Rather's carefully planned revelation of the fake documents purporting to be President Bush's National Guard file, actual document examiners blogged their analysis showing the documents were fake.

Irrefutable evidence proved that Rather's documents were forgeries.

In classic covert operator, and now PC, style, Rather admitted nothing, denied everything, and made counter-accusations. He fought CBS's attempts at punishment. He was finally allowed to resign. He later filed a lawsuit, crushed on appeal, against CBS. He has yet to admit his attempts at disinformation.

Defining Deviancy Down

In 1993, Senator Pat Moynihan published an article in the *American Scholar*, titled *Defining Deviancy Down*. Moynihan's thesis was that "the amount of deviant behavior in American society has increased beyond the [normal] levels."

Moynihan, in his academic style, explained that America was embarked on a re-definition of "normal." Moynihan, a life-long Democrat, was actually providing an academic definition of the PC-Progressive "America sucks, and we must change it," attitude. But he could not bring himself to directly criticize his own political party and its main source of activism. He kept his critiques in *Defining Deviancy Down* to an abstract "societal" level.

That said, Moynihan nailed the PC-Progressive's attacks on normal America, and the results of those attacks—insane homeless people wandering our streets, 2 out of 3 black children born out of wedlock, 83% of black children dependent on federal welfare, and crime escalating out of control.

Bygone Taboos

In pre-PC America, there were taboos. There were words which could not be said. There were acts which could not be committed. There were people who were not fit for polite company. There were manners and acceptable dress—for men, and for women. Religion was accepted and expected. The Lord's name could not be used in vain.

To be a bastard, born to an unmarried mother, used to be a horrible stain on one's character. To admit to being a bastard was taboo. Now, the Centers for Disease Control reports that, in 2007, almost 40% of American babies were born to unmarried women. That rate rose from less than 20% in 1980. Taboo no more.

Another bygone taboo, one that was a marker for polite American society was "taking the lord's name in vain." In 2010, if a hip hop song doesn't take the lord's name in vain in the first three lines, it probably won't see airtime on MTV. The more raunchy and blasphemous, the better, it seems.

Respecting women and acknowledging the special role that women play in society led to social taboos and niceties. PC threw those taboos out the window, in the name of gender equality. PC has a schizophrenic view of these taboos. At the same time that it trumpets the absolute sameness of men and women (and those who aren't sure what they are), PC demands that women be protected and provided with special privileges. Affirmative action, sexual harassment laws, woman-owned business set-asides for government contracting, the effective outlawing of men's sports in colleges, and more special provisions are made for women.

Yet at the same time, the darling culture of PC-Progressives, hip hop, completely objectifies women as butt-wiggling "bitches" and "'ho's," only fit for shaking their groove thing for a dope-addled dude in baggy pants to grope.

Of course, in post-PC America, there are taboos. The taboos are just different. Taboos now are determined by PC. Criticizing our first black president is racist. Being against same-sex marriage is homophobic. Allowing a social club for men only is sexist.

The Origins of PC

As we'll see in *Willing Accomplices*, the PC message of seemingly high minded, elite questioning of the fundamentals of American society and culture provides Progressives in 2010 with a ready-made attitude. Many critics believe that PC came about because of the "hippie days" of the 1960s and 1970s. They believe that some sort of natural evolution, with national attitudes maturing from the "uptight" 1950s, through the hippie days, into the 1980s and finally reaching fruition during the 1990s.

What we'll see is that PC was created as an attitude and point-of-view in the early 1920s. It was inserted into American culture by selected agents of influence. The agents of influence, whether witting of communist intelligence guidance, or unwitting, were all Willing Accomplices in propagating the attitudes that became PC.

The attitudes were sharpened and practiced during the 1950s, when official America became aware of the extent of actual communist activity, and investigated many of the guilty. These investigations forced the PC payload underground, and in many ways, made it more attractive to a certain element. The 1960s was the era when the PC attitudes resurfaced, and began to flower above ground.

The 1980s was the decade when the PC anti-American culture infiltrated American government and most institutions.

Marxism-Leninism and PC

Tom West in his Claremont Institute article, "Marx and Lenin" noted Marx's goal of critical, "dialectical" discussion was not to arrive at the truth. Marx's goal was to use criticism to destroy the enemy.

We see this exact same tactic in PC. Nothing is ever up for discussion. Once a PC position is stated, one must either accept the position, or face the destructive wrath of the PC acolytes. Reason and logic are not welcome in discussions of PC positions.

Tom West goes on to point out that Marxist criticism is essentially emotional. And its fundamental "feeling is *indignation*." West points out that Marxist critics are set on "*denunciation*." They are not concerned with the fundamental humanity of their opponent. All that concerns the Marxist critics is the need to "*strike*" their opponent.

Tom West's Postscript

After a scathing expose of how Marxism-Leninism has polluted American culture, West says he does not understand how this could have happened. Like nearly all historians and critics who see the parallels between Marxist-Leninism and PC today, West cannot conceive of the covert influence operations that created PC. His "Postscript" is worth pondering here. He notes that "for some reason," scholarship on Marx has "not been satisfactory."

> One might wonder why an essay on "Marx and Lenin" needs to be written, considering that scholars have been writing on the subject for half a century and more. The unfortunate fact is that scholarship on this and other Marxian themes has in general not been satisfactory. For some reason Western scholars have been reluctant to call a spade a spade. The majority of them keep trying to assure us that Marx and Lenin are not such bad fellows after all. Why an entire class of educated people, including many at our most prestigious institutions of higher learning, should want to hide the truth about Marx and communism from others, perhaps even from themselves, is hard to understand. It may be that only a psychologist of the rank of Nietzsche could fully penetrate the phenomenon--historically unprecedented as far as I know--of the intellectual leadership of a strong and free society making every effort to find reasons not to criticize its main enemy and to denounce those who do criticize it.
>
> At work, no doubt, is the self-loathing that Paul Hollander detected over and over again in his study of the long history of favorable responses to communism by Western scholars

> and students. But whence arises this self-loathing? Nietzsche said that man would rather will nothingness than not will. People who have lost their faith that life has a higher purpose may believe, deep down and almost unnoticed, that their life is not worth living. Thus the definitive refutation of Marx may not even be possible until the leading classes in our society are once again composed of men who reject root and branch the modern idea, stemming from Descartes, Hobbes, and others, that human life has no ultimate meaning beyond what human beings themselves will that it have.

Glimmer of Hope

Regardless of the apparent terrible current situation, it is impossible to give up hope for our country. Every day PC-Progressives around the country wake up, realize they've been living a lie, and have a conversion.

David Mamet, an American playwright and film director recorded his conversion experience in an article he called, "Why I am No Longer a Brain-Dead Liberal."

Mamet realized one day, while listening to National Public Radio that their point of view made him grit his teeth in disgust and rage.

He realized that in his PC-Progressive world-view, he "accepted as an article of faith that government is corrupt, that business is exploitative." He blamed his PC-Progressive views on his being a "child of the '60s."

He realized that the essence of his unthinking "brain-dead liberalism" shaped his attitude about life, his country, and the people around him. It was: "everything [in America] is always wrong."

But at the same time, he realized that everything in his own life was *not* always wrong. He came to the realization that he was holding two mutually exclusive points of view, at the same time. One was the PC-Progressive, American is "a state where everything was magically wrong and must be immediately corrected at any cost."

And the other was the reality he lived in every day—that America was a vibrant, energetic, striving country based on the American Constitution, which balanced powers to weaken each branch of government, and to allow capitalism to improve our lives. And he realized that this two-track mind was making him crazy.

For a self-professed brain-dead liberal to see the light must have required a huge act of will-power. The PC-Progressive way is the easy way. Scorn and hate. Elitism and disdain. Dropping the pose also costs you all of your PC-Progressive friends. But in the long run, you stay sane, and you live in the real world. That's not a bad compromise.

Chapter 5

Lenin's dilemma—what is to be done?

The West, and especially America, has developed a strong methodology of indoctrination of their proletariat. Their schools fill the children's heads with the myths of American exceptionalism. Their press daily is filled with lies about the glorious Socialist revolution. And their centers of entertainment create propaganda films that glorify their racist, imperialist wars of domination. These, my comrade, are the keys to the hearts of our enemy.

***Vladimir Lenin**, recreated conversation, 1919.*

Dawn of the 20th Century—Ripe with Promise

At the dawn of the new century, in 1900, the world was ripe with promise. Steam-powered locomotives, running on steel rails, opened up vast swaths of unsettled territory in America's west. America's Civil War had freed the slaves.

Industry was advancing steadily, making more and more goods available to more and more people. Scientific advances were making people's lives, in capitalist countries, better and better. Scientists and industrialists were laying the foundation for the healthy lives of comfort that we, in capitalist countries, enjoy.

Transportation, communications, medicine, energy, finance, and consumer goods, all were advancing steadily, making lives easier and better in capitalist economies.

Spread of Freedom

The U.S. had just trounced an old-line colonial power, in the Spanish-American war. We inherited Spain's colonies, in the western hemisphere, and in Asia. America shouldered her burden, and set about preparing Filipinos and Cubans for their coming liberty and free elections. Destruction of the vestiges of centuries of colonialism seemed to bode well for people laboring under the yoke of oppression around the world.

Scientific Advances

Electric wires were slowly spreading their life-giving and labor-saving power throughout the civilized world. Advances in medicine were curing more and more diseases. The telegraph was spreading around the world, making exotic countries seem nearby, and increasing the speed of communications. Information was becoming available to more and more people.

Real science was advancing by frog-leaps, one discovery after another. Practical and theoretical scientists were digging into the world, examining and dissecting animals, vegetables and minerals.

Roentgen, a German physicist, produced X-rays, winning the first Nobel Prize in physics. The Curies were experimenting with uranium in France. Henry Ford had created his first gasoline engine-powered vehicle. Thomas Edison was busy inventing in New Jersey. Darwin's theory of evolution had gained prominence.

Spiritual Turmoil

For all the advances in science, and the resulting physical improvements in life, the spiritual realm was in turmoil, especially in Europe. Traditional religions were questioned, and rejected by many. A seeming side effect of acceptance of science was a simultaneous rejection of religion. Organized religion, in many places, was in crisis. In search of a new truth, many people turned to spiritualism, séances, mediums, exotic religions, and other roads to a higher truth. Mankind's inbred sense of the divine, which cannot be erased, was intact. But, in the absence of traditional religion, mankind sought new avenues to experience the divine.

Social Sciences

Science also had spawned a new breed—"Social" Sciences. Clad in scientific garb, and spouting jargon incomprehensible to normal people, social theoreticians hitched their wagons to the shooting star of science.

The long tradition of utopia-seeking cults, dreamers and scammers, each with its own unique blend of prescriptions and proscriptions required of followers, continued in Europe and in America.

Previous utopian cults were driven by religion, like the Shakers, or were cults of personality, like the comically failed Transcendental community of the Alcotts in New England.

But now, visionaries, dreamers, and cult leaders found that they could cloak their utopian rantings in science, and achieve more respect. At least from a certain sector of society.

Marx's Science

In the United Kingdom, Friedrich Engels had supported Karl Marx, both German sons of hard-working fathers who created wealth with capital, providing capital so that Marx could spend time creating his new "science," Marxism. Marx's theory was that all human society was the result of "class struggles." He imagined that the under-class, his "proletariat," was exploited by the upper-class, his "bourgeoisie," which controlled the government, his "state."

Marx's "science" imagined an inexorable natural evolution, arising from a struggle between the classes. His fevered theory predicted that the under-class would rise up in revolt, and destroy the upper-class's state. The end result would be a classless utopia of human kindness and good will, in which no one would ever want for anything. All would share in the bounty of the Earth, selflessly and without want. Each would provide the community of mankind with the fruits of his talents, and each would be provided according to his needs. Heaven on earth, promised Marx.

Change Marx Believed In

Even better, Marx's new science called for action. No navel-gazing for this new class of social scientists. Marx's 1845 Thesis number 11 noted that, "The philosophers have only interpreted the world, in various ways; the point is to change it."

Oh yeah, Change, baby. Join the scientific wave of the future. Ride the change into utopia.

The New Testament

Marx's imagined science came complete with a testament, *The Communist Manifesto*, published in 1848. Communism, aligned with socialism, by the turn of the century, had gained followers throughout Europe. The fake science was replete with "immutable laws" of human societal evolution, predictions of progress, and promise of a coming utopia. Marxism used a common formula, well-known to confidence hucksters around the world—identify a real problem, cloak your solution in mystic symbolism and high-sounding scientific language, dangle utopia in front of the rubes, and then sit back and watch the fun.

Frauds, Scams and Cults

Almost concurrent with Marx's labors to produce Marxism, Sigmund Freud was giving birth to another fake science, Freudian psychoanalysis. Freud's mish-mash of high-minded scientific-sounding "laws" and a catalog of stock diagnoses and symbolic dream interpretations could have been lifted directly from a Sioux medicine man's stock in trade. But Freud cloaked his nonsense in pseudo-scientific language, and he wrote feverishly and often.

Freud's fake science soon won adherents around the world. Like Marx, Freud cloaked his scam in mystic symbolism, high-sounding scientific language incomprehensible to a non-believer, and promised a utopia to the true believers who performed the secret rites of the clan. It is likely not a coincidence that the fake science of Freudianism arose and fell nearly simultaneously with the fake science of Marxism.

It is also likely not a coincidence that both Marxism and the cult of Freud arose at the turn of the 20th century. The wide-spread rejection of traditional religion, and its answers for social and personal problems, left people drifting through life. They still had personal and social problems, but the ready-made answers found in church were missing. This might explain why the false idols of Marxism and Freudianism were so easily foisted upon European societies, which were in such turmoil after centuries of religious and social wars.

If the pseudo-science, cult-like aspects of these two false sciences sound familiar to 21st century readers, maybe it's because we are experiencing a similar wave of cult-pseudo-science. More on the Gaia cult in a later volume. Suffice it to say for now that "Green is the new Red."

Bolshevik Revolution

The opening decades of the 20th century were not kind to Russia. The weak, decadent and ineffective royal family spiraled into a death dance with spiritualism and self-absorption. The Czar's wife deepened a strange relationship with a conniving holy man, Rasputin. Normal Russians and the nobility grew concerned for the future of their country.

The international socialist-Marxist-communist spirit had swept Europe during the last half of the 19th century. Marx and Engels gained followers across Europe.

The Czar and his bumbling military entered a disastrous war with Japan.

The revolution began in 1905, and unfolded in slow motion over the next 12 years. The Czar allowed an elected representative body, the Duma, and a constitution. But the communists were not satisfied, and kept pushing for more.

In 1914 Russia entered World War I, joining England and France against Germany and the Austro-Hungarian Empire. The Czar may as well have signed his own death warrant. The Russian military was a massive weight on the Russian economy. The Czar's incompetent leadership incensed Russians, on the left and the right. The war effort weakened, and finally caused the collapse of the centuries-old feudal monarchy.

Early in 1917, the Czar was overthrown by a coalition of revolutionary parties—the Kadet Party, the Mensheviks, the Bolsheviks, the Social-Revolutionary Party, and the Social Democrats. Forming a Provisional Government, the newly free Russians attempted to run their country.

Lenin, the International Revolutionary

Vladimir Lenin, the Marxist writer and agitator, was out of the country as he usually was when there was violence or arrests. Lenin had transformed from the bookish son of a czarist education bureaucrat. He became a revolutionary after his older brother was executed in 1887 for plotting a terrorist attack.

Lenin was arrested for revolutionary activities in 1895, and exiled to Siberia in 1897. After three years internal exile, Lenin fled abroad. In the next 17 years he lived and traveled in Germany, Switzerland, and England, among other places.

He joined other Russian and international exiles, and wrote widely on Marxism, socialism, and revolution. His writing was thick with theory and analysis, awash with the rumors and back-biting of the revolutionary social whirl.

In 1902, Lenin published the answer to what he called "The Burning Questions of our Movement." *What is to be done?* detailed Lenin's prescriptions for immediate action. Lost in the weeds of international socialist in-fighting, his main point was the requirement for a newspaper of their own.

He returned to Russia after the 1905 revolution, but quickly fled to Finland when the monarchy cracked down. He wandered Europe for the next ten years, with his wife, Krupskaya, usually by his side.

Lenin's fellow Bolsheviks, Trotsky, Kamenev, Stalin, and Zinoviev all had been arrested, exiled—to Siberia and abroad and joined forces with various non-Russian socialists.

During this period, the Imperial security service, the Okhrana, penetrated the revolutionary groups with informers and agents provocateur. The Okhrana were brutally efficient. The revolutionaries studied their methods. The communists would later copy and improve upon many of the Imperial secret police techniques, including torture, false confessions, labor camps, internal exile. One of their favorites was covert action operations—disinformation, covert influence, and infiltrating opposition groups to manipulate their actions.

Lenin and the Revolutionaries Underground

From the time of his first arrest, till his final return to Russia in 1917, Lenin led an underground life. Everything he did and said, printed and published, was monitored by the Okhrana and its agents, in Russia and abroad.

The international revolution—Marxist, socialist, or anarchist was watched by European governments closely. Their finely balanced state of affairs, monarchies side-by-side with democracies, was fragile. Each European power engaged in power diplomacy, making and breaking alliances with other states. The alliances could shift at any moment.

Every European power had agents throughout the continent, and the world. Revolutionary Marxists were courted by Kaiser-worshipping Prussians. Strange bedfellows were the order of the day. The Russian revolution swerved back and forth—first a representative Duma was elected, and then a government was formed, with Kerensky playing key roles. All the while, WWI raged, and the Germans plotted.

The German goal was for the anti-war Bolsheviks to gain power. Lenin and his cronies made noises indicating they were ready to enact a "separate peace" upon assuming power. Divide and conquer was attractive to the Germans, who were fighting a two-front war.

Careful plotting by Germans, German agents of various nationalities, and Russian agents of the Germans swirled throughout the continent. Lenin received support payments from German agents. As Kerensky's Provisional government sagged, the Germans offered Lenin a deal he couldn't refuse. Packing up his wife and other trusted allies, but leaving Willi Muenzenberg in Switzerland, Lenin allowed himself to be sealed in a German train, and transported across German territory, in order to make his return to Russia, to finish his revolution.

It's likely that the German spymasters who made that deal with the devil came to regret their decision.

Revolutionary Tradecraft

In order to meet and communicate with his fellow socialists, Lenin, and all his contemporaries, became masters of what we call today clandestine tradecraft.

The actions and attitudes necessary to conduct business without being detected by hostile authorities, tradecraft allowed the revolutionaries to come to the cell meetings secure in the knowledge that they had not been followed. Cells of revolutionaries formed and disbanded constantly, a moving target was more difficult to find.

Tradecraft allowed the revolutionaries to secure safehouses for meeting and to locate printing presses. Their tradecraft allowed them to smuggle papers, money, valuables, people and other cargo into and out of Russia.

Their tradecraft developed full cover legends for their revolutionary comrades, back-stopped by aliases, fake official documents, passports, letters of recommendation, and more.

Their tradecraft developed "revolutionary names" for each of them, to provide another layer of security for their clandestine meetings. No revolutionary went by his birth name. Lenin's birth name was Ulyanov. Stalin's birth name was Dzhugashvili. Trotsky was born Bronstein. Dzerzhinsky went by various aliases during the Revolution. Christopher Andrew pointed out, in *The Sword and the Shield*:

> The Cheka's intelligence operations, both at home and abroad were profoundly influenced not merely by the legacy of the Okhrana but also by the Bolsheviks' own pre-revolutionary experience as a largely illegal clandestine underground. Many of the Bolshevik leadership had become so used to living under false identities before 1917, that they retained their aliases even after the revolution.

The revolutionaries perfected covert actions. The newspaper and pamphlets were the internet of their day. Access to printing presses was paramount for communications and propaganda.

Counter-intelligence vetting of recruits and contacts was developed to an art form. Interlocking rings of trust, with introductions and members vouching for new arrivals, background investigations, and intense interviews to determine loyalty were the basis of survival for the revolutionaries.

Running operations to infiltrate other groups, the tsar's police or soldiers, or even rival revolutionary groups, was handled by skilled veterans of Okhrana operations. Some Bolsheviks had worked as covert agents for the Okhrana, some had experienced the covert tactics as targets of the tsar's secret police. All Bolsheviks were steeped in clandestine techniques and practices, either as victims or as perpetrators.

Covert Action to Return Lenin to Russia

German diplomatic records reveal that during the years of World War I Lenin was in contact with, and received funds from, German espionage officers and sources. The Germans, intent on destroying their massive enemy to the east, encouraged Russian revolutionaries of every stripe. The Germans believed that a collapse of the tsarist government would force the Russians to capitulate, allowing the Germans to focus on the French and English.

Lenin maneuvered among the Russian revolutionary exiles in neutral Switzerland, making deals and making contacts with agents from many of the belligerent powers.

The tsar signed papers in February 1917 formally abdicating his power. Lenin, through German espionage contacts, arranged to be transported back to Russia, on a German train. The train was required to be sealed, with no passengers boarding, or exiting, during its transit of Germany.

The Germans clearly knew the danger represented by the revolutionaries they sent to Russia in that train. They sealed the Bolsheviks up to protect society from them, like the revolution-infected rats that they were.

At his greeting ceremony in St Petersburg, Lenin foreshadowed his ruling style. Piggishly ignoring the assembled Provisional Government officials, Lenin turned to the red-flag-waving masses and harangued them with the praises of international revolution, "Sailors, comrades, we have to fight for a socialist revolution, to fight until the proletariat wins full victory! Long live the worldwide socialist revolution!"

Lenin, the Bolsheviks, and Espionage

"Our cause is an international cause, and so long as a revolution does not take place in all countries our victory is only half a victory. Or perhaps less." *Vladimir Lenin, October 1917.*

Lenin understood implicitly and explicitly the power of espionage and covert conspiracies. His experiences as a revolutionary socialist and communist, organizing both in Russia and other European countries could be used as a tradecraft primer for covert espionage operations. From the use of aliases, safe houses, disguises, cutouts, cell operations, sleeper agents, surveillance detection, countersurveillance, surveillance, intelligence gathering, counterintelligence, cover companies and organizations, cloaking of true organizational objectives, Lenin's work ran the gamut of espionage operations. Trotsky, a dedicated revolutionary and communist theorist, confirmed the Bolsheviks' absolute reliance and reverence for clandestine, illegal, operational methods.

Sydney Hook, an American communist, who studied his faith in Soviet schools for foreigners, later rejected Soviet totalitarianism and went on to craft a career as a "philosopher," explained the necessity for Lenin to practice conspiracy, covert influence, and infiltration:

> Infiltration into the key positions of trade unions, cooperatives, and citizens' groups must be skillfully planned especially in sensitive areas. Sympathizers and fellow-travelers are to be groomed to show a false face to the enemy. Popular issues are to be exploited to fan discontent with the status quo into raging hostility.

The Russian Revolution ingrained in the Bolshevik veterans, who were, after the Revolution, the new Soviet government, a culture of conspiracy and covert methods probably unmatched in any ruling government in modern history. The innate dishonesty required to conduct covert conspiratorial espionage was imbued in each and every Bolshevik during the revolutionary years, and was suffused throughout the entire history of the Soviet Communist Party and all its satellite parties.

Lenin's Comintern strategy was a child of his Russian strategy. Instead of relying on bullets and dynamite, he used covert methods to "distribute ideological bombs through a network of party members and supporters across Russia."

Andrew noted that:

> From almost the beginning of the civil war in 1918, in keeping with the Bolshevik tradition of operating under false identities, the Cheka began sending officers and agents under various disguises and pseudonyms behind enemy lines to gather intelligence. By June 1919 the number of these "illegals" was sufficiently large to require the foundation of an illegals operations department.

Thus, the Bolsheviks, from the top to the bottom, knew about covert, clandestine, and, in their own words, conspiratorial operating techniques. They immediately instituted a network of illegals, working around the world, under various covers, not just official Soviet, or diplomatic covers.

This mode of political operating was ingrained in them. They understood and practiced clandestine tradecraft, and continued to do so, after their victory in 1917.

Turn to the West

Flush with his success in Russia, Lenin surveyed the international scene and began plotting the spread of his dictatorship by the Elite

Vanguard. Just as he had distributed ideological bombs covertly during the Russian Revolution, using the network of covert operators the Russian Communist Party had nurtured, he now turned his attention west.

While he saw Western Europe as ripe for revolution, in the wake of the destructive world war just ended, he also realized that the United States was a sleeping giant that had been awakened by its first foray into a European war. He began planning his strategy for spreading the revolution to North America. The red Army in tatters, along with much of the rest of the European continent's forces, Lenin and his minions focused on what they knew best: covert actions.

Intelligence in Bolshevik Soviet Union

After their victory, and ascension to power in Russia, the communists put in place a security and intelligence structure. The communists learned from their experiences working against the Czar's Okhrana security apparatus. The communists, by necessity, had become expert covert operators during their decades in illegal opposition.

The Okhrana penetrated the communists' ranks with recruited agents. The czar's security service arrested and interrogated legions of communists. The communists created an extensive counter-intelligence corps to ensure their anti-czarist operations' security. As they developed their organization, the intelligence function grew.

After the Bolshevik revolution, Russia descended into nearly five years of Civil War. Lenin's communist Reds, after seizing power from the non-communist members of the Provisional Government, attempted to bring the rest of Russia under their control. The "White" non-communists fought the Reds outside Moscow and Petrograd.

During the Civil War period, Lenin established, via his trusted Polish communist, Felix Dzerzhinsky, a counter-revolutionary secret police, the Cheka (Russian acronym for the All-Russia Extraordinary Commission to Combat Counter-Revolution and Sabotage).

The Cheka quickly established itself as the masters of the Red Terror. Class enemies, real enemies, counter-revolutionaries, those who displeased the new Russian rulers, were liable to be arrested and summarily executed—usually with a bullet to the back of the neck.

The Bolsheviks practiced Active Measures from the moment they seized Russia. During the early to mid 1920s, the Soviet Union's intelligence apparatus, the forerunner of the KGB, was focused on operations against counterrevolutionaries. The Soviet intelligence goals, as noted by Christopher Andrew, were not only to "... collect intelligence... but also to penetrate and destabilize..." adversaries.

American Naiveté

Throughout the period of European socialist revolution, the U.S. was relatively insulated. Though an American Socialist Party did arise, and European refugees set up foreign language parties in exile, the American political environment was little affected by the European upheavals. Insulated from the ferment by the Atlantic Ocean and by the American spirit of individuality, the U.S. public did not see the true face of the revolutionaries.

Even American involvement in WWI did not bring the American public into significant contact with the communist schemers.

During the decades of revolutionary conspiracy and tradecraft, while the Bolsheviks and their socialist friends perfected lying, cheating, counterfeiting, and using aliases, Americans perfected our reliance on trust and social mobility

Even when the U.S. realized the importance of clandestine work, we continued to be naïve about our own vulnerability to communist tradecraft.

Leninism

The winter of 1918-1919 was long and cold across Russia. The Bolshevik government fled to Moscow, in fear of the German army pressing St Petersburg. Lenin's power consolidated as the Civil War turned his way. His ruthless purges of counter-revolutionaries, the Red Terror, had created a fear, a raw, hard, cold fear layered over the crusted snow banks.

Communist Party insiders knew, as they had for several years, that their true goals had nothing to do with their stated goals. They knew that they had to lie about both their goals, and about the methods they intended to use to achieve those objectives. They believed that the utopian end justified their means. Purges and counter-revolutionary witch-hunts were useful tools.

With his experience as a true believer, and as an observant reporter of the human experience, Sydney Hook explained how the philosophy of "the little guy" and utopian peace and love on earth was actually a twisted human-hating cult:

> The psychology of Communist conspirators cannot be grasped without knowledge of their ideology. They are not, at least at the beginning of their careers, criminally base, but inspired by a resolute fanaticism to do what they imagine is the work of History. They care little for human life because they are prepared to sacrifice their own upon command. They are unmoved by human compassion because they regard it, like genuine pacifism, as a sign of weakness and hypocrisy. They are untouched by love of country because to them it seems an anachronism and because the Soviet Union is their true, and voluntarily chosen, country. They are rarely moved by argument and evidence because their hearts and minds are encased in the triple-plated dogmas of Marxist-Leninist-Stalinism which enables their substitute for religious faith to triumph over experience. Initially drawn to Communism by a laudable desire to diminish social injustice and human distress, they soon become corrupted by the means they employ. Their capacity for total sacrifice wedded to their belief in total solutions is the source of both their intransigence and danger.

Hook, looking back after he had abandoned the cult, explained the seemingly insane embrace of a doctrine, by seemingly sane and intelligent people, which was dedicated to destroying their own culture and fully functional way of life:

> Men are sometimes seized and made over by a vision of an Ideal in a manner quite different from what we would expect in view of their education and environment. Some visions intensify the powers of normal perception to discriminate between fact and wish, to recognize alternatives of action, and to weigh the moral costs of choice among them.

Hook quotes Trotsky, to explain how the communist elite vanguard believes it protects the masses from themselves: "If the dictatorship of the proletariat means anything at all, then it means that the vanguard of the class is armed with resources of the state in order to repel dangers, including those emanating from the backward layers of the proletariat itself."

Manipulation of the Philosophy

Many a Party hack had lifted himself out of rags and into the comfort of Party privilege over the corpses of those he had denounced. "Reactionary" and "Counter-revolutionary" were powerful words. Words meant things, but not the way that they had before October 1917. Now the Party hacks discovered that, following their leader's example, words could be made to mean almost anything.

Lenin's Need for Speed

The assassination attempt in August 1918 created a growing urgency in his restless thoughts. The global workers revolution, in which the proletariat would rise to overthrow their oppressors, the capitalists, was stalled. His tactics of manipulating the infant Russian democracy, followed by violence and a coup would be difficult to mimic in other countries.

The "science" of Marxist historical evolution was proving to be more than a little off in its predictions.

The pesky workers were not rising up across the globe. In fact, even the Russian workers had not done that. Lenin and his Party faithful had been forced to use various covert tactics to prod and poke the workers into any action at all. Communist agents infiltrated unions and guided their agendas in aggressive directions.

Agitators were placed in the media, in entertainment, and in academia. The army and the navy were infiltrated with Communist Party faithful. Lenin had learned well the failings of Marxian theory when faced by human nature. But he had also learned well how to overcome those failings. Covert actions and conspiracy were powerful tools.

Easy Picking—Americans as Suckers

In 1917, U.S. President Wilson used the power of executive order to create the Committee on Public Information (CPI). Wilson turned America's first propaganda agency over to a Democrat Party marketer–journalist turned Progressive cheerleader, George Creel. The CPI, widely known as the Creel Committee, was charged with building support in the U.S. for Wilson's decision to join WWI. Later, the Creel Committee took on the job of influencing foreigners; however the American home front remained its major market for peddling Wilson's call to arms in the European war.

Charles Edward Russell, dean of Columbia's Teachers College, fresh from a survey of Russia with the Root Commission, wrote to Wilson, urging the president to target Russia with propaganda designed to appeal "to the Russian's passion for democracy."

Wilson forwarded Russell's letter to Creel, with the comment, "It seems to hit very near to the heart of the subject [propaganda in Russia]..."

Creel and his advertisers took to the task with gusto. The iconic "Uncle Sam Wants You" posters were Creel Committee products. The Committee demonized the German foe, moving the American public slowly to support the war. The popular image of "the Hun" was a CPI advertising product.

However, Americans were not the only targets of the CPI's influence campaigns. The CPI had a foreign section. According to the New York Times, in July of 1918, Edgar Sisson was appointed general director of the foreign section of the CPI.

The foreign section included "agencies of the committee in Europe, Asia, and South America, the divisions comprised in the foreign section are the foreign cable, foreign mail, foreign films and pictures, work with the foreign born, and the present division of foreign educational work, the last becoming the executive division of the section."

Sisson, with no experience in Russia, landed in the revolution-torn country in the fall of 1917, just after the Bolsheviks overthrew

Kerensky's Provisional government. On his team, in the foreign educational section, was William F. Russell, dean of a college in Iowa, the son of the advisor to the president who was the dean of Columbia University's Teachers College. The younger Russell would later serve as both dean and president of Teachers College.

Communist connections to Columbia Teachers College are numerous and puzzling.

Sisson spent all of 90 days in Russia, including time during which he gathered what were later proven to be an Active Measure disinformation forgery operation, the Sisson Papers.

These papers purported to prove that Lenin and Trotsky were German agents, and the Bolshevik government just a front for the Kaiser. While there was a hint of truth to the charges, which German diplomatic archives later proved—that is, that Lenin did receive support from German espionage agents—Sisson's papers were a distraction. As an example of an Active Measure, the Sisson Papers affair would be an interesting study. It is not clear who produced the forgeries.

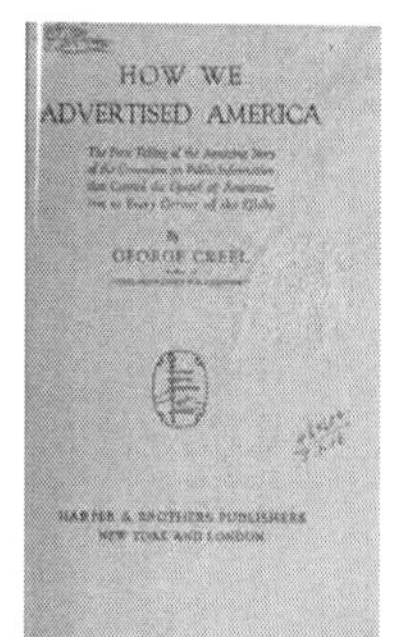

In his short time in Russia, Sisson widely broadcast, around a million copies, a pamphlet on President Wilson's Fourteen Point plan for peace. He also provided money to support Bolshevik propaganda efforts, supposedly against the Germans, but more likely in support of the communists. In all, Sisson's time in Russia was probably less than useless operationally.

William Russell and the Bolsheviks

The Bolsheviks, during wartime alliances with the U.S., both WWI and WWII, mastered the art of maximizing benefits from the relationship while giving away minimal information. Lenin and Trotsky allowed the Creel Committee to use Russia as a platform for its propagandizing. All the while the communists were observing the Americans, gathering assessment data. The cynical veterans of decades of underground revolutionary espionage activities observed the Americans and marveled at how naïve the Americans really were.

Many Americans left Russia, after diplomatic service or service in the Creel Committee, with a clear-eyed understanding of what the

Bolsheviks were all about. However, many Americans left Russia in thrall to the communists.

One who observed and understood was the Creel Committee foreign educational section member, and future dean of Teachers College, William R. Russell. He was in Russia soon after the Bolsheviks seized power and spent considerable time there, working on Creel propaganda against the Germans, for the Bolsheviks, and later against the Bolsheviks. Russell described how he saw the communist tradecraft:

> The way they worked their way to the seizure of power was as follows: Talk about peace, talk about social equality, especially among those most oppressed. Talk about organization of labor, and penetrate into every labor union. Talk on soapboxes. Publish pamphlets and papers. Orate and harangue. Play on envy. Arouse jealousy. Separate class from class. Try to break down the democratic processes from within. Accustom the people to picketing, strikes, mass meetings. Constantly attack the leaders in every way possible so that the people will lose confidence. Then in time of national peril, during a war, on the occasion of a great disaster, or of a general strike, walk into the capital and seize the power. A well-organized minority can work wonders.

Russell's spot-on understanding of how the communists worked, based on his own on-location observations in Russia during the revolution should have been useful to him during the next two decades of his work at Columbia. Yet, under his nose, communist covert influence agents like George Counts, who was under Russell's supervision at Columbia's Teachers College, used the exact tactics he described—talking, publishing, orating and haranguing, breaking down democracy from within, attacking the leaders, making people lose confidence—to destroy American society.

Competing American Amateurs in Revolutionary Russia

As Lenin, Trotsky, Stalin, and the Bolsheviks struggled to establish their fledgling dictatorship of the proletariat; President Wilson brought the U.S. into the war against Germany and its allies, Bulgaria, Turkey, and Austria-Hungary. Wilson's diplomacy with his Russian allies, who surrendered to Germany in the Treaty of Brest-Litovsk in March of 1918, at the same time, was led by competing delegations of amateurs.

Edgar Sisson was dispatched to St. Petersburg as the special representative of the Creel Committee to the Russian government. Apparently, his responsibility was to influence the Bolsheviks. At the same time, according to William Hale, a military psychological operations officer in WW2, in a 1961 article, Wilson sent "a cloud of assorted troubleshooters...each of them independent of the next, and all of them amateur."

The mass of amateur diplomats included the American ambassador, David R. Francis, "an elderly St. Louis grain dealer and Democratic politician." Francis spent more time with his "French tutor," Madame Matilda de Cram, than in dealing with the deteriorating diplomatic situation.

The American Red Cross Mission to Russia, a highly political group financed by American businesses with interests in Russia, was led by a multimillionaire copper magnate, William Boyce Thompson. His deputy, Raymond Robins, was a Progressive party orator who had found God, but no gold in the Alaska gold rush, was in love with his actress sister, and married into money.

Robins became the de facto American interlocutor for the Bolshevik government. Robins, in a 1920 book, claimed that he met with Lenin an average of three times a month during the time he was in St Petersburg and Moscow. Robins styled himself "Colonel Robins," though he had no military background, as did the rest of the Red Cross delegation, made up of dozens of colonels, majors, and lieutenants.

In his diary on the day the Bolsheviks seized power, Robins wrote, "A great day in Russia and the world....What an hour, o my father, Amen."

The military attaché, General William Judson, was the only one of the American diplomatic corps leadership who had any experience with Russia, as an observer of the disastrous Russian war against Japan earlier in the century.

These competing American diplomatic missions set up a confusion of cross-purposes that was skillfully manipulated by Lenin, Trotsky, and their skillful espionage professionals, to the benefit of the communists. In fact, the Red Cross delegation, with Robins as its spokesman, set up "diplomatic" contact with Trotsky after the Bolsheviks seized power, without the knowledge of Ambassador Francis.

Ambassador Francis was intimately acquainted with the royal family of Russia and its hangers-on. He had a limited understanding of the Bolsheviks and their leaders. He was attached to the diplomatic whirl of parties and receptions, royal balls and dancing. The revolution ruined his party.

Consul General Maddin Summers, in Moscow, was a Foreign Service professional valued by Francis because of his marriage to a Russian noble. A vice-consul, Robert Imbrie, who evacuated the embassy in St. Petersburg as the Germans advanced, later returned as the only official diplomatic presence in the city for five months, April to September, 1918. He was beaten to death by a mob in Tehran in 1924. His pitifully ineffective attempts at gathering intelligence exemplified the out-of-touch American diplomatic efforts, and the heavy British influence in manipulating the Americans' nascent intelligence collection efforts.

Imbrie, in a memorandum for the record, breathlessly reported on his "Information Service" set up to collect "military information regarding the Germans, and also political information." Imbrie detailed his amateur intelligence collection network, and the difficulty he encountered selecting men "whose discretion, energy and military knowledge fitted them for the duties assigned." His report makes it clear that Imbrie enjoyed playing spy. He provided scant details, however, on the operation in which two "women were employed because of their intimacy with certain of the Bolshevik leaders."

Imbrie's boast that his Service was "in possession of exact information...of the Bolshevik forces, their armament and so forth" would have been news to the Bolsheviks themselves, since it's unlikely at that time that they knew the strength of their own forces. Imbrie was simply another amateur playing in a game against professionals. It would be unlikely that his collection operations were not compromised by the Soviets from the first report to the last. In fact, the American amateur collection operations were infiltrated and busted at an early stage. British and French espionage operators, cynically manipulated their "idiot little brother from across the Atlantic." The Europeans dragged American diplomats into a spy plot. The British master of deception, Sydney Reilly, seems to be the master-mind of the collection efforts, in which he used American operator Xenophon Kalamatiano to run the network of Russian collectors.

When the Bolsheviks, with their iron control of the operating environment, inevitably exposed the network, it was the American Kalamatiano, who took the rap. Busted, with his Russian agents confessing all, Kalamatiano's own operating notes were enough to hang him. The Cheka discovered a list of Kalamatiano's agents, listed by encrypted number, hidden in his cane.

Kalamatiano confessed all under Cheka interrogation led by Jacob Peters and Dzerzhinsky, and was swiftly sentenced to death. The British consul, Lockhart, arrested at the same time as Kalamatiano, was quickly released in a swap for a Bolshevik diplomat, Litvinov. Kalamatiano suffered another several years in communist prisons before he was released for Bolsheviks held by the U.S.

As Hale observed in his critique of American diplomatic efforts, the American faction was, "Ridden with rivalries and cross-purposes that added to the general misunderstandings now arising between the United States and Russia..." He noted that the divided American diplomats, official and unofficial, "were no match for the monolithic Lenin and Trotsky, who knew precisely what they wanted..."

A newspaper report in 1920 described the Americans in Russia as enveloped in a "bewildering fog in which the American mind loses its way, and its patience, and presently gives the whole thing up as insoluble and casts it aside." The Russians knew very well the American impatience and incapacity for intrigue. Americans, in their sheer good will and energy, were easy targets for Russian espionage and intelligence

Hale's diagnosis of the final result of the diplomatic dance between the Americans and the Bolsheviks during the winter of 1917-1918 was "...the breakdown of relations that had existed between the two countries for over a century."

Alexander Gumberg—the Prototype Soviet Covert Influence Handler

The handful of competing groups representing the U.S. government in Russia lived totally under the control of the revolutionary guard. The communist intelligence and security service had a field day. Able to control the minutest detail of the Americans' lives—housing, food, travel, transportation, down to personal relationships—the communists observed, assessed, controlled and guided the Americans, according to the best interests of the Bolsheviks. It appears that no American who was present in Russia at that time left a record that indicated any of them had a clear understanding of the Russians' operational savvy and ruthless exploitation of the Americans.

The Bolsheviks manipulated the Americans—none of the principal players spoke Russian—by providing "translators." In what became the KGB's standard operating procedure, these translators were usually agents of the communist intelligence services. In a totalitarian society, the KGB easily co-opted those Russians who were not actually KGB officers or agents.

These co-optees were not affiliated with the KGB, but were required to do as ordered, and report to the KGB. These guides and translators were provided, by the KGB, to any visiting American who had potential use as a future covert influence agent, or just to control the perceptions of the visitors. Academics, journalists, politicians, American socialists and communists, and anyone else who might influence the enemies of Russian communism, were targeted in this way.

In Bosnia, when American forces entered the country in 1996, after the U.N. intervened, the Soviet-trained Serbian intelligence services ran operations virtually identical to the Bolshevik model. A high-ranking Serbian intelligence officer, after defecting, explained to me how he had managed the program of providing "interpreter/guides" for Western military and civilian officials. He detailed how, within one or two days, a week at the most, he had full assessment details on his targets.

If the target needed alcohol, or drugs, or girls, or boys, the Serbian "translator" provided for his needs. If the target needed to feel good about himself as an important person, hob-nobbing with bigwigs, the translator met that need, too. Whatever the target needed, the translator provided. In many cases, the Serbians' efforts resulted in a recruitment.

Gumberg, the KGB, and the Americans

Robins' guide and translator, who provided him entrée to the Bolsheviks, was Alexander Gumberg, a Russian-American whose brother, Sergei Zorin (his revolutionary alias), was a high level Bolshevik.

As a young adult, Gumberg worked on the American Menshevik Russian language newspaper, *Noviy Mir,* in New York during the time that Trotsky spent in the city. Like Trotsky, Gumberg's family had roots in Elizavetgrad, in modern day Ukraine.

While in New York, Trotsky wrote for Gumberg's paper. Gumberg, like many Russian socialists, returned to Russia as the revolution unfolded. His connections and sentiments were with the communist revolutionaries in Smolny Palace. He went to work immediately, as we'll see.

Gumberg came to America as a refugee, in early adolescence; apparently his family remained in Russia. During the course of researching this book, I discovered a cache of Gumberg's personal letters to a romantic target in the Bronx, New York.

These revealing documents, held in the private collection of Reverend Raymond Cannata, a relative of Gumberg's love interest, Esther Siebel, reveal that Gumberg was a true socialist believer, from his early youth. The milieu in New York, where he studied and worked, was pure radical chic—he taught and studied at the socialist Rand School, and addressed his friends as "comrade."

Some of Gumberg's personal letters to Esther Siebel, starting in 1914, were written on the *Noviy Mir* newspaper letterhead, and revealed Gumberg to be immersed in the revolutionary world, a committed socialist, three years before the Bolshevik revolution.

The final series of letters, beginning in the first week of April, 1917, to the young radical woman, now romantically entwined with another comrade, Spencer Brodney, were written during Gumberg's crossing of two continents, en route to his first operational work against the Americans in St. Petersburg.

Gumberg's journey, via train across Canada, then steamship, the Empress of Russia, to Japan and China and finally a train across Siberia to St. Petersburg, was concurrent with Leon Trotsky's return to Russia. However, Trotsky left New York and the *Noviy Mir* on about March 27, 1917, by way of the Atlantic.

Gumberg told the girl that eating at the ship's table, crossing the Pacific, was like being in the office of the *Noviy Mir*. Evidently the Menshevik paper's staff was all returning to Russia at the same time, including Gumberg's Bolshevik brother, Sergei Zorin.

Gumberg related to Siebel, in a letter dated April 14, 1917, that he and his brother earned the enmity of their socialist traveling companions because they had paid extra for single cabins.

Gumberg, Robins, KGB Executioner, Bolshevik Vice Foreign Minister

In a gushingly naive biography of Robins, a photo, taken in St. Petersburg during the early days of Robins' Russian sojourn, shows a group of men and a boy apparently just before or after some type of event, gathered around two cars.

Robins in full Red Cross military uniform, with great coat and campaign hat, boots and leggings, stands with a group of Russians in front of the official Red Cross automobile, a Pierce Arrow. Leaning on the car's radiator grill, separated from Robins by a jaunty American flag flying from the right front fender, is Jacob Peters, identified in the caption as the "Cheka chief in Moscow."

Peters is clearly a man in his element. He is relaxed, both hands in his overcoat pockets, legs crossed at the ankles. A ribbon decorates Peters' lapel. A pork pie hat, brim straight across his forehead, tops off the portrait of a cool and smug communist. He, along with the man to his left, is at ease, while the most of the rest of the group, including Robins, appear to be at attention. Peters' face is set in a grim smirk.

Peters, known as the "Chief Executioner of the Russian Revolution," was famous as "the most sinister figure of the Red Terror." The New York Times in 1919 reported that Peters was killed in a bombing at the Kremlin. But other sources report that he survived the bomb, and died in Stalin's 1938 purges. Regardless how he died, Peters lived as a thug, before and during his time as a leader in the Cheka. As a refugee in London, before the revolution, he brazenly murdered three policemen in a robbery, raising money for the proletariat.

On Peters' left is Leo Karakhan, a Bolshevik foreign affairs specialist, later Soviet ambassador to China, Far East expert, and Assistant Commissar of Foreign Affairs of the Soviet Union. In the time period of Robins' visit to Russia, Karakhan was the secretary of the Bolshevik delegation to the German armistice negotiations in Brest-Litovsk. Karakhan, tall and dark, sports a goatee and mustache, his dark overcoat seems to be dusty. His hands are in his overcoat pockets, and his body is turned toward Peters. He is solemn and serious.

After being recalled to Moscow from his ambassadorship in Ankara, in 1937, Karakhan was executed with a bullet to the neck, during Stalin's purges. In the New York Times, a "special cable" from Moscow, at the time of Karakhan's recall, likely from Walter Duranty, assured Americans that the recall was "for personal reasons." Karakhan had been known as "the master spy of the Bolsheviki in the Far East," and was the first Soviet ambassador to China, where he ran extensive espionage operations.

To Karakhan's left is a boy, of ten or twelve, proudly at attention, standing slightly in front of the rest of the group, in full Red Cross uniform, a spitting image of the American "colonel." The boy is identified as "the Russian boy mascot of the American Red Cross Commission."

Coolly off to the mascot's left, hands behind his back, is Alex Gumberg, Robins' secretary/assistant, and KGB handler. With a waist length brown leather jacket and military cap, wearing knee length boots, Gumberg could pass for a soldier, or a driver. His smooth, round face is boyish and he seems slightly ashamed of something, like he was just caught with his hands in the cookie jar.

The picture is a study in contrasts. Self-assured, dressed up in a play uniform, totally out of his element, Robins, officious and ridiculous at the same time, playing at diplomacy, a child in a deadly serious man's game, is surrounded by some of the century's vilest, cruelest, most devious, most cunning international conspirators. Robins is fresh and innocent, unaware of the true nature of his companions. He believes that his bosom pal, his "American secretary/translator," Alex Gumberg, is doing his bidding. Robins seemed oblivious to the fact that Gumberg worked for Peters' organization, and therefore, Robins also was working for the good of the Soviet revolution.

Gumberg and the American Committee for Public Information

Gumberg also "worked for" Sisson in the CPI's Russian delegation. Sisson, another guileless American, reported in his autobiography, *One Hundred Red Days: Personal Chronicle of the Bolshevik Revolution*, that Gumberg was "my interpreter." At least Sisson could see that there was the potential for danger with Gumberg, but being a stranger in a strange land, not speaking the language, and being responsible for influencing the population, Sisson needed a guide and language man. Sisson noted that Gumberg was "one of the most contradictory, and at times one of the most powerful of the odd figures of the Revolution."

Sisson's belief that Gumberg "did not associate himself with [Trotsky] or the Bolsheviks," in the summer of 1917, reflects his abject misunderstanding of Russia and the tradecraft of the communists. Like other Americans, he must have imagined that Gumberg's visit to Russia could be compared to Sisson visiting relatives in Omaha—with no understanding of the total control the communists exerted on those who fell under their strong hand.

During the fall and winter of 1917, Sisson noted that Gumberg was "acting as interpreter and handy man for American groups," as if the wily KGB operator was good for fixing broken faucets and reading menus. And it's very likely that Gumberg did just those things, building rapport and relationships as he smoothed out the difficult circumstances these Americans found in St. Petersburg, Moscow, and Vologda.

Sisson, in his book, relates his concern that Gumberg, upon returning to America, might have thought of injecting Bolshevik ideas into the American system. Sisson had Gumberg over to his New York hotel, where Sisson, "sat him down alongside me, told him that he was so close to Trotsky that he ought to have absorbed knowledge of the elaborate game of the winter, that I sought no admission from him, had no threats for him, but would expect him...to 'keep out of politics' while the war lasted."

Sisson, demonstrating his, common for an American with no background in dealing with Bolsheviks, lack of understanding, relates that, after he advised Gumberg to avoid politics in America, Gumberg "smilingly gave [that pledge]." Sisson hoped Gumberg kept the promise, but "never made any effort to find out if he did." Sisson's final word on Gumberg was dismissive: "A mighty man in

Russia, he was powerless in America." If only Sisson knew the power Gumberg wielded, both in Russia and in America.

Gumberg's brother, Sergei Zorin, was hailed as an "architect of the Great October Revolution" in a contemporary work of art, a porcelain platter, which he signed along with only 15 others, including Lenin, Trotsky, Lunacharsky, and Zinoviev. Zorin served as the Soviet Minister for Posts and Telegraphs, before falling from favor during Stalin's reign, probably due to his closeness to Trotsky.

Gumberg's Work against American Journalists

Little did Sisson know that Gumberg had been active throughout the year—escorting and translating for a group of American journalists, likely identified by Bolshevik intelligence as Willing Accomplice targets. John Reed, an American communist later named Soviet consul to New York, and Reed's lover, American communist Louise Bryant; and Albert Rhys Williams, the American socialist reporter who addressed the Congress of Soviets in 1917 with "greetings from the Socialists of America...we come here to learn its lesson and to express appreciation for your great achievements."

Williams' memoirs note Gumberg's presence, without further comment, as a participant in a celebratory romp the night that the Winter Palace fell. Reed, Bryant, Williams, and Bessie Beatty, a San Francisco reporter, the final member of the group squired by Gumberg, all received insider access, thanks to Gumberg and his Bolshevik bosses.

All four seem to have dedicated the remainder of their lives to supporting the Soviet Union. Bryant later married the first U.S. ambassador to the Soviet Union. Even Williams' wife, Lucita Squier, already a writer for silent movies in 1917, wrote a glowing review of Willi Muenzenberg's covert influence Moscow film studio, Mezhrabpom-Russ, in a San Francisco paper in 1930.

Gumberg's Ops against American Politicians

Three more prominent Americans were targeted and used by Alex Gumberg. Former Indiana governor James Goodrich, in 1921, was accompanied by "his interpreter," Gumberg, during his inspection trip for the Famine Relief Commission. Predictably, Goodrich returned to America singing the praises of the Russian peasant.

Sometime in the 1920s or early 1930s, Gumberg brought former governor of Wisconsin Robert LaFollette into the fold.

Senator William Borah, the chairman of the Senate Foreign Relations Committee, became enmeshed with Gumberg in the late 1920s. Gumberg and Robins pressed Borah for help in obtaining diplomatic recognition for the Soviet Union. Gumberg also worked with Borah on business deals for Russian and American interests.

Gumberg in America, Post-Revolution

After his work for the Bolsheviks against Robins and the Red Cross delegation, Gumberg returned to the U.S. He worked as a director for the KGB's cover provider for its operations in America, AMTORG, in New York City, in the textiles division. He then was a director for Chase Bank, and served as a director-without-portfolio for Floyd Odlum's Atlas Corporation, an investment conglomerate. In his obituary in the New York Times, Gumberg was described as a "financier."

Gumberg's KGB Operations—Long-Lasting Effects

It appears that Gumberg was responsible for recruiting and handling Robins during the volatile days of the Bolshevik revolution in 1917 to 1918. Gumberg's Robins operation was a template for future KGB influence operations. Gumberg assessed Robins' motivations, and effected such a powerful recruitment of the Red Cross official that Robins loved the Russian manipulator as a brother. When Gumberg died, in 1939, Robins wrote to Odlum:

> Alexander Gumberg was the best informed, and most luminous, loyal and courageous intelligence in all the Allied embassies and missions in Petrograd during the most critical months of the Russian Soviet Revolution. On intimate personal terms with Lenin, Trotsky, Dzerzhinsky and Chicherin he knew every member of the First Council of the Peoples Commissars. Loving his native land, yet wholly loyal to his adopted country, he worked valiantly for understanding and economic cooperation....He returned with me [to the U.S.] seeking to help in the true interpretation of the significance...of Russia under the Soviets for America.

In a letter to Gumberg (addressing his handler in the third person) in 1937, Robins gushed, "Almost twenty years I have known and trusted and loved Alexander Gumberg, sharing as we have in the Hope of this Supreme Revolution of all time, having known LENIN [*sic*] and his matchless mind and daring in the service of the liberation of the Group of Toil..."

Robins returned to the U.S. where he was a force in Republican Party politics. As one of the first Willing Accomplices, he spread the KGB payload far and wide, advocating for American recognition of the new communist state, and for expanded trade with the Soviets. He drifted along, claiming expertise on all things Russian, based on his pitiful few months in Russia. It appears he never realized how he had been used as an influence agent.

He cracked up in 1932, though. After disappearing from a speaking engagement in Chicago, he was found in North Carolina, using a fake name, claiming to be a coal miner from Kentucky. This incident was blamed on "amnesia," and Robins recovered, and lived to a ripe old age. However, it's clear that Robins showed symptoms of some sort of mental illness for much of his life. Could he have suffered from the strain of guilty knowledge?

Template for Muenzenberg

It appears that these first, highly successful operations to recruit Willing Accomplices for influence operations may have served as templates for Muenzenberg's later operations. However, the difference seems to be the payload for these first influence targets—Reed, Bryant, Williams, Beatty, Robins and Goodrich. In the early days of Bolshevik rule, when Gumberg was working his magic, Lenin and Trotsky still believed that the global socialist revolution would sweep the world in no time. So the payload that Gumberg slipped into the naïve Americans' heads was that the Soviet Union was a legitimate nation, very much like America during its revolution, and was deserving of American respect and recognition. Implicit in this payload was a promise of bountiful profits for capitalists who played nice with the Bolshevik.

This is in stark contrast to the later objectives of Soviet covert influence agents—destroying American culture and society. A positive influence goal made sense, during the heady, early days of the new country. As the Civil War dragged on, and it became clear that no other nation would fall to the Reds, the influence goals changed as well. We'll examine those payloads soon.

The Kremlin, a palatial dining room converted to a conference room Late March, 1919

Lenin had convened the Communist International earlier that month. Even though the meetings had the air of rushed urgency, and the delegates were not quite representative of global Communism, Party pronouncements rang with the inevitability of global victory for the Party. The world had yet to grasp the reality of Communism and the tools required for successful Communist victories.

No one understood the need for these tools better than the crippled Polish nobleman that Lenin installed as the first chief of the KGB, Felix Dzerzhinsky. He not only understood the need for them, he was a skilled covert action practitioner.

The atmosphere in the Kremlin on this chilly early spring morning was ripe with ambition and terror. Ambitions of spreading their revolution, like an infection, through the world. Terrified by the realization that their theories were being proven ridiculous by only two years of reality.

Little could the revolutionaries have dreamed that the operation set in motion this morning would echo through the next century. Or maybe they were supremely confident of their plan. Regardless, they did not imagine their fledgling state would collapse of its own impossible, inhumane, cruel weight after eighty years of rule and millions of lives snuffed out; while the operation begun on this day would relentlessly shape global politics for decades after the collapse of the Soviet Union, the unmasking of communism, the disintegration of the KGB, and the grisly deaths of many of the individual espionage officers who turned their leaders' ideas into intelligence operations.

"Good morning, Comrade Secretary."

The Polish-born chief of the Russian Communist Party's intelligence service was as close to Lenin as anyone. Their shared experience of jail and labor camps, revolutionary conspiracies, civil war, and now their complicity in the Red Terror created bonds tighter than a blood relationship.

His accented Russian voice was slightly high-pitched, but today it was hoarse. He had been up half the night with deputies of the Extraordinary Committee he led against counter-revolutionaries. His tirade of screamed epithets at his devoted cadre of blood-thirsty Chekists had been intended to motivate them to increase by a factor of ten the round-up of counter-revolutionary scum.

The Terror he created would be perfected in the next several decades, and one of today's co-conspirators, a Georgian thug who used the nom-de-revolution Stalin ("Steel") would hone the Terror to a fine point.

"Comrade Commissar, it's a fine morning."

Lenin sipped fragrant hot tea, his face wreathed by the steam from the glass cup in a silver holder. His face was calm and serene, betraying no hint of the internal physical and psychic pain he suffered. Two bullets, lodged in his body from an assassination attempt less than two years before still felt like fire in his bones.

The table was laid with a sumptuous breakfast of pastries, bread, caviar, and pots of spiced tea simmering in golden samovars on a side bar, heated with charcoal. Serfs quickly and silently served their communist masters, heirs to the throne of the Russian Caesars. The czars and their nobility replaced by new royalty and nobles, the Commissars and functionaries of the Russian Communist Party.

Terrified of their masters, the revolutionary slaves simply adapted to life under the new regime, with little to no change in their existence. They mixed the teas to create a traditional Russian brew, using an array of samovars of dark and spiced tea, and a samovar of hot water.

"What's the delay in Petrograd, comrade? Counter-revolutionaries and saboteurs need to feel the steel of our proletarian blades before they kneel in submission."

The blunt rejoinder from Stalin was typical. He had no time for niceties.

"Typhoid, comrade. We dare not enter the city until the fever has subsided."

"Fever be damned! Root out, crush and destroy the Whites and saboteurs!"

Stalin's swarthy features reddened with anger.

"It will be done, comrade."

Lenin, ignoring Stalin's detour, invited both men to sit. Stalin took a sip of the tea at his place, and spat it out.

"Saboteur! Bring me tea, not a woman's piss! Strong tea for a strong man, you Chechen dog!"

A serf scuttled forward from the side-bar, retrieved the General Secretary's glass cup, and created a new mixture, his hands trembling. Never looking at Stalin's face, averting his eyes lest they meet the terrible gaze and call attention to himself, the serf slid the new, stronger brew past Stalin's right elbow.

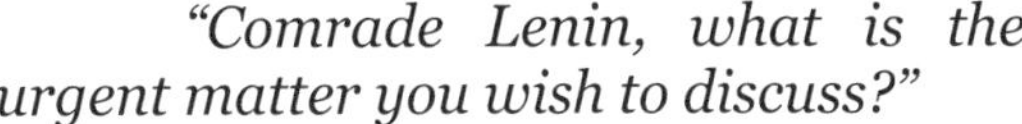

"Comrade Lenin, what is the urgent matter you wish to discuss?"

Again, the blunt approach of the Georgian.

"Have a pancake, comrade."

Lenin slid a plate of blinis stuffed with caviar toward Stalin. Dzerzhinsky quietly watched the two power brokers spar. He knew that his place was to speak when spoken to. Although he was not shy in disagreeing with either of the two sides of the double-headed monster which ruled the fledgling communist state, he also sensed the air of desperation in both men, and knew the depravity either was capable of. Even he far underestimated the depths of cruelty to which the two communist dictators could descend. He quietly sipped his strong tea, and nibbled buttered toast.

Lenin began:

"The American counter-revolutionary army is on the move in Vladivostok and Archangelsk. Our forces have harassed them. However, it is clear that our men offer only token resistance. The capitalists want our gold, our timber, our land. We face threats on all fronts, comrades. The glorious revolution is in mortal jeopardy. Let us prepare the destruction of this vile enemy."

Stalin grunted his assent. He noisily sipped his tea, his mustache dripping with the sweet beverage.

"And what can be done, dearest comrade? Our Siberian winter is effectively destroying them, even as we speak. We have more immediate concerns closer to home."

"Exactly, Stalin, my dear. The expedition of the American mercenaries will end as did Napoleon's. Their failure is assured. Yet, the willingness of the capitalists to invade our fatherland, even as the glorious revolution provides a model for the American proletariat to follow, is my concern. They are too strong, too brash, too uncivilized, too unsophisticated. They do not listen to reason, as do our European brothers."

Lenin daintily sipped his tea, more dilute than Stalin's, and quickly finished a caviar loaded pancake. Continuing, he alternately fixed his intelligence chief, and his deputy with his implacable gaze.

"Our propaganda and agitation among the American soldiers is bearing fruit. Our Polish comrade has more information....?"

Dzerzhinsky, caught by surprise, expecting discussion of the situation in Petrograd, quickly shifted his attention to his operations in the Far East.

"Our agents have met daily with American proletarian soldiers. We have been successful, my comrades. As we have worked in the royal army, so we work in the capitalist army. We are providing our agents with text for a petition. The American soldiers are easy to work. They are innocent, and unaware of our methods. We have recruited two, as unwitting agents, who think they are helping their comrades. The petition is in their hands now, and our officer has a meeting with the local agent in a week's time. Our control is superb, as usual, and we expect excellent results."

"That's fine, comrade. Your operation is fine. But what we need is much deeper than this expedition. It is a glimpse into the heart of the American proletariat, and how they are manipulated by the capitalists."

Lenin, warmed to his subject, the organization of conspiracies. Understanding the motivations of the Anglo-Saxon, German, and Western European mind was one of the areas in which he believed himself to have superior understanding. His extensive relations with the German secret services, German socialists, and his lengthy residence in Western Europe gave him much data for understanding the West.

"Our scientific approach to dialectical materialism is blunted by the confusing propaganda the capitalists flood over their proletarian masses. The masses are blinded by 'patriotism,' 'rugged individualism,' the American myth of "exceptionalism." They accept their chains and do not realize they are slaves of a corrupt and dying system."

Stalin, finished with his first cup of tea, motioned impatiently for a refill. The Chechen dog he had cursed earlier obediently fetched the Communist Commissar a new glass. This one, however, the dog had prepared specially. In the small kitchen just off the meeting room, the Chechen servant had unbuttoned his fly, and rubbed his penis around the rim of the tea glass.

"Taste the seed of my Chechen nation, you Georgian son of a whore!"

He silently commended his handiwork to his brutal master.

Stalin slurped the strong tea, imported from Georgia, with satisfaction.

"Yes, comrade, I, too, am concerned with the American problem. What is your proposal?"

Lenin strode to a floor length window and threw it open to the March breezes. Both Dzerzhinsky and Stalin had lit cigarettes to enjoy with their tea. Lenin, detesting the smell of the "filthy weed," introduced the fresh air into their meeting room. He continued, with his back to the smoking pair:

"It is simple, my courageous General. We continue the same operations which gained our victory in Petrograd, and all our victories. Even our Russian proletariat needed to be prepared. We infiltrate, penetrate, and control the channels of indoctrination of the masses. The West, and especially America, has developed a strong methodology of indoctrination of their

proletariat. Their schools fill the children's heads with the myths of American exceptionalism. Their press daily is filled with lies about the glorious Socialist revolution. And their centers of entertainment create propaganda films that glorify their racist, imperialist wars of domination. These, my comrade, are the keys to the hearts of our enemy. Comrade Gumberg made great strides, but he is only one man. We penetrate these channels; insert our messages of truth and reality: that America is a racist, imperialist, hate-filled, hegemonic, xenophobic, nest of capitalist vipers fixated on global exploitation of labor to fill the coffers of American capitalist swine. When we control those channels, and can insert our truths, the American spirit and morale will wither, decay and rot. The tendrils of our conspiracy will choke off American exceptionalism like a cat smothers a baby, in its cradle."

"Your mind is the fertile soil of genius, comrade."

Dzerzhinsky sensed the proper place for his comments to be inserted in the conversation. His mind, thinking in operational terms at all times, understood immediately how to run this operation. Without sharing details with his superiors, he already knew who to call on. Radek, the German propagandist, was already running similar operations against the Germans and Europeans. His tool, Muenzenberg, would be a fine operator for this requirement.

"Allow me to build a capability and report back to you in a week, comrade. At that time, it will be possible to provide details on our capacity and the necessary funds required."

"Funds are not an issue, comrade. This issue is of utmost importance and is not subject to financial controls. Diamonds and gold are available in whatever quantity is necessary. Strike at the core of the imperialist pigs! Slice open the heart of the American capitalist beast and bring it quivering to me! We will strangle them before they realize there is a hand on their throat."

Lenin now trembled himself, like the serfs who served him, but his shaking was not due to terror. His excitement was nearly unbearable. A quick operation to destroy the hated American spirit would provide him with unbridled joy. The anticipation of Dzerzhinsky's conspiracy already brought him an electric thrill. He was a genius, and he knew it.

"To the west crimson light will shine in the near future, comrades! And so we call this operation Crimson Sunset. Now, let me see the list of counter-revolutionaries liquidated last night, my Polish comrade."

Lenin's Dacha, Gorki
January 21, 1924

Lenin's palsied body twitched, his heart fibrillating wildly, his fevered brain presented him with a vision. The vision was so wild and terrible that what was left of his mind was shattered.

He saw a vast communist army crushed under the might of American technology.

Then, in the next instant, another cinematic vision appeared to the Soviet dictator—a melding of the USSR's hammer and sickle on a red field with the American red, white and blue.

In the foreground, American workers marched victoriously, arm in arm with Russian workers, under the new banner, accompanied by huge printed placards bearing motivational slogans. Peace, Hope, Believe, Change.

Vladimir Ilyich Lenin, the power-hungry architect of communist domination of the world slipped from consciousness and met his maker. He had not labored in vain. A faint smile curled up the corners of his rapidly cooling lips.

Stalin—Marxist-Leninism Perfected

The failings of Marxism in the real world, even after Lenin's adjustment of adding the Vanguard of the Proletariat to guide the ignorant masses to utopia, were glaringly obvious to objective observers. Most especially to the desperate men who now sat atop the communist throne in the Kremlin. Stalin was active in the revolution for nearly 30 years. Even before Lenin's diseased brain failed, Stalin maneuvered. He placed his lackeys in positions of power.

When he became Comrade Number One, his main goal was to consolidate power. Of course, he used Marxism-Leninism to explain this move. Tom West described Stalin's outlook:

> Only one man, the wisest and strongest of all, can be entrusted with the task of building socialism. And this man must not flinch from inflicting mass killings, deliberate famines, and torture involving the suffering and deaths of

> many millions of people. The Wise Man must employ whatever means he deems necessary to root out the millions of enemies of the people so that he can lead men to perpetual peace, happiness, and total communization.

The beautiful theories of Marx, Engels, and Lenin were now become flesh—the flesh was Josef Stalin. The requirement for communist leaders to force, coerce, bully, murder, maim, torture, kill, starve, imprison, shoot, destroy, exploit, and otherwise dehumanize its subjects, all for the greater common good, was demonstrated for all the world to see during the reign of Stalin.

Truth vs. Wish Fulfillment

How much reality would it take for true believers to realize the awful truth about the beautiful theory? How many dead before believers lost their faith? Could the horrible truth be hidden? If it could, for how long?

Some of the elite members of the Communist Party inside Stalin's prison nation were rewarded with luxurious lifestyles. How long could they be bought off? How much suffering could the masses endure before they threw off the yokes of Stalinist slavery?

It would appear that the endurance of the Russian masses was greater than anyone could have guessed. It took more than 60 years of violence against human nature before the long-suffering Russians gained their freedom.

What we'll see here is that the same suspension of reality exists today. PC believers put their faith in a discredited, utopian dream vision, and ignore reality. They seem prepared to sacrifice as many humans as did Stalin, in order to save humanity.

Although the sacrifices will begin with their opponents, of course—today's American PC believers can rest assured that the PC boot will be on their necks, all in due time.

The question is only how long it will take before the inhumane ideology of American PC-Progressives eats its own. Just as Trotsky felt the cold steel, as did Kamenev, and Zinoviev, millions of other true believers in Russian communism met their bloody fates.

Chapter 6

Soviet Active Measures

Active Measure operations differ from collection operations in one very important aspect—*the effects of Active Measure operations can continue forever.*

Human Intel *Collection* Operations.

Say "KGB spy." What do most people envision when they hear these words? Those who have watched too much TV or movies see assassinations and fancy weapons. If you're more grounded in reality, or a historian, you likely see the Rosenbergs, Kim Philby, Rick Ames, Jim Nicholson, John Walker and his family, or Alger Hiss.

These were all recruited agents of the KGB. Most of their work for the KGB was *collecting* and reporting secrets to the Russians. The Rosenbergs collected secrets on America's atomic bomb production program. John Walker *collected* secrets on the U.S. Navy's communications encryption systems. Jim Nicholson reported secrets about the CIA's operations and personnel (including my own life story and personality assessment, which he reported to the

KGB when he was my operations instructor, severely curtailing my operational options).

Each of these agents *collected* and reported secrets to their handlers. These are the prototypical intelligence agents. Most historians who study the KGB and its operations focus on these types of agents—*intelligence collectors*.

From the point of view of managing espionage operations, collection ops are resource intensive. Collectors need to have headquarters defining the requirements for collection. Headquarters are directed by policy makers, who identify unanswered questions they'd like answered. Targeters identify people that might have access to information to answer the requirements. Case officers hit the streets, meet, assess, develop and recruit agents in response.

Once intelligence collection agents are recruited, case officers must meet them securely, keep them motivated and focused, collect the secrets, and write reports based on the collected secrets. Requirements must be constantly refined and communicated to the collectors. The agent must be directed and his reporting fine-tuned.

The human intelligence collection enterprise is a highly resource-intensive and finely balanced affair. If any one of the steps is compromised or disrupted, the whole operation can be ruined. If the agent loses his access, the operation is over. If the agent dies, is arrested, or incapacitated, or loses his access, the collection operation is over. When the Rosenberg op was disrupted, there was no more product, no more secrets—the op finally died with the communist agents in the electric chair.

The most striking weakness of human intelligence collection operations is their limited life-span. As soon as the policy makers no longer are interested in the intelligence produced from the operation, it is over. Very quickly what was once hot, high-level, intelligence becomes historical trivia.

No matter how well the intelligence collection apparatus works, no matter how skillful the analysts, targeters, and case officers are a human collection operation is limited in duration. It has a life-span. It has a birth, and a death. When it is over, it is over. Once the agent is no longer providing information, once the information is no longer needed or timely, the operation is over. It is dead. The information becomes history, not intelligence.

There are no lingering after-effects when a human collection operation is over. When it's over, it's over. No more intelligence reports, no more interest in the information. The agent is terminated, the relationship ended.

Active Measures Can Live Forever

Now let's consider different sorts of intelligence operation. They are linked to human collection operations in that they also have important roles for human agents. Soviet intelligence called these other types of operations **Active Measures**. U.S. intelligence terminology is different. But most of the operations the Soviets called Active Measures would be **Covert Action** in American terminology.

Active Measure operations differ from collection operations in one very important aspect—**the effects of Active Measure operations can continue forever**. This is the root of *Willing Accomplices*, and a fact that is overlooked by almost all historians and commentators. It's worth repeating, with emphasis: ***The effects of Active Measures can last forever***.

For example, let's say a politician, Mr. Jones, intent on impugning the integrity of a political rival, Mr. Smith, during an election, plants false stories about Mr. Smith in the popular press. Let's say Mr. Jones accuses Mr. Smith of siring a child out of wedlock. The stories about the child are picked up by other media, and repeated. The Mr. Smith takes "the high road," and ignores the stories about the child. So, there is no printed evidence of Mr. Smith refuting the false stories. Mr. Smith wins the election, and goes on to achieve national prominence.

Fifty years later a historian is researching a book on Mr. Smith. The historian uncovers the contemporary press accounts of the bastard child. Of course, these press accounts are false, part of the active measure of denigration/disinformation. But the historian finds the false stories repeated in numerous publications, with no balancing denials by Mr. Smith. The historian includes the story of the bastard child in his book on Mr. Smith. The bastard child story, seemingly dead and buried decades earlier, now takes on a life of its own.

The book is used as a reference for encyclopedia (today, Wikipedia) articles about Mr. Smith. The encyclopedia is quoted and referenced hundreds of times, becoming the standard reference article on Mr. Smith. The "bastard child" story is now embedded in history, and lives forever.

While most Active Measure operations require human agents to initiate and run, once the operation is moving, it becomes a virtual perpetual motion intelligence machine.

The most striking example of the perpetual effects of an Active Measure operation is PC today. PC is a direct result of the communist covert influence operations, which planted their payloads in American academia, education, media, and Hollywood. PC's accepted anti-American dogma is nearly directly quoted from the messages implanted by Willi Muenzenberg, as we'll see in a later chapter.

Birth and Control of Soviet Active Measures

From the early 1920s through the beginning of World War 2, the KGB conducted a flurry of recruitments in America. While there is no record of the ratio of intel collection operations to Active Measures, Andrew's reading of the Mitrokhin notes shows that by spring of 1941, the KGB's "agent network in the United States numbered 221."

A former chief of Active Measures in KGB headquarters, an experienced case officer who had been the KGB's COS in Vienna in 1961, in his unpublished memoirs said,

> [Active Measures] did get an early start in Soviet Russia. Lenin's longtime revolutionaries who took power in November 1917 were so imbued with clandestine tricks that it was second nature to transmute them into government policy.

The KGB Active Measures specialist, who rose to the rank of general in 1967, said that the goal of KGB Active Measures since 1923 was, "upsetting the counterrevolutionary plans and activities of the opposition."

As the Soviet Union evolved into Stalin's dictatorship, the KGB received orders to step up Active Measures. One goal was "weakening or misleading...our adversaries."

This Active Measures connoisseur and leader claimed that his specialty was the "intellectual approach to clandestine intelligence," in contrast to "the more mechanical approach of 'practitioners.'"

The KGB general in recounting his experience with Active Measures said that these operations were controlled from the highest levels of the Soviet government. He described his specialty:

Active Measures' were clandestine actions designed on the one hand to affect foreign governments, groups and influential individuals in ways favoring the objectives of Soviet policy and, on the other hand, to weaken the opposition to it. Such actions might or might not involve misinforming an adversary by distortion, concealment or invention, but in practice we got better results by exposing truth—selectively. We usually made the distinction clear. When someone would propose a measure, for instance, we would frequently ask him, 'How much deza [disinformation] is involved in it?

The KGB general discussed keeping intelligence collection operations separate from Active Measures, "We tried to avoid using...foreign journalists whom we had recruited as information sources [note: intelligence collectors]. That would expose their true political sentiments and reduce their ability to gather intelligence from circles hostile to us." This clarifies the KGB's tendency, at least in the Cold War era, to compartment its Active Measure operations from intelligence collection ops.

The KGB general described his Active Measures group using the British defectors, Guy Burgess and Kim Philby, in their ops. The British turncoats were most useful in turning the Russians' English translations into vernacular English. The KGB officer notes that Burgess, while difficult to work with—the Russian describes having to deal with the young boys Burgess introduced as "his girlfriends," supplied by the KGB—did produce good work for the KGB. On the other hand, Philby was less useful, and provided input mainly through his case officer, Yuri Modin.

The KGB specialist carefully differentiates his operations, during the Cold War, from those of the International Department (ID) of the Central Committee of the Communist Party of the Soviet Union (CPSU). He admits that both the KGB's Active Measures groups and the ID were "attacking some of the same targets by developing campaigns and demonstrations..." And KGB officers would usually be the conduits for clandestine payments to the ID's covert influence fronts—"international organizations of lawyers or peace lovers or students..." But he notes that there was no "single coordinated program" of Soviet Active Measures.

The KGB general is adamant about the bureaucratic differentiation of the operations run by the ID—which was the successor to the Comintern's OMS—from the KGB proper's Active

Measure operations. From an outsider's perspective, this is interesting because it confirms analysis that Muenzenberg's Covert Influence operations were run under cover of the OMS.

The Active Measures specialist described covert influence operations:

> To deliver our policy line to key foreign government people in ways that did not seem to come from us, we would use friendly Westerns who were close to them. Our assets—sometimes just trusted persons without being fully recruited agents—included political activists, journalists, scientists, or government and military officials—and even sometimes businessmen. Sometimes we would get our own diplomats to drop 'indiscreet' remarks to their Western colleagues.

In the end, the main goal of Covert Influence Active Measures against the U.S. was to move political and public opinion "away from the conservative parties that were opposing our policies," in the words of a KGB Active Measures manager.

Taxonomy of Soviet Active Measures

Thomas Boghart, writing in the CIA's Studies in Intelligence, provided a taxonomy of the activities that the Soviets considered Active Measures. According to Boghart, "The basic goal of Soviet active measures was to weaken the USSR's opponents — first and foremost the "main enemy" (*glavny protivnik*), the United States — and to create a favorable environment for advancing Moscow's views and international objectives worldwide." Weakening and if possible destroying the U.S. was most effectively and efficiently done by attacking from within. Striking America's inner strength required hitting its cultural transmission institutions. As we'll see, they did just that.

Disinformation or Deception is planting false stories, usually in media not affiliated with Russia or the KGB. These operations never reveal the sponsor of the information. A disinformation operation could be an activity as simple as starting rumors. Forging documents, letters, orders, treaties that cast the target in a bad light is another form of deception or disinformation.

A classic disinformation campaign illustrates the longevity of Active Measures. In 1983 the KGB planted a false story in an Indian newspaper. The story, the "payload" of the operation, attributed to an unnamed American scientist, claimed that the AIDS virus was created by American bio-weapons laboratories. The initial publication did not have much of an impact. But in 1985, the sprout began to grow. A Soviet newspaper took up the initial claims, and elaborated—now the Russians claimed that not only had the Americans created AIDS, but also that they had purposely infected Haitians, homeless, homosexuals, and drug addicts in experiments to test the disease.

The story was picked up, amplified, added to, and exaggerated, until, during the U.S. presidential election campaign in 2008, we learned the preacher of Barack Obama's Black Liberation Theology church parrot the payload. In April 2003, twenty years after the America-invented-AIDS Active Measure operation began, Reverend Jeremiah Wright thundered from the pulpit of Trinity Church of Christ in Chicago, "The government lied about inventing the HIV virus as a means of genocide against people of color."

At the time, Barack Obama, who would five years later be the President of the U.S., was an active participant in Wright's racist congregation. Did Obama sit in the pews the day Wright delivered this KGB Active Measure payload? It's not clear, but it is clear that Obama did not reject Wright's virulent Soviet-inspired anti-American rants until they became public in 2008.

Denigration Operations during the Cold War are probably closest to the early Soviet Comintern-covered Muenzenberg covert influence operations designed to destroy the American culture. The goal of these was, just as Muenzenberg's goal, to destroy American exceptionalism, to destroy specific targets—individual people, organizations, or countries. Although the KGB does not make a distinction between covert influence and denigration, there is a fine difference. However, to the KGB operators, these were just another *deza* operation.

The KGB specialist describes a couple of denigration operations. One was designed to destroy the NATO Secretary General Joseph Luns. The KGB circulated "false allegations that he had misused official funds." The op proved successful when Luns retired a year later. The KGB officer heard, "through agent sources that these allegations, though unproved [since they were untrue], had indeed played a role in his departure."

The KGB general also claimed that his office ran a denigration operation against the German scientist, Werner von Braun, who helped America with its rocket program, after WW2.

In Oleg Gordievsky's book *KGB: The Inside Story*, he described a forgery planted by the KGB in the United States in 1982:

> In late October the Washington main residency implemented Operation Golf, designed to plant fabricated material discrediting the U.S. ambassador to the United Nations, Jeanne Kirkpatrick, on the unsuspecting American correspondent of the London New Statesman. On November 5 the New Statesman duly carried an article entitled "A Girl's Best Friend," exploring "the often secret relationship" between Jeanne Kirkpatrick and South Africa. The article included a photograph of a forged letter to Ms. Kirkpatrick from a counselor at the South African embassy conveying "best regards and gratitude" from the head of South African military intelligence and allegedly enclosing a birthday present "as a token of appreciation from my government." The use of the word "priviously" [sic] indicated that, as sometimes happens with its forgeries, Service A had forgotten to check its English spelling.

Propaganda is an overt, loud, in-your-face communication that does not attempt to disguise its source or intent. A poster declaring "The Soviet Union is the Fatherland of all Peace-loving Peoples" is propaganda. Radio Moscow broadcasts are propaganda. Propaganda is like advertising that is not ashamed to be advertising. The Voice of America is a U.S. propaganda channel, albeit much more subtle than most communist propaganda ever was.

Foreign Communist Parties were almost all controlled by the Soviet Union. Anything that an indigenous communist party, for example the Communist Party of the United States (CPUSA), did or said was tightly controlled by the KGB. The Soviet Union's leadership, through the KGB, the Comintern's OMB, the KGB, and other means, provided funds and the party line for the CPUSA. The leadership and membership of the CPUSA parroted the Soviet party line from the beginning of the party through the end of the Soviet Union.

Control of supposedly independent political parties, in the free countries of the West, provided the KGB with many opportunities for Active Measures. The long-time leader of the CPUSA, Earl Browder, inserted the Soviet line in political discussions. His status as an "independent, American" politician was taken for granted by naïve American journalists. Thus, Browder's Stalinist point of view was reported as an authentic American point of view, throughout his tenure in the CPUSA.

Front Organizations were used to influence unsuspecting Westerners, from the earliest days of the Soviet Union. The controlling hand of the KGB was hidden from view of members of the fronts, and from the media. The first fronts began as seemingly spontaneous international organizations to provide relief to the Soviets during the famine of 1921. The famine was caused by a combination of drought, communist seizures of crops, and lingering effects of the Russian Civil War, ended just a year earlier.

Working for the Comintern, Willi Muenzenberg, the brilliant and energetic German communist, veteran organizer, and confidante of the Bolsheviks, headed the Foreign Committee for the Organization of Worker Relief for the Hungry in Soviet Russia. This committee was created by Lenin as a counter-balance to the embarrassing fact that the American government was actually providing real aid. Herbert Hoover directed an organization, the American Relief Administration, that actually fed millions of Soviet citizens every day.

Muenzenberg created an intertwined network of fronts that raised millions of dollars, mostly in the U.S. Americans were suckers for fronts. In response to Muenzenberg's front organization entreaties, Americans poured in contributions to help the starving proletarians in the Soviet Union. In contrast, Europeans were less receptive to the communist Active Measure. Muenzenberg was frustrated with the amount collected in Germany, France and England. He turned his attention to the fertile operating ground in North America.

Muenzenberg created another front in the U.S., the Friends of Soviet Russia (FSR) society, which he used to raise funds, ostensibly for famine relief. The front made political statements, such as the FSR famine fund-raising letterhead logo, "Give without imposing imperialistic and reactionary conditions as do Hoover and others." Muenzenberg learned from this first success, and went on to much greater front successes during the years between the World Wars, as we'll see later.

Paramilitary Operations are clandestine military operations, such as training of insurgent or guerilla forces. A good example of this type of operation was the CIA's training and insertion of forces on Cuba during the Bay of Pigs fiasco. The KGB has funded and armed a wide variety of guerilla and terrorist groups active against the U.S. and its allies—for example, the Palestine Liberation Organization and the Viet Cong.

Kidnapping and Assassination are two facets of the same Active Measure, sometimes known as wet ops. The Russian communists had none of the moral and legal constraints that the U.S. faces during peace-time (or at least during a non-declared war). They were ready to employ physical violence to meet their intelligence goals. The KGB planned and carried out the assassination of Trotsky in Mexico. The KGB likely was instrumental in the killing of Bulgarian journalist Georgi Markov in London. Recently, it is likely that the KGB's successor planned and carried out the killing of ex-KGB whistleblower Litvinenko, also in London.

Covert Influence involves inserting a desired message (the payload) into the culture of an enemy. The origin and intent of the message is hidden by using an Agent of Influence. The Agent is usually a native of the enemy culture and has access to the targeted culture's communications line. If the objective was to influence the American planning for the war strategy conference with the Soviet Union in Yalta, the KGB would seek an agent within the U.S. government who was involved in those talks. The agent of influence, ideally someone close to the planners, respected and knowledgeable, would be provided with the Soviet line. Whenever possible, the agent of influence would argue the Soviet line, as if it was his own. An agent of influence never reveals his true master, and sometimes is not even aware of his being manipulated.

Some agents require a "fig-leaf," an ostensible excuse for their actions. Even though they likely understand the reality of what they are doing, it is sometimes psychologically easier to deny the reality, and maintain independence from the case officer running them. A good case officer understands this, assesses his agent's personality, and provides the agent with a fig-leaf if necessary.

For example, it's likely that George S. Counts, an extremely productive covert influence agent, was provided a fig-leaf that masked the true identity of his handlers. He was provided with massive amounts of payload material, which he parlayed into a successful career as America's premier expert on Soviet education. The payloads he inserted into American education and academia resonate today, in PC attacks on American exceptionalism.

While it is likely that Alger Hiss, a recruited Soviet spy, provided intelligence collection services to the KGB, the secrets to which he had access were nearly of no value, when compared to the value he could provide as an agent of influence. Hiss was involved in policy formulation in the Department of State, and was a major player in the strategic planning talks between Roosevelt and Stalin in Yalta.

Covert influence is the classic example of a Soviet Active Measure that has no expiry date. As we'll see, the KGB, with Muenzenberg providing the operational and organizational savvy, ran a brilliant covert influence operations designed to destroy America's self-pride and sense of exceptionalism. Muenzenberg, crushed by the pitiless might of Stalinist oppression, likely never dreamed that his creation of hate-America-first would grow and spread like kudzu, creating PC and weakening his target, right up to 2010.

Using experienced operatives and highly compartmentalized operations, the KGB sought to insert covert influence "payloads" designed to call into question the fundamental bases on which American society and culture had been built. Many progressives eagerly carried out these covert operations for the Communists. Others not involved in the operations received the covert messages and accepted them as gospel.

The agents of influence denigrated American patriotism, capitalism, and individualism, and called into question American foreign policy, all of which seemed to form the philosophical basis of an elite attitude, which coalesced during the Great Depression and was nurtured and strengthened by the American transmitters of the KGB's covert influence operations: journalists, screenwriters, and professors, among others. A Willing Accomplice in Hollywood, in the 1950s, commented that by participating in the anti-anti-communist groups, "I would be spared the agony of thinking my way through difficult issues: all the thinking would be done for me by an elite core of trained [thinkers]..."

The goal of the KGB's covert influence operations was to make Americans feel that their country was bad. The KGB utilized Willing Accomplices to spread the message that America was an evil, racist, imperialist war-monger and that Communism was a benign, noble experiment designed to rid the world of corruption, oppression and injustice. Muenzenberg used his fronts as cover to run innovative and staggeringly successful covert influence operations against the U.S.

PART TWO

DESTROY THE AMERICAN SPIRIT

Chapter 1

Covert Influence

These Communists know what they are doing. They follow their orders. Particularly would they like to dominate our newspapers, our colleges, and our schools.

***William F. Russell**, Dean Columbia Teachers College in a 1938 speech to the American Legion.*

Our future teachers will be able to discuss their own histories and current thinking drawing on notions of white privilege, hegemonic masculinity, heteronormativity, and internalized oppression.

***University of Minnesota teacher training program**, 2009.*

Following the express instructions of the leadership of the Communist Party of the Soviet Union, beginning with Vladimir Lenin, the KGB implemented massive covert influence operations soon after the end of the Russian Civil War. The goal was to destroy the core moral fabric of American society.

Taking advantage of the intellectual and philosophical climate of the early 1900s, the Soviet intelligence apparatus began what would now be called in intelligence circles “intelligence preparation of the battle space” to move the world towards the inevitable dictatorship of the proletariat. Covert operatives realized that America's greatest strengths were its proud exceptionalism and belief that freedom and liberty were part of all men's divine destiny.

Prior to and during the Russian Revolution, Bolshevik head Vladimir Lenin and his cronies learned the value of conspiratorial practices and the value of disinformation, propaganda, agents of influence, and other Active Measure techniques. Russian society and culture were uniquely suited for these practices of secrecy and espionage. Trotsky described his first experience in Communist agitation, saying "[w]e knew...contacts with workers demanded secret, highly 'conspiratorial' methods. And we pronounced the word solemnly, with a reverence that was almost mystic."

The Bolsheviks employed these tactics during the time of the czars, and the Russian Revolutions. The Bolshevik coup, culminating in the October Revolution of 1917 was a textbook application of Active Measures preparation of the battlespace, followed by kinetic paramilitary action. Throughout the ensuing Russian Civil War, the Bolsheviks improved their knowledge of Active Measures, and all forms of espionage. By the time they consolidated their power, during 1920, they were experts in all forms of espionage and Active Measures.

The main target of covert influence operations was the Soviet Union's main adversary, of course, the United States. The covert operations, in which KGB officers recruited and ran agents, were aimed at influencing "Innocents," (the term Soviet covert operatives used to describe Westerners who believed their lies) and were their Willing Accomplices, doing the Communists' bidding, wittingly or unwittingly. The KGB identified and focused on the three areas of a free society that pass on its cultural heritage: the media, academia/education, and entertainment. In addition, they focused their efforts on vulnerable governmental policy-makers, particularly in the State Department.

Using experienced operatives and highly compartmented operations, the KGB inserted covert influence "payloads" designed to destroy the fundamental bases on which American society and culture had been built. Many American Progressives eagerly carried out these covert operations for the Communists. Others American Progressives not involved in the operations received the covert messages and accepted them as gospel.

As Whittaker Chambers explained the methodology, "The communist underground worker in the United States, who had failed as a political organizer decided that he 'might try writing, not political polemics, which few people ever wanted to read, but stories that anybody might want to read -- stories in which the correct conduct of the communist would be shown in action and without political comment.'" Thus hiding the wolfish communist underpinnings of the stories in sheep's clothing.

The messengers denigrated American patriotism, capitalism, and individualism, and called into question American foreign-policy, all of which seemed to form the philosophical basis of an elite attitude, which coalesced during the Great Depression and was nurtured and strengthened by the American transmitters of the KGB's covert influence operations: journalists, screenwriters, and professors, among others. A Willing Accomplice in Hollywood, in the 1950s, commented that by participating in the anti-anti-communist groups, "I would be spared the agony of thinking my way through difficult issues: all the thinking would be done for me by an elite core of trained [thinkers]..."

This attitude of uncritical acceptance of the dictates of the elite opinion makers has all the trappings of a cult. We'll see that this attitude has much in common with today's PC cult.

American Flirtation with Domestic Covert Influence

Partly in response to the communist revolution, Woodrow Wilson's Progressive administration tried its hand at overt propaganda. In April, 1917, Wilson formed America's first 20th century propaganda group—the Committee on Public Information (CPI). The CPI's main objective was to bring the US into WWI, and to weaken German power. The CPI's targets were both domestic and international. Among the international targets was Russia. Conflicting objectives created confusion, however. The Bolshevik threat to American business interests in Russia was of concern, but a strong communist Russia was also a powerful deterrent to German power. The CPI was disbanded after operating for two years. The effort left a bad taste in Washington's mouth, but created some native expertise.

After Wilson's short-lived stab at the influence game, it was only after World War 2 that America began to understand the rules of the game. When we belatedly tried to play, it was too late. The Russians had the upper hand. The KGB and its predecessors had infiltrated and begun to twist to their benefit the most intimate domains of our culture.

KGB Covert Influence Payload

The goal of the KGB's influence operation was to make Americans feel that their country was inherently bad. The KGB utilized Willing Accomplices to spread the message that America was an evil, racist, imperialist, foreigner-hating war-monger and that Communism was a benign, noble experiment designed to rid the world of corruption, oppression and injustice.

Babette Gross, wife of KGB agent Willi Muenzenberg, told Stephen Koch, that Muenzenberg taught his operators that "You do *not* endorse Stalin. You do *not* call yourself a Communist. You do *not* declare your love for the regime. You do *not* call on people to support the Soviets. Ever. Under any circumstances." And then Gross, in her ninth decade, more than fifty years after her beloved Willi's body turned up rotting in a French forest, revealed to Koch the smoking gun of the Soviet covert influence payload:

> You claim to be an independent-minded idealist.
>
> You don't really understand politics, but you think the little guy is getting a lousy break.
>
> You believe in open-mindedness.
>
> You are shocked, frightened by what is going on right here in our own country.
>
> You're frightened by the racism, by the oppression of the workingman.
>
> You think the Russians are trying a great human experiment, and you hope it works.
>
> You believe in peace.
>
> You yearn for international understanding.
>
> You hate fascism.
>
> You think the capitalist system is corrupt.

This is the message that Muenzenberg implanted in his operators. This is the message they communicated to their influence agents. This was the message that filtered throughout the American media, throughout American Schools of Education, throughout American elementary, junior high, and high schools, throughout Hollywood. Willing Accomplices in those domains repeated the payload, and variations. This payload was the most effective influence operation of all time.

This payload exactly matches today's PC-Progressive message. Soviet covert operators propagated it through American Innocents, who wittingly or unwittingly, spread the anti-American message throughout American culture. It created a vile, self-loathing among normal Americans.

Covert Influence Methodology

In a covert influence operation a payload is secretly inserted into some part of the enemy's communications channels. The ultimate goal of covert influence is to transform the enemy in a way that is useful to the attacker, to prepare the battlespace.

In a typical covert influence operation an intelligence officer targets someone who has potential as an agent of influence. The target is chosen for access to a desired channel of communications (the Comintern intel operators targeted American media, academia, and Hollywood). The intelligence officer uses standard recruiting tradecraft to become friends with the targeted agent of influence. Appealing to the identified vulnerabilities of the targeted agent, the officer burrows into the target's life.

The targeted agent of influence may, or may not, know that he is dealing with a hostile intelligence service, even after he is recruited. The agent might provide his services because he believes in the message, or she may work for pay, or maybe for some other gratification. In the actual operation, the espionage officer provides the recruited agent of influence with the payload. The agent of influence inserts the payload into his communications channel. Once the payload is inserted, in the form of a news story, an editorial, a speech, a book, a lecture, a movie, a radio program, a song, a play, or any other form of communication, the payload takes on a life of its own.

Covert influence operations are little understood, or studied, even by intelligence case officers who recruit influence agents, and place the influence payloads with the agents. Case officers work in a bureaucracy which requires constant administrative reporting—status updates, requirement generation and feedback, validation of reporting sources, budget allocation reviews, personnel performance reviews, and more. Case officer evaluations and promotions are based on progress towards objectives during the reporting period—annually, usually, but sometimes even shorter term, quarterly or monthly.

The chief assigns a case officer to answer that requirement. The case officer is busy with multiple operations at the same time. His intelligence collection operations are easily measured—how many intelligence reports did his assets produce this quarter? How many agents did the case officer recruit this year? How many technical operations did the case officer participate in? What was the feedback from analysts on the intelligence reports the case officer wrote?

A case officer's effectiveness seems to be easily measured by these quantifiable factors. And maybe these are good measures of the case officer's work. However, these measures fall apart, and are very poor yardsticks to use when a case officer is conducting covert influence operations.

Immediate Measurement of Covert Influence Impossible

Attempts to manage clandestine operations as if they were like any other corporate activity ignore the unique and esoteric aspects of these operations. Their results, especially of covert influence operations, can be difficult to measure.

When the goal of an operation is to *covertly* create an attitude, or change perceptions, or create negative feelings about a person or country or policy position, how can the effectiveness of the operation be measured? Maybe the only real measurement of an effort to change attitudes would be to conduct a poll.

Influence Opinions and Attitudes—Public Relations and Advertising

Covert influence operations are much like advertising and public relations campaigns. Their goal is to get in the mind of their target audience to guide their actions, thoughts, and feelings about a certain issue.

PR Campaigns—Denigration Campaigns

Public relations campaigns try to influence the public's attitudes, usually in a positive way, toward a product, or company, or person. This type of influence campaign is usually overt, conducted out in the open. A good example of these campaigns is an election.

Candidates run a public relations and advertising campaign. The traditional (until the 1980s) objective of an American campaign was to create a positive image of the candidate. "Negative advertising" began to dominate political ad spending from the 1990s until today.

Negative advertising is a form of a public relations campaign virtually identical to a denigration campaign in covert influence operations. Usually, political negative advertising is carried out overtly—via TV or internet ads, with the disclaimer: "This advertising was paid for and approved by the candidate."

Public relations, on the other hand, involves a candidate's PR flacks making friends and feeding stories to the media, or other influencers. When a media member is of the same political bent as a candidate, the PR flacks' job is made much easier. The PR worker might just feed a sympathetic journalist a rumor about his candidate's opponent. Or maybe provide an exclusive report on the opponent's relationship with a photographer on the campaign bus.

The resulting insider expose of the candidate's opponent could be called a denigration covert influence operation. The result is the same as the Soviet's covert influence operations against American culture. The target is discredited, by a seemingly unbiased and trustworthy source. A certain segment of the population accepts the negative insinuations.

Covert influence operations do not carry disclaimers identifying the sponsor. George Counts' books denigrating American culture never had a note at the end saying: "This book brought to you by the Soviet Politburo and the KGB."

The KGB learned quickly to make friends with, co-opt and recruit the main drivers of American culture, in the heady, scary, and exhilarating period after they seized power in Russia. A full scale PR denigration campaign was set in motion, aimed at destroying the main adversary of the U.S.S.R.

DNA of Advertising Payload—I can't believe I ate the whole thing

In 1972, advertising agency Wells, Rich, Greene created a television commercial for the antacid, Alka-Seltzer. Its payload was the tagline "I can't believe I ate the whole thing." The commercial was an instant hit.

In internet terms, the payload went viral. The tagline was named one of the "ten best quotes of the decade" by Newsweek magazine.

Jokes, stories, and repetition around the water cooler spread the payload around the U.S. Nearly 40 years later many people can still quote the commercial's tagline. The DNA of this commercial payload is evident, and can be identified in various media.

Advertising payloads are easily tracked, with massive text databases available for searching online. In the same way, we can track the KGB's covert influence payloads, as we'll see later in this chapter.

Measuring Covert Influence Results

The message can influence consumers for the rest of their lives. All it takes is one time exposure, and consumers' beliefs and attitudes can be changed. Reading a book or an article, hearing a song or a radio show, seeing a movie or a play are potentially life-changing experiences. The communist covert influence message was intended to change individual and societal morals and values.

The result of the Muenzenberg payload's dissemination throughout American society is now clear. A healthy, happy, productive nation of citizens, blended in the great Melting Pot, had set aside their differences when they became Americans. After Muenzenberg's influence op, the same people were converted into a confused mass of self-interest groups, torn apart by PC divisions of race, gender, ethnicity, income, class, language, sexuality.

DNA of Covert Influence Payloads

Although it is difficult to measure the results of covert influence operations, we can track the payloads from the ops. This analysis is very much like DNA testing. First we isolated and identified Muenzenberg's core message. This core message is the unique DNA profile that can be traced and tracked. The next step is to compare the DNA profile of the core message from the covert influence to messages from later sources.

A good fit, or even an exact fit, still does not allow us to know exactly how that message made its way from the mind of the elite Soviet espionage corps to the mouths of American students or screen-writers. A match allows us to show that today's PC message is nearly identical to the communist covert influence payload from the past.

Let's examine one DNA match—in the Academic/Education domain. The KGB targeted this domain as one of the main conduits to attack and shape the attitudes of the future—American children.

Payload Tracking—KGB Covert Influence Operation—George S. Counts

George S. Counts, PhD, was a professor of Education at Columbia University's Teachers College (TC), from 1927 till his retirement in 1955. Coming to Columbia with no background at all in Russia, he was hired by TC's International Institute (a Rockefeller Foundation grant recipient) to be its Russia expert.

Counts traveled to the Bolshevik country, to study its education system. In short order, he developed astounding contacts in the U.S.S.R. (Note: Full details of Counts' development, recruitment, and handling as a KGB covert influence agent will be covered in a separate chapter.)

Counts was easy pickings for the KGB. Arrogant, and ignorant, he was easily manipulated. A Russian graduate student, Anna Osipovna Perlmutter, was co-opted by the KGB to handle Counts. She worked as Counts' administrative assistant for his entire career at Columbia. A Jewish refugee from the Pale, she left Odessa and arrived at the dock in Hoboken in 1910, age 16. Her family had preceded her by several years, and she left at least an older sister in Odessa.

Her family (mother, father and six brothers and sisters) settled in Chicago. She evidently stayed in Russia when her family fled the pogroms targeting Jews in the early 1900s. Anna graduated from a teachers training institute in St. Petersburg in 1910. Upon arrival in America, Anna separated herself from her family. By 1924, she earned a Masters in Education from Clark University in Massachusetts, while her family remained in Chicago. Her thesis at Clark was on the "History of Education in Russia."

Working with Counts at the TC International Institute, Anna was a real expert on Russian education, fully fluent in both Russian and American English. Counts spoke no Russian at all when he arrived in New York—Rockefellers' new "Russian Education Expert."

Anna traveled to Russia with Counts, where he used his unbelievable network to gain access to Soviet officials in Education and other areas. With not a hint of irony or apparent self-awareness, Counts returned to Columbia from a trip to Russia in 1929. Soon after, he reported, "This little volume came to my desk...sent to me without comment by a Russian friend...aware of my interest in both education and social planning."

The little academic was, after only a couple of months visiting Russia in a span of less than two years, ready to style himself as an expert in Russian education. Unless he had thrown himself into full-time study of Russian, and immersed himself in the culture and language, it is impossible that Counts was, after only two years, capable of translating a Russian book into English.

Yet this is exactly what he claimed to do. The book, which "came to his desk," from a "Russian friend," was an internal propaganda training book, *New Russia's Primer*. It was designed by the Soviets to introduce their school children to the communist five-year plan. The Soviets internal propaganda system was well-developed. They understood the need to inject communism into their citizens' lives at an early age.

The five-year plan reflected Stalin's central-planning pipedream of creating a communist economic powerhouse. The entire Soviet economy proved to be completely untenable and imaginary.

However, at the time, 1930, America was ripe for exposure to the socialist/communist lies about the superiority of a centrally-planned economy. As the Great Depression tightened its grip on the U.S., the spry little Teachers College professor prepared to seize the spotlight.

In 1931 Houghton Mifflin published *New Russia's Primer: The Story of the Five-Year Plan,* by M. Ilin, translated from the Russian by George S. Counts, Associate Director of the International Institute and Professor of Education in Teachers College, and Nucia P. Lodge, Research Assistant in the International Institute.

We see that Anna Osipovna has transformed herself into Nucia Lodge. And we see that the dapper professor Counts modestly claims that he translated the book, while grudgingly crediting his KGB handler.

The payload of this unbelievably brazen covert influence operation is straight out of Muenzenberg's manual.

Muenzenberg's payload: "You think the capitalist system is corrupt...You're frightened...by the oppression of the working man...You think the Russians are trying a great human experiment..."

Counts' New Russia's Primer:

> In America the machine is not a helper to the worker, not a friend, but an enemy. Every new machine, every new invention, throws out upon the streets thousands of

> workers. In glass factories one person now makes three thousand bottles an hour. In former times such a task required seventy-seven men. This means that each machine for the making of bottles deprives seventy-six men of employment. And the American worker despises the machine which takes away his bread.
>
> But how is it with us [Russians]? The more machines we have, the easier will be the work, the shorter will be the working day, the lighter and happier will be the lives of all.
>
> We build factories in order that there may be no poverty, no filth, no sickness, no unemployment, no exhausting labor—in order that life may be rational and just...We build in our country [the U.S.S.R.] a new, an unheard-of, a socialistic order.

The newly-minted "Russian expert" from Columbia delivered the KGB payload directly into the cultural heart of America. "Capitalism is corrupt! Russia's experiment is working!" screamed his text.

The Primer was a selection for Book-a-Month Club members in May 1931, and 46,000 members chose it. Counts' first influence project was a best-seller for seven months, and ranked eighty-first on the list of nonfiction bestsellers from 1921-1932. Cloaked in his non-partisan, academic-research cover, Counts delivered the anti-capitalist payload into schools, universities, and living rooms across America.

Of course, at the same time that Counts published this covert influence coup, Stalin was in the midst of forced collectivization of huge swaths of Soviet society. Dissenters were rounded up and shot. Or sent to the gulag, where they were worked to death, in the most inhuman conditions imaginable. Counts, who had visited Russia at least twice by 1931, could have witnessed the unimaginably squalid lives of normal Soviet citizens, if he had wanted to do so. Maybe he did, maybe he did not. We'll probably never know, but we do know that he continued pouring out covert influence payloads for another decade.

Counts cloaked his KGB payload in his work in Education with his participation in "non-ideological" organizations, like the Progressive Education Association, and the Philosophy of Education Society, for which Counts edited the journal *The Social Frontier,* beginning in 1934.

Counts continued publishing, speaking, and teaching that "the age of individualism was over," and that it was time to accept "collectivization" in the American economy. Counts continued advancing his KGB covert influence payload, always rejecting any suggestion that he was a communist, or inspired by socialism, cloaking his "philosophy of education" in Progressive terms.

Counts founded the Social Reconstruction philosophy of Education—the root of which was the need to "change America." A tenet of Count's approach was that America needed to be changed. He voiced, and repeated, over and over, the KGB's influence payload of his shock at what was happening in America.

After Stalin's 1939 pact with Hitler, Counts began to distance himself from the "collectivist" approach to economics, and in the 1940s launched a new publishing career, again with Anna "Nucia" Perlmutter Lodge as his translator. This new phase, clearly after a break with the KGB, focused on the negatives of the U.S.S.R. and its education system. Yet he never renounced his earlier works. And amazingly, Counts' covert influence payload is still required reading in many schools of education.

Counts' DNA in PC-Academia and Education

Counts' payload, directly from the mind of Willi Muenzenberg, is now found in nearly every American School of Education. One example: the University of Virginia's Curry School of Education's Social Foundations program's website homepage, in 2010, trumpeted the ideals of Social Reconstructionism, and explicitly traced their philosophical roots to George S. Counts, the KGB agent:

> Our history as a graduate program in Social Foundations goes back to 1970, but we are linked to a broader field of inquiry pioneered at Teachers College, Columbia University in the 1930's and now encompassing most major universities in the United States. Like John Dewey, *George S. Counts,* and Harold Rugg, we insist that educational activities must be evaluated in terms of their social as well as their pedagogical outcomes. Like our colleagues in Social Foundations across the country, we maintain that there is much more to education than schooling and that there is much more to schooling than the technology of educational practice.

Claiming solidarity with their "colleagues in Social Foundations across the country," the Virginia Education Academics reveal the extent of the success of the KGB's Counts influence operation. They trumpet their adherence to Counts' social Reconstructionism, and implicitly champion Counts' call for the end to individualism and the need to become a collectivist society.

The University of Minnesota's College of Education and Human Development, in a teacher training redesign program, spells out the desired outcome. Note that there is nothing about teaching kids how to read, write, spell, and understand the beauty and uniqueness of American history, do math, understand science or anything else that would actually help the young Americans appreciate and function in their country and world:

> Our future teachers will be able to discuss their own histories and current thinking drawing on notions of white privilege, hegemonic masculinity, heteronormativity, and internalized oppression.

Muenzenberg's payload screams out from these poor PC-addled academics' every sentence. Thanks to Counts, the KGB's DNA-print is all over this 21st century American teacher training initiative.

Teachers graduate from American Schools of Education filled with zeal to "change American society." Their courses are filled with calls to "change" their students. These calls for change are nearly always calls to create a PC social order, and rejections of traditional American values like individualism, free enterprise, and responsibility. And yet, every year, American students seem to fall farther behind the Chinese, the Japanese, and the Russians in nearly every measure of academic success. Change? Surely it's needed. But not Counts', and the KGB's, version of change.

The same DNA tracking of Muenzenberg's payload is just as fruitful in the other domains targeted by the KGB—Hollywood and the media. Many American movies, most PC-media offerings, from news to entertainment shows have at least one strand of Muenzenberg's anti-American DNA threaded into their theme or message. Try analyzing the theme of a movie, TV show, or Diane Sawyer news story.

Chapter 2
The bureaucrats

The overarching societal influences, measured in decades, resulting from the ops of long-dead agents and KGB officers, are only of passing interest to him, even though he understands the analysis. He has difficulty seeing past his own bureaucratic boundaries.

KGB bureaucrat's mindset.

Latter-Day KGB Operator's View

A KGB general, active in covert influence ops in the 1950s to the 1970s, like most operators, was unable to understand the long-term effects of his work. While proud of his work, and its effects, because of the KGB's lack of a bureaucratic history (beyond revering the memory of the Chekists), he was unable to understand that the effects of the KGB's covert influence ops were long-lasting—measured in decades, not quarters.

The general believed that his ops (and he was only concerned with the ops that he ran), "...influenced Western political parties, groups and organizations; they weakened some of our most potent adversaries; they even shifted some public opinion and may have shaken Western solidarity."

And yet, the general, maybe out of false humility, finished his short memoir with a protestation that his ops were not as influential as many gave them credit for being.

I believe that the general suffers from the common bureaucrat's affliction—I-am-the-world syndrome. Because of his in-depth participation in three decades worth of operations, he is unable to pull back and look at the longer-term view. He is stuck in a mode of examining one tree in the forest—his own operations—missing the holistic view, the effects of a century of KGB covert influence operations on the Main Adversary.

This tree-in-the-forest view is also common among American clandestine operators. As this project has progressed, an experienced clandestine operator has read drafts. While he grasps the overall thesis, and sees the societal level impacts, he is unable to extricate himself from the grasp of his own agency. His main concern with the effects of PC on America is how PC affects his former agency—when did it first become policy, who ordered the policy, when was it ordered, how was it implemented—he is unable to step away from his bureaucratic tree to see the historical forest.

The overarching societal influences, measured in decades, resulting from the ops of long-dead agents and KGB officers, are only of passing interest to him, even though he understands the analysis. He has difficulty seeing past his own bureaucratic boundaries.

Ashburn, Virginia 2007

The turban-clad Sikh driver whipped the dark gray Washington Flyer Ford Crown Victoria into my driveway. The trip back to Washington from the Middle East was a relief. On the same charter plane was the woman deputy who had insisted the chief fire me. The chief, a thin, faded gray non-entity, was the epitome of the stereotypical useless bureaucrat. Scared to death that he would make someone in power angry, his default operational setting was "if you don't do anything, you can't be blamed when it goes wrong." Clearly that mode had worked wonders for his career. He was chief of a huge office outside the U.S. Americans were missing or held hostage by enemies and terrorists in his area of operations. Yet his major concern seemed to be playing inter-agency politics to keep his nose clean.

The opportunity to free a group of four American hostages had cropped up unexpectedly. I'd seized the chance, and started mustering the resources needed to begin tracking down the location of the suffering Americans. In short order, however, a domestic American federal law enforcement agency claimed supremacy over the case. Trying hard to make up for the failures made evident on 9/11, they now claimed any case that involved "a crime against an American," no matter where it happened in the world. Careful preparations and discussions with their agents led nowhere.

I briefed the little gray man. He deferred to his subordinate, my classmate. My old friend assured me that it was our operation, we had the resources and the know-how to do it, and the law enforcement guys were playing in a field far outside their skillset.

The lady deputy never said a word. At the planning meeting that night, the cops went ballistic when I told them we would handle this case. On cue, the group (they never traveled alone, always at least three showed up for every meeting) bounced to its collective feet and berated me.

The next morning the cops came to the office to meet the thin gray man for the first time. I arranged the meet-and-greet in an effort to be collegial, introducing the newly arrived law enforcement chief to the also newly-arrived thin gray man. An hour later, I got a phone call.

"Where are you now?" the voice of the lady deputy.

I was in my hooch, a four bunk trailer in the compound, just in front of a bomb shelter, "I'm in my room."

"Don't go to any more meetings outside the office. Come see me as soon as possible." The lady's voice oozed superiority.

Offered a choice to sit in a basement corner with the analysts for another two months, or to take the next flight home, I packed my bags.

Enjoying the sound sleep of the innocent, I was oblivious as the Boeing passenger jet cruised at 35,000 feet over northern Europe. Twelve hour days, seven day weeks had piled one on top of the other for the last thirty days. After bunking down every night, I devoured books on Soviet espionage. I was getting a good feel for the subject. Back in Virginia, with some involuntary free time, I dived into researching the covert-influence-created-PC theory.

I was stunned to discover no published study of communist covert influence operations against the U.S. And, of course, there were no studies on the effects of the apparently non-existent covert influence operations against America. I searched the CIA's library, and unclassified reference materials. I talked to Hayden Peake, the CIA's super-historian. He referred me to some tangentially related reports on Active Measures, but had no leads on KGB covert influence.

Back to square one, I started with a Bing search on "covert influence operations." The first page was all about American covert operations. (Redo the search in 2010, and the first page, besides my own articles on Soviet ops, now includes the old CIA covert operations, and the PC media's own recent interest in the subject. Of course, they're not interested in uncovering how they became so slanted against normal Americans. The first PC media article is from The New Yorker. Their "reporter at large," Jane Mayer, discovers that the Koch brothers have "funded stealth attacks on the federal government." Oh my! Conservatives are against the Obama administration! Stop the presses!)

The American definition of Covert Operations does surface. Spelled out in National Security Council (NSC) Directive 10/2 (June, 1948), it is an action carried out by American forces, so that "U.S. responsibility for it is not evident to an unauthorized person, and that if uncovered the U.S. government can plausibly disclaim any responsibility..."

The Directive goes on to specify what actions might be included as Covert Operations, "propaganda, economic warfare; preventive direct action, including sabotage, anti-sabotage, demolition and evacuation measures; subversion against hostile states...and support of indigenous anti-communist elements in...the free world."

But, in the first five pages of Bing results, nothing on the KGB's covert influence operations against America. So, I recalibrated my search. Let's start with KGB and communism in America. This proved more fruitful.

The Venona decryptions are the logical place to start. Over to Amazon.com, I ordered the experts' books on the recently declassified and released treasure trove of KGB cables. Historians Haynes and Klehr, and Herbert Romerstein both have excellent books on the cables. In the meantime, better get the Mitrokhin files too. Christopher Andrew, a British historian, with close ties to British intelligence, worked with the former KGB archivist, Vasili Mitrokhin. They produced a couple of volumes based on notes Mitrokhin had smuggled out in his clothes, during his long career in the KGB.

I found that John Earl Haynes, now a Staff Fellow at the Library of Congress, was part of a team of three who gained access to Comintern files, during a brief opening in the early 1990s. He'd written widely about the files he viewed, and is an expert on the early KGB. Using my headhunting skills to find him and establish contact, I set up a meeting in his office on Capitol Hill.

Romerstein, on the other hand, is reclusive and doesn't answer inquiries, email or phone calls. No luck there. I'd have to forge on without his input. Now that I was immersed in this fascinating world of the past, with frighteningly massive implications in the present, I barely noticed the breaking news from my last post. Knowing how the domestic law enforcement agency operated, it was clear that the headlines were the answer to the cops' demand to the hostage-takers, after I'd left. The terrorists: "Want proof of life? Here it is." The headlines: "Severed Fingers Delivered to American Embassy in Belong to Five American Hostages."

Later that month, new headlines: "Battered Bodies of Hostages Found in Streets." The message to the American domestic law enforcement "hostage experts:" "You're on my turf, infidel!"

My worst nightmare come to life. The only way to stay sane when you are a tiny cog in a huge bureaucratic grist mill is to realize that you are essentially powerless and just go with the flow.

The little gray men and nasty little women, not caring about the lives in the balance, zealously and jealously guard their careers and perks—private jets, special protection details of massively armed guards in Raybans and goatees, unmarked helicopters, billions in funding to use as they see fit. The lives of five Americans are less important to the little gray bureaucrats than a fly buzzing around their heads. Their inflated egos only sense threats to their fiefdoms. A dead American here, a dead American there—what's the difference?

Nothing I could do now, except press on, applying my skills to a problem outside the bureaucracy. My determination to expose how covert influence ops had created PC grew stronger.

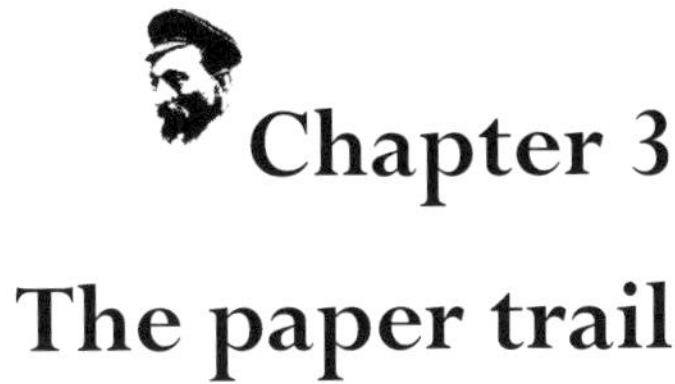

Chapter 3
The paper trail

If ever there was a service that can keep compartmentation, the KGB is it. They were wonderful at compartmenting their ops

Tennet Bagley, former CIA case officer, Soviet ops expert.

Soviet intelligence operations have been studied by numerous researchers. There is a dearth of primary sources for communist espionage. However, a few sources have surfaced since the fall of the Soviet Union. Mitrokhin, the Venona files, and Vassiliev are the most prominent. The bulk of these sources deal with collection operations. Most historians have focused primarily on collection operations.

KGB covert influence operations are usually glossed over by intelligence specialists and cultural commentators. The files and cables made public by the collapse of the Soviet Union have illuminated many communist intelligence collection and recruitment cases. Yet the same files reveal precious little about covert influence operations. Why?

Covert influence and other Active Measures, as mentioned earlier, are among the most highly compartmented espionage operations.

The KGB's operations were driven by a dysfunctional system—the CPSU leadership, from the Politburo down, was trapped in a feedback loop with the KGB. The leadership, dealing with the potential of the total collapse of communism, demanded justification from the intelligence apparatus.

In fact, the Marxist-Leninist philosophy that provided the underpinnings of the Russian Communist worldview **required the communist political and security apparatus to do its utmost to destroy capitalist societies.** This philosophy also required its adherents to believe that the capitalist world was constantly plotting against the international communist movement.

Projection as Evidence

The KGB was unable to report on reality to its masters. It was trapped in a spiral of blaming its adversary—the U.S.—for all problems. This mindset, as the USSR collapsed in 1991, could be viewed as an example of the psychological phenomenon of transference.

Projection is a type of mental gymnastics that neurotics use to rid themselves of their guilty feelings. In this interesting psychological exercise, the sick person accuses others external to himself of exactly the same symptoms from which he suffers.

The neurotic KGB had for many years, in fact decades, been running destabilization operations against the Western world, including its main adversary, the United States. These operations were run "regardless of cost."

As the USSR's political system disintegrated in the early 90s, KGB leadership "blamed its disintegration on an imperialist plot masterminded by the United States." KGB analysts warned Gorbachev, that "the United States had become a "vulture swooping over the Soviet Union" plotting to "incite our people to hate each other" and to "pour oil on the flames of our internal discontent". Other senior KGB officers "publicized previously classified conspiracy theories about a legend on American plots to subvert the Soviet Union and undermine its global influence."

In the late 70s, the KGB chief, Andropov, reported that the USA was "regardless of cost recruiting agents within the Soviet economy administration and scientific research and training them to commit sabotage. Some of the Soviet Union's current problems derived from America's secret sabotage offensive."

Mitrokhin Only Saw Fraction of KGB Files

The record, as exposed by Mitrokhin, and the Venona intercepts, provides voluminous evidence of the KGB's diligent operations against the United States' political underpinnings. Although former KGB officers have been apparently open about their own and others' operations in the West during communism's heyday, it's clear that we still are only seeing the tip of the iceberg. *Mitrokhin himself admits that he did not see the vast majority of KGB files on operations in the United States.*

Even if with complete visibility into the KGB's files, which, as any intelligence officer knows would be nearly impossible, as they exist today or as they existed in 1991 at the fall of the Soviet Union, they would still only provide a keyhole view of a vast and complicated intelligence operations universe.

Files Purged

The KGB, beginning in the days of the Russian Revolution, was a highly compartmentalized organization. In addition, beginning with Lenin, and especially during Stalin's rule of terror, the KGB, as in all of Russian society, was subjected to targeted and random purges of suspected counterrevolutionaries. These purges, affected the KGB from top to bottom.

The terror had the same effect on the KGB that a lobotomy would have on the brain of a human. Whole sections of the institutional memory of the organization were erased in a fell swoop. An intelligence organization is based on information, files, and knowledge sharing. A lobotomized intelligence organization continues to function. But its institutional memory is erased.

While the human resources of the KGB were purged, there is ample evidence that the KGB's files were also purged. Mitrokhin told a story to Christopher Andrew about gaining access to a file on Stalin in the KGB's archives. The file folder remained; however, the contents were missing. It had been purged. When, or by whom, was not noted, in the file, or by Mitrokhin.

The true history of the KGB's operations against the United States washed down the gutter in the basement of Lubyanka prison in the Kremlin. Washed away and forgotten, memory cleansed by blood spurting from the skulls of KGB managers and operators executed by Stalin's henchmen.

Primary Sources? The Paper Trail

What documentary evidence do we have of KGB operations? What are the primary sources? Are these sources actually primary? Is the availability of these sources restricted, now or in the past? Are these sources complete and unbiased? Is absence of evidence in these sources actually mean that there is no evidence of Active Measures or covert influence operations? Was the brief window of availability, in the months and years just after the fall of the USSR sufficient to provide researchers access to the complete intelligence archives of the KGB? Has the KGB, or its successor, controlled access to available files? Did the CIA, or other non-Russian intelligence agencies control access to files? Did the non-Russian intelligence agencies release everything in their control?

If we acknowledge that virtually all of the files and primary sources available on KGB operations are limited and controlled by various organizations with ulterior motives, does that mean that we cannot confirm our hypothesis? Let's look at some of the "primary sources" that have been used to study KGB operations.

Venona Documents

Venona is the code name of a wire-tapping and code-breaking operation carried out during the early 1940s. Cables transmitted between the Soviet embassy in Washington and Moscow were intercepted and recorded. Although the cables were encoded in a virtually unbreakable system, mistakes by Russian operators gave code-breakers a chance. A massive operation, staffed with dozens of analysts, went to work on the cables. During the course of a couple of decades, Americans, with British help, were able to decode some text from some of the cables.

Besides being encoded electronically, the KGB cables also used code-names within the text. True names were seldom used, for both officers and agents. Even if the full text of a cable was decoded, analysts were left with text that was not clear. A secondary decoding process had to be undertaken to reveal true identities of the personalities in the cables.

The existence of the Venona project was not publicly acknowledged for decades. Only in the mid-1990s did the U.S. finally acknowledge the project, and release some of the intercepts and analytical notes.

The entire known Venona database of decrypted Soviet cables amounts to just over three thousand cables. These cables were collected during the period 1940 to 1945. Thousands of cables were intercepted, but only around three thousand were fully or partially decrypted.

The Venona cables, while sensational in the sheer number of Soviet agents revealed, are mostly routine intelligence operational messages. KGB case officers, and station management, are seen in the Venona cables dealing with mundane aspects of running intelligence collection agents and operations. The issues that must be dealt with in running someone who is committing treason against their country are wide ranging and can be quite complicated.

For example, the cables on the handling of Elizabeth Bentley, who had become a KGB surrogate case officer by default after the death of her KGB lover/handler, show the complexities of dealing with headstrong agents.

As interesting as these Venona cables are, it is very likely that they are only the tip of the iceberg of KGB operational traffic generated by covert operations in the United States. While the KGB's routine operational discussions are revealed to us, we completely miss the KGB's covert influence operations.

The Venona decryptions include no documents regarding covert influence operations. When they discuss KGB Active Measures, they focus mainly on deception and disinformation, both of which are more blatant and require extensive documentation and coordination—spelling out the false message, producing draft forgeries, honing the forgeries, and recruiting agents to place the disinformation. All of which requires much back and forth conversation. In an intelligence bureaucracy, this "case management" requires messages, cables, memoranda, and other communications.

To put some perspective on the miniscule sample of operational messages represented by the Venona cables, a busy intelligence station, even with just a handful of case officers, could easily send and receive a hundred messages in one day. Several hundred in a week, and tens of thousands of messages in a year. Venona's total database of cables is just three thousand—a couple of weeks worth of messages—a miniscule sample of the KGB's operations during that five year period. The KGB, by the time of the Venona intercepts, had been operating in the U.S. for more than twenty years.

In *The Venona Secrets* Romerstein discusses cables that reveal Harry Dexter White as a KGB agent who performed both collection and influence operations. White, Assistant Secretary of the Treasury in the Roosevelt and Truman administrations, was a Harvard economist. Otherwise, *Venona Secrets* sheds virtually no light on KGB covert influence operations, strategic or tactical, and nothing on the Lenin-era ops.

Mitrokhin's Notes

Mitrokhin was a KGB librarian. During the course of many years, after souring on communism, and maybe plotting revenge, he took notes on various KGB files that passed through his hands. After offering his treasure trove to the Americans and meeting rejection, the British accepted him and his trunk full of KGB secrets.

Andrew's book on Mitrokhin's files has no entry in the index under "Covert Influence." He admits that "Mitrokhin's information...is not comprehensive," and, noting the vastness of the Soviet intel bureaucracy, "Mitrokhin did not have access during his KGB career to the files of the GRU's American agents and did not note references to these agents in KGB files."

Lacking access to the GRU, the Soviet military intel organization, and the Comintern and other non-KGB organizations, Mitrokhin's notes are less than comprehensive.

Andrew notes that the GRU's recruited agents included, Alger Hiss and Julian Wadleigh both State Department officers; Harry Dexter White, an employee of the Treasury Department; and George Silverman. "Like the Cambridge Five, the Washington moles saw themselves as secret warriors in the struggle against fascism." In Wadleigh's own words, he had "... offered my services to the Soviet underground in Washington. As one small contribution to help stem the fascist tide."

While Mitrokhin does provide a massive amount of information, we must realize that he was one archivist, in a huge bureaucracy, in one espionage organization which kept tight compartmentation of its operations, and files. His notes are another tantalizing snapshot of a huge intelligence organization's vast file system.

According to Andrew, Mitrokhin's notes (and Venona cables) reveal the extent of the KGB's success in penetrating America's young intelligence service, the CIA's forerunner, the Office of Strategic Services (OSS). Recruited assets included Duncan Chaplin Lee, the personal assistant to the OSS Director, General

William Donovan. Other OSS penetrations included Maurice Halperin, J. Julius Joseph, Donald Niven Wheeler, "Soviet agents at OSS headquarters were probably well into double figures. Communists... have been identified in the Russian, Spanish, Balkan, Hungarian, and Latin American sections of the OSS's R&A division and in its operational German, Japanese, Korean, Italian, Spanish, Hungarian, and Indonesian divisions."

Vassiliev's Notes

Alexander Vassiliev was a former KGB case officer. He resigned as the Soviet Union was collapsing in the late 1980s. He became a journalist, and covered some intelligence related issues. After the fall of communism, the KGB's successor agency, the SVR asked Vassiliev to work with an American author, Allen Weinstein, on a project involving KGB files on operations against America.

Sponsored by the KGB, Vassiliev sat in their offices, with KGB officers monitoring him, and read KGB files. He was allowed to make notes. His notes finally filled eight notebooks, which "someone" mailed to him in London after he fled Russia. The plan for the book called for Vassiliev to write outlines of cases, or issues. Those outlines would then be read and cleared for publication by a KGB censoring committee. Then Weinstein would edit, add, subtract, and interpret, according to his own, separate knowledge of the issues.

The resulting Weinstein book, *Haunted Wood,* did not name any new American spies. But it did provide confirmation of the espionage activities of suspects, including Alger Hiss, and a Congressman Dickstein, of New York. Weinstein did not receive full access to Vassiliev's notes compiled while reading KGB files.

Vassiliev later worked with Haynes and Klehr, after his partnership with Weinstein ended. In the introduction to his book with Haynes and Klehr, *Spies: The Rise and Fall of the KGB in America*, Vassiliev provides a glimpse into the file review process.

He details the two types of files, of the "many" other types, on which he focused his research. He only read "operational correspondence" files, and "personal files." The personal files concerned specific agents, while the operational correspondence included administrative issues, logistics issues, security issues, as well as some agent handling issues.

As an ex-KGB case officer, he also provides a glimpse into the narrowness of a typical case officer's areas of interest. Working as an ops officer in the KGB's U.S. department, he was ignorant about the history of KGB operations in America. His focus was on the operations that were happening in the here and now, that affected him. If he knew what was good for him, a KGB officer's focus ended at the tip of his nose.

Vassiliev also explained that in order to get a file from the archives, a KGB case officer "needed special permission...and had to explain why [the file] was needed." He provides a glimpse into the Soviet system, "Believe me, you would not want to explain to the boss why you wanted to know more secrets after some of your colleagues had been executed for high treason."

On his methodology for selecting files during his research project, Vassiliev is a bit fuzzy. He "got materials from the early 1930s." And later, "files from the 1920s." But he is very clear that he was not allowed into the file room. In fact, he was only allowed to sit in a separate building, far from the archives. His file requests were couriered by a KGB public affairs officer to the archives. The public affairs officer then hand-carried the files back to Vassiliev's office. Two public affairs officers sat in the office with Vassiliev during the entire two year research period.

Vassiliev detailed how he carefully fooled his minders, requesting the more general operational correspondence files, when his KGB minders refused to provide personal files of specific agents. He was able to glean some information from the ops correspondence files, evidently accidentally misfiled from the personal files.

We must conclude that the KGB carefully shielded its most precious secrets from the Weinstein/Vassiliev project. Vassiliev admits that the KGB refused to provide any files from either their illegal (non-officially covered) department, or their scientific and technical intelligence department.

A pretense of openness, yet still maintaining tight compartmentation. A limited, modified, let-it-all-hang-out approach to transparency. The Vassiliev project, once again, demonstrates the miniscule amount of information the KGB allows to be revealed about its operations. Even Vassiliev's careful notes, as extensive as they are, fill only eight composition books. This is not even a drop in the vast ocean of the KGB's operational files.

With the arrest of ten KGB illegals in the U.S. in 2010, some of whom had been working since the time of the U.S.S.R., it's clear both that the Russians continue to target America, and that they continue to tightly compartment their operations.

Library of Congress, Washington D.C.
July 2010

I hate driving in to D.C. Traffic has always been bad, with traffic bottlenecks. Now the socialist grabbers in charge of the city have revenue-enhancing speed camera traps everywhere. They place the cameras in a speed transition zone—where the limit goes from 45mph to 25mph in a hundred yards, with a barely noticeable sign. Parking is even worse. Parking signs are completely indecipherable. One signpost might have four signs attached, all with conflicting guidance on parking hours and regulations. Parking enforcement officers hover all over the city, waiting to pounce on confused motorists and tourists. It seems that D.C.'s kleptocracy has decided its easiest pickings are from out-of-towners. I avoid coming into the city at all costs. But there's no other way to meet with John Earl Haynes in person. His office is on Capitol Hill, in the Library of Congress, smack in the middle of the city.

The insane maze of one way streets, diagonals laid out over a grid, roads closed for construction, and now the post-9/11 security measures make finding any address a maddening task. I quickly find that the Library of Congress has several branch buildings, in a couple of locations around the Hill. Finding a two hour limit parking space in front of a building marked "Library of Congress," I'm exultant. I beat the bastards! The security guards tell me otherwise. Wrong building. Not too far from the right one, but the Washington heat and humidity is a killer. I'm running late for the appointment with Haynes, it's 95 degrees and wilting humidity. Sort of reminds me of the jungles in the Philippines.

The building is impressive. It's the Library of Congress main building, across the street from the Capitol, with an impressive dome atrium. Haynes's office is in the "Scholarly Colonnade." Lazy and ignorant security guards at the entrance don't know how to give directions to the Colonnade. I wander off, looking like a tourist, and find a map of the building. Locating the Colonnade, I realize that I can't get there from here. At the end of a hallway is a door, marked "Alarm will ring if door is opened." It's a back entrance into the Colonnade. And it's ajar. I step in, no alarms ring. Now, just need to find the right desk. Navigating the two level maze of cubicles and offices, with a confusing numbering system, doesn't lead me to his desk. Finally, I have to ask again. A lady at a desk on the upper deck doesn't know how the numbering system works. She goes into a back office and emerges with another lady, a veteran of the Library. She points me in the right direction.

Haynes is away from his desk when I finally find it. A note says that he's at the gym, and will return. A bust of the first Cheka chief, Dzerzhinsky, gazes implacably down at his cubicle. I settle into an empty adjacent cubicle, and review my notes. My main question for Haynes regards a White Russian (Cossack) general, Yakhontoff. George S. Counts, the KGB covert influence penetration of American education and academia, had introduced Yakhontoff to Counts' publisher, John Day. Contemporary newspaper stories detailed Yakhontoff's lecture tours of America extolling the virtues of Soviet Russia. It appeared that the KGB had used Counts as a "social broker," to extend the network of another of their influence agents, Yakhontoff, in addition to using Counts for influence ops.

Haynes appeared after his workout, a trim, athletic man, pleasant and unassuming. His database doesn't have any specific details on Yakhontoff—there is a passing reference in testimony from Thomas Bisson to Congress's Special Committee on Un-American Activities (SCUAC) in 1943. He listened to my covert influence idea, and like most historians, focuses on documentation. That's easy for them, because they can make a lot of hay from a few documents. He described his access to the Comintern documents, and the complete lack of access to the OMS Comintern documents—the Comintern department that likely provided cover for the KGB influence ops run by Muenzenberg.

Making my way back to the car in the blazing D.C. heat, I realize that I understand the covert operating style of the KGB much better than the premier American historian of KGB operations. My clandestine operating experience provides an understanding that historians lack. Haynes is a sterling researcher and has a clear understanding of the Soviets' ill will towards our country, but no feel for operations.

Damn! Another parking ticket. Pay it quick, or the PC-DC police will boot me.

Comintern Files

John Earl Haynes and Harvey Klehr, co-authors of several books, including *Venona: Decoding Soviet Espionage in America* scored a coup in 1993. After the fall of the Soviet Union, Haynes and Klehr were allowed access to the CPUSA files in the archives of the Comintern in Moscow.

The absence of the covert influence operations from what we have seen of KGB files so far is likely due to the fact that Muenzenberg ran the operations under the auspices of Comintern. As Stephen Koch noted, "The Comintern was... shaped from its inception by the two leading passions of Lenin's political personality: his obsession with secrecy, and his preoccupation with absolute power."

In his books, and in conversation with me, Haynes noted that the Comintern files, which were open only during a short period for selected researchers to access selected files, were "immense." He also said that "most sensitive intelligence-related material was removed when the Comintern was dissolved or at some later date." He noted that he believed the KGB and the Comintern had cooperated when the Comintern was dissolved in 1943, in Haynes' words, "to change the Comintern's political networks into intelligence networks."

This is surely a misunderstanding of Soviet espionage operations. The Comintern was, from its beginnings a tool of the Russian leadership. The Comintern, and its connections, and operations were Soviet intelligence networks from the first day of their inception, till the last day of their existence. While there may have been a separate bureaucracy to control and manage the Comintern operations, they were KGB operations, with no doubt. There is absolutely no evidence of any kind that Soviet intelligence officers ran rogue, uncontrolled, de-centralized operations outside the purview of centralized espionage control exercised from the very top of the Soviet leadership.

The KGB-successor intelligence agency has not released files from the Comintern-covered intelligence operations. We cannot let absence of evidence force us to muzzle our intellectual and analytical capabilities, to arrive at the logical conclusion that the Comintern provided excellent cover for espionage. And that the Comintern was used for extensive espionage operations, throughout its history. These operations included some of the most sensitive, compartmented, and effective operations undertaken in the history of the KGB.

While the Comintern archives, according to Haynes, are immense, Haynes mentions in his book *The Secret World of American Communism* that he and his co-authors were able to review about “a thousand files”, compromising several “score of thousands of documents.”

His book reproduces only ninety-two documents from the Comintern files, dealing with the Communist Party of the U.S.A. The documents are concerned almost exclusively with the bureaucratic support of underground and routine communist party affairs. These documents are extremely interesting (accounting logs documenting the PC saint, John Reed’s receipt of millions in gold and valuables from the Comintern. Reed, the Alex Gumberg-handled journalist, was the subject of a PC-Hollywood hagiographic movie, *Reds*), but there are no real operational documents. Haynes told me that the records of the OMS were never made available to him.

David McKnight, an Australian historian, also had access to the Comintern files. He notes “the significant absence in the records...of Comintern intelligence branch, the International Liaison Service (OMS), and its director Osip Piatinitsky,” in his *Espionage and the Roots of the Cold War: the Conspiratorial Heritage.*

It seems that Haynes had to prioritize his limited amount of time in the Comintern files. He focused on the CPUSA files. He said that after a short period of cordial communications with the staff in the archives, he and his team faced a hostile reception from the Russian archivists. When the Russians realized Haynes and his colleague were not from the CPUSA, as they evidently believed initially, their access to the files was terminated.

Haynes’ work is remarkable in what it did does reveal. However, it is clear that he only saw a tiny fraction of the documents detailing Comintern clandestine operations in America.

While some of Haynes’ Comintern documents do discuss cover arrangements, there is no detailed information on the operations that the cover is designed to enable. Cover arrangements are only a means to an end, but are not the operation.

Restricted Files and Compartmentation

Covert influence operations are one of the most highly compartmented subsets of intelligence operations. The CIA and the KGB are more alike than they are different. The bureaucracy and operational recordkeeping of intelligence, much like the bureaucracy of a military force, is similar across cultures. In covert operations, one of the most important aspects is security. "Need to know" is a near sacred tenet of intelligence operations. Operational recordkeeping includes various levels of compartmentation, all designed to protect operational information from being disseminated to those who do not have a need to know.

Clandestine intelligence operations require massive amounts of information, communications between supporting elements at headquarters and in the field, and the field operators. Planning, directing, managing, reporting results all require writing formal and informal reports. Recruiting an agent requires vetting, testing, checking, and handling. Each of these activities involves communications, writing, and discussion.

According to Stanislav Levchenko, a former KGB case officer, the operations of each bureaucratic group within the KGB "... are highly compartmentalized. The directorates cooperate with each other only when it is strictly necessary."

Another ex-KGB case officer, Oleg Kalugin, remembered being allowed to open a file clearly marked DO NOT OPEN, only after being indoctrinated into the case by a security officer. Another KGB case officer detailed how every night the COS in his station would use needle and thread to hand-sew certain files closed.

Tennent Bagley, a CIA case officer, who specialized in working against the KGB during the 1950's and 60's, told me, "If ever there was a service that can keep compartmentation, the KGB is it. They were wonderful at compartmenting their ops."

While routine operational matters are discussed in correspondence which is available to all personnel in the relevant office, operations requiring greater secrecy and compartmentation are only discussed and written about in channels which are not open to everyone. These "restricted" channels may be handled by only a handful of headquarters and field personnel.

In the computer age, these channels are computerized records which are only made available to the proper subset of personnel. In the days of paper files, compartmentation and restricted handling involved a variety of different methods and means. These included hand written notes, typewritten reports which were not disseminated electronically, but were delivered by couriers between stations and headquarters, and even oral briefings.

A complicated case, during the course of a year, could generate three or more physical file folders, each two inches thick, filled with case documentation, support and operational. For a long running case, as for example, our case studies of covert influence agents George S. Counts and Walter Duranty, both of whom seem to have been active for a decade or more, the physical file holdings of the intelligence bureaucracy could easily fill a dozen or more two inch thick file folders.

Access to classified information is predicated on the concept of "need to know." Only those that have a legitimate connection to running, supporting, managing, or vetting a case are allowed to see the file. And those who do see the file may only see the bits and pieces that are relevant to their expertise. For example, the officer who decides what sort of communications gear to provide an agent might only see information about the agent's technical capabilities. This need-to-know principle applies to all covert operations.

A case involving high level targets, or sensitive technology or covert action can be handled in a way that restricts access to the file even more tightly. These restricted cases are not even acknowledged to exist, outside of the small number of officers who are "read in" on the case. Others, even in the same office or department, may not even know that the case exists.

A Tiny Fraction of the Tip of an Iceberg

I feel quite comfortable asserting that the documents that have come to light, as of today, regarding KGB covert operations, are not even the tiniest fraction of the tip of the iceberg.

It is likely that the Comintern's OMS section provided cover for the KGB's covert influence operations against the U.S., during the earliest, and most effective, days of Lenin's operation to destroy the Main Adversary. It is likely that the documentary evidence from those operations will never see the light of day, if it still exists at all. But, for sure, those documents have never been open to Western researchers—yet.

We are left with the vitally important task of using our knowledge of covert operations, case management, human intelligence recruiting and handling, and other relevant skills to sort out and analyze the vast covert influence operations the KGB unleashed on America, ultimately creating the Progressive ethos and the Obama administration.

Recreated Covert Influence Ops Cable

Although we don't have copies of the covert influence ops cables that the KGB generated during its ops, a KGB case officer would have written one after his first meeting in Moscow with Walter Duranty. A recreation of that cable is below. Each covert influence operational file would have been crammed with dozens, hundreds, of cables like this.

TO: CENTER

FOR: NA/JOURNALISM, NA/CI, NA/CA, NA/COPS, C/NA/COVINFL,

REF:

A. WASHDC 05734 (14 JAN 1921)

B. CENTER 006832 (25 JAN 1921)

C. WASHDC 05990 (23 JUNE 1921)

ACTION: REQUEST DOMESTIC JOURNALISM DEPARTMENT PROVIDE AUTHORIZATION FOR SPECIAL ACCESS FOR SUBJECT. THIS ACCESS WILL BE USED TO INCREASE SUBJECT'S VALUE TO HIS HOME OFFICE, AND TO MAKE HIM MORE DEPENDENT ON OUR SERVICE, VIA C/O. ALSO, REQUEST ENCRYPTION, AND PROVISIONAL AUTHORITY (PA) TO BEGIN ADVANCED DEVELOPMENT FOR THE EVENTUAL RECRUITMENT OF SUBJECT AS A COVERT INFLUENCE AGENT.

1. SUMMARY: ON 25 AUGUST 1921 CASE OFFICER (C/O) VLADIMIR N. OGELOVNY MET WITH AMERICAN JOURNALIST WALTER ((DURANTY))(SUBJECT) PER REF A PLANNING. C/O, UNDER MININT TRANSLATOR/INTERPRETER COVER ESTABLISHED HIMSELF AS SUBJECT'S FIXER, BUILT RAPPORT WITH SUBJECT AND BEGAN IN-DEPTH ASSESSMENT AND DEVELOPMENT. IN ADDITION, C/O PROVIDED SUBJECT WITH A "WELCOME GRANT" OF USD150 TO COVER HIS INITIAL LIVING EXPENSES. DETAILS FOLLOW.

2. IN ACCORDANCE WITH REF C ITINERARY, SUBJECT ARRIVED VIA TRAIN FROM RIGA. PER REF B PLAN, C/O MET SUBJECT AS HE CAME OFF THE TRAIN. C/O INTRODUCED HIMSELF AS SUBJECT'S PERSONAL MININT TRANSLATOR/INTERPRETER. C/O PROVIDED ASSISTANCE TO SUBJECT WHEN HE ENCOUNTERED REF B PLANNED "CONFRONTATIONS" AT IMMIGRATION AND CUSTOMS.

3. IMMIGRATION PROBLEM: SUBJECT'S VISA DID NOT BEAR THE "PROPER AUTHORIZATION" STAMP. C/O, IN FULL VIEW OF SUBJECT, TOOK IMMIGRATION OFFICER ASIDE, FOR A "CONFIDENTIAL DISCUSSION," WHICH INCLUDED PASSING A SMALL BILL TO THE IMMIGRATION OFFICER. (SEE FINANCIAL ACCOUNTING FOR FULL DETAILS OF TRANSACTION. C/O RETURNED TO STATION

IN THE EVENING TO COLLECT THE MONEY FROM THE IMMIGRATION OFFICER. FULL RECEIPTS PROVIDED IN ACCOUNTING.) SUBJECT WAS VISIBLY UPSET WHEN IMMIGRATION INITIALLY REFUSED HIM ENTRY. C/O ALLOWED SUBJECT TO CONTINUE VERBAL ALTERCATION FOR AT LEAST 5 MINUTES. BY THAT TIME, SUBJECT WAS EXTREMELY ANGRY. C/O ALLOWED THIS ENGINEERED FRUSTRATION TO BUILD TO NEAR A BREAKING POINT BEFORE STEPPING IN TO ASSIST. IN SHORT ORDER, C/O HAD THE CONFIDENTIAL DISCUSSION WHICH RESULTED IN SUBJECT'S BELIEVING HE HAD RECEIVED SPECIAL TREATMENT, THANKS TO C/O. AFTER MOVING PAST IMMIGRATION, AND BEING ALLOWED ENTRY TO THE SOVIET UNION, SUBJECT COMMENTED TO C/O THAT HE WAS GLAD TO HAVE SOMEONE LIKE C/O ON HIS SIDE.

3. CUSTOMS DILEMMA: PER REF B PLAN, AT THE CUSTOMS INSPECTION, SUBJECT'S LUGGAGE WAS OPENED AND ALL ITEMS WERE EXAMINED CLOSELY BY COOPERATING CUSTOMS OFFICIALS. SUBJECT, AFTER THE CONFRONTATION AT IMMIGRATION WAS STILL UPSET. WHEN CUSTOMS OFFICERS SET ASIDE A VARIETY OF HIS PERSONAL ITEMS, WITH THE DECLARATION THAT THESE WERE CONTRABAND, AND NOT ALLOWED INTO THE SOVIET UNION, SUBJECT EXPLODED. AT EXACTLY THIS TIME, C/O INTERVENED. C/O WAS AGAIN ABLE TO PLAY THE ROLE OF SUBJECT'S PROBLEM SOLVER. C/O AGAIN "BRIBED" THE CUSTOMS OFFICER, IN FULL VIEW OF SUBJECT.

4. FIXER: BY THE TIME C/O HAD MANEUVERED SUBJECT TO THE HOTEL, C/O SOLVED SEVERAL MORE "DILEMMAS" FOR SUBJECT. AS A RESULT, C/O'S ROLE AS SUBJECT'S PERSONAL "FIXER" WAS IMBEDDED IN SUBJECT'S MIND.

5. ASSESSMENT: C/O USED THE TIME ON TARGET DURING THE DRIVE TO THE HOTEL TO BUILD RAPPORT AND ASSESS SUBJECT. HE IS VAIN, EGOTISTICAL, INSECURE, AND SELFISH. HE EXHIBITS DEEP DISDAIN FOR HIS JOURNALISTIC COLLEAGUES, AND HARBORS DEEP GRUDGES AGAINST HIS SUPERVISORS. SUBJECT BELIEVES THAT HIS POSTING TO THE SOVIET UNION WILL PROVIDE HIM WITH A VEHICLE TO RISE ABOVE THE MASSES, TO BE RECOGNIZED FOR THE STAR THAT HE TRULY BELIEVES HIMSELF TO BE. C/O ELICITED SUBJECT'S PROFESSIONAL AND PERSONAL DETAILS WITH MINIMAL EFFORT, ESPECIALLY AS THE WINE FLOWED DURING DINNER. C/O'S SKILLED DEVELOPMENT OF SUBJECT, AND MASTERFUL ORCHESTRATION OF THE BUREAUCRATIC OBSTACLES AT THE AIRPORT, THE HOTEL, AND A ROADBLOCK ON THE WAY TO DINNER, HAVE BROUGHT SUBJECT TO THE REALIZATION THAT HIS SUCCESS IN THE SOVIET UNION WILL DEPEND UPON C/O. AS C/O DROPPED SUBJECT AT HIS HOTEL, NEAR THREE IN THE MORNING, SUBJECT GUSHED THAT HE FELT LIKE C/O WAS HIS "NEWEST BROTHER." C/O BELIEVES THAT SUBJECT'S NARCISSICISTIC PERSONALITY WILL PROVE MORE VULNERABLE TO AN EVENTUAL RECRUITMENT PITCH THAN THE AVERAGE DEVELOPMENTAL. C/O BELIEVE THAT SUBJECT HAS ALREADY BECOME DEPENDENT ON C/O'S ASSISTANCE, AND WILL ONLY BECOME MORE SO AS THE RELATIONSHIP DEVELOPS.

6. PLANS: C/O WILL CONTINUE TO MEET SUBJECT REGULARLY, CONTINUING THE GUISE OF TRANSLATOR/FIXER. C/O BELIEVES SUBJECT HAS GLARING

NEEDS THAT WE CAN MEET. HE HAS GOOD POTENTIAL TO PROVIDE A PLATFORM FOR ACTIVE MEASURE OPS AGAINST THE MAIN ADVERSARY.

------------END----------END------------END-----------

Chapter 4
Cold War influence ops

Civilization as we know it is to be completely destroyed or completely changed.

***Whittaker Chambers**, former American communist, in* Witness, *his monumental expose of communist espionage in America*

Stalin purged his intelligence services of any potential threats during the late 1920s through the early to mid-1930s. The skilled KGB operators, officers and agents, who penetrated to the core of American society during the early days of Soviet rule, were virtually wiped out.

Yet an institutional memory of these revered "Chekists" remained with the KGB, and lingers to this day.

The irony of Stalin's cleansing of the KGB is that he removed the most productive and effective operations officers, at a time when their operations were beginning to bear fruit. The beauty of their covert influence operations was that the payloads, once inserted, like a virus implanted in healthy tissue, spread their destruction without the need for controllers.

During the post-WW2 Cold War years, the KGB was reinvigorated, and took up where their Chekist ancestors had left off, prior to the purges.

The Soviets, buoyed by their participation in the victory against Germany in WW2, redoubled their efforts against the U.S. According to Andrew in *The Sword and the Shield*, the U.S. continued to be "the main target for KGB active measures as well as for intelligence collection."

Andrew recounted how "A conference of senior KGB officers ... reaffirmed a priority... 'our chief task is to help to frustrate the aggressive intentions of American imperialism... we must work unweariedly at exposing the Adversary's weak and vulnerable points...'"

As Andrew explains, "what was euphemistically described as 'exposure' was in reality [fabricated] disinformation ..." The Active Measures feverishly created were mostly "influence operations designed to discredit the main adversary [the U.S.]...."

Although America was its main target, the KGB did not neglect operations against America's allies, specifically the United Kingdom (UK).

British Targets

During WW2, the KGB made full use of its small army of British recruited agents. Using Comintern cover, KGB officers pierced the heart of British society. One of the best of their networks was known as the Cambridge 5. These agents, spotted and recruited as students at Cambridge, eventually worked their way into British targets. They held sensitive positions in British intelligence services, foreign service, other government, journalism, and academia.

These agents were prolific spotters and assessors of other Britons, providing leads to KGB officers for many more British agents. These agents were used for covert influence, when possible. As Andrew explained, one of them,

> Peter Smollett... head of the Russian department in the [British] wartime Ministry of Information... [used] his position to organize pro-Soviet propaganda on a prodigious scale. A vast meeting at the Albert Hall...to celebrate the 25th anniversary of the Red Army included songs of praise via massed choir, readings by John Gielgud and Laurence

> Olivier, and was attended by leading politicians from all parties. The film USSR at War was shown to factory audiences of 1 1/4 million. [In one month] alone, the Ministry of information organized meetings on the Soviet Union for 34 public venues, 35 factories, 100 voluntary societies, 28 civil defense groups, nine schools and a prison; the BBC in the same month broadcast 30 programs with a substantial Soviet content.

One of the Cambridge Five, Kim Philby, a high-level British foreign intelligence officer, fled to Moscow, just ahead of arrest by British counter-espionage investigators. During years of suspicion that he was a Russian agent, Philby perfected the art of Andemca (Admit nothing. Deny everything. Make counter-accusations.) Within the British intelligence agency, Philby was supported by a loyal group of friends. He deflected criticism and investigations by "cleverly presenting himself as the innocent victim of a McCarthyite, witch-hunt." His 30 years of service to the KGB were repaid with a new life in the Soviet Union. He died a drunk and shattered man, decades later.

American Targets

Elizabeth Bentley was an American covert operations agent. After a long career of covert operations for the KGB, mostly acting as a courier, handler, and eventually as a surrogate case officer for her KGB handler (who was also her lover), Bentley realized the horrific nature of the system she served. She turned herself in to American counter-intelligence, and told her story, including naming names of the American agents she handled for the KGB.

Bentley told the story, recounted in Andrew's book, of a meeting with her new KGB case officer at a restaurant in Washington. The Russian case officer forgets that Bentley is actually an American, and reveals his true feelings about Americans: "I hope the food is good... Americans are such stupid people that even when it comes to a simple matter like cooking a meal, they do it very badly."

The KGB officer's attitude towards normal Americans—rubes, hicks, unsophisticated clowns—provides insight into the mind of American Progressives, whose attitudes were formed by the KGB's influence payloads. Bentley's case officer, realizing his mistake continued, "I'd forgotten for the moment that you, too, are an American."

Bentley's insight into the KGB's operations was a shot across the bow of the American Progressive establishment, and marked the beginning of an American awakening to the communist threat.

The Progressive response to Bentley's revelations also marked the beginning of the Progressives' overt practice of the communist response to exposure. She was reviled as a slut, a repressed Pilgrim, a blonde bimbo, and many more attacks. Admit nothing, deny everything, and make counter-accusations.

Bentley's revelations to the FBI's New York field office "identified [some of those] supplying information to 'the Soviet espionage system:'... Assistant Secretary of the Treasury, Harry Dexter White, OSS [predecessor to the CIA] executive assistant Duncan C. Lee and Roosevelt's former aide Lauchlin Curry.

American Intelligence Penetrated Extensively

The Venona cables and other sources besides Bentley and Chambers have revealed numbers of KGB agents working in America's foreign intelligence agency, the Office of Strategic Services (OSS), during the early Cold War era, "well into the double figures."

The KGB agents in the OSS, according to Andrew, included Maurice Halperin, J. Julius Joseph, and Donald Niven Wheeler. Agents and/or communists in the OSS analytical division worked in sections dealing with Russia, Spain, the Balkans, Hungary, and Latin America. In the OSS's operational division, KGB agents and/or communists worked in sections targeting Germany, Japan, Korea, Italy, Spain, Hungary, and Indonesia.

These agents were surely used for intelligence collection, but it is likely that they were responsible for influencing both analytical products, as well as operations.

The extent of the penetration of the OSS is breath-taking and reveals a systemic failure of imagination, and savvy. This failure clearly was on the part of the highest levels of the new espionage agency, and demonstrates their total misunderstanding of America's sworn enemy.

OSS leadership, made up of President Roosevelt's Wall Street and Ivy League lawyer chums, even spent time in Moscow exchanging information and planning operations against the Nazis. These naïve, or possibly sinister actions, provided the KGB with inside knowledge of the operational philosophy, capabilities, and personnel of the OSS's successor agency, the CIA.

Post-War KGB Operations in America Curtailed

After WW2, Bentley's testimony, Chambers' information, and other counter-intelligence actions forced the KGB's operations underground. Their collection ops and Active Measure ops, as well, were forced to retrench. Many officers and agents were recalled to Moscow, to avoid arrest, after each of the defections of KGB officers and agents.

Rudolf Abel, ultimately exposed and arrested, served eight years as the KGB's illegal COS in New York. During his tenure, his job of spotting, assessing, and recruiting new agents was made much more difficult by the transformation of the operational environment, mainly the "postwar decline and persecution of the [Communist Party of the USA]," according to Andrew.

In fact, the CPUSA ceased to be a factor in assisting the KGB's espionage in America the day in 1949 that Eugene Dennis, the CPUSA's General Secretary, and 10 other leaders of the Party were tried, convicted and jailed of crimes involving "the forcible overthrow of the [U.S.] federal government. The conviction of "more than a hundred other leading Communists...on similar charges" in 1951 was the final body blow to the illegal, immoral, and inherently anti-American charade of a native Communist Party in America.

CPUSA Neutralized, Marginalized, Eliminated as Influence Threat

The fiction of the CPUSA as a threat has captured the attention of generations of historians, politicians, and amateur espionage researchers. The CPUSA was, from the early 1920s until its crushing in the early 1950s, nothing more than a covert arm of the Communist Party of the Soviet Union (CPSU). It was directed, funded and controlled from Moscow. Anything and everything the CPUSA did was a direct reflection of Soviet direction.

The mistaken focus on the CPUSA continues to this day. Researchers, down to 2011, still focus on trying to prove that this or that individual was a "card-carrying member" of the CPUSA.

Such proof is useless. Carrying a card, paying dues, attending meetings, or taking part in other CPUSA activities demonstrates more than anything that such a person was not of use to the communist movement.

Anyone who was operationally useful did not join the CPUSA. They also limited their apparent links to communism, or the fellow-traveler social circles.

The actual threats to America, as we will see, limited their connections, and require counter-intelligence analysis to reveal their status, and the damage they have done to America.

Forget about communist "Dupes," and the need to expose and confirm links to the CPUSA. Focus not on words, but on deeds. Forget about the 21st century CPUSA. It is a fossilized joke made up of semi-crazed iconoclasts. They are not a threat to America today.

The threat to America today is already in our universities, our schools, our media, and Hollywood. The threat is PC and its Progressive advocates. Their roots are not in the CPUSA. Their roots are in the covert influence agents who poured anti-American payloads into our culture, while at the same time, the anti-CPUSA ghost-busters bungled around hunting card-carrying commies.

Pitiful Wretches—NSA Employees Defect

By the 1960s, the KGB was extremely careful in its operations inside the U.S. Normal Americans realized that communism was not a valid path to utopia, and the genocide of the last 40 years was slowly being revealed. The FBI stepped up pressure on KGB officers and their targets. This made collection operations more difficult for the KGB. They relied more on defectors, who were not well vetted before arriving in Russia.

Two Americans defected, in 1960, in a case that reveals the depth of the success of the communist influence operations. Two National Security Agency (NSA) employees, William Martin, and Bernon Mitchell, both cryptographic mathematicians, were both intelligent and book-smart, but lacking in street smarts. They seem to have believed the anti-American influence payloads, and the overt Soviet propaganda—at the same timing buying into an anti-American line, and believing that the Soviet Union was some sort of heaven on earth for all mankind. They were upset that NSA had violated the airspace of other countries without permission, and that American authorities intercepted Soviet propaganda from the U.S. mail.

They left a note behind after they fled for Russia. Andrew describes the note as,

> a lengthy denunciation of the US government and the evils of capitalism in that bizarre eulogy of life in the Soviet

Union, including the claim that its emancipated women were "more desirable as mates."

Their utter naiveté is revealed in this rationale for defecting. Seeking "desirable mates" could rank with the most pitiful reason for anyone to have thrown away a promising life in America.

From the most free and just nation in the history of the world, these two eggheads fled to one of the most tyrannical, despotic dictatorships in modern history—hoping to get more dates. These two could be the poster-children to counter the Progressive-PC influence line.

Less than two years later, 1962, the NSA defector formerly known as Martin, now going by a Russian name, Sokolovsky, was disgusted with the realities of life under Soviet communism, and probably also with his dating prospects. He approached an American on the streets of Russia, and begged for assistance to get his story out to the Western world.

In a declassified CIA memo, Martin was quoted as telling the American he met in the streets of Leningrad that he was "greatly disillusioned and disappointed with what he found in the USSR and was looking for outside help to leave Russia."

This case, and many more like it, illustrates both the success of the covert influence payloads in convincing Americans that their country was a horrible pit of injustice and horror; and the success of convincing naïve eggheads that communism was the path to nirvana.

The Martin and Mitchell case should be required reading for all American students. Interest in their case has been revived by PC-Progressives, but unfortunately not as an object lesson in rejecting covert influence.

Instead their case is now used as an object lesson in the horrors of American McCarthyite "homophobia." Because investigators initially suspected that the pair were homosexual lovers, government efforts focused on the potential security risks of homosexual employees.

Since they were not homosexuals, both married women in Russia, the elevation of their case as an example of "homophobia" becomes another example of PC over-reach.

Bobby Kennedy—Influence Agent

In 1961, the KGB embarked on a new twist of covert influence. The objective of the operation was to, as Andrew documents, "demoralize the West by persuading it of the growing superiority of Soviet forces."

KGB officers, working under a variety of covers, implanted this influence payload. In what must be considered a success of the highest possible level, a KGB colonel, military intelligence officer, operating under TASS cover, assessed and developed the callow Attorney General of the U.S., whose power far exceeded his job title. As the younger brother of the young President, Bobby Kennedy was one of the President's closest advisors, 35 years old at the 1961 inauguration.

The military career of Bobby Kennedy, a dilettante who thrived under the patronage of his millionaire bootlegger father, may best illustrate the special dispensations he received, throughout his short life.

Bouncing between boarding schools during WW2, just before he turned 18, apparently to avoid the draft, Kennedy enlisted in the Navy. He was immediately accepted into the Navy's special training program for college-aged officer candidates, sort of an early ROTC. He, of course, was accepted at Harvard's version of the program. He did nearly two years in the program, bouncing from Harvard to Bates, and back to Harvard, until the Navy commissioned a ship named after young Bobby's brother, the U.S.S. Joseph P. Kennedy, Jr., surely on the command of Daddy Kennedy, the Democrat power broker.

In February, 1946, Kennedy used his father's Progressive patronage power to obtain a discharge from the officer candidate program, to serve as an apprentice seaman on the USS Kennedy.

It doesn't take much imagination to realize that the peripatetic Bobby Kennedy's 119 day tour as a seaman on his daddy's ship had nothing in common with a typical seaman's sea duty. Arriving on February 1, he left the ship on May 30, and was discharged, honorably from the Navy.

Supported by the Kennedy family's house newspaper in Boston, he flitted about the world, pretending to be a reporter for a few trips, until he finished law school.

He was immediately ensconced as a lawyer in the Department of Justice in Washington DC, for three months, before his daddy got him a job as a prosecutor in Brooklyn. He only lasted at that job for four months, resigning to "manage" his brother's Senate campaign.

After the successful campaign, daddy again pulled strings, and young Bobby landed a job with, ironically, Senator Joseph McCarthy's Subcommittee on Investigations.

His tenure with McCarthy was more than seven months, a long time for this daddy's boy on the move. He left the Senate job to work for, no surprise, daddy Kennedy, supposedly working on government reorganization.

It took his father seven months to get young Bobby his next gig, as chief counsel for the Democrat minority in the Senate. Eleven months later, bouncing Bobby became majority counsel, when the Democrats won back the Senate from the Republicans.

Bobby, not quite 30 years old, with no real world experience, settled into the warm comfort of the sinecure arranged by his daddy, in the shadow of his big brother, the anointed Democrat savior, and waited for the 1960 elections, which daddy Kennedy planned as a coming-out for his favorite surviving son.

Bobby again "managed" a John Kennedy campaign, this time a successful one for President, in 1960, and was rewarded by his daddy and big brother, with the plum appointment to be the Attorney General of the United States.

On his first day in the highest law enforcement office in the country, Bobby Kennedy was barely 35 years old. Outside his blatantly political job as a Democrat counsel in the Senate, he had held a handful of positions, usually for a few months at the most.

It appears that virtually all of the "jobs" he held were arranged by his family political connections—119 days on the ship named for Daddy Kennedy's favorite son, four months as a prosecutor in Brooklyn, seven months as a counsel in the Senate, seven months working for his daddy, until he joined his brother in the Senate, for nearly seven years.

From the point of view of a Russian case officer, working against this shallow, callow, punk daddy's boy, elevated to a position of nearly absolute power in his brother's administration, would be child's play.

The KGB likely began probing multiple avenues of approach to the callow kiddie crowd in the White House, soon after their ascendance in January 1961. Maybe they already had established contacts with Bobby Kennedy, during his international travels, through Europe, the Middle East, India, Vietnam and Japan, as a student, pretending to be a journalist. Students on the make, traveling through these areas would have come to the attention of the KGB in each of the countries he visited. Especially a student who was the son of the corrupt Democrat ambassador to London.

The KGB approach that clicked with the naïve Attorney General was the approach of a military intelligence colonel operating under cover as head of the Washington bureau of the TASS news agency. It may be useful to read ahead to the next chapter for the testimony of Ismael Ege, about the KBG's use of TASS for operational cover.

In a classic piece of operational tradecraft, the KGB case officer, Georgi Bolshakov, represented himself to his target, Bobby Kennedy, as a "back-channel" conduit to the Kremlin. This is a common operational ruse, useful to convince otherwise wary targets that the information they share will go straight to the highest levels.

This ruse is also useful against targets in influential positions, for example a kid Attorney General, the most trusted advisor to his brother, the President of the U.S. Against these targets, the ruse is expanded to include a ruse within a ruse—that the target is also receiving confidential details in an "information exchange."

After accepting a "personal relationship" with the Bolshakov, Bobby Kennedy opened up to the espionage professional's developmental operation. Kennedy invited the KGB officer to his home, and met with him dozens of times.

For a developmental operation, this is a rather accelerated schedule. It seems that the KGB was ready to err on the side of aggression, due to the need to implant influence messages with the young administration.

In stark contrast to the dilettante know-it-all Bobby Kennedy, Bolshakov was an expert at his profession. He had joined the Soviet intelligence system in 1943, served throughout WW2 and followed that with a three year graduate level training program in intelligence operations. He developed excellent English language skills prior to his posting to Washington.

The superbly successful development of the Attorney General by a man who was clearly Soviet intelligence would seem shocking by today's counter-intelligence standards. At the time, evidently the Kennedys could do no wrong. Even today historians writing of this espionage operation give Bobby Kennedy an unwarranted benefit of the doubt.

Andrew, discussing Bobby Kennedy's use as an influence agent, says that Bobby seemed to be, "forgetting that he was dealing with an experienced intelligence professional who had been instructed to cultivate him," And that "the president's brother became convinced that 'an authentic friendship grew' between him and [the KGB officer]."

There is absolutely no reason to give Kennedy the benefit of any doubt. He was simply an arrogant, ignorant, spoiled rich man's son playing at international affairs. He was playing against talented, experienced, well-trained professionals. He was no match, and was out-witted, out-gunned, and out-maneuvered.

The relationship seems to have terminated when the Russians manipulated the out-witted Kennedys during the Cuban missile crisis. The KGB case officer, after influencing the Kennedy administration's view for several months, provided a disinformation payload to young Bobby, who swallowed it, hook, line and sinker.

In a conversation recorded in the Oval Office, between the President and his little brother, the two neophytes, playing at power politics seem to come to the realization that they've been played for fools. Bobby tells his brother that he'd had lunch with his KGB handler that day.

President: "What did he say?"

Bobby: "He said this is, this is a defensive base for the Russians. It's got nothing to do with the Cubans."

President: "...They're lying...This horror about embarrassing me in the election.... But they didn't tell you there were missiles there."

Bobby: "No. Remember, I told you that."

A member of the President's cabinet, later the same day joked about the potential consequences of a war that might ensue over the Soviet missiles in Cuba. Speaking to the Defense Secretary, Robert McNamara, an unidentified meeting attendee said, "Suppose we make Bobby mayor of Havana."

The KGB's influence operations officers, in the field, were far superior to the Soviets' decision makers, analysis, or ability to capitalize on the nearly unbelievable operations run by the field officers.

Recruiting, or at least co-opting, the Attorney General of the United States, by the KGB, is the operational equivalent of a grand slam home run, Triple Crown, Three-peat, MVP, World Cup, and a Super Bowl championship, all rolled into one.

The leadership of a banana republic, or an African former colony, where a young colonel as the President, after a coup, installs his even younger brother in his cabinet, might be seen as susceptible to a cabinet member being targeted and played by an ops officer. Such a country would be a ripe target for a case officer's plucking. But to consider the leadership of a super-power to be susceptible to such a blatant influence operation is shocking and nearly incredible.

The fact is, though, that the Bobby Kennedy operation happened, and has been known for some time. Exact details remain sketchy due to most KGB documentation, as discussed earlier, being under the control of the KGB, while the Kennedy side of the story is controlled by the PC hagiographers who seem to believe that the Kennedys truly were the America's Camelot. Exposure of truths that tarnish the haloes of the Kennedy brothers is not encouraged by the PC keepers of the legend.

However, the relationship between Bobby and Bolshakov is known. Bolshakov's true status is known. We know what KGB officers do. We know how they operate. We know their operational goals. We know what Bolshakov told Bobby. We know the story that Bobby believed—he had a "back channel" to the Kremlin to avoid diplomatic sclerosis. We know that Bobby eventually realized he'd been used. And we know that none of the American players ever admitted the whole truth.

Bobby told the Russian ambassador that if it became publicly known that he had accepted a deal with the Russians to remove U.S. missiles from Turkey in exchange for the Russians removing their missiles from Cuba it "could cause irreparable harm to my political career in the future."

Chapter 5

KBG case officers speak

Communism is not worth to fight for. For the contrary, it was necessary and worth to fight against communism, to fight by all means if we wish the spiritual values of mankind do not submerge into the dark seas of evil.

***Ismael Ege**, former KGB case officer, after defecting, in testimony to Congress.*

Interstate 85 South, near Butner, North Carolina
March, 2008

Driving back to North Carolina is bittersweet. It's amazing how my stomping grounds have grown and changed in the last thirty years. From a pleasant little backwater, reviled by Northerners as a den of redneck racists, Carolina is now inundated with Yankees fleeing their high tax dystopias of union money-grubbers stealing tax-payers blind. The Northern influx started with a vengeance in the late 1980s, as retirees poured into the Outer Banks, the Asheville mountains, and the Raleigh-Durham-Chapel Hill Research Triangle. A pleasant four-season climate, low taxes, a right-to-work state (little union control of industry), friendly and courteous people, natural beauty, world-class universities and medical facilities—it was a well-kept secret. Until it wasn't.

Nasty-tempered Yankees changed much of the culture of Carolina. Working part-time after graduate school, looking for a real job, I graded writing tests in Durham. Of the fifty or so graders that I worked with during those six months, I was the only North Carolinian. The rest were all Yankee refugees. I admired their choice of states, however their complaints grew, "Why can't ya find a good beh-gul around hee-ah?" they whined. Unfortunately, besides their appreciation of the weather in their new home state, they also brought their Yankee attitudes, and politics. Within twenty years of the influx, Carolina went from being represented in the U.S. Senate by the dean of conservatives, Jesse Helms, to a Democrat, Kay Hagan, who rode Obama's coattails to D.C. in 2008. The Northern influx altered the political balance in North Carolina, at least for the interim.

I make my way to the conference, in downtown Raleigh, through somewhat decrepit city streetscapes. Seems they're trying to come back with an urban renewal plan. The history museum, venue for the conference, features an interesting exhibit on waterfowl hunting. I shoot virtual ducks during breaks in the conference.

Good to visit Raleigh, but also good to be heading back to Northern Virginia. The mix of old Carolinians with international espionage is a bit disconcerting. Hitting I85 North is a relief.

Cold War KGB Active Measures Case Officer

The 2008 Raleigh Spy Conference drew my attention for its featured speakers—including retired CIA case officer Pete Bagley. Bagley ran ops against the KGB for most of the Cold War. He wrote books, some with his former opponents in the KGB, after his retirement. His focus for this talk was on his then recently published book on the KGB defector, Yuri Nosenko. His book, *Spy Wars*, dissects, from the viewpoint of a counter-intelligence case officer (Bagley was the first case officer to handle Nosenko, upon his defection), what Bagley believes was a massive Active Measure operation against the U.S.

Bagley believes that Nosenko, a KGB case officer, was actually sent by the KGB to implant a deception payload, with the ultimate goal of influencing the CIA and the U.S. policy-makers' beliefs about the U.S.S.R. and the KGB.

At the Spy Conference, besides interviewing Bagley, and bouncing my covert-influence-created-PC theory off him, I met an even better source—an ex-KGB case officer, Andrey S., who left the KGB when the communists lost power, and came to the U.S. after trying his hand at business in Latin America for a few years. His 20 year career as a KGB case officer was focused almost entirely on targeting Americans and American institutions. He served in the KGB station n Washington for six years in the late 1970s to 1981, under Third Secretary cover. And at the KGB station in New York, under United Nations cover, for five years. He was KGB COS in a Latin American country at the end of the Soviet Union's reign.

He plans to write a book, detailing his operations against America, under the title *Target America.* I told him that title has already been used—*Target America: the Influence of Communist Propaganda on U.S. Media*, by James Tyson.

During a long lunch in Raleigh, Andrey explained the KGB's Active Measures, and targeting Americans. His targets in Washington were the intelligence agencies and Congress. He doesn't warm up enough to provide details on his targets, and I don't press him. Andrey, like most KGB officers whose memoirs I've read, is not well-read on the history of KGB ops against America. He is nearly totally focused on his own specific operations, during his own specific time frame. This confirms the extreme compartmentation of KGB ops, and explains how ancient operations are unknown except to the small handful of those who ran or managed them.

Of course my counter-intelligence antenna is on high alert in dealing with Andrey. My assessment is that he is telling the truth about who he is, and about the operations he ran. While it may not be the *whole* truth, that is to be expected. Andrey is in a tight spot for residency status. He had a sponsor to immigrate, and helped out this consulting firm with lectures to U.S. intelligence and law enforcement agencies, on the subject of Russian tradecraft. But this company did not follow-up on its promises for a green card. Andrey, who did not defect, but left Russia when communism collapsed, is left in the position of not being able to return to Russia, which is under the control of his former KGB colleagues.

Yet he also does not yet have established immigration status in the U.S. either. He was still in that precarious status, right up to the end of 2010.

I respect the need for Andrey to hide the exact identity of his American recruits, but he has no reason to obfuscate the general approach to Active Measures that the KGB took, at least during his tenure.

He told me that he ran "aggressive CI operations against the CIA...operational games; double agent operations." He was an expert at "assessing and recruiting American targets in the U.S. and third countries." He ran and supported operations against Americans, including "recruitment approaches, Active Measures, false flag" approaches.

According to Andrey, throughout the 1970s, until the fall of the Soviet Union, KGB case officers were required by KGB headquarters to come up with Active Measure operational plans. Each reporting period (quarter, half-year, and annual) case officers' output was evaluated, mostly on numbers of proposals, not so much on effectiveness. KGB covert influence operations were also suggested to the field station by KGB headquarters.

A typical Active Measure op, conceived by a New York station case officer, and run out of New York, involved creating fictitious groups of "Mothers of Minority Soldiers." The objective of this operation was to weaken the morale and unit cohesiveness of the American military, during a time when the KGB believed the U.S. was gearing up for an invasion of Nicaragua. These "Mothers" groups, which only existed on KGB paper, then sent out press releases to Hispanic and black media. KGB headquarters forgery and documents groups provided authentic-looking letterhead for the groups. They also produced pamphlets.

The mailings called for mothers of minority soldiers to join the groups. The pamphlets and press releases all claimed that "black and Hispanic soldiers are most likely to be on the front lines of the coming war against our brothers in Nicaragua."

The case officer ran this operation just like a public relations or advertising campaign. He bought a mailing list of black and Hispanic media. After the false materials were prepared in Moscow and received in New York station, the case officer addressed and stamped, by hand, the envelopes. The packages had to be mailed from a neutral area, not from the Russian consulate. The case officer ran extensive surveillance detection routes, sneaking across the 25 mile radius boundary the FBI imposed on Russian diplomats.

The results were not measurable, but the case officer got credit for effort.

KGB COS Vienna—Active Measures General

In an unpublished memoir, a former KGB COS in Vienna, Austria detailed how he was recruited by Ivan Ivanonich Agayants, at the time (1961) the chief of KGB "deception" operations. The KGB case officer's descriptions of his career inside the fabled Active Measures group are mostly inside politics. However, he does shed some light on the extreme importance that Soviet policy-makers, the Politburo, placed on Active Measures. He comments, when he was offered the Active Measures job that "it offered the opportunity to...move into direct support of our foreign policy." The KGB COS ultimately rose to the rank of KGB General, running the Active Measures headquarters element.

This offhand comment demonstrates the powerful results the Soviets believed their Active Measures were capable of producing. These operations are not mere intelligence collection. These operations have the potential to make a historical difference, tilt the political playing field to favor the communists.

Agayants, according to the KGB COS, learned his craft at the knee of a KGB legend—Artur Khristianovich Artuzov. Artuzov's career ended with a bullet to the brain during Stalin's purges. According to the KGB COS, Artuzov ran legendary deception operations, beginning in the early 1920s, including TRUST, which used fake dissident organizations, and other deceptions to lure self-exiled enemies of the Bolsheviks back to Russia. The "counter-revolutionaries," convinced by Artuzov's deception operation, thought they were joining an effort to overthrow the Bolsheviks. In reality, the entire "anti-Bolshevik" organization was a sham, totally controlled by the KGB. The unwitting Russian patriots, lured back by the fake promise of saving their country, ended up rotting in communist prisons or dead.

Val Aksilenko, Afghanistan

Val Aksilenko was a KGB case officer, who specialized in the North America Department, and served as the chief of the Washington branch. Aksilenko told me in a conversation in 2008 that he led, planned, and implemented extensive Active Measures work against the U.S. In the last period of his career in the KGB, he worked on the Afghanistan issue for the USSR.

During the Soviet Union's war in Afghanistan, Aksilenko led an intelligence unit under cover in the Russian Academy of Science until 1988. He then moved to a staff position on the Council of Ministers of the USSR in the Kremlin, working undercover in the Foreign Economic Committee.

Gorbachev insisted that the warring Afghan factions must be reconciled and tasked Aksilenko's group with that goal. Aksilenko visited Afghanistan, and spoke with the two sides—the Najibullah government, and the mujahedeen rebels. He used western Europeans as intermediaries to contact the mujahedeen. The KGB veteran called his covert influence op "Triangle."

Aksilenko was tight-lipped on details about his operations against America, only confirming that he ran multiple covert influence operations against multiple targets in the U.S., throughout his career.

Ismael Ege, Military Case Officer, 1930s to 1941

On October 28 and 29, 1953, a former KGB (military intelligence, GRU) case officer, testified about communist espionage operations against the U.S. before the U.S. Senate Committee on the Judiciary's Subcommittee to Investigate the Internal Security Act, and Interlocking Subversion in Government Departments.

The subcommittee chairman, Senator William Jenner, of Indiana, was the only Senator present at the hearing in room 110 of the United States Courthouse in Foley Square, New York City.

Robert Morris, the subcommittee counsel, led the questioning of Ege. The defector from the communist country, in emotional and dramatic terms, detailed his personal journey. He was born in Orsk, in the Urals, in 1904. In 1920 he trained as an educational propagandist for primary school teachers.

Ege volunteered to come to America, after his defection, to share with the Senate details of how the KGB operated its targets, tactics and techniques. The case officer, who was trained in military engineering, deployed to Germany and Turkey under journalist cover, as a Telegraph Agency of the Soviet Union (TASS) correspondent.

Ege detailed for the committee how the communists used journalist cover to both collect intelligence, and for covert influence. He explained to Senator Jenner that the communists viewed Americans as naïve and unable to understand that a journalist could actually be an intelligence operator.

Targeting technical intelligence collection in developed countries, including the U.S., Ege deployed to Germany in 1941, under an alias, using TASS cover, as the deputy chief of TASS in Berlin.

When Germany declared war on the Soviet Union, in June of 1941, Ege, as a civilian (under his cover name and occupation) belligerent, was arrested and interned for three weeks. He was released in an exchange for Germans held by the Russians, after just three weeks in a concentration camp.

Ege explained to the subcommittee how he came to be a communist, his experience mirroring that of red-diaper-babies in America. He said that when he joined the "All-Union Communist Party of the Bolsheviks" in 1921, at 17 years of age, he was "young, emotional, and unexperienced [and] believed that communism would bring happiness, freedom, equality, and the same degree of political freedom to the national minorities of the former Tzarist Empire of Russia."

Ege said that he joined the army, believing that "it was an instrument of peace...not of...aggression."

Working his way up the ladder of promotions in the army and the Communist Party, however, he began to see the "true face of communism, of Soviet dictatorship, and its weapon of aggression—the Red army..."

Living in interesting times, Ege was there at the dawn of the communist dictatorship, and saw "the bloodshed, the horrors of the liquidation of uprising against the Soviet tyranny in the Middle Asia and Trans-Caucasuses, collectivization and of forced labor, the purges, the Soviet-Finnish War, the occupations of Baltic countries and Bessarabia."

As Ege thought about the actions he witnessed and read about, as a Party member, and intelligence officer, he became "terrified and ashamed for the cruel methods of Soviet [*sic*] government."

The despair and emotion is evident as Ege, in his foreign-accented English, explained the inner conflict that communist tactics and techniques caused within his own heart:

> I was having spiritual conflict with myself. Finally, I asked myself the most important question: Was it worth it to fight for communism? Was communism a right kind of

> prescription against the social disease called by many as crisis of human society?

At the same time, the 1920s through the early 1940s, that American Willing Accomplices were turning a blind eye to the clear evidence of communist atrocities, this young man, split by the monumental decision to reject everything he had been taught and believed, did the right thing. In his own, less than perfect, English he told the Senator:

> I am proud to declare that in the end of 1930s, while still living and working in the USSR, I was able to answer those vital questions in the positive way and to make up my mind to break with the Soviets whenever chances would come.
>
> My answers were these:
>
> Communism is not worth to fight for. For the contrary, it was necessary and worth to fight against communism, to fight by all means if we wish the spiritual values of mankind do not submerge into the dark seas of evil. That is because communism is Godless, is unscientific, is outmoded.

After sharing his conversion experience, Ege explained the organization of Soviet intelligence, its techniques of using cover, and the bureaucratic in-fighting inherent in the KGB, military intelligence, and the Comintern's intelligence arm.

Ege explained that the Comintern was the highest level of Soviet intelligence operations, reporting directly to the Central Committee of the Communist Party of the Soviet Union. Although he was operating against the same targets, he never saw the Comintern operations documents.

The compartmentation of Comintern ops was airtight, and Ege never saw their cables or reports.

Ege detailed an operation he oversaw, "Seven Brothers," in which young Russian intelligence officers, after espionage training, were sent to America, under student cover and aliases, for undergraduate and graduate study.

Ege described his military and intelligence training in "policies and the party line." The party line was always, "the United States of America was enemy No. 1."

As he related the story, Ege figured out the communist party line was against the U.S. because "The United States of America is for freedom, for free enterprise, for the dignity of the individual, and for principles of western democracy."

While the Soviet Union, his native land, the land of his youth, education, and indoctrination, was "the most totalitarian state where the individual is not free. He is a slave of the state."

Ege explained how he used his TASS cover against the American press for covert influence operations. The visit of any American journalist to the Soviet embassy, requesting an interview with a Russian official, generated excitement in the embassy's espionage offices.

When the American arrived, the espionage managers called Ege, "Downstairs is a foreign American correspondent," and then showing their own belief that the Americans were as crafty as themselves, "perhaps spy. Find out, of course, is he spy or not. If he is spy, for what agency is he working."

Then the espionage manager's directions concluded, "Find his background and, finally, in some future try to use him."

Ege, summing up his relatively limited experience working against the American media, said, "That was double-face play always with every correspondent, every press attaché..."

These Soviet case officers represent the final stages of the communist clandestine operations against their Main Adversary. In their stories, we can see the remnants of their professional ancestors. Maybe these glimpses of recent communist operations, and glimpses into their minds, can help us to better understand the minds and operations that are no longer available for study.

Chapter 6

Active Measure ops

Any clandestine operation is, by definition, a conspiracy.

McCarthyite Conspiracy Theories

It's interesting to note that some critics of exposing the KGB and communist operations against America call efforts like *Willing Accomplices*, which report on communists and their anti-American operations "McCarthyite," or "conspiracy theories."

The fact is that both of those epithets are more true than the critics probably know. First, McCarthy's basic investigational premise, that the U.S. was the target of a concerted infiltration strategy, for collection and influence, by communists, both foreign and domestic, was fundamentally correct. He may have misinterpreted some evidence, and may have been a bit more forceful in his accusations against some targets than was warranted. McCarthy may not have fully understood the methods and targets of the communists, but that's understandable—he wasn't a counter-intelligence specialist.

But then again, almost no contemporary of McCarthy's in America, outside a handful of KGB defectors who had been directly involved in the operations, understood the Soviets, the KGB, the American communists, and the massive anti-American collection and influence operations.

And the fact is that, although McCarthy did uncover communist infiltrations of the U.S. government and other organizations, he also very likely missed huge numbers of communists, intelligence collectors, influence agents, and other Willing Accomplices of those who sought to harm America.

As for this work, or others which examine communist espionage operations against the U.S., being called "conspiracy theories," one can only chuckle, and quote Bart Simpson "No duh!" Again, the critics are onto the truth, and probably don't even know it.

A Clandestine Operation is a Conspiracy

Any clandestine operation is, by definition, a conspiracy. The procedures involved in covertly meeting, gathering intelligence, planting covert influence payloads, communicating, paying, tasking, and otherwise running an espionage operation are known as tradecraft. Tradecraft is nothing more, or less, than techniques of conducting a covert conspiracy.

So, if critics wish to rail against this analysis as conspiracy-mongering, I surely will not argue with them. All my efforts in this research project are focused on exposing the KGB conspiracy to destroy the American spirit. This conspiracy involved the entire Soviet government, each and every communist party member, in the U.S. or elsewhere, every KGB officer, and untold multitudes of American, and foreign, Willing Accomplices, recruited or co-opted to promulgate that nasty payload that begat anti-American Political Correctness.

These groups, and others, worked together to secretly run operations against America and her allies, in order to soften them up for the global spread of Marxism-Leninism, as the communist cult leaders had predicted.

It is difficult to imagine a better organized or more wide-spread conspiracy than the one that existed during the high point of Soviet influence in the world. That high point lasted from October 1917 through the late 1980s, or so.

Sometimes the conspiracy was well-led and successful. Sometimes the conspiracy was led by dunces and was ludicrous in actions and results. But always, the KGB conspired to destroy America.

Conspiracy? Si, se puede! Yes, they could, and yes, they did!

KGB Ops Put Homosexuals in Closets Everywhere

Christopher Andrew's excellent overview of the KGB, written with the ex-KGB archivist Vasili Mitrokhin, is based on Mitrokhin's smuggled notes from KGB files, as well as Andrew's own research from other sources.

The KGB, after WW2, ramped up its Active Measures, other than covert influence, operations against the U.S. One of the Active Measures operations they practiced was the denigration campaign, using disinformation, forgeries and other techniques.

One of the KGB's main target's, because of the Bureau's responsibility for counter-espionage, was J. Edgar Hoover, long-time Director of the FBI.

In the late 1960s, the KGB embarked on a series of Active Measures designed to destroy the pugnacious Hoover. The op began with "fabrications of [Hoover's] homosexual affairs." Andrew noted, however, that the KGB "spoiled a plausible falsehood by surrounding it with improbable amounts of conspiracy theory. It sent anonymous letters, intended to appear to come from the Ku Klux Klan," to American newspapers.

The KGB's forged letters accused Hoover of favoring certain homosexuals for promotion, in return for sexual favors.

The KGB's forgeries ramped up the accusations against Hoover with a claim that he had "been engaged for several decades in a larger gay conspiracy to staff the CIA and the State Department with homosexuals."

Andrew details another KGB Active Measure, this one in 1977, "[a KGB] officer in New York, posted a forged FBI document to the California-based magazine Gay Times reporting that [Senator Henry] Jackson had been an active homosexual..."

The consistency of this theme seems to betray the lack of creativity of the KGB's operational planners.

Racial and Religious Targets

The KBG used racial tensions in the Great Adversary's society for operational traction, as they had since the early cases of Sacco and Vanzetti and the Scottsboro Boys.

The KGB took on Active Measures operations targeting Martin Luther King. In 1967 they planned to "discredit [King] and his chief lieutenants by placing articles in the African press," according to Andrew.

At the same time, the KGB also planned "to forge and distribute through illegal channels a document showing that the John Birch Society, in conjunction with the Minuteman organization, is developing a plan for the physical elimination of leading figures in the Negro movement in the US."

Andrew reports another operation, intended to make use of the tensions among rival ethnic and racial groups in the U.S.:

> In 1971 [the chief of the KGB] personally approved the fabrication of pamphlets full of racist insults purporting to come from the extremist Jewish Defense league...at the same time, forged letters were sent to 60 black organizations, giving fictitious details of atrocities committed by the [Jewish Defense League] against blacks...

As late as 1984, KGB Active Measures plans included racially inflammatory provocations:

> In 1984 [KGB] officers in the Washington residency mailed bogus communications from the Ku Klux Klan to the Olympic committees of African and Asian countries.

As the Soviet system slowly self-destructed, its most energetic defenders were the KGB.

In 1978, the KGB concocted a bizarre denigration campaign against Carter's National Security Adviser, Zbigniew Brzezinski. The apparent goal was to discredit Brzezinski. In the operation, the KGB "drafted a bogus report on ...Brzezinski ... which... declared that the Zionists had compromising information on his private life would seriously discredit him." They slipped a copy of this report into the open window of an American diplomat's car in the Israeli capital.

Even as the Soviets courted western media with Gorbachev's perestroika, in attempts to cling to power, the KGB continued Active Measures:

> [During the Gorbachev era, KGB] forgeries were used to promote media campaigns... in 1987, a forged letter from the [US Director of Central intelligence]... on plans to overthrow the Indian prime minister... in 1988, bogus

> instructions from Reagan to destabilize Panama... and in 1989, a fabricated letter from the South African Foreign Minister... referring to a sinister but nonexistent secret agreement with the United States.

As Andrew notes, the Gorbachev era boasted one of the most virulent Active Measure operations. And as noted in an earlier chapter here, that operation echoes to this day, with President Obama's spiritual mentor, advisor, and pastor, Jeremiah Wright's spreading of the fake communist attack payload:

> Probably the most successful anti-American active measure... promoted by a mixture of overt propaganda and covert action by [the KGB], was the story that the AIDS virus had been manufactured by American biological warfare specialists... the story received major news coverage in over 43 world countries.

Even as the Soviet Union collapsed, the KGB called together its operators in September 1990 to remind them that "work on active measures is to be considered one of the most important functions of the KGB's foreign intelligence service."

Chapter 7

21st century Russian covert influence ops

As long as injustice and poverty remain dominant, the struggle will continue.

***Vicky Pelaez**, Russian covert influence agent, El Diario, December 1, 2009*

Russia is a proud country, and its people are proud of their heritage. The Soviet Union was superpower, and the KGB was a dominant player in global affairs for decades. The fall of the Soviet Union was a blow to the national pride of Russians. The loss of superpower status was a blow to Russia's national ego.

The rise to power of Vladimir Putin, a KGB case officer, should be a clue to those who are paying attention that the former Soviet power brokers did not just fade away. Putin's reign is a reprise of the dictators of the Soviet Union.

Russian industry is controlled by an oligarchy of tightly knit, well-connected families. Many are KGB veterans.

The Russian clandestine service still stands, virtually unchanged from its communist days. The current name of the service really does not matter. For all intents and purposes, it is still the KGB, and we'll call it the KGB here.

When Putin ascended to power, he took over a demoralized Russian society. His regime needed a Main Adversary as a symbolic enemy to rally the electorate. America, in the throes of the Global

War on Terror, was enmeshed in foreign wars, taking on al-Qaeda and the Axis of Evil.

The brazen employment of American global military power seemed to Putin like a slap in Russia's face. America's obliteration of the Afghanistan government and its "shock and awe" obliteration of Saddam Hussein's regime in Iraq must have made Putin long for the good old days of Russian global might.

Regardless of Putin's inner thoughts, we now know that he ordered a concerted KGB operation against the U.S. Even as a ring of more than ten KGB officers and agents was uncovered and rolled up in 2010, we must realize that, just as in the 1920s, this is surely just the tip of a Russian espionage iceberg.

From the make-up of the agents and officers arrested, it appears that Active Measures, and specifically covert influence operations, are as important to the Russians as ever. It appears that the Russians may understand the effects of the KGB's ancient covert influence ops, and are, even today, in 2011, piling on, inserting more "America sucks" influence payloads into the culture.

Propaganda Today: Russia Today—RT—in English and Spanish

- Russia is actively operating the full scope of Active Measures. Their overt propaganda unit cranks out anti-American messages into the heartland of the U.S. via the Putin government-owned station Russia Today (RT). It is broadcast via satellite across the U.S., by local digital broadcast throughout the Washington DC and New York City metro areas, and also on some American Public Broadcasting System digital subchannels.
- RT also offers full Spanish language broadcasts, focusing mostly on news, for Latin America.

Watching a day of RT is like taking a time machine trip back to the 1960s, or for that matter, like watching the PC-Progressive stalwart MSNBC.

Regular programs include several American commentators. One young lady is the "talent" for "The Alonya Show." In perfect idiomatic English, Alonya rails against America, broadcasting from RT's studios in Washington DC.

Recent Alonya shows have included PC-Progressive takes on Big Oil, the persecution of Julian Assange, the Koch brothers' class warfare, Wisconsin governor Scott's struggles against public unions, a Mother Jones reporter's exploration of the travails of female reporters, the Center for American Progress's analysis of the Egyptian coup.

So That's Where Air America Went!

Another of RT's America-based programs is "The Big Picture with Thom Hartmann," a sneering, bespectacled version of Keith Olbermann. Hartmann rants about American conspiracies against peace-loving minorities everywhere. A little due diligence on this PC-Progressive gabber revealed that he was a refugee from the failed PC-Progressive talk radio network Air America.

Recent Big Picture shows included the Wisconsin union battle from the point of view of the Campaign for America's Future and ThinkProgress.org. Thom took on the U.S. Army's use of psychological operations on Congressmen in another program. Thom takes Obama's side in the budget battle against "draconian cuts the GOP is proposing." Thom sponsored a young PC-Progressive journalist's visit to the conservative CPAC, and discussed Big Oil's subsidies in another.

Between Ms. Alonya and Mr. Hartmann, their shows play 4 hours between 6pm and midnight on the east coast.

RT Spanish, broadcast in the US, is much more strident in its anti-American tone. Evidently the Spanish language programmers are less bound to an attempt to appear unbiased. The Spanish language programs seem to have come from 1960s Cuba. Constant documentaries on American war crimes in Vietnam, and Soviet war heroes from the Great Patriotic War are interspersed with news broadcasts about American atrocities in Afghanistan and Nicaraguan social justice advances.

The striking thing about the RT broadcasts is their almost exact duplication of the KGB's covert influence and propaganda payloads from the 1920s right through the fall of the USSR.

Alonya and Hartmann join a long line of PC-Progressive Willing Accomplices, ready to denigrate and demean their country. Surely they are not getting rich from their work at RT, but it's clear from watching them that they are getting a good dose of PC-Progressive elitist hauteur.

Russian Covert Influence—Pelaez and the Hispanic Press

The FBI arrested fiery New York columnist, Vicky Pelaez in late June, 2009. An editor and writer for the Spanish language newspaper *El Diario La Prensa*, she was charged with being an unregistered agent of the Russian government. Her arrest was part of a sweep of nine other KGB officers and agents working in and against the U.S.

The 10, after breathlessly pleading their innocence, eventually pled guilty to conspiracy, and were all transferred to Russian custody.

Pelaez's far-left, anti-American columns won accolades from American Progressives, and from some in the Hispanic diaspora in the U.S.

Released on bail to home detention during the Fourth of July long weekend, she was ultimately swapped, along with her KGB case officer husband, for a handful of Russians convicted in Russian courts for spying against their own country. None are American officers, and only one appears to have had any contact with American intelligence.

As soon as the deal was rushed through the American courts, nothing more was said by officials on the west side of the Atlantic. The KGB operatives returned to heroes' welcomes in Moscow, including Pelaez.

The KGB provided Pelaez with free housing, and a monthly stipend of $2000 for the rest of her life.

Pelaez's Payloads

A sample from a Pelaez editorial in El Diario, translated from Spanish scorched the policies of her adopted country: "...refusing to hear ... the popular resistance and the opinion of the majority of countries in the world, the Big Boss [the United States] supported the putchists' ... illegal [Honduran] presidential elections..." Pelaez finished her anti-American rant, written in her comfortable suburban house in Yonkers, NY, with a tired revolutionary screech, "as long as injustice and poverty remain dominant, the struggle will continue." (El Diario, December 1, 2009)

Case Study in Penetrating America's Cultural Transmission Belts

For nearly a century, Russian intelligence operations have exploited our openness, and the American commitment to individual rights. The Russians know that an American, regardless of origin or recent citizenship, is allowed to speak freely and criticize the government. To exploit our weaknesses, the KGB has honed their influence techniques. They prefer to use leftists, minorities, and women (Pelaez is a three-fer, combining all three desirable attributes) as their agents.

The template of the Pelaez operation is familiar to experts in Russian covert influence operations. In the early 1920s, the KGB targeted a foreign-born journalist of dubious background, Walter Duranty.

Today we see the same pattern of influence operations against the American media. One of the most important demographic slices in America is the Hispanic population. With Spanish language media providing direct targeting, covert influence operators find targeting Hispanics quite easy.

Pelaez arrived in New York in 1988 and established herself as an expert on leftist issues. She burrowed deep into the Spanish language press. From journalist to commentator, she editorialized freely. She was widely quoted in Hispanic media, and frequently highlighted by Cuban propaganda vehicles.

Russian Covert Influence Template

Russian covert influence operations would seem to be following a well-worn path of tradecraft. Using tried and true recruiting techniques, the Russian operators methodically assess the motivations of their targets. Using the targets' unique motivations, the KGB recruits them as agents. They become Willing Accomplices in anti-American influence operations. Sometimes the agents are witting of their KGB control, sometimes they are not. From the FBI's reports, it appears that Pelaez was likely fully witting of her KGB sponsorship.

Pelaez, originally a citizen of Peru, infiltrated the US after a suspicious, one-day "kidnapping" by Peruvian communist rebels. Soon after, she was granted asylum to enter the US. Ironically, her asylum request was apparently based on the threat of retribution from the communists.

In the Russians' Pelaez case, the intelligence officer's development and recruitment of the targeted journalist included marriage. This is a level of commitment and dedication that very few free world intelligence services can demand or expect.

A steamy combination of true belief in her message, infatuation with her recruiting officer, substantial lifestyle benefits (a free ride to New York City and US citizenship) seemed to motivate Pelaez.

Her influence work at the Hispanic newspaper in New York is typical of covert influence payloads. She denigrated the US and its policies, at the same time she lauded Latin American dictators, with the payload masked as her "point of view." It is likely that her influence work changed the attitudes and beliefs of hundreds or thousands of those exposed to her intel operations

The use of a Russian-born immigrant, hiding in plain sight as a KGB controller is classic Russian tradecraft. A husband acting as controller for a wife is uncommon, but not unheard of. Pelaez's husband appears to have confessed to the FBI, admitting his birth in Russia and his work for the KGB. It's likely that his role was as a principal agent, acting as the go-between for his wife and their KGB handlers.

Federal prosecutors brought the Russian spies to court several days after their arrest. Pelaez was a pitiful sight. She appeared dazed and confused, a Hispanic housewife snatched from her kitchen.

Dazzled by Jason Bourne and Jack Bauer, and ignorant of the most effective forms of espionage, Americans didn't know what to make of the pudgy Peruvian-born journalist. Seemingly, the main concern the media was the plight of her children. The Huffington Post speculated that she was betrayed by her handling officer—her husband.

Many Americans were distracted by the slutty daughter of a KGB officer, Anna Chapman, caught peddling her wares as a swallow (KGB's term for the bait in sex-traps). Little did Americans realize that the frumpy journalist, Vicky Pelaez, was the latest warrior in a century-long, vicious attack on America. The sex-kitten was just a shiny bauble to distract us.

In the early days of the struggle for world domination between the USA and global communism, American statesmen were clueless about the enemy they faced. They were clueless about the rules of the struggle. They were ignorant of the communists' tactics. And they arrogantly refused to learn.

In 1929, more than a decade after the Bolsheviks had imposed communism on Russia, the American Secretary of State, Henry Stimson, politely declined to take part in espionage, averring that, "Gentlemen don't read each other's mail."

The Bolsheviks, however, were not gentlemen. In 1929, the Russians were already reading our mail, even as we refused the offer to read others'. The communists had, so to speak, slipped into our house at night and were living in our basement. The communists were playing a game that America had never understood. Even at that early date, they were winning. Their strategy: covert influence operations.

The Russians today continue to use the exact same strategy.

PART 3

COUNTER-INTELLIGENCE

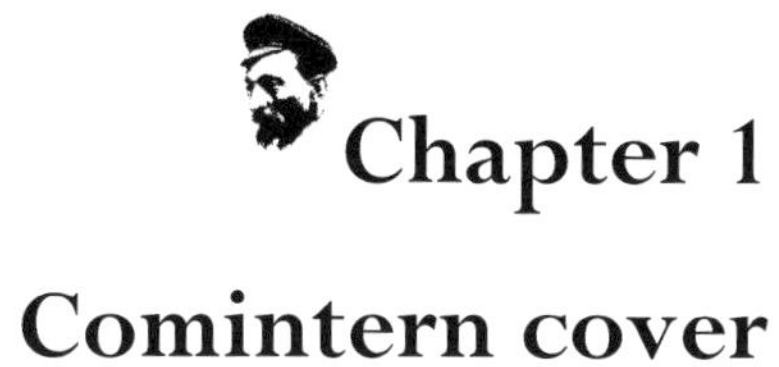

Chapter 1

Comintern cover

The [Comintern] illegal organization...made use of covert offices... the illegal organization kept its papers [and] files...separate from...the normal Party organizations.

Günther Nollau

Communist International

In 1919 Lenin was in the middle of a vicious civil war. He lacked the capability to project military strength across his borders. Lenin conceived a plan for the global spread of communism using his party's proven covert capabilities. He established the Communist International (Comintern).

This ostensibly independent group of communist leaders from around the globe was actually a front for Soviet political control. It also provided cover for international intelligence operations.

After Stalin seized the reins of Soviet power, he strengthened the covert ops begun by Lenin, even as he ruthlessly murdered many of the operators. Though he did away with the Comintern, its intelligence operations continued.

Extravagant Funding

The Comintern, both its overt and covert sections, enjoyed an almost unbelievable "river of gold" funding from Lenin. At one meeting in March 1922, according to Raymond Leonard in *Secret Soldiers of the Revolution*, the Comintern received "three times the sum spent to combat famine in Russia that entire year."

This huge investment in efforts to spread communism across the globe reflected Lenin's belief that a world revolution was "both imminent and necessary for the practical survival of the first workers' state."

At the same time, the pressure on the Soviet Army's covert action arm was intense. The CPSU expected action from the Red Army. The expectations raised put scrutiny on the Army in this "dangerous political whirlwind, because it was the only organization capable of organizing armed insurrection abroad."

The first Chairman of the Executive Committee of the Comintern (ECCI), Gregory Zinoviev, Lenin's long-time comrade, expected the Red Army to achieve revolutionary success in other countries. As the early days of the communist nation gave way to year after year of revolutionary failures in other countries, "the traditions of conspiracy and revolution shared by the leading figures [of the Red Army] and the Comintern ensured that Soviet espionage would continue to bear the stamp of revolution."

Comintern Offices for Espionage

The official regulations of the organization, the Comintern Statutes, in Article 12, laid out the general plan for espionage in America:

> The general situation...in... America forces the Communists of the whole world to create illegal Communist organizations alongside the legal organizations. The Executive Committee is charged with ensuring that this is brought about.

As Nollau noted in his 1961 study of the Comintern, the Soviet Union used the international connections provided by the Comintern network of foreign offices for both overt and covert work. In the parlance of the communists, "legal" and "illegal" work. From the beginning of the Comintern in1919, until its demise in 1943, the Soviets exerted absolute control over the organization.

The Soviet communists applied a façade of international democracy to the management and organization of the group. But the truth was that the Soviet communist party applied strict and brutal control and discipline to the Comintern.

While running Comintern offices in plain view, and establishing open relationships with foreign communist parties, the KGBs at the same time used the Comintern and its employees for clandestine operations.

The Comintern, with its widespread presence around the world, provided nearly perfect cover for intelligence operations. As internal bureaucratic struggles restricted the effectiveness of both the KGB and Soviet military intelligence, the Comintern carved out a niche for itself, separate from, but allied with the KGB. The Comintern's espionage operations enjoyed support from the top echelons of the Soviet Communist Party, including Lenin.

Intelligence officers operated under Comintern cover "using aliases derived from forged or stolen identity papers." As they perfected their techniques, they created support mechanisms to create cover legends, companies, and personas for an army of covert operators.

International Liaison Department—KGB's Niche

After Lenin's death in 1924, control of the world revolution was part of the spoils in the internal struggle for dominance in the Soviet Union. Espionage operations of the International Liaison Department (Russian acronym: OMS) of the Comintern "actually increased, especially in...the United States..."

The OMS was, for all intents, the international branch of the KGB. While there were bureaucratic structuring and restructuring exercises throughout its existence, the OMS was absorbed into the KGB after the Comintern collapsed. For our purposes, we will consider the OMS as a KGB branch. This bureaucratic niche, not part of the KGB, but not really part of the Comintern either, allowed the OMS to fly under the radar. Its living between two worlds ensured the secrecy and compartmentation of its operations, at the time and today. The OMS was never publicly mentioned by Comintern functionaries.

Although his study focused on Red Army intelligence, Leonard ventured a guess that hit the nail on the head. "Most early Comintern intelligence operations in the United States may in fact have been directed from Berlin by Willi Muenzenberg." This astute observation struck at the core of the Comintern cover for operations to recruit Willing Accomplices.

Hiding in Plain Sight

The Soviet Union was recognized by, and established diplomatic relations with, most countries in Europe, Asia, Africa and South America. The OMS used diplomatic cover for its officers in these countries.

The OMS COS in Berlin in 1923, during the time the KGB was fomenting a revolution in Germany, had a staff of more than 25. He was under cover as a Press Department diplomat in the Soviet embassy.

According to Gunther Nollau, the OMS station in Copenhagen worked out of a commercial cover office, an architect and engineering firm. The most common technique for Comintern cover was for OMS espionage operators to work in a foreign country overtly as a staff member of the an affiliated labor union. But their more important duties were clandestine. For example, during the 1930s, when steamships accounted for the majority of international travel, many the KGB had many agents who were seamen. The Comintern, under cover of seamen's unions, established bases throughout the U.S. and Europe.

These bases and the agents they controlled gave the Comintern communications channels around the world. The agents in charge of these bases were KGB agents and natives of the country in which they operated.

The bases functioned as clandestine rallying points for Comintern agents. The agents provided passports, other official documents, contacts, and served as message centers for other agents arriving, departing, or passing through.

The base chief was also responsible for a budget, receiving and disbursing funds from Moscow. These bases provided a network of support around the world. An agent could travel from Europe to America for operations, and enjoy logistical, financial, and other support. Whatever KGB officers or agents required was available in this global network of clandestine operations bases.

The legal and illegal operations of Comintern officers were closely coordinated. Illegal espionage activity and agents were compartmented from the legal activities of host country communist parties. Strict compartmentation of espionage activities militated that overt communists in host countries were strictly prohibited from participating in illegal intelligence operations.

If a host country communist party member had special access to a target, before he could take part as an agent, the KGB required the candidate to sever all ties with the party. The longer the candidate's overt relations with the party, the more difficult it would be to create a cover identity.

The solid clandestine tradecraft of the KGB made future counter-intelligence investigations of suspects difficult, and sometimes impossible. Cover stories, multiple aliases, conflicting documentary records contribute to confusion about certain individual's affiliation. In the end, the only sure way to identify a Willing Accomplice is by careful analysis of their life as a whole.

Arnold Deutsch—KGB Recruiter

The case of the Cambridge Five, the long-term KGB agents affiliated with the British university is illustrative of the Comintern and KGB hand-in-glove relationship.

The KGB-trained full service case officer who built this network was Arnold Deutsch. According to Christopher Andrew, he was a Comintern true believer. Sent to England as a NOC, Deutsch developed a method of identifying promising young men who were toying with communism. After careful development, Deutsch convinced them to renounce overt connections to Marxism, and instead to focus on achieving positions of influence.

His resulting penetrations of English intelligence, military, and diplomatic offices were spectacular in their results.

His successful recruits who have been indentified include British citizens Anthony Blunt, Guy Burgess, John Cairncross, Donald MacLean, and Kim Philby.

Recent research by Roland Perry seems to confirm that another Deutsch success was the American Michael Straight.

Straight, raised by wealthy parents in an unconventional British school, went on to run his family's magazine the New Republic, and to fund numerous covert influence front organizations, as well as to work for the U.S. State Department.

Comintern in America

The United States did not recognize the Soviet Union until 1934 (with the help of Willing Accomplice Walter Duranty, discussed in detail later). Because the Soviets lacked diplomatic facilities in

America to provide cover, intelligence officers working for the Comintern in the U.S. had to create stations of non-official cover (NOC) officers—or in the Soviet terminology, "illegal residencies." These cover mechanisms included the Soviet's trade group, Amtorg.

This standard operating procedure for the communists, with their decades of experience in running secret conspiracies, seemed to befuddle most foreign governments, and especially the Americans. During the Comintern's period of most active operations, roughly the whole of two decades—the 1920s and 1930s, American security and counter-intelligence, such as it was, all but allowed the Comintern free rein to operate in the U.S.

Covert Comintern operators like Alexander Gumberg, Willi Muenzenberg, Otto Katz, Nucia P. Lodge, and dozens of others escaped American scrutiny and investigation, for the most part.

And yet, during those two decades, Comintern covert operators ran rampant across the American cultural landscape. They planned and executed devastatingly effective covert influence operations against a wide swath of American society.

KGB Control of Comintern Agents

The Comintern was an organization that reflected Marxist-Leninist strategy and tactics almost perfectly. To outsiders, the Comintern appeared to be an international grouping of communist parties, striving together for the common good, assisting the proletariat in spreading the glories of Marxism-Leninism across the globe. A variety of third world, second world, colonial, postcolonial, and other oppressed peoples communist parties were represented in the Comintern. From the Comintern headquarters in Moscow came ringing calls to solidarity with the proletariat.

One of the best indications of the total control that the KGB applied to Comintern agents is their methodology when foreign agents visited Moscow.

In reality, however, the Comintern was just like every other Soviet-controlled organization. The foreign members of the Comintern were subjected to Soviet discipline. A visit to Moscow for a Comintern meeting, while surely a treat for an African wannabe Stalin, since all expenses were paid, could also be an extremely harrowing experience. More than once, Comintern delegates from foreign countries were roused from sleep. They responded to the fabled "knock on the door at midnight." KGB goons took them from their cozy foreigners' hotel, and they were never seen again.

Especially after Stalin was in power, suspicions, internal strife, and accusations of betrayal stalked every foreign Comintern agent.

Ruth Fisher, a German agent, arrived in Moscow in 1925 for consultations with the ECCI chairman, Osip Piatinitsky. Installed in the KGB's favorite hotel cum prison, the Lux, near the Kremlin, Fischer's passport was confiscated by Piatinitsky upon arrival.

The mastermind of the KGB's covert influence operations against America, trusted with millions of communist dollars for use in his front companies, not even Muenzenberg was trusted to keep his own passport when he visited Moscow. Luckily for him, his network of old Bolsheviks helped him secure his permission to leave.

Hundreds of other foreign Comintern members were not as connected or energetic as the covert influence mastermind. Once in the Soviet Union, they lost free will and liberty. Their small lives were swept into the maw of the great humanity-loving, but human-hating communist machine. Their corpses, lumps of rotting materialistic flesh, their souls casually discarded in the atheist ether, were tossed into trenches and covered in lime to speed decomposition. Absolute control of body, mind, and spirit was required by the KGB. And this control was achieved in nearly every instance.

Comintern Tradecraft

Nollau's research uncovered the tradecraft used by OMS officers working as NOCs in America (and elsewhere). Their secret lives required that they be as inconspicuous as possible, and they must appear totally harmless. They could never carry compromising material in public. They could not have contact with known communists. All safehouses must be carefully selected and vetted, including the owner.

Compartmentation of espionage operations required using a different alias for each operation. Safehouses and covert meeting sites must be rotated frequently. Strict punctuality was required.

The Comintern's counter-espionage and counter-intelligence bureau, the International Control Commission (ICC), struck terror in the hearts of communists around the world. The ICC kept voluminous files on all comrades. Any undue curiosity about issues not directly related to one's duties could bring a visit from the ICC, followed by the KGB.

The OMS NOC offices kept their files and papers strictly segregated from the Comintern's normal bureaucracy.

OMS Control of Spanish Civil War International Volunteers

In Spain the KGB ruled with an iron fist over the international fools who came to support Soviet imperialism. The communist intelligence officers carried out assassinations of suspected collaborators, established KGB prisons in Spain, duplicating the reign of terror that Stalin was overseeing at the same time in Moscow.

Under the cover of the Comintern's OMS, the KGB managed every detail of the communist operation in Spain—vetting volunteers, assigning them to duties in Spain, indoctrination and training, counter-intelligence investigations, arrest and detainment, and executions of the hapless nit-wits.

The KGB assigned an officer, George Mink, to the foolish Americans who formed the Abraham Lincoln Brigade to fight in the Spanish Civil War. These fellow travelers were duped by the work of Willing Accomplices into assisting the Soviet Union's first military adventure abroad.

Mink was apparently responsible for ideological purity and counter-intelligence. Nollau reports that an American communist in Spain with the Brigade testified that Mink murdered several American volunteers, some shot from behind on the battlefield.

Stalin's Purges Decimate Comintern

The Old Bolsheviks who had headlined the Comintern's first ten years were, to the man, accused and tried for horrific, imaginary crimes. They were some of the first heads to roll in Stalin's blood-letting. Trotsky, the firebrand philosopher with blood on his hands, was accused of treason, espionage, philosophical divergences and more. Radek, the gnome-like propaganda expert. Zinoviev, the Comintern's rock.

Bukharin, former editor of Alexander Gumberg's newspaper in New York City, *Novy Mir,* and former editor of *Pravda,* and former Chairman of the Comintern.

While the brutality of the communists to each other nearly matches their brutality to their opponents, it is difficult to feel sorry for them. Bukharin, during his salad years at the pinnacle of Soviet power, defined the blunt instrument of the communists' power, the Dictatorship of the Proletariat:

> Dictatorship of the proletariat allows "no freedom (such as liberty of the press, speech, meetings, unions, etc.) for the bourgeois enemies of the people...

One must wonder what Bukharin thought of the lack of freedoms when it was he who was considered a "bourgeois enemy of the people."

Each of the communist thugs was accused by Stalin and his thugs of heinous crimes—plotting assassinations, collaboration with the Gestapo, espionage, sabotage, and ideological deviancy.

Anyone of an intellectual and political stature sufficient to pose a threat to Stalin was purged. The only Old Bolshevik who escaped the murderous Georgian's wrath was Lenin—only because he was dead.

Andrew Meier's *The Lost Spy* provides an in-depth study of an American OMS agent's life and death. Cy Oggins, a Columbia University graduate, zealous communist, seems to have signed on as an OMS courier and low-level support agent. Under various commercial covers, he provided services in China, Europe and America for a decade or more.

Oggins was called back to Moscow for consultations, during the purges. Enduring rounds of interrogation, he eventually met the fate of so many loyal communists—place: Lubyanka; tool—bullet; location—brain.

Concurrent with Stalin's purges of the Comintern were purges throughout the communist workers paradise. Tim Tzouliadis in *The Forsaken: An American Tragedy in Stalin's Russia,* details the sorry lot of another group of Americans, some of whom were foolish communists, but most of whom were desperate for jobs.

The Americans immigrated to Russia during the early years of the Great Depression. Stalin needed their technical expertise. They built factories, engineered roads, bridges, dams, and buildings. They provided skilled labor, agricultural expertise.

During Stalin's cleansing, virtually every American living under the Dictatorship of the Elite Vanguard fell under suspicion. The vast majority were either executed or sent to the Gulag—a vast network of prison camps where they suffered in subhuman conditions. Few survived the camps. A bullet in the brain was kinder.

Other foreigners suffered even worse. The only Polish Comintern official who was not purged was Dzerzhinsky's widow. Even a 70 year-old Comintern veteran disappeared, never to be seen again.

Among Yugoslav communists who paid the ultimate price for being in Russia while Stalin was consolidating his power were four former General Secretaries of the Yugoslav Communist Party.

The Danish representative to the ECCI disappeared without a trace. Norwegian Communist Arthur Samsing, visited Moscow in 1936—was never seen again.

And last, but not least, Willi Muenzenberg, Lenin's own covert influence genius, was an Old Bolshevik with ties to Radek, Zinoviev, and Trotsky, among others. His successes under Comintern and commercial cover were unprecedented. Wily operator that he was, Willi avoided the trap of returning to Moscow for consultations. A cat and mouse game ensued, but the end was the same as for all loyal communists, just a different means—Muenzenberg's corpse was found under a tree in France.

Entire sections of the ECCI were whittled down to just a few survivors.

In the end, the Comintern was dissolved, its espionage operations absorbed into the KGB. In the early days of heady communist aspiration, it provided a perfect cover and platform for the KGB's covert influence operations. Willi Muenzenberg was the master of the Comintern's covert operations.

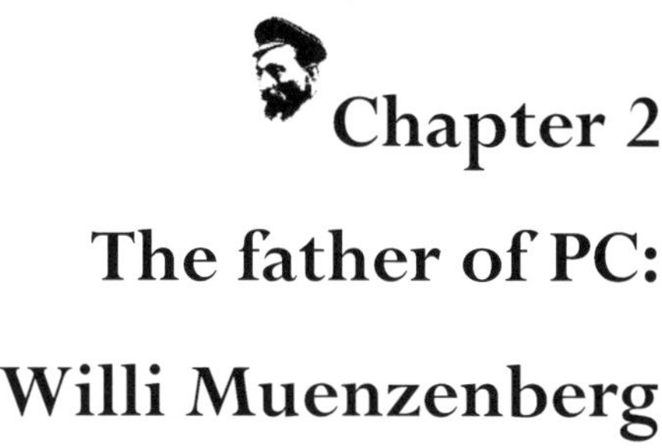

Chapter 2

The father of PC: Willi Muenzenberg

To criticize or challenge Soviet policy was the unfailing mark of a bad, bigoted, and probably stupid person, while support was equally infallible proof of a forward-looking mind committed to all that was best for humanity and marked by an uplifting refinement of sensibility.

Stephen Koch, Double Lives*, on the attitude implanted in American society by Muenzenberg's influence operations.*

Sean McMeekin, in *Red Millionaire: A Political Biography of Willi Muenzenberg, Moscow's Secret Propaganda Tsar in the West,* scoured Comintern records and produced a detailed portrait of the wily German from those records. However, McMeekin seems not to understand the nature of covert operations. His analysis is nearly totally of the public nature of Muenzenberg's work. Even McMeekin's title reflects his conclusion—that Muenzenberg was a rather inept businessman who built an empire, while at the same time managing "propaganda" for Moscow.

Though he includes "secret" in his title, McMeekin never pierces the intentional fog of espionage. He seems to have relied mostly on the financial records and correspondence of Muenzenberg's commercial cover entities. By their very nature, espionage commercial cover entities are unlikely to be profitable, and are constantly in need of money.

Cover records are designed to confuse as much as to record the truth. For an operator, dealing with bureaucratic paymasters is frustrating and requires constant justification and massaging. Read in this light, by an experienced intelligence operator, the records that McMeekin used in his research reveal the extent of Muenzenberg's cover entities, and his masterful exploitation of the access they provided.

McMeekin's conclusions also reflect a misunderstanding of Russian Active Measures. Propaganda's overt in-your-face presentation was not Muenzenberg's strong suit. Although he did produce much propaganda, Willi was the master of the covert approach, which was ultimately much more effective, as we'll see in my analysis. That said, I rely greatly on McMeekin's biographical details for my review of Willi's life below.

On the other hand, Stephen Koch's *Double Lives: Stalin, Willi Muenzenberg and the Seduction of the Intellectuals,* comes much closer to the reality of the Comintern genius's covert operations. Koch appreciates, and captures, the covert fundamentals of Muenzenberg's front operations. Koch only misses the results of Willi's operations against the U.S.—that is, the current state of American politics, PC-Progressivism that nearly perfectly mirrors Willi's anti-American influence payload.

Otherwise, Koch's impressionistic book on Muenzenberg is as close to the truth as we're likely to find. My contribution is to analyze Muenzenberg's operations with an experienced covert operator's point of view, and to tie his operations to their results today.

Communist to the Core—Willi's Life

Self-Promoter, Leninist, Energetic Recruiter

Born in Prussia in 1889, Willi Muenzenberg was the youngest son of a military veteran. His father, Karl, affected the arrogance of a Prussian officer, but lacked the discipline required for service. He settled into a nomadic post-service life.

Karl, according to Willi's later autobiographical articles, which may or may not be near the truth, abused Willi severely. When Willi was fifteen, Karl was shot dead while "cleaning his pistols."

A lackluster student, but one who loved to read for pleasure, young Muenzenberg's future was uncertain. Willi tried barbering, as an apprentice, and didn't take to it. Soon after his father's death, Willi took a menial job in a shoe factory. A natural organizer, Willi gravitated to a debating society, the Workers Educational Association Propaganda, bringing a group of his teen-aged laborer buddies.

The radical chairman of the Association spotted Muenzenberg's potential and guided the youngster through a course of readings on Socialism, Marxism, and radical philosophy.

Muenzenberg recruited more young laborers to join the Association, and it was soon rebranded the Free Youth. His mentor moved up the Socialist bureaucracy to head the state Socialist movement.

Thus, Muenzenberg began his lifelong pattern of vigorous recruiting and influence, undertaken for the communist cause with the support and protection of a mentor.

A few years of agitation, organizing, writing, pamphlet producing, harassment by the authorities, arrests, and political in-fighting laid the groundwork that Muenzenberg would build on the rest of his life.

Muenzenberg followed Socialist comrades to Switzerland, where they installed him as a pharmacist's assistant in Zurich. His boss allowed him as much time off as he wanted. Willi threw himself into Socialist and anarchist youth activities.

He created publications and reached out to other youth organizations. In short order, Willi won the right to lead Switzerland's largest Youth Socialist organization.

With the outbreak of World War in 1914, Muenzenberg proved himself in the Socialist community with his impassioned speeches for international solidarity, and opposition to workers marching off to "die for capitalism."

Taking advantage of international Socialist connections, and his location in neutral Switzerland, Muenzenberg organized an anti-war Youth Socialist conference. The Russian delegation, including Lenin's lover, Inessa Armand, were the most vocal and influential. The result of several consecutive conferences was a new International Youth Secretariat, with Willi Muenzenberg selected to be its Secretary.

At this conference Muenzenberg first met Lenin, and likely other of the Russian's communist clique. Trotsky, Radek, Zinoviev, and other prominent Bolsheviks are sure to have attended the conferences. Soon after, the international socialists held a secretive convocation at Zimmerwald, near Bern. There they hashed out a plan for the way forward for international Socialism. Lenin argued for his Elite Vanguard approach to guiding the world revolution.

In 1915, Muenzenberg published the first number of his organizations magazine, the *Youth International*. He now had the attention and readership of 30,000 Socialist members around Europe.

Lenin attended Muenzenberg's Youth group meetings in Zurich, arguing with Willi on fine points of Socialist theory and doctrine. Muenzenberg and Lenin established a personal friendship, solidified by shared political aspirations.

Lenin's plan for infiltrating the world's armies, recruiting soldiers into world socialism, after which they would lay down their arms, won Muenzenberg's support. Muenzenberg became a committed follower of the Russian revolutionary.

Muenzenberg was by 1915 wholly involved in Socialist and revolutionary politics. It's likely that his income and support was solely through the various organizations he ran and belonged to. It appears that he mastered the intricacies of fund-raising for his own support during his involvement in international Socialism, while in Switzerland. He would never again want for monetary support.

Lenin and Radek Leave Willi in Zurich

German covert action operators provided Lenin with virtually unlimited funding, as the Russian political atmosphere deteriorated into chaos. The German objective was to undermine the Russian Czar's war efforts.

In April, 1917, the Swiss clique of communists, including Lenin, Radek (photo, left), and Zinoviev, all Muenzenberg comrades, were packed into a train across Germany, bound for Stockholm, en route to Russia. On the heels of the February Revolution in St. Petersburg, Lenin and his German backers smelled blood in the water. Lenin's theories were about to meet the test of reality on the ground in St. Petersburg, the imperial capital of Russia.

Muenzenberg accompanied the communist group to the train station in Zurich. Either Lenin or Radek told him, "Either we'll be swinging from the gallows in three months, or we shall be in power." Willi chose not to accompany them. His German citizenship put him at risk of being detained for military service as they passed through Germany.

Instead, Willi plotted a route to meet his comrades in Stockholm. He did visit Stockholm soon after the Russians left Switzerland. Radek was installed by the Germans in Sweden, and it's likely that Muenzenberg conferred with the German message-master there.

Regardless of what he did in Sweden, Willi returned to Zurich, where he heard the news of the Bolshevik seizure of power in Russia, the October Revolution of 1917.

Within a week, Muenzenberg was in a Swiss prison, after violent protests by Socialists in Zurich. As his future was considered by the Swiss authorities, Muenzenberg wrote them a letter. He laid out his Socialist philosophy, explaining that he rejected violent overthrow of governments, in favor of an approach that included "years of relentless education and propaganda." This glimpse into the mind of the covert influence maestro reveals the blueprint for his later operations.

Released and then re-arrested, Muenzenberg became a political hot potato for the Swiss. No other European state would agree to receive him, and the Swiss would not consider sending him to Germany, due to his status as a draft resister there.

The Swiss considered deporting the communist to the U.S., but were told that Muenzenberg would not be welcome under any circumstances. This is curious because at nearly the same time, Trotsky and his entourage of revolutionaries had found refuge in New York.

The Menshevik, soon-to-be-Bolshevik, along with Alexander Gumberg, and Bukharin, had written for the *Noviy Mir* Russian language revolutionary organ from the Lower East Side of Manhattan. They had just left the U.S. for Russia in the spring, just in time to arrive for the Bolshevik seizure of power.

Muenzenberg remained in Swiss prisons for another year, until November 1918. With a Socialist government running an exhausted, defeated Germany, the Swiss deported Muenzenberg to his homeland.

Post-war Germany

Post-war Germany was in a tremendous state of flux. Soon after Muenzenberg's arrival, the German Communist Party, allied to the Bolsheviks, was founded. Muenzenberg missed the foundation meetings, but was involved in the party soon after.

A hot revolution, led by radical communists, was quickly put down. Willi was arrested and jailed, as a communist radical. He remained in jail through the spring of 1919, when the first congress of the Communist International was held, establishing the Comintern. Although his old comrades invited him to the conference, Willi was not released from confinement until later in the summer.

With an additional warrant issued for his arrest, Muenzenberg made his way to Berlin, arriving in late October 1919.

From his new base of operations, still moving constantly to avoid arrest, Muenzenberg established contact with the new Comintern. The Russians established a front company in Berlin, from which they funded the German Communist Party.

He established the Communist Youth International, funded by a wealthy Swiss patron, and received Bolshevik money. Keeping a low profile, to avoid German police, Willi was not liked by the Berlin Comintern officer. Despairing of achieving his previous high status and power again, Muenzenberg planned to attend the second conference of the Comintern, scheduled for July 1920, in Moscow.

Soviet Union—Comintern Baptism

After greeting his old friends, like Zinoviev, in St. Petersburg, he watched, along with a crowd of a hundred thousand others, a theatrical reenactment of the Bolshevik storming of the Winter Palace. The cast and crew of more than twenty thousand put on a not-to-be-forgotten spectacle for the thrilled international visitors.

Moving to Moscow, the former imperial palace of the Kremlin was the site of the Comintern gatherings. Lenin's address, from a throne room, sealed the impression of Russian dominance of the communist movement.

While the Russians pretended that the Comintern was, as its name implied, truly international, it was clear to all delegates that the Russians were "more equal than the other pigs."

Muenzenberg next met with his friend, Radek, the newly installed executive secretary of the Comintern. Although no records exist to document their meeting, later events make it easy to surmise that Radek, the consummate covert influence operator and Muenzenberg brainstormed the influence operations that were to change the world.

During his stay in Moscow, Willi networked with his former friends from Swiss exile, most importantly, Lenin. Lenin and Muenzenberg joked about Willi's doubting the Russian's predications of failure of any attempt to seize power in Russia by force. Lenin good-naturedly rubbed Muenzenberg's nose in the overwhelming communist success.

Leaving Moscow, Muenzenberg was flush with a cache of czarist diamonds. The new currency of revolution, seized from their imperial predecessors, the Bolsheviks' control was solidified as much with their monetary support as their communist piety.

In addition to the Soviet wealth, Muenzenberg returned to Berlin with the end of his Youth International all but a certainty. The Comintern had no place for independent thought, or action. At the next Comintern congress, in July 1921, Willi's Youth group was stripped from his control.

Russian Famine

One of Lenin's first jobs for Muenzenberg was to manage the public relations response to the horrible famines that swept through the Soviet Union in 1921. Embarrassed by the efficient and effective American famine relief efforts, led by Herbert Hoover,

Lenin demanded an immediate, world-wide communist hunger relief program. In his first high-level, global operation, Muenzenberg was appointed to run the effort.

American Fronts

After floundering in Europe, which was tapped out emotionally and financially, Willi hit his stride in America. He sponsored the Friends of Soviet Russia (FSR) committee, which found that Americans were suckers for the Muenzenberg pitch.

Money rolled in faster than the FSR could spend it. Branch offices were established across the U.S., from the east coast, through the Midwest, and on to the west coast. Muenzenberg must have seen the potential for using these fronts.

The American market was fertile and receptive. American leftists, admiring the Soviet experiment from afar, were itching to be involved.

Muenzenberg's energetic management and ideas merged with energetic action and efficient American organization. The FSR emblazoned their logo on wearable buttons, creating both a fund raiser and an indication for those in-the-know of the wearer's caring humanity. Willi began to get a good feel for the American market.

Herbert Hoover, understanding what the Soviets were all about, saw through Muenzenberg's fundraising cum propaganda. Hoover called the communist bluff in public relations pieces in New York papers. Willi learned that more subtlety would be needed in future work in the U.S.

At the same time Muenzenberg raised money for "famine relief," his publications presented Soviet communism to Americans as if it was a happy picnic of rosy-cheeked farm boys and girls.

While Hoover's actual famine relief operation fed 11 million people daily, Willi's influence operation only fed twenty thousand photogenic children.

With a flood of American cash coming in from the FSR, Muenzenberg further infiltrated the American left with an "industrial assistance" program. More cash from American donors flowed into Muenzenberg's front companies, ostensibly to aid Soviet workers.

Clandestine Influence Operations

Willi likely honed his clandestine tradecraft training during this period. He was closely tied to a variety of Comintern and KGB officers, visiting Moscow often, establishing front companies and cementing bonds with his Comintern mentors, Radek and Zinoviev, and of course Lenin.

It's likely that he met with the KGB head, Dzerzhinsky. The KGB chief would have given him broad guidelines for his influence operations.

The KGB had been quite successful in influencing the Americans already. Alex Gumberg was still working in America, continuing to run the operation that he had begun during the heady days of the Revolution in St. Petersburg.

Now Dzerzhinsky, and his staff under OMS cover would have directed the German master of influence to concentrate on the American "market." Gumberg had made heady inroads with the diplomatic, corporate, and legislative targets in the States: he was running Raymond Robins, and was working his contacts to wriggle deeper and deeper into corporate America.

Lenin's vision to bring America to its knees required penetration of the wellsprings of its civil identity, the "transmission belts" of American culture.

This is when Muenzenberg's fertile and active operational mind likely grasped the requirements of the operation. He'd seen Americans hungry for a way to express their superior humanity. His "famine relief" operations fleeced thousands of their pennies. He was surely full of operational ideas.

All he needed was the time and the target. Both would come soon enough.

German Revolution

From 1920 through 1923, Muenzenberg was active with his Communist Youth groups, working out of Berlin. As Germany convulsed in reaction to the new political realities after the end of WW1, successive waves of right-wing and then left-wing upheavals swept over the country.

Willi kept his head down, likely learning his covert work, while doing Comintern overt youth proselytizing and organizing. Until January 1923, when Muenzenberg wrote an article in a German communist journal urging German comrades to struggle against the “enemy [who] resides in our own land,” the nascent Weimar Republic government. Even while the French occupied a piece of Germany, Willi’s communist line echoed the Russians from 5 years previously—forget the foreign invaders, overthrow the bourgeious native government.

Comintern Anti-fascist Front

In 1923 with Lenin slowly fading after a series of strokes, the Comintern began deploying the anti-fascist front strategy. The dying Commissar’s dream of destroying the capitalists from within was ready for deployment. Zinoviev, Radek, and Lenin likely had pegged Willi Muenzenberg as the perfect engine to run this operation for several years. It’s likely that his preparation including running commercial cover ventures, fund-raising, and Comintern work—all provided a nearly perfect cover and network to begin on of the most powerful covert action operations of all time.

On 18 May, 1923, Muenzenberg took control of a new front organization. His overt cover for covert influence operations was the Action Committee in the Struggle Against Fascism and War.

Willi launched his ops quickly. A campaign to spin the Soviet Union as under imminent threat from capitalist countries, “Hand off Soviet Russia,” brought the first wave of western Willing Accomplices under Willi’s control: Albert Einstein, Henri Barbusse, and American author Upton Sinclair all lent their names to the op. They and more Accomplices were all charter members of the “Society of Friends of the New Russia.”

Friends of Soviet Russia in Chicago

In early 1924, Willi’s operation shifted focus to America. The FSR was growing like a mushroom, and moved its headquarters to Chicago.

With cover activities that included raising money for hungry children in Germany, as well as the Soviet Union, the FSR gained American adherents in droves. Some wrote to the offices asking for pictures of the hungry children they were paying money to feed.

With a focus on American targets, Willi began to wrap up his cover operations in Germany and Russia that were taking up much of his time and attention. By December 1925, Muenzenberg’s full time and attention was on the Comintern’s premier covert action operations.

Mezhrabpom-Russ—Willi Goes Hollywood

McMeekin, researching the Comintern's cover business accounts, analyzes Muenzenberg's foray into the movie business on an overt level, as he does all of Muenzenberg's activities. Again, he misunderstands the purpose of a cover business.

Sometimes espionage operations require commercial cover to allow the operators to gain access to their targets. In the case of the Russian film company, Mezhrabpom-Russ (Russ), Muenzenberg must have had his operational sights set on penetrating one leg of the three-legged stool of American culture—Hollywood.

In October 1923, Willi established Russ. His access operation paid dividends immediately. He sold half the Russ shares to a consortium of unidentified American movie investors. Likely these were Hollywood insiders angling to gain access themselves to the Russian market. Muenzenberg's Hollywood gambit was on.

"Anti-fascist" Fronts

In 1926, Willi stepped up his flurry of anti-fascist front organizations. He opened operations of the League Against Colonial Oppression, with covert Comintern funding. This name is a preview of Muenzenberg's genius for mining the issues that touched the soft souls of the American liberal elite. Yearning to be relevant and holier-than-thou, these elites responded to Willi's tune. Being against Oppression was a slam dunk. Being anti-colonial was fashionable.

Willi's jumped into action with the new League. He held a "Conference Against Imperialism," in Brussels in January 1927. With an eye on the Main Adversary, Willi invited black American delegates from the American National Association for the Advancement of Colored People (NAACP), and the American Negro Labor Congress. Their voices against the American oppressors joined with India's Jawaharlal Nehru, standing in for Gandhi, and Chiang Kai-shek, in addition to other notables who became the first PC-Progressive fashionable elite—the brilliant physicist Albert Einstein probably was the most famous Willing Accomplice.

Propaganda Press—Hiding in Plain Sight—Popular Fronts

Hiding in plain site may be the best way to describe Muenzenberg's covert influence operations. He skillfully and energetically combined at least two Active Measure operations. His techniques of running both overt propaganda combined with covert influence may never be understood by intelligence professionals again. His brazen use of his well-known standing as the communist press impresario to conceal covert operations would never pass muster with timid operational bureaucrats after Muenzenberg was gone—whether they were Soviet or American bureaucrats.

Muenzenberg's tactic of forming "Popular Front" organizations with no apparent ties to communism was a stroke of genius that continues to be used to today. His blending of Comintern objectives and themes, covered by apparently non-ideological organizations with high-minded names and lofty pronouncements sucked in Willing Accomplices around the world, and especially in America.

Willi ran the Kosmos Publishing company for the Comintern, and the German Communist Party, putting out Soviet Russia in Pictures, the Evening World, Berlin in the Morning, and the Owl's Mirror—all overtly communist propaganda rags. He segmented his communist market into demographic slices—*Children in Battle*, *The Pioneer* (for teenagers), and *The Women's Path*.

Soviet Russia in Pictures did wonders for promoting the Russian Elite Vanguard—Willi's bosses—with covers devoted to Stalin, Lenin, and his KGB boss Dzerzhinsky. Propaganda and sucking up to his masters were in Muenzenberg's bag of tricks.

More Cunning Methods of Agitation

In the depths of the global Depression, Muenzenberg held a convention of his International Worker Relief front organization in Berlin in October 1931. Willi's rhetorical line was straight out of the Comintern's playbook—he noted that the capitalist system was on its last legs. But his comrades' task was to "speed up its collapse and force it through completely everywhere."

To speed up the great class war, which would result in a Red triumph, Muenzenberg shared the framework of his covert action operation. He wasn't a Red Army soldier, but his strategy would surely destroy the enemy. He told them that they had to "shake up the millions who are not yet aware. We must awaken their hearts and their minds." This awakening however, required "new, more cunning methods of agitation."

Willi scorched the air with his communist promises. Together they would destroy the "bourgeoisie in all countries."

But this would require them to convince the workers of "the rightness of our cause." Slightly miscalculating the length of his operation, he promised in "two years or three, proletarian dictatorship will come."

In the summer of 1932, Muenzenberg assembled a cast of Willing Accomplices in Amsterdam. As the world hurtled toward WW2, and his own Germany was close to falling under Hitler's control, Muenzenberg rallied his Innocents to denounce French imperialism! The Comintern flavor-of-the-month was denunciations of the capitalist European countries.

Political Battles in Germany—Hitler's Rise

Muenzenberg, installed as a German Communist Party candidate, was elected to the Reichstag. He was fighting on the front lines of the Comintern's global revolution strategy, toe-to-toe with the National Socialists in Germany through the 1930s.

Instead of being blood enemies, however, the Nazis were many times the lesser of two evils, in the eyes of the Comintern. This period, during Stalin's consolidation of power, saw dissenting communists and socialists targeted by Muenzenberg's machine. Ironically, during the rise of Hitler's National Socialist fascism, the Soviets were rabidly attacking other socialists as "social fascists," code for dissenters from the Stalin line.

As old Bolsheviks were cleansed from the system by Stalin's purges, Trotskyite became the worst label to tag a communist.

Muenzenberg happily toed the Stalinist line. He tagged the German Socialist Party as "class traitors," in editorials and commentary in his publications and speeches. At the same time, there were elections in Germany in which the Nazis and the Communists teamed up to defeat the Socialists. Weaving in and out of the rhetorical jungle, Willi zigged and zagged along with the Party line, as dictated by the Kremlin.

Now I Have Them

When Hitler finally took power in February 1932, his wrath turned immediately on the Communists. Muenzenberg's press conglomerate was shut down, one by one, within a month.

Within a year, the German parliament building, the Reichstag, was burning, probably set alight by a communist. It was all the excuse Hitler needed to crack down on his opponents. Telling his Nazi acolytes, "Now I have them," he ordered the extermination of

Hitler's Bolshevik enemies. Four thousand German Communists were arrested in one night, in the German province of Prussia alone.

Muenzenberg the Fugitive

Willi fled his native country for France. The Nazis were hot on his trail. With a bit of luck, he avoided the storm troopers searching for him. He used espionage tradecraft to obtain a false ID, and crossed into France. There he likely made contact with the Comintern illegal support base, and with their documentary support, made his way to Paris. Within a month, he and his wife, Babette Gross, were accepted by the French government as political refugees.

Working quickly, Muenzenberg recreated his cover publications, and refocused his overt propaganda on the Nazis. In Paris, he created the German Freedom Library, the World Committee for the Relief of the Victims of German Fascism, and publishing operations Imprimerie Francaise, Editions du Carrefour, and Editions Sociales Internationales.

Brown Book

The World Committee became the front for Muenzenberg's production of the *Brown Book*, an Active Measure masterpiece that surely became the standard for future KGB disinformation. Working with his hand-picked band of covert operators, including Arthur Koestler, Muenzenberg created an alluring tale that enchanted anti-fascists around the world. The book claimed to be a research project into the conspiracy to set the Reichstag alight.

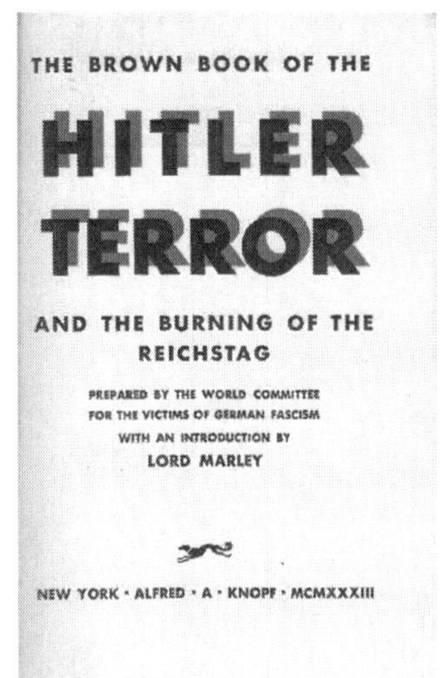

THE BROWN BOOK OF THE
HITLER
TERROR
AND THE BURNING OF THE
REICHSTAG
PREPARED BY THE WORLD COMMITTEE
FOR THE VICTIMS OF GERMAN FASCISM
WITH AN INTRODUCTION BY
LORD MARLEY
NEW YORK · ALFRED · A · KNOPF · MCMXXXIII

Muenzenberg and his men skillfully blended a carefully measured brew of lies, truth, innuendo, forgeries and real documents into a toxic recipe that blamed the Nazis for the fire.

According to McMeekin, the *Brown Book* was "a fraudulent hack job." The logic of Nazi responsibility for the foul deed was so compelling that the fact that it was not true seemed not to matter. Again, Muenzenberg created a template that his PC-Progressive descendants would copy again and again. In June

1933, Muenzenberg was in Moscow, surely to coordinate further operations with his OMS and KGB bosses.

Following the Moscow meeting, Willi put together a unique Active Measure, again a template for future Willing Accomplice operations, a piece of disinformation theater—a "counter-trial" of the Nazis for the crimes "revealed" in the *Brown Book*. Of course the trial had no legal standing, but Muenzenberg's publicity and public relations work, compiling a list of Willing Accomplices from the U.S. and Europe, and gaining press coverage from all over the world, created a global sensation.

The *Brown Book* and the counter-trial created enough publicity and pressure on the Nazis that the trial in Leipzig only convicted the one Communist who had been found *in flagrante delicto*, sweating in the burning parliament. The other Communists were acquitted. The return to Moscow was triumphant. The world-wide publicity was a victory for Willi Muenzenberg.

American Interlude

After the burst of energetic operations focused on the Reichstag fire trials, Muenzenberg settled fitfully into his exile in Paris. He established overt propaganda organs, and worked his Comintern fronts.

He took what was evidently his only trip to the U.S. in July and August of 1934. He held rallies in Boston, Washington D.C., Chicago, Cleveland, Milwaukee, and in Madison Square Garden in New York City.

At the rally of thousands of communists in New York's Madison Square on July 6, 1934, Muenzenberg addressed the crowd in German. His speech was then read in English. He appeared with Earl Browder, the chairman of the American Communist Party, and other American communists. He was greeted with a standing ovation. His speech predicted a World War to start in Germany within the year.

On July 27, 1934, Muenzenberg addressed another rally of communists in New York, this time at the Bronx coliseum. Interestingly, the Times now reported that Muenzenberg "predicted that there would be no war in Europe." In the three weeks between the two New York rallies, it would appear that Stalin's opinion had swung. As always, Muenzenberg reflected the Party line in public.

We see Willi's brilliant organizational touch in the sponsors and affiliated groups at his rallies—the Anti-Nazi Federation and the National Committee to Aid the Victims of German Fascism in the Bronx. Muenzenberg was billed as "the international secretary of the Movement Against War and Fascism."

In the Bronx, 35 women delegates to the International Women's Congress Against War attended the rally, in preparation for their planned visit to Paris for an August 4 convocation of their front group. The communists at the rally voted to "hold a demonstration at the pier," when the women were scheduled to leave on July 28, the next morning.

The Bronx rally also denounced President Roosevelt and the governor of California for the recent raids on foreign born workers. They protested "the brutal Fascist and police terror used against workers on the West Coast."

Muenzenberg's visit to the U.S. coincided with virulent strikes in various locations across America. The *New York Times* reported a German newspaper's warning to the United States that Muenzenberg represented a danger to American society.

The Worm Turns in Paris

Back in Paris after his whirlwind tour of the Main Adversary, Willi was faced with upheavals in his organizations. The Frenchman Barbusse, a former Muenzenberg lieutenant, was developing his own Comintern-backed Active Measures stable. Barbusse took over many of the publications that Willi had managed previously.

But Barbusse's reign lasted less than a year, ending with his death in August 1935. Muenzenberg jumped back into action and feverishly created more Popular Front organizations, attempting to keep up with the head-snapping twists and turns of the Comintern.

Stalin's purges were destroying more and more of Willi's mentors. Thousands had already been purged. How long could Willi avoid the knock on the door at midnight?

Purge, Purge, Purge

In the first show trial that Stalin orchestrated, in August 1936, Zinoviev, Willi's old Bolshevik mentor, his friend since their time with Lenin in Zurich in 1916, was charged with crimes against the state. He cravenly confessed, and was summarily executed.

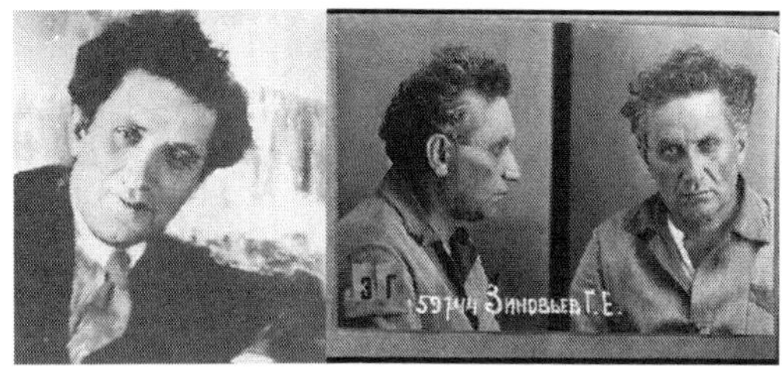

Grigory Zinoviev—before and after torture.

Muenzenberg surely wondered what the smell was that followed him everywhere after that trial. He was tightly linked to all the old Bolsheviks who represented threats to Stalin's consolidation of absolute power. He was barred from a meeting of the ECCI in Brussels.

Summoned to Moscow, Muenzenberg must have brazenly thought that he was untouchable. Upon arrival, he arranged a meeting with his ultimate mentor and protector, the gnome-like old Bolshevik, Karl Radek. Muenzenberg only then learned that Radek, too, had just been arrested.

The ECCI chairman refused to meet with Muenzenberg. With his wife, Willi holed up in the newly constructed Hotel Moskva on Red Square, near the Kremlin and the Lubyanka, headquarters of the KGB. The Comintern ordered Willi to remain in Moscow, to "work in agitprop." All of Willi's work in Paris was taken over by others.

The Comintern's International Control Commission (ICC), the counter-intelligence and counter-espionage committee responsible for KGB-led investigations of members now informed Muenzenberg that he was charged with "lack of revolutionary vigilance."

Surely the old covert action operator must have realized that he was in great danger. Ever the operator, Willi cooperated with the ICC, and publicly denounced his old friend, Zinoviev, and supported the death sentence. Evidently, this bowing to the ICC earned him a reprieve. He and Babette Gross were allowed to leave Moscow, and returned to France.

Propaganda as a Weapon

In the winter of 1936-37, Willi took a rest in a sanatorium near Paris. He used this opportunity to finish off a text on propaganda—*Propaganda as a Weapon.* Intended to reveal the Nazi's use of treacherous propaganda, Willi must have gotten an illicit thrill at the irony of the communist master of Active Measures calling out

Hitler's Goebbels as a dastardly abuser of the fine art of propaganda.

Purges Without End

In the middle of that productive winter for Willi, his old friend Radek, broken by the KGB, confessed. Like all of Stalin's targets, he said whatever they wanted him to say. Radek told a tale of anti-Soviet terrorist activities and espionage for Japan and Germany. His prison sentence became a death sentence when KGB thugs beat him to death in his cell.

The pace of arrests, interrogations, and terror stepped up with the coming of spring 1937. Even as the flowers opened with the promise of a fresh beginning, Willi's friends and associates were rounded up by the ruthless KGB. Comintern associates disappeared into the KGB's dungeons. Some came out, some did not.

KGB surveillance covered Muenzenberg's movements in Paris, and occasionally demanded that he come to Moscow for consultations. Clearly spooked, Muenzenberg delayed and avoided the inevitable.

Willi played both ends against the middle, in a last ditch effort to save his skin. Embroiled in Comintern in-fighting, he wrote directly to Stalin to denounce fellow German Communist Party leaders, advocating for himself to be elevated to leadership in the German Party. When that didn't work, Willi, in a mark of true desperation, threatened to reveal the Comintern's espionage operations.

With Muenzenberg's ECCI protectors executed or in prison, Stalin seemed to be in no mood to respond to either threats or groveling from the covert action operator. The KGB stepped up demands for Muenzenberg to report to Moscow.

Comintern officers, terrorized by Stalin's purges, began turning. One KGB officer published a letter in Switzerland calling Stalin a traitor. His body was found in the streets soon after. Walter Krivitsky, another KGB NOC officer, unwilling to carry out assassinations of fellow communists, defected to America, where he would later publish a book on his life in Stalin's intelligence service. He died mysteriously in Washington D.C. in 1941.

The ECCI chairman, tiring of Muenzenberg's games, demanded that he come to Moscow in September 1937. In response, Willi played what must have felt like his trump card. He wrote back to the Comintern boss, trumpeting his days of "collaboration with Lenin." With no effect.

The back and forth with the Comintern continued for another year, into 1938. The KGB and the Control Commission were itching to get their hands on one of the last surviving remnants of old Bolshevism. Finally, in February 1939, unable to coax him back to Moscow, or to deal with him in France, the Comintern formally expelled Muenzenberg from the Communist Party.

Willi the White

Expelled from the Party he loved, Willi was at loose ends. Excoriating him as only a former lover can, the Comintern poured scorn onto its former star. This was not difficult for the Comintern, but it was difficult and painful for Muenzenberg. He seemed to be torn, feeling the wounds as if they were to his own flesh when his former comrades called him a "White," a counter-revolutionary.

But Willi still needed the stimulation of work and the excitement of a cause. He ginned up a German Unity Party. He sloganeered against the delaying tactics of the Popular Front—irony piling upon irony.

When the Stalin-Hitler non-aggression pact was signed in August 1939, Willi was finally immune from the whiplash effect active communists felt. They had to change their tune, to stay in harmony with Moscow. For the first time in twenty years, Willi could disagree openly. The Soviet quid for the Nazi quo was Poland. When the Red Army invaded Poland in September, Muenzenberg's spleen vented. He declared that "Socialist Russia is no more," and that Stalin was a counter-revolutionary.

As cathartic as his brief period of honesty must have been, he was not fated to enjoy it long. As a German citizen when the Nazi army invaded France in May 1940, Willi was ordered, along with his compatriots, to an internment camp. The German advance necessitated his camp's evacuation less than a month later, on June 20.

In the confusion of the mass evacuation in advance of the German onslaught, Muenzenberg, with a small group of fellow prisoners, fled toward the Swiss border. No one ever reported seeing Willi alive again. His body, a rope knotted around the neck, was found in October 1940 decomposing at the foot of an oak tree. Did the KGB catch up with him? Did he finally despair of regaining something like his old power? It's unlikely the truth will ever be known.

Covert Influence—Willi's Operations

Muenzenberg—Unparalleled Expertise

The most far reaching, and ingenious Soviet covert influence effort was the global operation run by Willi Muenzenberg, a German Communist with close ties to Lenin dating before the Russian revolution, as well as to Karl Radek, the Soviet Union's master propagandist. Stephen Koch's excellent book on Muenzenberg, *Double Lives* (2004), provides a glimpse into the man's soul, and an accounting of his operational philosophy and some of his covert influence operations.

With direction from the very top of the new Communist government in Moscow, Muenzenberg set out to establish, maintain, and enlarge a vast network of Communists, and Willing Accomplices in the media, entertainment, and Western governments to spread the one true faith, Communism. It seems that Muenzenberg was a perfect fit for this task. "He was in his element inventing the right news angle; planting the right story at the right time; heading off this or that opponent with this or that burst of bad news."

Need for Belonging, Acceptance and Esteem

Human beings have a complex set of physical and psychological needs. The psychologist Maslow identified the hierarchy of human needs. Starting at the base of a pyramid, the most essential needs are food, shelter, and security.

Maslow's pyramid of human needs works up from food and shelter to the ultimate need, at the top of the pyramid, for self-actualization—becoming all that you are capable of being. In between are psychological needs—belonging, acceptance, esteem, love.

These human needs are what marketers, con-men, advertisers, public relations flacks, and other manipulators use to move their merchandise.

Good salesmen instinctively understand human needs. The key to advertising has been described as "sell the sizzle, not the steak."

In the early 20th century, the emerging fields of public relations and advertising were in their infancy. American attempts at influence were relatively crude, like the Committee for Public Information. Crude, yes, but their work laid the foundation for American public relations, advertising, and influence.

Unfortunately, our enemies were much further along in understanding influence. Willi Muenzenberg was the master.

Cloaked in his overt propaganda organizations and Popular Front cover groups, hiding in plain sight as it were, Muenzenberg ran an interlocking, tightly woven network of covert influence operators.

The results of Willi's operations were like a snowball rolling downhill. Forming a small ball of snow, in a level meadow, you push it toward the mountain slope. It takes a lot of energy to keep the snowball rolling. Yet, even as you push it, it picks up more snow, grows bigger, and begins to gain momentum. When you reach the edge of the slope, and give it a final shove over the edge, the snowball slowly rolls down the slope, growing in both size and momentum as it rolls.

On the way down the mountainside, the snowball, now huge, dislodges more and more snow, until finally an avalanche ensues. The entire mountainside releases its load of snow, and a devastating mass of frozen death wipes out everything in its path as it roars down the mountain.

Willi's covert influence operations required a massive amount of energy to keep them rolling. Once the operations caught momentum, and then after Willi and his operators were dead, the snowball moved on its own, the payload of his influence ops became the perceived wisdom of an entire class of American political Willing Accomplices. Only after Willi was long dead did America suffer the full effects of his ingenious influence operations. In fact, only after the entire communist infrastructure in Russia had collapsed did we begin to see the full effects of the Muenzenberg application of Lenin's plan to destroy the Main Adversary.

As the great American showman, P.T. Barnum might have observed of his fellow countrymen, "There's a sucker born every minute." And early 20th century American suckers were unique. An appealing blend of innocence, naiveté, energy, good-will, humor, religion, and positive energy made Americans different from Europeans.

The sheer scope of the American mind and continent was a psychic shock to Europeans. Once over the shock, however, a sophisticated European intent on deceiving Americans had the upper hand. Even today, when advertisers want to impress their audience with sophistication, the voice they use in their ads almost always has a British accent. PBS TV movies seem to require actors to speak in British accents.

The Muenzenberg Creed

Muenzenberg's wife succinctly explained her husband's operational payload to Koch in an interview in the 1989. She provided the lyrics to the communist covert influence creed, beautifully rendered, almost poetic. The Muenzenberg creed was:

> You do not endorse Stalin.
>
> You do not call yourself a Communist.
>
> You do not declare your love for the regime.
>
> You do not call on people to support the Soviets.
>
> Ever.
>
> Under any circumstances.
>
> You claim to be an independent-minded idealist.
>
> You don't really understand politics, but you think the little guy is getting a lousy break.
>
> You believe in open-mindedness.
>
> You are shocked, frightened by what is going on right here in our own country.
>
> You're frightened by the racism, by the oppression of the workingman.
>
> You think the Russians are trying a great human experiment, and you hope it works.
>
> You believe in peace.
>
> You yearn for international understanding.
>
> You hate fascism.
>
> You think the capitalist system is corrupt.
>
> You say it over and over and over again.
>
> And you say nothing, nothing more.

Emotionally Involving the Innocents

R.N. Carew Hunt observed that Muenzenberg manipulated Americans' emotions. Instead of just asking for money for starving Russians, Muenzenberg's fronts urged Americans not to donate to charity, but to show their solidarity with the victims. An appeal to the heart instead of the head, the Comintern learned quickly, was more successful. Marx's dialectic, totally based on logic, was discarded for emotion.

Once Muenzenberg and his agents realized the unique American response to these emotional appeals, they built on their expertise with repeated use of this technique. Americans seemingly could not get enough. They donated money, time, and products. They wore ribbons, buttons, and pins showing their solidarity with whatever cause the communists peddled.

Willi understood fronts as cover for action from his long experience in the communist movement. Striking while the iron was hot, Willi and his KGB agents and officers, established a myriad of what he called Innocents Clubs. They were the nexus of the Willing Accomplices who would transform American culture—Hope and Change incarnate.

In fact, his covert influence operations were usually undertaken under the cover of "Popular Front" organizations. These were the Innocents Clubs. They provided the intelligence officers direct access to the Innocents, who were ignorant of the real nature of Soviet Communism, who believed that they were acting in the international spirit of anti-fascism.

These cover organizations provided the emotional charge that the suckers needed, tying their good intentions to an ostensible cause—anti-fascism, the Scottsboro Boys, Sacco and Vanzetti, peace, anti-war, labor support, living wages, immigrant rights, racial justice, social justice—name the radical, liberal, social cause, and it's likely that Willi's men had a group for you to join.

Many of these Willing Accomplices were

> true believers, people with no secret agenda, but with dewy moral dreams about a radical new Soviet-led, socialist "humanism". With a light sneer, Muenzenberg referred to this vast soft horde of the radical devout as "Innocents." His own phrase for the fronts he created to guide and direct their earnest but, politically naïve commitments was "Innocents' Clubs."

Koch's Analysis—Willi and the Innocents—Willing Accomplices

In 1989, Stephen Koch interviewed Muenzenberg's widow, Babette Gross. She was at Willi's side during much of his covert influence career. She had shared his mind, as well as his bed. Still carrying the torch for her idol, she provided Koch a glimpse into that mind, and into his strategy and tactics, and his essential influence payload.

As Koch described Willi's operations, he "was the first Grand Master of two quite new kinds of secret service work, essential to this century, and to the Soviets: the covertly controlled propaganda front, and the secretly manipulated fellow traveler."

According to Muenzenberg, "the Revolution needed middle-class opinion makers – artists, journalists, people of good will, novelists, actors, playwrights... humanists, people whose innocent sensitivities weren't yet cauterized to numbness by the genuine white hot radical steel."

The covert influence operations he ran made good use of these Willing Accomplices. Even while the cynical Soviets, who had seen the revolution, the Civil War, the infighting, the purges, the tortured confessions of "counterrevolutionaries," secretly despised the fools, Muenzenberg's covert strategy required "organizing the intellectuals."

The KGB was quite successful recruiting with front organizations in Europe. In America, Willi's "apparatus...sought to organize the intellectual elite, particularly wherever that elite was in formation, for example in colleges and universities. Precisely the same people who instituted the Cambridge penetrations supervised parallel operations in New York and Washington, in the Ivy League..."

These intellectuals, these Western Willing Accomplices were usually non-communists. This allowed the Accomplices to maintain deniability, while the Communist covert influence operators manipulated them for the greater good.

Even as stories began to leak out of the true horrors occurring in the Stalinist utopia, the Willing Accomplices studiously averted their eyes, and listened with rapt attention as their Communist case officers denied everything.

The Willing Accomplices' job was to "reassure the non-Communist world that despite appearances, all was well, Utopia really was a-building; that they had been over to see the future, and the socialist future was sweet and good."

Birth of PC-Progressive Form—Uplifted Sensibilities

Once Muenzenberg grasped the realities of his American target, his goal morphed to take advantage of the unique American psychology. As described by Koch, based on his interviews with Muenzenberg's wife, the covert operator created the style, form, and substance of PC-Progressivism.

> His goal was to create for the right-thinking non-Communist West the dominating political prejudice of the era; the belief that any opinion that happened to serve the foreign policy of the Soviet Union was derived from the most essential elements of human decency. He wanted to instill the feeling, like a truth of nature, that seriously to criticize or challenge Soviet policy was the *unfailing mark of a bad, bigoted, and probably stupid person, while support was equally infallible proof of a forward-looking mind committed to all that was best for humanity and marked by an uplifting refinement of sensibility.* [my emphasis]

Here we see a precise description of PC-Progressivism at the moment of its birth. Muenzenberg created the easy way out for those who craved acceptance and the illusion of being on the side of the enlightened. Those who care.

At the same time, this formula sets up the PC-Progressives as being better than the non-carers. Those who do not follow the politically correct path are "bad, bigoted, and probably stupid." PC-Progressives who follow the party line revel in their superiority, their caring, their intelligence, their loving souls, and their clear elevation above the masses.

Muenzenberg standard modus operandi was twofold, he used co-option and denial—"co-option of liberal democratic opinion; denial of communist motives. He organized in all the media: newspapers, film, radio, books, magazines, and the theater. Every kind of 'opinion maker' was involved: writers, artists, actors, commentators, priests, ministers, professors, 'business leaders,' scientists, psychologists, anyone at all whose opinion the public was likely to respect."

The high standards of covert influence operations that Muenzenberg set, his techniques, his targets, and his methods proved to be extremely sound and productive. The subtle infiltration of targeted organizations, publications, or other media by a communist intelligence officer, or agent, who uses "opinion makers" to plant the desired covert influence payload became the Soviet's standard operational approach. And not only the Soviets use the standard approach, even today, other intelligence agencies have adopted this covert influence operational modus operandi.

Muenzenberg created a network of operational specialists. An early success of the "Muenzenberg men" was their covert influence operation carried out to deflect Western attention from the communist forced labor camps. The truth, which had been reported by some left-wing press outside Russia, ran the risk of alienating the Soviet's Western supporters. So Muenzenberg cranked up his covert influence operations.

So efficient and so effective were Muenzenberg's techniques that his formula created the mold from which PC-Progressive responses to exposure continue to flow today. His "job was to distract press attention by accusing the accusers, deflecting attention...." We'll examine this more fully in the chapter on Andemca—Admit nothing, deny everything, make counter-accusations.

Spanish Civil War Willing Accomplices

In the exciting years between the world wars, communism built upon its triumph in Russia by adopting an anti-fascist identity. The Spanish civil war became a proving ground for many American Communists and fellow travelers. Muenzenberg built on the relationships forged during these days.

"The writers, artists, journalists, scientists, educators, clerics, columnists, filmmakers, and publishers, either under [Muenzenberg's] influence or regularly manipulated by his "Muenzenberg men," form a startling list of notables from that era, "Ernest Hemingway to John Dos Passos to Lillian Hellman to George Grosz to Erwin Piscator to Andre Malraux to Andre Gide to Bertolt Brecht to Dorothy Parker... to Kim Philby and Laurence Duggan, Guy Burgess and Alger Hiss, and Anthony Blunt and Whittaker Chambers."

Embedded within the Comintern—Secret Agents of Opinion

While Muenzenberg's men worked themselves into positions in which they could be used to collect intelligence, "*they were first and foremost professional propaganda agents, the secret agents of opinion.*" [emphasis mine]

The organization for which Muenzenberg performed his covert influence magic, "the real Comintern was a core of disciplined professional revolutionaries, put in place to enforce Leninist hegemony throughout the socialist movement worldwide.... It ran its own propaganda network and had its own secret service...linked...to the other Soviet secret services."

The Comintern, as a public organization, enjoyed the ability to produce press releases and other public information. Muenzenberg's men burrowed into this organization, providing public cover for their covert activities, "with deep cover espionage networks."

Plausible Deniability

A technique of intelligence operations is sometimes referred to as "deniability." This is how policymakers, prime ministers, presidents, and other decision-makers are able to cushion themselves from the realities of intelligence operations. Obama pronounced, with a straight face, that there were no "boots on the ground" in Libya. As a practitioner of the PC-Progressive creed, dissembling and hiding motives and actions behind a screen of verbiage is second nature to this President. His effortless lying is reminiscent of the masters—Lenin and Stalin.

The Comintern provided another level of deniability for Lenin and the Soviets. So Muenzenberg worked for a secret intelligence organization within a secret cover organization running secret operations against secret targets.

However, in the true Soviet tradition of trusting no one, "the evidence is strong that two of Muenzenberg's principal lieutenants, Louis Gibarti and Otto Katz, were... agents of the [KGB] as well."

Interlocking circles of intelligence officers, informants, counter-intelligence reporters, each carrying out covert operations as well as watching and reporting on their colleagues, are all defining characteristics of the Soviet intelligence system.

Of these practitioners, "Gibarti ranks as a founding father of the modern mingling of propaganda with espionage and covert action."

The KGB's global covert influence operation, managed by Muenzenberg developed contacts and "maintained networks of agents working with creative artists, with actors in the film world, with writers and journalists."

With the cynicism that is typical of a human intelligence operator, Muenzenberg had no illusions about the people whom he recruited and manipulated. Muenzenberg, who understood the grim reality of Soviet communism, having been present at its birth, and intimately acquainted with its midwives, chose to live outside Russia, until his death.

PC-Progressive Substitute for Religion

As religion had promised, and delivered, salvation and the opportunity to do good works while on earth, to its believers, for Willing Accomplices membership and participation in the rites of Muenzenberg's front organizations "served as a substitute for religious belief...[and]...a role in the search for justice in our century."

With the neat approach of "defining who was guilty in society," Willi offered secular absolution from their sins for all those who opposed the guilty. A mass hunger for "righteousness" made this an appealing "illusion" for millions of Americans.

Communism—Love That Dare Not Say Its Name

Marx's original theory held that the masses of laborers and farmers would rise to create the Dictatorship of the Proletariat. Unfortunately this starry eyed bit of theory was dimmed by a bitter dose of reality. The Russian Revolution and the civil war demonstrated to the Communists that the proletariat was incapable of the role assigned by Marx. Lenin, ever the pragmatist, adjusted the Marxist dogma, and arrived at the approach that is still known as Marxism-Leninism.

This approach has the elite intelligentsia, the Vanguard, doing the thinking for the vast unwashed proletariat. These elites know what is best for the rest of their countrymen, and, for that matter, for the entire world. Their role is to drag the proletariat, kicking and screaming, bleeding and dying, into the glorious future of global socialism.

The Vanguard, acting for the proletariat, installs a dictatorship. The theory is that the elite dictatorship will evolve into Marx's Dictatorship of the Proletariat. In reality, the Dictatorship of the Elite has continued indefinitely in each and every communist country.

Because the elites' role is so important, so crucial to proper Marxist-Leninist historical evolution, nothing can be allowed to stand in the way of their beautiful ideas. Their status as special anointed arbiters of history and culture provides them with unparalleled power. Regardless of the actual results of the elite's actions or policies, including seizing and eliminating private property and businesses, massacring millions of real or perceived enemies, they can always claim good intentions.

Muenzenberg tapped into these good intentions and put them to work, with Willing Accomplices believing they were working for anti-fascism, peace, brotherhood and all the other beautiful intentions. Muenzenberg's operators assured the Willing Accomplices "that despite appearances, all was well, Utopia really was a-building; that they had been over to see the future, and the socialist future was sweet and good."

And yet, Willing Accomplices, in love with Soviet Utopia dared not utter the name. Because of the inherent clash between reality, theory, and practice, "Stalinism does not permit people to be honest about their politics."

The Soviet covert influence operators applied classical intelligence recruitment techniques. "Every resource of manipulation, from rudimentary group psychology to plain bribery, was used to keep the ranks of the famous and influential left safely Stalinist in everything *except* name. *As for the name, that had to be avoided at all costs.*" That name, of course, was Communism.

Destroy the Land of Opportunity

While standard Marxist dogma required parroting the party line of global communist revolution, Stalin was more realistic. His objective became much more easily achievable, denigration of the American culture and social system.

> Stalin had no serious interest or belief in a mass-based American revolution.... The apparatus of American Communism would be directed instead toward discrediting American politics and culture and assisting the growth of Soviet power elsewhere. It sought not the outright

> destruction of the American democracy, however much that might be desired, but practical influence on its culture, the placement of agents who would over the long term seek to smooth and promote the advance of Soviet influence and assist the apparatus in its work of espionage.

Once Muenzenberg had established the form of Political Correctness, Stalin's objective of influencing the American culture became the substance, the covert influence payload. The glorious Revolution was the myth upon which the Soviet Union was being constructed, the rival myth competing for global attention was a country where the streets were paved with gold, the USA.

> For the world proletariat of 1925, a leading counter-myth to the myth of revolution was, by far, the myth of America. That vision – the notion of the melting pot, the Golden Door, the Land of Opportunity – this is what held the real political attention of the International. To the Bolsheviks, this was the true American menace.

The objective of Lenin's Active Measure operation was to create and sustain a worldwide anti-American campaign that would focus its appeal upon the mythology of its appeal to immigrants. The goal was to

> instill a reflexive loathing of the United States and its people as a prime tropism of left-wing enlightenment.... The United States had to be depicted as an *almost insanely xenophobic place, murderously hostile to foreigners*. [my emphasis]

As part of Stalin's overarching plan to influence, in ways helpful to the Soviets' own goals, American society and culture, another payload was added to the covert influence arsenal.

> Insiders came to call this plan, the "peace conspiracy."... by the middle of 1928, [Muenzenberg's covert influence] apparatus...had seized upon pacifism as the principal issue of the hour, and it continued to promote "peace..."

Racist America

Any niche that the influence operators could dig their fingers into was exploited. Following Muenzenberg's creed, American racism was one of the prime niches.

Feeding them what they liked, disdain for normal Americans, Muenzenberg, took a grain of truth and used it as a wedge to destroy.

> If the American adversary culture rightly saw the oppression of blacks as the society's great institutionalized crime, Stalinism would take the highest of high ground on the "Negro question." No matter that Stalin ruled a country where a significant part of the population languished in what amounted to slave labor camps – where indeed a significant part of the economy was based on the forced labor of millions.

Hate America First Operations

Now Muenzenberg had created the form, and the Soviet hierarchy had provided the substance of the hateful philosophy–hate America, everything it was, is, and will be. Every good left-winger would know without thinking just what to think. All that was left was to go forth and spread the gospel.

Muenzenberg's men understood the code and were well-trained and practiced in covert tradecraft. They developed extensive networks of Willing Accomplices. In his KGB operation, the intelligence officers "...arranged the celebrities into guided and controlled networks, assigning agents to their management, focusing on given communities in the arts, in journalism, in the academy...."

The covert influence operations, by making use of Innocents, who were admired and influential led to such successful results that "once a fashionable opinion was properly launched, it would quite spontaneously develop and grow among the ranks of enlightened people.... [Muenzenberg's men] called this ripple effect in cultural politics 'rabbit breeding.'"

Church of PC-Progressivism

Muenzenberg's Innocents Clubs could just as well be called the first united congregations of the "Church of PC-Progressivism. For what these groups offered members was

> a substitute for religious belief. He offered everyone, anyone, a role in the search for justice in our century. By defining who was guilty in society, Willi offered "innocence" to anyone who "opposed" it. People hungering for righteousness seized upon the new illusion by the millions.

Target: Hollywood

Hollywood especially was attractive to the Muenzenberg operation. After all, it controlled the imagination of the country, its dreams, its hopes, its desires. Hollywood movies reached throughout the vast spaces of the North American continent, and spread around the world. Movies directly accessed raw human emotions provided a direct link to targets' heartstrings.

Willi's KGB covert influence officers and agents circled Hollywood, searching for openings. According Ronald Radosh in *Red Star Over* Hollywood, the KGB was "focused on...Hollywood..., seeing the Popular Front as a way of dramatically increasing power there."

Muenzenberg regarded Hollywood as critical to the effort to undermine American culture. A communist screenwriter explained to Congress that the covert influence operation of the Popular Front years was based on the fact that "Hollywood 'influences the country not only culturally but politically."

He went on to explain that what he considered "the Popular Front," but what was actually Muenzenberg's influence operations, aimed to "subtly insert ideology 'in an ordinary John and Mary movie,...[rather] than to put in a whole thesis."

Otto Katz—Recruiter in La-La Land

It appears that Muenzenberg began the Hollywood operation with a star KGB influence operator, Otto Katz, who operated under various aliases, including Andre Simone in California. He also assumed the identity of an anti-fascist fighter, "Breda," in many developmental encounters with Willing Accomplice fronts.

Katz, a fascinating character and the subject of many books himself, led a life roughly parallel to Muenzenberg's. Koch noted that "Muenzenberg...in 1924 had discovered a very young Otto, already a covert communist...Otto was possessed of almost legendary charm; he had a great theatrical gift for spinning at will the illusions of unearned intimacy."

"The illusion of unearned intimacy" may be the best description of a case officer's developmental technique that has ever been written.

Katz worked with Willi in Berlin before the Nazi takeover, and was on the Brown Book writing team in Paris. He was likely, at the same time he served Muenzenberg, reporting to the KGB on Willi's actions and attitudes.

Katz worked for the KGB in Spain, where he directed the British Willing Accomplice, Claud Cockburn. Katz was subjected to a show trial in Czechoslovakia in 1952, after which he was executed by his communist overlords.

In 1935, Muenzenberg's covert influence operation against Hollywood hit high gear. Otto Katz made his first visit, and personally organized the Hollywood Anti-Nazi League. As Breda, Katz made stirring speeches against the fascist threat, winning the hearts of the movie colony's elitists. Katz took to the Hollywood scene like a pig to slop. His cover legend included a story of his having been Marlene Dietrich's secret lover, or husband. The writers and artists adored him, and wrote him into movies—notably the character of Laszlo in *Casablanca* was probably modeled on Katz. Or modeled on Breda. Or modeled on other lies Katz told.

Regardless of the truth, Katz's mission in California was a smashing success. As Koch noted, "Katz spent his days among the stars, a companion to the theater folk, and in the ambience of the international cinema."

The key to recruiting espionage agents, whether for stealing secrets, committing treason, or for use in covert influence operations, is the ability to see deep into men's hearts and to fathom what it is that makes them tick, their motivations and vulnerabilities.

With this understanding, gained only through extensive time on target, breaking bread, sharing wine, pouring out your heart, and listening to your target pour out his heart, a skillful case officer, like Katz, crafts a recruitment pitch that hits all the right chords. The pitch plays to the target's vulnerabilities, promising to provide the missing ingredient in the target's life.

Adversary Culture—Elite Attitude

Clearly what was missing in many an American intellectual's life during the early decades of the 1900s was a defining cause or movement that would raise them above the "moron millions."

Koch noted that Muenzenberg and his operators saw the relationship of American intellectuals with their own society, and sensed a vulnerability. Koch called the intellectuals who loathed their own society the "adversary culture."

His operational genius was that he understood "what the adversary culture believes sets it apart from the vast hypocritical and second-rate middle class to which it belongs..." This cultural self-loathing appeared to be the main common denominator among Willing Accomplices, in Hollywood, the media, and academia. They were better than the masses.

Radosh, quoting an actor during the 1940s, noted that Muenzenberg's Popular Fronts expressed what "everybody wanted to hear...it became comfortable, even fashionable," to be a Willing Accomplice.

In this actor's unself-conscious admission, the communist covert influence operations fulfilled his need for acceptance, and his need to be perceived as being better or more enlightened than the masses.

The Accomplices' human need to belong, and to believe, created the PC-Progressive template: their membership in the caring-group "was an indispensable part of their integrity, their intelligence, and their independence. They needed to *believe*."

The fact that their belief system was essentially Stalinist did not matter. They simply ignored that reality, and enjoyed the feeling of superiority they gained from belonging.

As Koch said of the KGB's recruits who collected intelligence for the Soviets, "Living that lie in blind self-righteousness, all of them threw their great talents into the service of tyranny and a tyrant's fraud. But it was such a convincing fraud! It felt so necessary! So true! The embers of that fiery conviction still burn..."

Moron Millions

Dorothy Parker, one of Katz's Willing Accomplices, wrote the script for a movie directed by the great Alfred Hitchcock, *Saboteur* (1940). She shared writing credit with Peter Vertiel, the son of Salka Vertiel, host of Popular Front meetings in Hollywood.

The story concerns a network of Nazi spies conspiring to sabotage America's defense industries. Hitchcock's hero eventually has a face-to-face confrontation with the head of the Nazi spy network.

Parker and Vertiel delivered the communist covert influence payload, letting the Nazi spy give voice to the Willing Accomplice point of view:

> K: Why is it that you sneer every time you refer to this country [America]? You've done pretty well here, I don't get it.
>
> T: No, you wouldn't. You're one of the ardent believers, a good American. *All the millions like you, people that plod along without asking questions. I hate to use the word stupid, but it seems to be the only one that applies. The great masses, the moron millions.* Well, there a few of us who are unwilling to troop along. A few of us who are clever enough to see that there is much more to be done than just live small complacent lives. A few of us in America desire a more profitable type government. When you think about it Mr. Kane, *the competence of totalitarian nations is much higher than ours. They get things done.* [emphasis mine]

Parker and Vertiel's exquisite disdain for the unwashed masses of America is disguised by giving the lines to the Nazi. But the attitude is all Willing Accomplice: Superiority. Moron millions. We know better than you. Totalitarian nations get things done. If only we were in charge. This pesky democracy thing is really hurting our country.

The Willing Accomplices, the elite of Hollywood, carefully distanced themselves from the Moron Millions. The elites, the chosen, "were clever enough to see that there was much more to be done." These Willing Accomplices quietly and secretly were doing their duty. Destruction of the moron culture and society from within.

Target: Media

While Muenzenberg's operators had to visit Hollywood to effectively penetrate that American cultural transmission belt, reporters and journalists, commentators and writers effectively came to him.

The Russian Revolution brought a gaggle of American media to Russia. In the early days of the revolution, the KGB set up an effective operation to control these journalists, and to bring them under direct development and recruitment.

While some journalists were already in the Communist camp, like John Reed (whose body is buried in the walls of the Kremlin), others were less convinced of the rightness of the Bolshevik cause.

Bessie Beatty was a rich girl from southern California. While a student at Occidental College, her connections seem to have landed her a job at the Los Angeles *Herald*. Without finishing her senior year, in 1907, she went to Nevada to report on a mining strike. This reporting somehow turned into a hagiographic book on the upper classes, *Who's Who in Nevada*.

Her book allegedly caught the attention of editors of the San Francisco *Bulletin*, Fremont Older, who hired her and let her write her own column.

In 1917, Bessie was 31 years old, still working for the *Bulletin*. Her beat was women's and children's issues. Older sponsored her to travel to Russia alone, to cover the revolution. Without speaking Russian, clearly with no background on Russian issues, but probably well-disposed to the social issues, Bessie arrived in St. Petersburg.

She fell in with the John Reed journalism gang, including his wife, Louse Bryant, and Albert Rhys Williams. This group was under development by Alexander Gumberg.

Gumberg, working under the forerunner of the KGB, assessed and developed this group. He fed them access to the Bolsheviks, translated for them, and provided the story line for their journalism, the original covert influence operation. He escorted them to the Winter Palace the night after it was taken by the communists.

Beatty was an ideal covert influence recruit. She wrote glowing accounts of the wonderful advances the Bolsheviks introduced in Russia. She interviewed an all-woman battalion near St. Petersburg.

Louise Bryant mentions Beatty often in her later writings about her time in Russia. Beatty herself wrote a glowing account of those revolutionary days when she returned to the U.S., *The Red Heart of Russia*.

She became a staunch advocate for the Bolsheviks, like many Willing Accomplices, especially in the early days. She testified in support of the Bolsheviks before a Senate committee. She returned to Moscow in 1921, and produced a series of articles based on interviews with Soviet leaders, Lenin, Trotsky, Chicherin, and Kalinin.

Beatty later wrote for MGM studios, and became host of a long-running radio show. Her unique blend of advice and chit-chat was sort of like the Oprah of her era.

Beatty's covert influence work for the Bolshevik's was brief, but intense. It does not appear that she entangled herself with the Muenzenberg fronts after her trip to Moscow in 1921. However, her recruitment during the revolution was a template for future operations. It's likely that Muenzenberg modeled his operations on those of Gumberg.

The goals of Gumberg's influence ops were more focused on achieving diplomatic recognition of the Soviet Union than Muenzenberg's later goal of destruction of American society.

Beatty was an accomplished Willing Accomplice. She was not alone. Many journalists exposed themselves to the influence operation. Many were co-opted or recruited. We'll examine Walter Duranty as a case study later. However, we should not forget that dozens, probably hundreds of journalists were Willing Accomplices, setting the stage for today's domination of the media by the PC-Progressive group-think.

Target: Academia

John Dewey was a driving force behind the 20th century changes in educational philosophy in America. Respected as an educator and philosopher After admiring the communists from afar, Dewey visited Moscow in 1928, on invitation of the Soviet Education Minister Lunacharsky. Evidently Dewey advised the Soviets on establishing a new education system.

One could argue that Dewey was the father of communist education. While in Russia, he would have been handled very carefully by the KGB. He would have had a handler, likely his "translator/guide," who meticulously noted his vices and virtues. In a very short time after his arrival, the KGB would have a full assessment for co-opting or recruiting another Willing Accomplice.

The handler, at the direction of the KGB, arranged for Dewey to observe various activities and schools, all carefully pre-arranged to make the best impression on this naïve Accomplice.

The professor responded wonderfully, from the KGB's point of view. In his book, written after his first visit, Impressions of Soviet Russia and the Revolutionary World, Dewey gushed like a lovesick school girl about "the marvelous development of progressive educational ideas and practices under the fostering care of the

Bolshevist government—and I am speaking of what I have seen and not just been told about."

Oh yes, Dewey assured us, he had *seen* progressive educational ideas in practice in Russia. And the wonderful Bolsheviks fostered those ideas.

Dewey hunkered down in the warm glow of his KGB handlers, and celebrated in his book, the "enormous constructive effort taking place in the creation of a new collective mentality; a new morality I should call it."

Implicitly, Dewey criticized American education in his song of celebration for the construction of a collective mentality. Clearly, Dewey laid the foundation for criticizing American education, and society, for its immoral individuality.

Fed the Muenzenberg covert influence payload, in the heart of the collectivist beast, Dewey lapped it up, asked for more, and returned to America, determined to spread the gospel.

Dewey was just one academic/educator developed and recruited or co-opted in the KGB's covert influence operation. His efforts as a Willing Accomplice continue to pay off, even in the 21st century. Along with his fellow Columbia Teachers College colleague, George Counts, Dewey can be credited with destroying traditional American education, and creating the PC-Progressive mess that our children suffer in today.

Chapter 3

Progressive response to exposure: Andemca

The people want democracy—real democracy, Mr. Dies, and they look toward Hollywood to give it to them because they don't get it any more in their newspapers. And that's why you're out here, Mr. Dies—that's why you want to destroy the Hollywood progressive organizations—because you've got to control this medium if you want to bring fascism to this country.
Dorothy Parker, to HUAC Chairman Martin Dies, 1940

In virtually all cases in which KGB intelligence operations, whether collection operations or active measures are exposed, the operatives' response is simple and effective. The response itself is a covert influence operation. The goal of the operation is to reduce the "blowback" associated with exposure of an intelligence operation. The multiple sub-objectives include denying the accused spy was in contact with Russians, or KGB agents. If this contact is exposed, then the objective is to deny that the contact was out of the ordinary, or that it was for intelligence purposes. If that is proven, then the objective shifts to destroying the accusers.

In a free country like the US, this covert influence operation is left to the Willing Accomplices in the media. The techniques of this operation are best explained by the covert action motto:

Admit nothing; deny everything; make counter-accusations.

Andemca

The KGB's accomplices perfected the technique of lodging counter-accusations. The effective response has usually been that they were fighting racism and fascism. That their accusers are racists and fascists.

When the House Un-American Activities Committee (HUAC), conducted hearings in the 1940s and 1950s, opponents said the hearings were "un-American." But the reaction to HUAC was muted compared to the reaction to hearings and investigations led by Wisconsin Senator Joseph McCarthy. The accusations against HUAC and McCarthy, trumpeted by the press, and seized on by Willing Accomplices for generations, made the communists, and fellow travelers exposed by the investigations PC-Progressive heroes.

McCarthy uncovered a vast network of communists throughout the federal government. While he did exaggerate some of the charges, and while he may not have been the most savory character himself, his investigations were productive and illustrative of the extent of communist intelligence collection operations in the U.S. government.

The media and academia hero worship of the Hollywood Ten, Alger Hiss, Walter Duranty, George S. Counts, Dorothy Parker, and other Willing Accomplices and communist agents was in itself a covert influence operation. Following the Andemca prescription, however, Willing Accomplices could not stop just with praising the guilty. They had to continue, attempting to destroy the innocent investigators, or at least to divert attention from the guilty communist spies.

Whitaker Chambers, Joseph McCarthy, Elizabeth Bentley, and anyone else who dared to tell the truth about Soviet intelligence operations and operatives faced the wrath of the PC-Progressive forces during their lifetimes, and after they died. Willing

Accomplices took to heart the "make counter-accusations" prescription. Chambers was smeared as a homosexual. McCarthy was smeared as a secret cross-dressing drag queen. Bentley was smeared as a sex-crazed, homely plain Jane. The forces of PC-Progressive "toleration" have been active in smears and counter-accusations ever since, *viz* the on-going attacks against Ronald Reagan, Rush Limbaugh, or Sarah Palin today.

Up to today, PC-Progressive acolytes still do not acknowledge the truth of the revelations about Hiss, the Hollywood Ten, and the communist intelligence collection operations uncovered by the Venona project, and the Mitrokhin files. And till today "McCarthyism" is one of the vilest accusations that can be made against foes of the destruction of American culture.

In PC textbooks, Hollywood movies, and the PC media, McCarthy is the ultimate "bad guy." The "Red Scare" is portrayed as a horrible time in America, with innocents nabbed off the streets, trundled away in dark sedans by men in trench-coats and fedoras.

In the PC cult mythology, the lives of well-meaning intellectuals were ruined by fascist, racist, hating white males. The fact is that these PC-Progressive attacks are straight out of the KGB's handbook for reaction to exposure—Andemca—and are part and parcel of the original covert influence operation, dating from the 1920s.

Chapter 4

Counter-intelligence methodology

You see, when it comes to fighting Communists I am a battle-scarred veteran. But after twenty years I cannot tell one by looking at him. If only he were a tall, dark man with bushy black whiskers, a bomb in his hand, a knife in his teeth, and a hand grenade in each pocket of his smock, I could recognize him. Only the leaders, however, proclaim their membership. The clever are silent, hidden, anonymous, boring from within. You can tell a Communist only by his ideas.

William F. Russell, 1938

Counter-intelligence Vetting—Lessons from Einstein

Counter-intelligence (CI) is a sub-discipline of espionage operations. The goal of CI is to determine the truth of a situation. Is your subject who he says he is? Does he have the access he claims?

CI requires an inquisitive, skeptical mind. It also requires one to doubt everything and everyone.

When Albert Einstein worked in the Swiss Patent Office, his credo was: "You have to remain critically vigilant. Challenge every premise. Challenge conventional wisdom. Never accept the truth of something merely because everyone else views it as obvious. Resist being credulous. When you pick up an application, assume everything is wrong."

This is the same mindset that CI requires. Just because people have been researching and writing about Walter Duranty, or Dorothy Parker, or George S. Counts for decades does not mean that they have come close to the truth.

A CI specialist cannot be deterred because a target makes counter-accusations, or accuses you of "McCarthyism."

Working as a case officer, one must maintain constant CI vigilance. You just met someone at an oil industry conference in Nigeria. This person claims to be an Egyptian working in Europe for a Mexican company, with a degree from a French school. There are so many facts that you either must accept at face value, or you must perform due diligence to get closer to the truth.

Mossad Assassination

The 2010 Mossad operation in Dubai, in which a team of more than ten espionage officers used false passports and aliases to travel in and out of the United Arab Emirates, illustrates the danger of taking identities and backgrounds at face value.

These highly skilled officers had one goal—to assassinate a Palestinian terrorist. Their false identities, disguises, and aliases got them into the country, into the target's room, and then out of the country. All in all, a highly successful operation.

The UAE CI analysis only later identified the group, and their aliases. More than a year later, there has been no news of any of the operators being arrested, or of their true identities being revealed.

Working in CI, one becomes used to constantly questioning—identities, motives, backgrounds—everything that makes an individual unique.

Espionage operators manipulate their environment by using false names, false backgrounds, cover stories, false employers, disguises, and other ruses to dispel suspicion of themselves or their motives.

My experience as a case officer, along with my experience as an executive recruiter, and street smarts developed during my partying days, and on the streets as a case officer, have all honed an acute set of "CI antennae" that help me to recognize CI issues.

My experience in vetting candidates for job placement, my experience working in headquarters on CI approvals all contribute to my acute CI awareness and analysis skill.

The research and analysis of the covert influence agents and operations in this book were, in effect, applied counter-intelligence vetting. In CI vetting, when someone is suspected of cooperating with a foreign intelligence service, the CI officer considers all aspects of the suspect's life and circumstances. No avenue is off-limits, no issue can be ignored. A piece of evidence that may be vitally important could be buried beneath a haze of lies, subterfuge, cover stories, falsifications, mis-directions, intentional forgetfulness, human errors, lost records, and other actions or inactions that obfuscate the truth. Careful CI vetting allows us to penetrate this haze, and get closer to the truth.

Rick Ames and Jim Nicholson

Rick Ames, a CIA officer spying for the Russians, should have come under suspicion for living above his means. He drove a car conspicuously more expensive than should have been affordable at his pay grade. He paid for a house in cash.

James Nicholson, another CIA officer who was recruited by the KGB, had unexplained foreign travel. He used the trips to both meet his handling case officers, and to visit girlfriends.

Jim was an instructor at the CIA training facility (the Farm) when I went through training. He had serious alcohol abuse issues then. We traveled to another city for surveillance detection training. Jim suggested we lunch at Hooters, where he proceeded to drink a couple pitchers of beer. Riding back to the Farm, Jim passed out, snoring through the entire trip. In retrospect, this was a CI indicator. Something was wrong in his life. So wrong that he needed to drink himself into oblivion in order to be comfortable with fellow CIA officers.

Cuban Double Agents

The CIA has been burned not only by its own officers spying for the KGB, but also by what it believed to be recruited agents, working for the CIA against foreign targets. The Cubans used controlled dangles against the CIA. The CIA recruited these dangles as agents. Solid CI vetting would likely have uncovered these double agents. Close examination of every aspect of their stories, scrutiny of their attitudes and demeanor could have provided clues to their true allegiance.

Khost Suicide Bomber—CIA Recruited Agent

In December, 2010 seven CIA employees died in a suicide bombing. The bomber was a Jordanian member of Al-Qaeda. The terrorist convinced inexperienced CIA officers that he was genuinely interested in helping America capture and kill terrorists. In a last testament video, released after his death, the terrorist mocked the CIA for its pitiful counter-intelligence vetting. He disdained the bagfuls of money offered by the uncomprehending American officers.

Close examination of the lifestyles and actions of each of these double agents would have provided evidence of their treachery. A CI officer must be aware of the global environment in which the suspects operate, with a grounding in what is normal and what is not normal. Small variations must be noted and explored. A seemingly insignificant statement, or action, might reveal an important detail about the suspect's cooperation with the KGB. No tidbit of information is too minor.

Close scrutiny of a subject's background, combined with interviewing that person, can provide an experienced CI officer with details necessary to form a conclusion about the subject's possible cooperation with a foreign intelligence service.

Foreign NOC Officer

I was able to determine that one subject, a candidate for agent status, had been dispatched by a foreign intelligence service, more than twenty years previously. During an in-depth interview, I explored her background in detail. Her story was that she had come to the US to open a company, along with her husband. My line of inquiry involved details of the business arrangement: who had funded the business, who were their partners in their home country, what exactly was the business supposed to be selling. These questions were seemingly impossible for her to answer straight. Any query aimed at details of her business resulted in ten-minute-long rambling stories about her and her husband's "friends."

Following up on the friends, who she said included a military officer, resulted in her rambling disjointedly about unrelated issues. Clearly I had hit a nerve with this topic. After further analysis, my final assessment was that she had been planted into the US in a long-term "seeding" operation. After setting herself up "in business," and receiving US citizenship, twenty years later, she approached the CIA to offer her linguistic services. Only my close and diligent CI investigation and inquiry resulted in the uncovering of her true affiliation.

This candidate had been "under development" by a CIA case officer for an extended period. In this case, as happens with double agents, the case officer was under development as much as the agent. The case officer, also a woman, of similar middle-age to the agent, empathized so strongly with the agent's personal story of a bad marriage, abusive husband, neglected children, that she did not pay attention to the agent's obvious CI issues.

"Falling in love with her agent" is applicable in this case. Once a case officer becomes too close to their agent, it is sometimes difficult to see the warts of the case. And if the agent is using development tradecraft against the case officer (establishing commonalities, developing rapport, solving personal problems), the closeness is exacerbated. In this case, the handling CIA case officer was enraged that I had been "mean" to her agent during the interviews.

Adikimbo and the Vicodin

In another case, an agent candidate (call him Adikimbo) had been under development by a case officer for more than a year. Adikimbo was supposedly providing details on foreign officials whom he met in the course of his international business travels. The best way to vet these contacts would be to ask Adikimbo to provide their names, titles, nationalities, business dealings, and other pertinent details. My questions were met with clear resistance. Adikimbo directly challenged me, asking why I needed this sort of information. From the initial elicitation to the final clear request for the details, nothing was going to get him to provide the details.

My continued attempts to determine just what Adikimbo's story was, and who he had actually been meeting with, and why, were fruitless. Later inquiries revealed that Adikimbo had been used to meeting with his case officer for drinks, and then more drinks, and chatting about his travels. Adikimbo had never before provided any details on his contacts. When it was clear that Adikimbo would not provide details, I brought the meeting to an end, said my good-byes, and left him with a glass of wine in the restaurant where we had been meeting.

The next morning, the agent, as part of the vetting process, was scheduled to meet with another CIA officer. When that officer knocked on the agent's hotel room door, he was greeted by a bleary-eyed Adikimbo. After firing up the hotel room coffee maker,

Adikimbo told the officer that he had been so "stressed out" after meeting with me, that he had come back to his room, taken three Vicodin (pain medication) tablets and drank another bottle of wine.

Adikimbo was hiding something, and my pointed questioning had, again gotten to its rotten core. In the end, it turned out that Adikimbo did not have any "high level contacts." He was just an ordinary schmuck, who had in the course of his business traveled to various countries.

He had been inflating the importance of his contacts and his work in order to impress his "friend," the recruiting case officer, and to keep the largesse of the CIA flowing. At least in this case the recruiting case officer was not enraged at the results of my CI probing. He accepted the results, and moved on. Adikimbo probably ended up in rehab somewhere.

Kevin Ricks

In 2008, I started using Facebook. In the initial rush of finding old friends and acquaintances, a high school classmate showed up in my Friends list. He was living in the Washington DC area, as was I. We had an email exchange. I found out that Kevin Ricks was teaching English nearby. I added him to my Friends list. He and I had graduated from high school in the same class at Roanoke Rapids High School, North Carolina. I hadn't talked to him since graduation night in 1978, 30 year previously.

Kevin was slightly off in high school, but that wasn't too unusual. I remembered his campaign for a student council position. All his posters had reference Elton John songs.

In the following couple of months, I didn't have any contact with Kevin, but as a Friend, I saw his exchanges with his other Friends. It seemed that all of his friends were adolescent boys, from high school age or just out of high school. I noticed several were foreigners, seemingly exchange students.

As a former teacher, and teacher of foreigners, Kevin's exchanges with the students seemed somehow odd. While I didn't really focus on the issue, after about a month of reading Kevin's wall postings, I un-Friended him. I told my wife that something wasn't right about him.

The next time I heard Kevin's name was in 2010, on the news. He'd been arrested for sexual molestation of a high school boy at the school he taught. As the story unfolded, before he finally pleaded guilty in federal court and was sentenced to a long stretch, a Washington Post reporter revealed that Kevin had been molesting students since the summer of 1978. My CI sense had been spot on. Something was not right with Kevin.

Vetting Commercial Recruitment Candidates

As an executive recruiter, I provide a one year guarantee to my clients for each candidate I place. If my candidate does not work out, that is if he either quits or is fired in that first year, I guarantee that I will provide a replacement candidate at no charge to my client. This guarantee is ample motivation for me to ensure that every candidate that I present to my client companies is ready, willing and able to do the target job successfully.

The criteria that define willing and able include not only the candidate's educational background and work experience, but also the harder-to-define "cultural fit." Some companies are loose and informal. Dot.com companies, who were most of my clients during the 90's, were notoriously informal. Foosball table in the lobby, beer in the fridge, shorts and t-shirt as the corporate uniform.

I had to know and understand all of these intangibles in order to determine if a given candidate was a cultural fit. On the other hand, I must understand the candidate's true personality as well. Many candidates, motivated to land a job, will say that they would be happy to work in an informal environment.

However, the truth is that many candidates were not good fits for the dot.com way of working, and left, unable to cope with the chaotic environment. The only way to determine a candidate's true motivations and feelings is to apply case officer skills.

I spent numerous hours with my candidates, either on the phone, via email, or in person, learning their personal interests, habits, likes and dislikes, desires, motivations, in effect what makes them tick. This understanding of their personal background, in addition to a deep understanding of their professional background, has given me a 100% successful placement rate. I have never had to provide a replacement candidate. My success is due, in large part to my vetting skills.

Not only the personal and cultural issues need to be vetted when considering candidates in a search. The first order of business is to determine that the background information the candidate provides on his resume is accurate and a true reflection of his life's work.

Close scrutiny of the resume and the candidate's other documents provides me with the ammunition I need to begin vetting. I focus on schools and degrees. I note dates and the length of each experience. I note significant duties and responsibilities. I research the schools, the degrees, the majors, the companies, supervisors, each fact in that candidate's background. Using the internet and other sources, I educate myself on each facet of the candidate. Once I have this base of knowledge, I begin conversations with the candidate. The conversations are not interrogations, nor are they interviews. These vetting conversations, using my case officer experience and training, allow me to build a complete picture of the candidate, personal and professional, and to vet his background and experience.

If a candidate says that he graduated from Bradley University in Peoria, Illinois, I might ask him what downtown Peoria smells like. The ethanol distillery makes the downtown smell like beer. This could lead to a conversation about drinking beer, or about the pluses and minuses of living in the Midwest.

I lead the conversation where it needs to go, constantly assessing the candidate and his answers. In this manner, in the course of five to ten hours of conversations with a candidate, I am able to vet their personal and professional backgrounds to the degree of certainty required for me to present them as a viable candidate to my client.

My highly developed ability to spot a story that is not straight, to understand what motivates a candidate or agent, to dive deeply into any subject or issue, and overall understanding of human nature across cultures, has resulted in a near-perfect track record in both intelligence operations and executive recruiting. I am aware of both my strengths and my weaknesses. Vetting and CI investigations are my strengths.

The point of these stories is to illustrate the necessity of pointed, probing investigations into the background, actions, words, associations, and every other facet of a subject's life and work. Nothing can be sacrosanct or off-limits when conducting CI research.

Application of CI Experience to Willing Accomplices

I approached the research into the subjects of this book in the same spirit of candid CI investigation that I have applied to any intelligence agent with or against whom I have worked in my career, or any executive candidate I have placed. A subject's simple denials are just that, denials, and mean nothing. Attempts to change the subject do not sway me. I focus like a laser beam on my subject, and follow the path, documentary, circumstantial or narrative, wherever it may lead.

It is with this spirit of truth-seeking, fully informed by extensive experience in espionage, that I have applied my skills to the issue of researching Soviet communist covert influence agents and operations against America. While no one can ever claim to be 100 percent accurate, I believe that my research and vetting skills and analytical conclusions concerning intelligence operations are among the best.

Weak American Counterintelligence

The target of the campaign, the American populace, was all but defenseless. There was no national counter-intelligence authority. No government agency was maintaining vigilance on the communists and their Willing Accomplices moving among us. There was no counter-terrorism agency to protect us from those who intended to destroy our way of life.

In the 21st century, Islamic extremists have philosophies and goals—American culture is sick and a threat, and therefore must be destroyed—similar to the 20th century communists. Now our entire security apparatus works to identify, track, engage and disrupt and destroy those who mean us harm. *Viz* Anwar al-Awlaki, an American citizen, Islamic extremist. Reports are that the American security system is working to assassinate him.

During the 1920-1950 era, the U.S. government labored under the misapprehension that the Soviets were our friends. Due to the Russians' taking our side against the Germans in WW2, it seems that Americans charged with protecting us from enemies, domestic and foreign, gave the communists a pass. In fact, the American counter-intelligence infrastructure, during the rise of the U.S.S.R., was minimal at best and incompetent at worst.

Responsible for identifying threats to America, it appears that the FBI and other national agencies focused less on "subversion," (except for the early 1900s focus on anarchists) and more on those planning physical violence. It was much easier to find an anarchist's bomb laboratory than it was to find the mental bomb laboratory of covert influence.

Besides the FBI, both the Army and the Navy had CI organizations during this era. It seems that these separate CI groups were not comprehensive, did not understand their enemy, and did not cooperate, or share information.

During WW2, the CIA's predecessor, the Office of Strategic Coordination (OSS), also had CI functions. However, the OSS was riddled with communist penetrations, and worked with the KGB against the Nazis. Thus, there was no real, effective, national CI office during the decades of maximum Willing Accomplice covert influence operations.

Although analysts and commentators, William Randolph Hearst among them, noted the potential for communist subversion, and spoke up about the problem, these voices were drowned out by Willing Accomplices.

Joseph McCarthy, the House Un-American Activities Committee, Richard Nixon, Roy Cohn, and others became household names during a brief period of anti-communist investigations. The irony, for America today, is that virtually all of the accusations made by the investigators, now vilified by the PC Willing Accomplices, were on target.

CI Methodology to Identify Willing Accomplices

My method of identifying Willing Accomplices relies on my expert analysis as an intelligence operator with extensive experience in recruiting agents for covert operations. I considered suspects who were active in the time frame of about 1917 to around 1940. This was the height of the KGB covert influence operation.

There are three indicators associated with individuals who were Soviet covert influence agents:

Visited the USSR?

Success not consistent with recent past?

Content of work consistent with Muenzenberg creed?

Each KGB Willing Accomplice I've identified was positive for these indicators—visits to Russia, success inconsistent with past, and content of work consistent with the Muenzenberg creed.

Those three indicators, I believe, are circumstantial evidence of a subject being a covert influence agent, a Willing Accomplice. Because we do not have access to the Active Measure cables, CI analysis like this is the best we can do to identify the Willing Accomplice agents.

An additional CI indicator is a subject's association with overt Communist organizations, or covert fronts, such as the Muenzenberg's Popular Front organizations like the Friends of Soviet Russia.

However, many people dabbled in these organizations, and even belonged to the American Communist Party, without performing services for the KGB. In fact, overt affiliation with Communist organizations is almost a disqualifier for the KGB to have used a candidate for covert influence.

This methodology to retrospectively identify Willing Accomplices, during the era of the KGB's maximum covert influence operations is effective, as we'll see.

However, there were surely Willing Accomplices who did not match the three indicators. That is, the KGB could have developed an influence agent outside the USSR. Thus, there are surely covert influence agents who never visited the USSR. However, the second and third indicators bring to light almost any covert influence agent.

The agent was likely to have enjoyed success, even if he had not been to Russia. And his point of view had to be consistent with Muenzenberg's creed, otherwise he would not have been influencing in the KGB's desired direction. So, even if the first is not met, the second and third indicators alone have the potential to identify agents.

These indicators are quite powerful. I believe that anyone who is positive for all three indicators, during the right era, can be considered nearly 100% as a Willing Accomplice.

First Indicator—Visited the USSR

The first indicator, visits to Russia, is one of the most important. In the Soviet Union, the KGB owned the turf, and could arrange absolutely anything required to advance an operation against an unsuspecting American target.

I interviewed a former KGB officer who worked against the American target in the USSR. He revealed that any American of potential operational interest who visited the USSR would come to the KGB's attention at the Russian embassy in Washington, upon submission of a visa application.

According to research gathered by Wolin and Slusser, published in 1957 in *The Soviet Secret Police*, aliens residing in the U.S.S.R. were always subject to intense scrutiny by the KG.

In any case, aliens were never left out of sight by the state security organs. Only the degree of surveillance varies.

Wolin and Slusser provide an interesting view of the development and assessment process:

> The subjects investigated by the state security organs in connection with aliens in the U.S.S.R. are in general as follows: business activities; personal and private life; character, nature, inclinations, weaknesses, habits, enthusiasms, interests; moral character; business and personal affairs (career, financial resources, family relations, etc.); political views and attitude to political events and developments; attitude to Communism in general and to the Soviet Union in particular; and all types of connections, visits, and interests in the Soviet Union.

The foreigner planning to visit the Soviet Union became a target before he even left his home country. And when he arrived in the Soviet Union, the real work began for the KGB:

> The work is carried out by a twofold method -- investigation by agents while the alien is still abroad, before he has been granted a visa to the U.S.S.R., and surveillance by agents on the territory of the U.S.S.R. Surveillance also extends to the members of the alien's family living with him in the U.S.S.R.

Anywhere in the Soviet Union that foreigner went, they would have been under constant observation by KGB co-optees, officers, or agents:

> State security agents are infiltrated among Soviet citizens working in foreign institutions located in the U.S.S.R., Soviet institutions specially established for aliens, and organizations serving the general public but used by aliens as well. Agents entrusted with surveillance of aliens may be secret collaborators of the state security organs or employees recruited in the establishments and institutions concerned.

According to a KGB case officer I interviewed, the KGB viewed journalists, academics, educators, and entertainers as some of their highest level targets. The KGB station in Washington would handle the application of any target of interest, and would notify KGB headquarters in Moscow immediately.

According to the KGB officer, a plan of operation would be put in place in Moscow. The visiting American would be surrounded by KGB personnel, from landing to departure. Every facet of the American's visit would be stage-managed and controlled.

The goal of such an operation is the same as the goal of any human intelligence (humint) operation: to obtain assessment data on the target, in order to obtain the target's cooperation in intelligence operations. The KGB would provide translators, tour guides, drivers, girls, boys, food, drink, drugs, or whatever the target's heart desired. The target would find himself in a fantasy world where his every wish could come true.

The target would discover a new best friend among the many people whom he met in Russia. This "best friend" would be the recruiting KGB case officer, or his surrogate. By the end of his visit to Russia, regardless of how long his stay, the KGB would have a thorough understanding of the target's motivations, personality, desires, needs, plans, hopes, wishes, habits, loves, hates, and every other personal quirk and fancy. The KGB excelled at identifying motivators, and in providing solutions to target's problems.

This assessment would result in a pitch, either overtly by the KGB, or covertly, by a cover organization such as a Friendship Society, a university, a company, or any cover mechanism that helped in the operation.

Some targets require the ability to maintain a "fig leaf" for their own mental health. Even though they may suspect that they are working for Soviet intelligence, the use of a cover organization or person allows them to maintain the fiction, in their own mind, and with anyone who might question them in the future, that they are actually in league with an ostensible "International Organization of Journalistic Excellence," or a Viennese cinema production company, or a German University research foundation. The KGB were masters at providing such fig leafs to their targets.

Regardless of the cover used, any American target active in the transmission belts of American culture would have been targeted by the KGB when visiting Russia.

The KGB so thoroughly controlled every aspect of Russian society and life that, from the beginning of the Soviet communist government, until the end, virtually nothing happened in Russia without the KGB's knowledge or control.

KGB Recruitment of Foreigners in Russia

In 1987, the U.S. State Department published a *Report on Active Measures*. Excerpted was an interview with two KGB officers, Stanislav Levchenko and Ilya Dzhirkvelov, originally published in the February 20, 1987 issue of *Russkaya Mysl*, a Parisian weekly. Both officers said they "were KGB agents directly involved in active measures operations prior to their defections."

These two case officers explained how pervasive the KGB's work against foreigners was in Russia. Specifically for covert influence, they said that no foreign journalist, or other target who could help in the influence ops, could escape the KGB's recruitment ops.

Dzhirkvelov had worked in the largest directorate of the KGB, "which carrie[d] out counterintelligence work against foreigners and Soviet citizens connected with foreigners," in the Soviet Union.

He said that, during his time in the KGB, his unit had specifically targeted journalists, because the KGB and the Soviet leadership "excellently understand that journalists are people who create public opinion in the West and are able to be used as agents of influence."

Dzhirkvelov explained that the KGB

> had detailed information on each foreigner arriving in the Soviet Union. We received this information from archived material and from our agents overseas. We were always interested in the past and present of an arriving journalists, his views, his hobbies, etc., that is anything that could be used with him during his time of work [in the USSR]. I myself personally worked with foreign journalists – Americans, Germans, and French.

For journalists who did not speak Russian, the KGB provided them with secretaries and translators. Each of these helpers was a KGB source. These sources, in many cases, became very close to their targets. In some cases, these sources would actually run the operation—as we've seen with Alexander Gumberg. We'll also see that Professor George S. Counts was handled by his "secretary/assistant," Nucia Lodge, throughout his career as a Willing Accomplice.

The KGB was responsible for all aspects of foreigners' lives in the Soviet Union, not even "a change of apartment [or] anything similar could be decided without the agreement of the [KGB's] Second Main Directorate."

In addition, the two KGB case officers noted that the KGB specialized in recruiting Russian "émigrés who are already in the West." They note that the immigrants can be controlled from Russia, even when they lived in America. This sort of control was most often done by threatening family members, or other types of blackmail or coercion. Sometimes such immigrants were willing to cooperate for other reasons—ideological or other.

Second Indicator: Success Not Consistent with Recent Past

Espionage case officers generally recruit agents by solving problems for a candidate agent. For an academic, problems in their profession might be lack of high–level publications. For a journalist, a professional problem might be inability to cultivate the right sources to beat the competition to the good stories. For a screenwriter, a professional problem might be that they don't fit in to the social scene in Hollywood.

A case officer can solve all of those problems, and more. A common misunderstanding of recruiting is that people commit espionage "for money." That is nonsense. No one is "motivated by money." The only character I know of who is motivated by money is Uncle Scrooge McDuck. He has a vault in his basement full of cash that he swims in. Other people are motivated by human needs. Very few people are so self-actualized that they are invulnerable.

Good case officers will find any target's needs, and solve those problems. In the case of most influence agents, those problems are professional.

Journalists need constant access to sources who can provide them with scoops. Academics need access to information they can use in their research. Hollywood screenwriters need the right connections to be able to work on good projects.

A journalist suddenly has access to a political figure who no other journalist has been able to interview. His scoop catapults him to the highest levels of journalistic excellence. He may win awards—like the Pulitzer Prize.

An academic is suddenly allowed to travel to an area to conduct research that no other professor in his field has been able to visit.

His ground-breaking research may earn him a place as an expert in his field.

A screenwriter is suddenly able to make the right connections to gain work in high-level movies. Her writing might win awards, or cement her reputation.

Personal success might also include new cars, new houses, international travel, high fashion, or other indicators of success that were not present in the recent past.

This is not an all inclusive list of indicators of sudden success. But this probably captures the majority of CI indicators.

When someone has been plugging along in their field for some time, with no remarkable success, and then they suddenly achieve a stunning coup that catapults them to the top of their field, my CI antenna go up.

When the subject's sudden success is in a field that is connected to the Russians, then it is fair to say that the chance of a simple coincidence is slim.

Coupled with recent travel to the Soviet Union sudden professional or personal success is highly suspicious.

Third Indicator: Content of Work Consistent with Muenzenberg Creed

The third major CI question is the clincher. If the first two are positive, and this one is too, it is fair to say that the subject is a Willing Accomplice, and performed covert influence work for the KGB.

The judgment of consistency with the Muenzenberg creed is not simple. The point of covert influence is that the message, the payload, is subtle, not overt propaganda.

Therefore, a CI analyst must consider the overall tenor of a subject's work, and focus specifically on issues that were of interest to the KGB most at the time of the work.

Thus, during the early days of the Soviet Union, when the KGB, in response to Stalin's demands, was working to influence the U.S. to recognize the Soviet Union diplomatically, an analyst must be on the alert for subtle support for that issue.

From the beginning to the end of the USSR, the KGB's goal in covert influence was to destroy the U.S. by undermining our culture, as reflected in Babette Gross's enumeration of the Muenzenberg covert influence creed.

The presence of one or more of the talking points from the Muenzenberg creed demonstrates the subject's point of view is in line with the anti-American influence payload, and is a CI flag.

CI Analysis Test Case—Known KGB Covert Influence Agent—Vicky Pelaez

To test my three-indicator CI analysis, let's run it against a recent example of a known KGB covert influence agent.

Vicky Pelaez was one of the KGB Ten, NOC officers and agents arrested in the U.S. during 2010. The Obama administration quickly sent the KGB officers and their agents to Russia, with few questions asked.

To an experienced case officer, and CI professional, the role of each of the 10 in the KGB illegal station was obvious.

Pelaez's role was covert influence agent in the Spanish language press. She inserted influence payloads that were virtually unchanged from Muenzenberg's operations. Why change a good thing when it's working?

First Question: Visit to Russia?

Pelaez did not visit Russia that we know of. However, she did subject herself to complete communist control, which was equivalent to visiting Russia during Soviet control.

In 1984, she was "kidnapped" for one day by communist rebels in her home country. She had been a sensationalist TV reporter in her native Peru for a few years. During the time that she was under the communists' power, she obtained an exclusive interview with their leader.

So, a stint under absolute control of communist intelligence is a "yes," for the first question.

Second Question: Success not consistent with recent past?

After Pelaez's "kidnapping," she had sudden access to sources of "news" that no one else had, and that she had never had before. She was suddenly an international celebrity. The articles she wrote, based on her communist sources were eagerly sought by international news organizations.

In 1986, Pelaez, it appears, took advantage of the illegal alien asylum law in the U.S. to gain residency in the U.S. Although she had never spent time in the U.S., her handlers faked her papers to appear that she had been in America long enough to meet the requirements of the law.

Once in America, with her Russian case officer husband, who was her handler, Pelaez was granted citizenship. She began work for Spanish language papers in the U.S. She was quickly successful, and built a middle-class lifestyle, with houses and cars, exceeding of her previous life-style.

By 2010, the U.S. asylum system had rewarded her with American citizenship. She had a high-profile job in New York, and a middle-class lifestyle, complete with a comfy home in the suburbs of New York City. Pelaez's material circumstances were definitely improved from her pre-recruitment life.

Third Question: Content of Work Consistent with Muenzenberg Creed?

Since her kidnapping, Pelaez's point of view, revealed in her articles, matched the KGB's anti-American point of view almost perfectly. She was known as a rabidly anti-American writer after her arrival in the U.S. Let's take a look at two bits from randomly selected articles, one from 2007 and one from 2009.

A sample from a Pelaez editorial in *El Diario* in 2009, translated from Spanish scorched the policies of her adopted country. She wrote that the U.S. refused to listen to "the opinion of the majority of countries in the world, the Big Boss [the United States] supported the putchists'...illegal [Honduran] presidential elections..."

Pelaez finished her anti-American rant, written in her comfortable suburban house in Yonkers, NY, with a tired revolutionary screech, "as long as injustice and poverty remain dominant, the struggle will continue."

In another editorial, written in 2007, Pelaez shared her opinion on English-speaking America's threat to Hispanic culture. In an anti-imperial screech that included a diatribe against McDonalds and Kentucky Fried Chicken, the Russian influence agent wrote: "[Gentrification] consists of eradicating national cultures and traditions, converting the world into a global village and allowing only the values of North American culture to develop."

The 2009 article is an elaboration of Muenzenberg's payload of American imperialism and fascism. Right out of the playbook of Willi's Willing Accomplice influence operation from the 1920s.

The 2007 article riffs on Muenzenberg's creed. Specifically Pelaez attempted to play the notes of the tune against America, as an "almost insanely xenophobic place, murderously hostile to foreigners."

It is clear that Pelaez's sentiments, as reflected in the contents of her work, are fully consistent with the Muenzenberg creed.

Final Analysis—Three Strikes and You're Out

So, we see that Vicky Pelaez, a known Russian covert influence agent, provides a positive result. Three out of three positive indicators show that our subject is extremely likely to be a covert influence agent.

She subsequently pled guilty, and was accepted by the Russian government in a spy swap. The Russians later provided her with a pension. Her husband acknowledged his status as a KGB officer living under an alias, and proudly asserted his loyalty to the KGB.

It's interesting to note that at the time of Pelaez's recruitment, 1984 at the latest, the Soviet Union still existed. Therefore, she was a KGB agent. When the Soviet Union fell, clearly the new Russia kept Pelaez on as an influence agent. Her payload may have been adjusted somewhat, but it appears that her message could have been written by Muenzenberg—America sucks.

With this analysis of the Pelaez case, we see that a known KGB covert influence agent is clearly identified using the 3-question indicator screening.

Thus, we can have confidence that this is a strong analytical tool to identify KGB covert influence agents. Now we can apply the tool to historical suspects.

PART 4

AGENTS REVEALED

Chapter 1

Willing Accomplice in Academia and Education: Dr. George S. Counts

Review

Up to this point *Willing Accomplices* has worked toward laying out the background to prove the hypothesis that KGB covert influence operations created Political Correctness and the Progressive political agenda in American today.

I've laid out my unique qualifications for conducting this CI analysis. We've examined the background of the KGB's covert action program, and its genesis with Lenin. We identified the reasons behind the Soviets' decision to create operations to destroy the American spirit and culture. We examined examples of KGB covert action operations, and heard from their case officers.

We identified the specific targeted domains of the KGB's covert influence operations—the transmission belts of culture—the media, education/academia, and Hollywood.

We explored the reasons that a paper trail has not yet surfaced publicly to provide documentation of the Comintern covered KGB covert influence operations.

We looked at a recent case of Russian espionage covert influence operations against the U.S., Vicki Pelaez.

We've explored Willi Muenzenberg's role as the covert influence genius who wrote the influence payload. And we've examined his use of the Comintern, cover organizations, fronts, and Innocents Clubs, to gain access to the pool of potential influence agents in America.

We looked at the American cultural milieu in the years between the World Wars. We explored the reasons that some Americans were vulnerable to a philosophy that denigrated their country while, at the same time, provided them with justification for feeling superior to the American "moron millions."

We saw how this feeling and set of beliefs inculcated by the KGB's operation, the Muenzenberg Creed, is nearly identical to today's PC-Progressive set of beliefs.

We've also studied a CI analysis methodology that provides a 3-question screening test to indicate whether a suspect can be considered a covert influence agent for the KGB.

Now let's put this all together, and identify some of Muenzenberg's American Willing Accomplices.

CI Analysis—Eight Decades Later

Conducting a CI investigation from 80 years distance may seem more difficult than examining a contemporary suspect. And it may be. However, it is probably easier in some ways, especially when considering covert influence suspects.

Covert influence leaves a large footprint, even when done subtly. There is a product—a newspaper article, a book, a speech, a movie, a lecture—something relatively public that communicates the covert payload.

The point of a covert influence operation is to influence the target culture. This requires mass communication. The KGB's Muenzenberg operation cranked out influence products by the ton.

Finding the influence production of our suspects is relatively easy. And analyzing the products is relatively easy, since we now have the benefit of Babette Gross's recitation of the Muenzenberg Creed. Prior to her admission of this Creed to Stephen Koch, one had to rely on a gut feeling that, for example, Walter Duranty was "Stalin's Apologist," and leave it at that.

Making the connection between a suspect's being an "apologist" for the communists, and his being an actual influence agent left a writer open to being attacked as a "conspiracy nut," or a "Red scare" fear-monger.

No longer.

We can now identify the gist of a suspect's influence message, boil it down to its essence, and compare this essence with the Creed.

Examining suspects from a distance of decades, we also have the benefit of easily available search tools—to find records of travel to Russia, for example.

We are also more or less immune to the tactics of Andemca that contemporaneous investigations met. Consider the absolutely horrific abuse that Senator McCarthy had to endure during his investigations of communists in the government, or the abuse heaped on the investigators of Alger Hiss.

The counter-accusations hurled by the PC-Progressives and their political predecessors complicate any investigation, and are liable to at least be a distraction. The benefit of conducting this analysis from 8 decades is that we will avoid some of those distractions. (Once the PC-Progressives catch wind of the conclusions in Willing Accomplices, however, the counter-accusations are likely to fly thick and fast.)

Let's use our 3-question analytical screening Willing Accomplice identification tool on selected suspects from the Muenzenberg era. We'll look at a suspect from each of the KGB's targeted domains, beginning with Academia and Education.

I selected these suspects based on the third indicator of the CI screening test—based on their public writings, pronouncements, speeches, by the content of their work being consistent with the Muenzenberg Creed. Once a suspect was identified as positive for the third question, I then researched in-depth the first two criteria to determine those answers.

Here are the results.

Carbondale, Illinois
August, 2009

The slow pace of the town in Southern Illinois's Little Egypt (the delta between the Mississippi and Ohio Rivers) is made even slower by the storm damage. A freak straight-line wind storm hit the town hard, several months before. Evidently the cost of clearing all the fallen trees exceeded the budget of the University, and the town. Across campus numerous huge trees and branches littered the wooded areas. Most of the green was cleared, and sidewalks were passable. The buildings, many of them thrown up during the GI Bill boom times of the 1950s and 1960s, appeared shabby and tawdry—concrete and brick, shorn of their protective trees.

It was a homecoming, of sorts. This is where I met my wife, where I completed most of my BA degree. Carbondale, home of Southern Illinois University. I'd spent two years after military service here. Bought my first home here—an eight by forty-eight foot mobile home. Worked in the library, delivered pizzas, ran a typing service, sold used cars to foreign students. Hustled and studied.

A couple hours' drive from St Louis, Carbondale's economy was clearly hurting. Ever since coal had dwindled as an industry, the delta region had almost no viable source of income.

The library was newly renovated. The old entry hallway, with a statue of D. Morris, where I had manned the security desk, had been converted to a side hall, and the statue moved out into the elements. Checking in with the Archives staff, I had to surrender my belongings, everything except a pencil and my laptop.

The archive attendant pushed out a cart loaded with boxes from the Counts collection. She only allowed me to browse through one box at a time. Waiting for the first folder, I thought back to the phone interview with my old SIU professor, Dr. Aikman.

Retired for the last twenty years, Dr. Aikman had taught in SIU's education department since the 1950s. He had known George Counts, and had been his colleague. Aikman's description of the elderly Counts, in SIU Education department faculty meetings, spouting Greek and shuffling to his seat, helped to make Counts real to me.

I'd taken many classes in the same rooms where Counts had taught. In my Teaching English as a Second Language undergraduate major, and then when I'd returned for graduate studies in Instructional Design, Education classes were prominent in my course load.

This was where I'd seen PC-Progressivism first hand for the first time. In Education classes, Counts' philosophy of collectivism, and American non-exceptionalism took center stage. Along with Dewey's child-centered curriculum, which denigrated the need for society to prepare children for actual roles in the economy, instead advocating for children to guide their own studies, Counts' and other Progressive Education ideas dominated the School of Education.

It was where I had discovered that there was surely no place for me in this PC-mafia dominated profession. I had learned how to plan and structure lessons, and how to be an Instructional Designer, but the ugly PC of Education scared me.

Spending time inside the secret lair of American Education schools would convince most people to keep their kids away from the brain-washing that graduates of Education schools are prepared to inflict on their students.

With great anticipation, I attacked the documents in the Counts collection. The first folder dragged me deep into Counts' personality and life. A handwritten autobiographical sketch for a listing in the Directory of American Scholars revealed his high self-regard.

Morning became evening as I examined his Soviet driver's license, Counts' arrogant, irritated eyes peering sideways from behind round, rimless gold spectacles, his neatly trimmed mustache framing his down-turned mouth (picture below).

He did not suffer fools lightly, and in this picture, he clearly felt he was dealing with a fool. His huge collection of typed, and later, hand-transcribed quotes on 3x5 index cards took up several boxes. His secretary had taken care of him well. In the years when Nucia Lodge had been his assistant, she had typed the cards. After he'd left Columbia, the cards were block letter, Counts' own handwriting.

Подпись владельца удостов

Срок настоящего удостоверения продлен

по 193 г.

Зав. Отд. печати НКИД

Counts must have been humiliated by the need to prostitute himself to a little jerkwater university. After decades of being quoted on the front page of the New York Times, being toasted by intellectuals and politicians around the world, influencing policies, how down-

market must Carbondale have been for Counts?

The Education School was housed in a three story brick building that looked a lot like an elementary school. After 30 years at Columbia's marble palaces, what did Counts think every morning when he crossed the parking lot on Clocktower Drive. Counts' attempts to change to world, his revolutionary calls to remake America, with blood and bullets, if necessary, had not led him to the halls of power. They'd led him to almost literally nowhere.

After two days of immersion in the remnants of Counts' scholarly life, I was left with more questions than answers. I'd discovered that there were almost no documents from before Counts' arrival in Illinois. His daughter, Martha, told me in a telephone conversation that he had destroyed his papers when he left Columbia, in the mid-1955. It seemed that Counts had overstayed his welcome there, maybe because of the heat of the anti-communist investigations, maybe because of his age, but Columbia asked him to leave.

And Martha said that, in a fit of pique, the little man had burned everything. For someone with such a massive sense of self-importance, of his own historical importance, and a massive output of writing, it must have been a huge undertaking, psychically and physically. His papers were surely his babies. He produced nothing in his life but thoughts and words. His papers represented his thoughts and words. What drove him to destroy the lot? Was there something that he wanted to hide?

His works in the fifteen years following his arrival at Columbia were revolutionary screeds extolling the superiority of collectivism and educational methods of indoctrination.

He had been in touch with myriad Soviets, American leftists, and Willing Accomplices. He had been a member and leader of many Willing Accomplice organizations. He must have had a huge collection of membership files, agendas, meeting minutes, planning documents, and more from his days as a Soviet stooge.

Having left the service of Soviet intelligence in the late 1940s, he must have panicked when he realized the evidence that had accumulated in his Columbia office. Did he destroy the incriminating items long before he left Columbia? Or did he not destroy them, and they are sitting in a box, in an archives or an attic somewhere even now, waiting for the truth to be documented?

Until his lost papers show up, I can only base my analysis on the remnants he left behind, which he must have believed to be non-incriminating: his Soviet drivers license; a notebook with contacts in Moscow he and Nucia Perlmutter had jotted down before his first visit; postcards the little professor collected in Russia.

Later items of great value he left in his Carbondale papers included a series of letters with his Russian companions from his driving trip across Russia, chronicled in his little book: A Ford Crosses Russia.

In early 1964, Counts attempted to raise funds to repeat his 6,000 mile car trip across Russia. He recontacted the Soviet handlers who had accompanied him, and pitched them the idea. A correspondence ensued, over the next couple years, as Counts futilely attempted to convince the communists to give him a visa to enter the USSR. The KGB, with a full file on the turncoat, would never authorize his visit. But the letters that resulted from the idea are full of unspoken secrets shared between comrades.

Taking a coffee break in Morris Library's soaring atrium, with a Starbucks kiosk brewing latte, Counts' rhetoric bounced around my brain. This little man talked and wrote, and wrote and talked. Enabled by the Soviets, he had ruined American education. I put down my grande cappuccino and gazed out on the storm-wracked campus through the huge atrium windows.

If only there was a smoking gun in those boxes—a note from his handling case officer, an accounting for expenses reimbursed by the KGB. But the clues and insights come thick and fast. More time in the archives could pay dividends. Intriguing leads to the archived papers of the John Day Publishing Company, at Princeton University's library, add an item to my to-do list. This is one search that probably won't be over soon.

Baltimore
February 1932

The hall was packed. A chilly February evening in the dead of winter. Yet the audience, packed into the small hall, standing room only, was steaming hot. The little wiry man, after his introduction by the chairman of the Progressive Education Association, stepped up to the podium.

In a strong tenor voice, he wove a hypnotizing tale. The world, as his audience knew it, was rotten. They raptly followed his rapid fire delivery. Fact piled upon anecdote, the mustachioed, bespectacled professor had seen the future—and it worked.

He plied the listeners with intoxicating tales of Russian peasants cooperatively creating their own learning communities. He told them that America's mythical rugged individualism was dead and dangerous. The audience would lead Americans, willingly or unwillingly, into the bright future of collectivist striving for the communal good.

He told the now spellbound American teachers how, in Russia, experts such as he used a five year plan to guide their efforts. He extolled the excellent results being achieved, ahead of schedule, by the brilliant technologists he knew in the Soviet Union.

Riding the wave of tension and excitement, George Sylvester Counts pounded the podium as he delivered his final pronouncement to the dumb-struck teachers: "If democracy is to be achieved in the industrial age, powerful classes must be persuaded to surrender their privileges."

The little professor strolled over to his chair to the left of the podium, on the stage, and sat down. Self-satisfied and smug, he smoothed his mustache. The audience, stunned, began to buzz. The teachers were not sure if they had heard right.

Counts stood up. He adjusted his coat, and approached the podium. He glanced at his notes. The crowd hushed. Counts declared, his high pitched voice echoing throughout the hall, "Ruling classes never surrender their privileges voluntarily!"

He went on, "If a bold and realistic program of education is not forthcoming, we can only anticipate a struggle of increasing bitterness terminating in revolution and disaster!"

Some in the assembly of Progressive teachers were unsure if they had heard the professor correctly. Had he just advocated the violent overthrow of the constitutional government of the United States? Was he advocating a revolution, and that it be led by teachers?

Many of the teachers crowded around Counts after his speech. Teachers questioned him. Hands thrust through the ring of questioners to slap his back.

In the first class compartment of the late train to New York that night, Counts was ablaze with fervor. He had done it. An almost direct call for violence. The repressed ardor for collectivism was finally released from his small breast. Now the world could see that he was a lion, not a Midwestern lamb. He folded the notes that Nucia Perlmutter had typed for his speech, slid them into his coat's inside pocket, leaned back in the richly upholstered chair, closed his eyes, and dreamed.

Counts' dreams were vivid and satisfying. He was the American Education Commissar. He'd seen how the Russians respected their commissar. He held complete sway over all education matters. He would create a five year plan, spelling out in excruciating detail, for the dunces he controlled, exactly how to achieve the goals set out in the Chairman's Five Year Plan.

Counts smiled in his sleep. The porter, passing by his compartment, looked in to offer service. The evil smile twisting the face of the little professor shocked the porter. He withdrew without a word, and made a mental note to avoid that compartment.

Background

His life was enmeshed in the sweeping arc of historic upheavals in American society, education, and academia. At the same time, he was drawn into, or stepped into, the titanic clash of civilizations—capitalism versus communism, American rugged individualism versus European sophist collectivism, republican democracy versus totalitarian dictatorship, and as can be seen in hindsight: good versus evil. George Sylvester Counts witnessed, and participated in, the tectonic shifts of American culture.

As we will see, the Russian communists built him a platform, and provided him with a message, which he delivered very effectively during a turning point in American history.

This professor of Comparative Education, knowing nothing about Russia, became in less than five years, a leading expert on Soviet education, and a "translator" of a Soviet primary school textbook that explained Stalin's Five Year Plan.

Counts' breathless explanations of the beauty and wisdom of collectivist central planning was accepted at face value by a guileless American public, not yet made cynical by the countless lies of the emerging forces of the American Left.

Counts' writings and speeches were so influential and powerful in American academia and education that his Soviet-provided messages have been, and continue to be, even today, among the most powerful and quoted theories in American Schools of Education.

His *Dare the School Build a New Social Order* speeches and publications galvanized the education industry. Teachers flocked to his Progressive movement, basking in his assertions that their profession, long a backwater, under-appreciated province of women and milquetoast young men, had the power to actually transform American culture.

The transformation into a collectivist utopia was, Counts assured them, within their grasp. All the teachers needed to do was to organize, unionize, and professionalize, become part of the Elite Vanguard, and they could have the prize.

My counter-intelligence analysis reveals, for the first time, the role of his "secretary/assistant" in the covert influence intelligence operation conducted by the KGB. Nucia Perlmutter Lodge was an almost perfect KGB covert influence handler.

The KGB's influence op used Counts as a channel to insert the Muenzenberg Creed covert payload into American education and academia.

Although Counts seemed to turn against his Soviet collaborators in his later career, he never renounced the point of view which made him a hero to anti-American forces. His books and the Counts Manifesto have influenced the training, education, and educational philosophies and practices of several generations of American teachers, including those teaching, and training teachers, today.

Early Life

Counts was born in Baldwin City, eastern Kansas in 1889, the third of six children in a farming family. His parents valued formal education highly and sacrificed to send the young Counts and his siblings to the good public schools in Baldwin. After graduating high school, Counts entered Baker College in his hometown in 1907, and graduated in 1911. All but one of Counts' siblings graduated from the College.

How many young Americans were fortunate enough to receive such an education? Counts' parents sacrificed to provide their children with this education, moving their household to be closer to a town which offered such fine education. Many families could not afford such a move, or were unaware of the opportunities. They made do with a simple education of ABC's, basics of reading, and simple math.

Some were able to continue through high school, learning a solid curriculum of math and science, history and language. But most American schools were not in the same league as that enjoyed by Counts.

Counts was afforded as thorough a classical education as an American boy on the Midwestern prairie could expect. He studied Latin and Greek. He soaked up the glories of ancient civilizations that had passed on their traditions to the young United States. He learned of the deeds of Greek and Roman warriors, heroes, gods, and goddesses. Young George soaked up a solid understanding of the foundations of American culture and civilization. He learned of the trials and tribulations, successes and defeats, and the myths and legends of the founding fathers of his own young country.

In short, young George Counts was the beneficiary of a thoroughly grounded, thoroughly American education. The roots of America extended through the centuries through English, European, Roman and Greek civilization, philosophy, and government. Democracy was a fragile thread that ran through this historical fabric. American education of Counts' era made sure that each student grasped this thread firmly and understood the foundations of American government and society.

Counts' solid grounding in logic, rhetoric, composition, writing and debate served him well throughout his studies, and his later career as an academic. He wrote long, well and often. An introduction to one of his books goes on for what seems like forever, as he weaves thread of detail in and out of the narrative.

At Baker, Counts studied "classical and scientific Latin; scientific and modern language; literature and arts, oratory, commercial, normal," subjects.

Wilson Counts, George's younger brother, inherited the family farm in Baldwin. George Counts' nieces and nephews recall a sharp contrast between the two brothers, Wilson and George. Wilson was an engaging and humble uncle who encouraged their interest in his gems and the farm life.

In contrast, a Kansas historian wrote that George, who would stay only several days during the weeks-long family reunions held annually at the farm from 1920 to 1960, would sit and rock on the front porch "lecturing long-windedly."

Academic Career

After earning his bachelor's degree, Counts taught high school science for one school year, and then served as a principal at another high school, both of these in Kansas. In 1913 Counts entered the University of Chicago, where he married a classmate, Lois Bailey, the daughter of a Methodist minister from Kansas, with whom he had two daughters, and remained married the rest of his life. He earned his doctoral degree in education in 1916.

From 1916 to 1920, Counts worked at a series of small colleges in their Education Schools. These included Delaware College (where he was the head of the department of education), Harris Teachers College, and the University of Washington. In 1920 Counts began work at Yale. He described his hiring by Columbia in the preface to a 1931 book—after a short stint at the University of Chicago in 1926, Dr. Counts was hired at the Teachers College of Columbia University (TC) in 1927.

According to his daughter, Martha Counts, Dr. Counts remained on the faculty at TC until his mandatory retirement at age 65 in 1956.

After several visiting professorships, Counts was recruited by Southern Illinois University (SIU) in Carbondale. His name brought immediate credibility to the rural School of Education in the coal-mining country in the delta of the Ohio and Mississippi Rivers. Art Aikman, an SIU Education colleague remembered him at SIU as a small, "bumbling, mumbling man" who kept to himself, made sage wisecracks in

Latin and Greek, sat in the back of the room at faculty meetings, and constantly smoked a pipe. Counts died in southern Illinois in 1974, weeks away from his 85th birthday.

Columbia Teachers College—International Institute

Teachers College (TC) of Columbia University, New York City. He was hired by the new President of TC, Dr William Russell, in 1927. Dr Russell succeeded his father in that post in the same year. Three years earlier, the Rockefeller Foundation had provided a grant to TC to fund the Teachers College International Institute (TCII).

According to Counts' daughter, Martha in an interview in July 2009, Russell recruited Counts because the Institute needed someone who was an expert on Russia. The fact that Counts was not a Russia expert did not seem to make a difference.

Counts' first foray into international education issues was probably where he networked into the TCII. He was part of a team of academic educators who went on a colonial government survey of the educational system in the Philippines in 1924-25.

His colleagues on that trip, according to a contemporary account in the New York Times, Dec. 20, 1924, included the TCII director, Paul Monroe; the Carnegie Foundation's Institute of International Education director, Stephen Duggan; Harold Rugg, another TCII professor; as well as several other TC professors.

Monroe's PhD was from the University of Chicago, like Counts. It's likely that they shared an alumni network, and probably shared similar philosophies of education. For sure, the months-long Philippines journey, via steamship, and their work on the survey placed Monroe, Count, and the TC professors in intimate contact for a prolonged period.

Confluence of Willing Accomplices

Interestingly, Duggan's son, Laurence Duggan succeeded his father to head the Carnegie Foundations Institute of International Education director from 1946 until his suicide in 1948. He jumped from his office window after his spying for the KGB was publicly revealed by Whittaker Chambers.

Duggan's mentor, Edward R. Murrow, also a staffer of the Institute of International Education, made Duggan's case a stable of his Andemca attacks against the largely accurate McCarthy investigations. The Duggan story played a prominent role in a recent PC-Progressive influence movie produced by George Clooney.

This is an interesting case study of all three cultural domains merging together, across the decades, for a covert influence triple whammy—a Willing Accomplice Hollywood director in 2005, creating a movie about a Willing Accomplice in the media who went after Joe McCarthy with an Andemca attack because his friend, a Willing Accomplice in Academia killed himself after being outed as a KGB agent in 1948.

The precise alignment of the main themes of Muenzenberg's covert influence ops could not have been brought together more neatly if Willi had planned it himself.

The Venona files reveal that the younger Duggan was a prolific KGB collection agent during his tenure at the U.S. State Department. And one must assume that he was, like Alger Hiss, also engaged in covert influence operations, at State, and later at his education foundation job.

Networked his Way to TCII

It would appear that Counts' close contact during the Philippines project with the elder Duggan, and the other TC professors, convinced the TCII director to bring Counts on as their "Russia expert" at TCII. In 1927, Russian expert or not, Counts joined TC.

Almost immediately, Counts packed up for his first trip to the Soviet Union. Spending the Rockefeller money (likely a sop to the institution where Rockefeller's two sons, Nelson and David both attended TC's "experimental" Lincoln School), which flowed into TCII at the rate of $100,000 per year, said funding promised for a total of 10 years, seemed to agree with Counts.

Up to 1927, Counts' research and writing had focused on parochial subjects: *The Social Composition of Boards of Education* (1927) and *The Selective Character of American Secondary Education* (1922). But now that he was deemed a Russia expert, he began to act like one.

Counts followed in the footsteps of his TCII boss—William Russell had worked in Russia during the final days of World War I, in the first (and last) official U.S. government propaganda unit, the Committee on Public Information. Russell had been in Siberia, providing American propaganda movies to the locals, exhorting the Russians to maintain their vigilance against the Germans.

While the effort was ultimately a failure, Russell surely built a strong network among the Russians he encountered there. The Bolsheviks were establishing themselves across the breadth of the Russian empire at that time, and were working the Americans heavily.

At Columbia, Counts (writing in the third person) recounted in the preface to a 1931 book, he was hired to be the "associate director of the International Institute, and professor of education in Teachers College...He served as special investigator of education in the Philippines...and in Russia in 1927 and 1929."

Counts claimed in the same book that his trip to the Philippines was in 1927. However, ship manifests document his travel on the SS President Jefferson, departing Manila on May 5, 1925, and arriving Seattle on May 28, 1925.

Counts' trips abroad for TCII were followed by a series of successful publications on Russia in 1929 and the early 1930's. These publications gained him a national reputation as a "Russia expert."

According to Counts, his travels in the Soviet Union included: "[In 1927] approximately three months in Soviet Russia traveling extensively by railroad, visiting institutions of many kinds, and engaging citizens from all walks of life in conversation."

Counts appeared to believe that he was free to go where and as he pleased. If there were any controls over his movements or actions, he was either unaware, or pretended they did not exist.

Handlers in the Ford Crossing Soviet Russia

When he returned to the Soviet Union, in 1929, he said: "I...remained seven months. On this occasion I took a Ford car into the country and during July, August, September, and October, drove approximately six thousand miles through the European part of the Union, from Leningrad across the Caucasus Mountains and from Odessa to Nizhni Novgorod and regions beyond."

Although he did claimed that he was "entirely alone" for just one-sixth of the journey, he still pretended that he could move about freely.

He did not detail who accompanied him, or the level of control they exerted, for the other five-sixths of the trip, "I shaped the route myself and motored entirely alone for about a thousand miles. The major object of the journey was to see at first hand the new construction which was supposed to be under way. It was an illuminating and thrilling experience."

In the SIU archives, Counts' letters reveal the identities of his 1929 companions. In 1964, Counts sought to relive his glory days, to return to Russia and drive his 1929 route again. He wrote to his handlers from the trip—Mikail Bernstein, and Johansen Zilberfarb.

Bernstein hints at the sort of relationship they had in 1929, in his letter from February, 1964, "The chief vice of your last *Challenge* was not that you criticized us but that you were clearly indiscriminant in your choice of sources and your 'ideological' allies."

The scolding tone of a scorned handler comes through in Bernstein's letter. He wants to rekindle the relationship, or at least get "time on target" again.

After his 1929 trip, Counts' daughter Martha said he took a sabbatical year in 1936, and again traveled in the Soviet Union.

As was common knowledge among Counts' contemporaries, no visitors to the Soviet Union in that time period went anywhere without advance coordination with "security," meaning the KGB.

During the latter part of his Columbia tenure, and for several years thereafter, Counts was involved in electoral politics. This included a stint as the President of the American Federation of Teachers (AFT). He ran for the U.S. Senate seat in New York on the Liberal Party ticket, a Party he helped to found.

Ultimately, his political ambitions bore no fruit, and he moved to rural Illinois, living out his life in obscure academia.

Educational Philosophy

Already a proponent of Dewey's Progressive Education philosophy when he arrived at Columbia, Counts became a member of a regular discussion group at TC that included Dewey, William Kilpatrick, and other proponents of radical educational reform.

According to a profile of the group, written in 1951, "This discussion group was probably the most powerful influence in Teachers College; it attracted some of the ablest men in the college, including Dewey, Counts, Childs, Watson, Brunner, Raup, Hartmann, Johnson, Newlon, Bagley, Elliott, the young Dean Russell himself, as well as many others."

The Counts Manifesto:

Individualism is Dead—Long Live Collectivism!

Counts' attitude toward education matured at TC, and with his visits to Russia. Following his publication of the Soviet Union's elementary school text-book, *The New Russia Primer* in 1931, Counts unveiled what I call the "Counts Manifesto." He made a whirlwind series of speeches to professional education organizations, including his Progressive Education Association (PEA) in 1932.

In his bold proclamation, printed as a series of pamphlets capturing his PEA speeches, as *Dare the School Build a New Social Order,* Counts broke with Dewey's ideas of child-centered education, and proclaimed the need for "imposition and indoctrination."

He argued that he and his fellow Progressives had been timid, had professed and theorized, and not acted in concert with their beliefs. Counts' argument was fundamentally Marxist, in tone and terminology, but never referenced Marx. His themes included class, class conflict, anarchy of extreme individualism, race hatred, reconstruction of society; democracy vs. industrial feudalism, capital must belong to the masses, not the favored few.

In his PEA speeches, He spoke (and spoke, and spoke, and spoke) condescendingly of "the masses," "the minds of the masses." He said "natural resources and all important forms of capital will have to be collectively owned."

Counts went on to demand that "the resulting system of production and distribution be made to serve directly the masses of the people."

He ended his speeches with a call to action to his fellow Progressive Educators, in effect a call to bloody revolution: "If democracy is to be achieved...powerful classes must be persuaded to surrender their privileges...this process has commonly been attended by bitter struggle and even bloodshed."

And, in a shot across the bow of the American bourgeoisie, Counts warned his comrades, "Ruling classes never surrender their privileges voluntarily."

Counts continued with his line of argument in later speeches and writing, toning it down for his audience, if necessary.

On Nov. 12, 1934, in an article headlined *Dr. Counts Sees New Social Era...Age of Individualism is Drawing to a Close...Asks Educators to Prepare Public for Collectivism*, he told the New York Times that "America has already entered an era of collectivism."

The Times commented that Counts' call for collectivist reconstruction of society was in accord with a related commission study that "urged educators to help the American people adjust themselves to the emerging collectivist society..."

Thus, the fundamental thrust of Counts' prolific writing during this period called for a revolution, bloody if necessary, in the American education system. His vision was for teachers to lead an inevitable reconstruction of American society.

Counts preached his manifesto throughout the 1930's, and up to the beginning of World War II.

He continued to publish books promoting his Manifesto, including: *A Ford Crosses Soviet Russia* (1930); *The American Road to Culture: A Social Interpretation of Education in the United States* (1930); *Soviet Challenge to America* (1931); *A Call to Teachers of the Nation* (1933); *The Social Foundations of Education* (1934).

Public Identification as an Influence Agent

His very public advocacy for collectivist revolution made Counts fair game for those who disagreed with him. The newspapers of William Randolph Hearst frequently published criticisms of Counts and his comrades. The Progressives did not take the criticism sitting down.

In multiple venues, both spoken and written, Counts and his supporters, practicing the covert action principle of Andemca when exposed, lashed out at the Hearst criticisms. Their responses were personal and, of course avoided the central point of Hearst's criticisms—that the Counts Manifesto was solidly anti-American and pro-collectivist.

Defection?

At some point in the 1940's, Counts made a 180 degree turn in tone and substance. Suddenly, with no explanation, he portrayed himself as an anti-communist. He proceeded to churn out several books on the realities of the Soviet Union. Yet, he never explicitly acknowledged that his earlier infatuation with the USSR was wrong.

He called himself an "anti-communist liberal" for the rest of his life, and got away with it. Not only did Dr. Counts have his cake and eat it too, but he had the frosting, the candles, and got to lick the bowl and the spoon.

Rejection of His American Roots

How to explain that Counts, after leaving his high school in Kansas, and obtaining a PhD in Chicago, turned on his roots? It would appear that his goal, after entering academia, and especially after his visit to the Soviet Union in 1927, was to repudiate everything that made up the core of his culture, but most especially the education system that had created him.

His lifelong professional quest seems to have been to destroy that which had created him. He preached the necessity of Progressive Education. This implied Change, with a capital "C." Things that had been done for decades needed to be Changed. Assumptions needed to be Changed. Attitudes needed to be Changed. Individualism had to Change to Collectivism. Counts saw the future, and had the prescriptions to cure America's ills.

Nucia Perlmutter Lodge—Counts' Assistant and KGB Handler

New York Harbor
October 4, 1910

The SS Noordam, a stalwart of the Holland-America line, blasted her whistle. The one-smokestack steamer smoothly slid through the Narrows, past Liberty Island. The pilot steered the huge ocean liner into the New York harbor. An early October chill, damp and windy, permeated the mouth of the Hudson. The twelve day passage from Rotterdam to New York had seemed like an eternity to the sixteen year old girl. She tightly gripped the railing. Her gloveless hands were cold, but she didn't notice. She shivered as she watched the Statue of Liberty glide by.

Thursday afternoon commuters jammed the ferries plying the route between the Jersey side of the Hudson and the Manhattan piers. The ferries buzzed around like fireflies, darting through the huge ocean-liner's plodding path.

The Noordam carried only first and second class passengers. With no steerage class passengers, she steamed past Ellis Island. Two tugboats guided the passenger steamship through the channel, up the river and into the narrow slots of the Holland-America pier in New Jersey.

Anna Nucia Perlmutter reached into the inner pocket of her simple but solid black coat, and counted the coins, without looking. Fourteen dollars, everything left from the savings her sister had slipped to her when she left Odessa two months ago. Chinsia had choked up, but kept her regal bearing, so important to her. When they had exchanged simple pecks on the cheek, Anna's oldest sister whispered in Yiddish, "Tell Mama I love her. Me and the kids will come as soon as we can."

Anna, so excited to be moving, after months of terrifying waiting in the remains of the crumbling Russian empire, didn't realize that she would never see her sister alive again. Hearing the catch in Chinsia's voice, she ignored it, and chirpily answered back, out loud, "Don't be silly Chinsy. I'll see you in Chicago!"

As positive as she pretended to be, Anna felt a deep pain leaving her sister and their home. The anti-Jewish pogroms in the last several years had split apart their tight-knit community. Anna, her parents and five brothers and sisters would be reunited in Chicago, but Chinsia decided to stay, with her new husband, to build a life together in Odessa.

Chinsia clinging to her arm, she'd climbed onto the agent's wagon, looking over her shoulder as the sway-backed horse pulled the rickety vehicle down the alley, to her destiny. Switching from wagon to train. Jewish welfare committee transit houses. Border crossings. Corrupt guards leering as she passed through the de-lousing showers. At the center in Hamburg she paid two marks for a bed and board: white bread, tea with sugar and milk for breakfast; thin meat and vegetable soup for lunch; milk and sugar in tea with white bread at night.

Now, as she inched down the gangway, her small bag packed with her clothes and books weighing down her thin arms, Anna mentally reviewed her mother's address. Her senses were bombarded by the smell from the Hudson River, the huge debarkation halls on either side of the Holland America's Hoboken pier number five, the broad paved streets with a tangle of telegraph wires and fine trees, just dropping the last of their leaves, the babble of six, eight, ten European languages, and the familiar Yiddish, stevedores calling, stewards urging passengers to move down the ramps, the pervasive stench of manure.

She knew that the immigration inspectors, after the health screening, would ask for her destination. And she was ready: Fannie Perlmutter, 1302 North Roley St, Chicago, Illinois.

She repeated it to herself again, in English. The difficult rhythm and tongue positions of the new language were easy for Anna. She was like a parrot. If she heard a word, in any language, she could repeat it.

Going down the ship's gangplank, Anna was behind the Hines family, Mrs. Hines, three girls and their little brother, Nechemje. Surie Hines, just a year older than Anna, became her new best friend during the crossing. The girls stayed close together, Anna appearing to be one of the Hines family, as they moved through the line into the Holland-America arrival hall.

The cavernous red brick building was organized like a cattle sorting operation. Chutes and stalls guided the mass of immigrants through the stations to the American immigration bureaucrats. Anna's second class ticket bought her out of the chaos of Ellis Island into the more gentile arrival operations at Pier 5. But that was no consolation to Anna.

Surie Hines and the family split off at the first chute. Anna touched Surie's arm, in a gentle gesture of good-bye. Surie, right arm loaded with a bag and a bundle, left hand holding little Neshe's hand, glanced at Anna and sighed, then disappeared into the crush of excited immigrants.

So easy to make friends. So easy to move on. So easy to blend in. So easy to make others think she was something she was not. The first in a series of new relationships developed and lost in Anna's new homeland. October 4, 1910—the first day of the transformation of a little Russian-Jewish girl into a covert communist operator.

Anna Nucia Osipovna Perlmutter Lodge was born in Odessa, in what is now the Ukraine, in February 1894. She seems to have used a variety of names through her life, but finally settled on Nucia, with the family name Lodge taken from a claimed husband (name and identity as yet unknown).

Her family, probably victimized by the recurring anti-Jewish pogroms which swept the region in the late 1800s and early 1900s, fled to America. Her parents, Joseph and Fannie Perlmutter, and Nucia's five sisters settled in Chicago, where they appeared in the 1910 U.S. census, without Nucia. The children are noted as speaking Russian, and the parents as speaking Yiddish. The family claimed to have arrived in 1910.

Nucia arrived in Hoboken, New Jersey, apparently traveling alone, in October 1910, when she was 16 years old, using the name Anna Perlmutter. She indicated her destination to be her mother's address in Chicago, and her next of kin outside the U.S. to be a sister in Odessa. Her native language was listed by the immigration agent as "Hebrew."

Nucia next appears in American records at Clark College in Worcester, Massachusetts, where she earned her Master's degree in Education in 1924, with a thesis titled *History of Education in Russia*. She called herself Nucia Perlmutter.

In a resume that she sent to Cossack General Poliakoff, who was seeking a translator for his Russian language memoir in 1966, Nucia claimed that she graduated from the Mariinsky Gymnasium in St. Petersburg in 1916. If that is the case, she must have returned to Russia after her original arrival in America in 1910.

Her great-niece, Amy Dennis, remembers Nucia's sisters not approving of Nucia and her academic activities dealing with Russia. Amy, whose grandmother was Rayousha, Nucia's oldest sister, said that her grandmother seemed to be a believing Russian Orthodox Christian. Rayousha had Russian icons all over her house. Until my CI research, Amy had not known that her ancestors were originally Jewish.

In fact, Amy said that her grandmother told her that the three sisters, Rayousha, Zenia, and Nucia arrived by ship in New York, soon after the revolution, in 1917. Rayousha said that she and Xenia had gone on to Chicago, and Nucia had stayed in New York to go to school.

According to Amy, "There was a strange thing going on in that household. Grandmother spoke lovingly of Russia, but didn't want to discuss what happened there. A cloud of repressed suffering hung in the air."

The secrets were so thick and impenetrable, that they drove Rayousha's only daughter, Lola Jean Kabrine, to flee the house at 16, and to finally go mad.

Lola Jean adored and idolized her aunt, Nucia. She listed Nucia as her next-of-kin when she enrolled at the University of Chicago in 1943. Lola Jean provided an address in Chicago for Nucia, who actually lived in either New York or Philadelphia at the time, while her own mother, Rayousha, lived less than 15 miles from the University.

The young girl symbolically reached out to her aunt, hoping for contact with her idol. Unfortunately, Nucia was busy. Even this desperate gesture revealed another layer of Nucia's cover—another name—Kay Lodge. So many names, so many places, one small woman.

Until 2010, Amy Kabrine Russell had no idea that the family had come to America with 6 sisters, father and mother. Nor did she know that they were Jewish.

She said that she met Nucia a few times in Chicago, growing up in the 1960s, "Nucia was a bit of an enigma. She was attractive, quiet, serious, small in stature, with dark hair."

It appears that Nucia's sisters' guilty knowledge of what Nucia was really about, and their family secrets, was likely to have created much of the fear and dread that haunted the family.

The mystery of the disappeared father, mother, and five children must also have been part of that heavy atmosphere. Did they die in the 1918 flu epidemic in Chicago? Did they return with Nucia to Russia and then get stuck during the Revolution? Whatever happened, it was not nice or pretty, for the matriarch and patriarch of the family, along with five of their children, seem to have been whisked down the memory hole, never mentioned or acknowledged again.

It's not clear how Nucia portrayed herself to her professional colleagues like Counts, but there is nothing to indicate that she shared her sisters' adherence to Christianity. It's also likely that her sisters had some idea that Nucia was involved with the Bolsheviks. Any Russian of that era knew that to return to Russia under the Bolsheviks was to put yourself under the direct control of the communists.

If we accept that Nucia returned to Russia to finish her schooling in St. Petersburg sometime between 1910 and 1916, that leaves eight years—from 1916 to 1924—unaccounted for in her life after receiving her diploma in St. Petersburg.

These were tumultuous years in Russia, including the revolution and civil war. Watch *Dr. Zhivago* to understand the turmoil.

If her Master's degree took two years of study at Clark, that still leaves 1916 to 1922 as unaccounted in her life.

I believe that Nucia, during those formative years, was deeply involved with the Bolsheviks, possibly in Russia and maybe in the U.S. Her American ties, with her family living there, made her an attractive candidate for KGB espionage work. Much like Alexander Gumberg, she could establish an American persona, totally non-threatening to her American targets.

The KGB's Comintern apparatus could even have sponsored her MA at Clark, preparing her for covert action operations. It appears that she returned to Russia after finishing her MA in Massachusetts.

According to Counts' daughter, Martha, the professor met Nucia on his initial trip to Russia in 1927, where she served as a translator, assistant and secretary to his delegation.

In her resume, Nucia seems to confirm this version of events. She listed her "Assignments in Soviet Russia:"

> **1927**: Interpreter and Secretary to a group of American educators and writers (Paul Douglas, George S. Counts, Stuart Chase, Rexford C. Tugwell, and others). Present at interviews with Stalin, Trotsky, Bukharin, Krupskaya, and many others. Travelled with the delegation from Leningrad to Moscow, Kiev, Kharkov, Crimea, and back to Moscow.
>
> **1929**: Appointed by Teachers College to do educational research in Soviet Russia for one year.
>
> **1930**: Had charge of the American educational exhibit in Leningrad as part of the International Exhibit.
>
> **1931**: Guided a group of American teachers on an educational tour in Soviet Russia.

If she met Counts on his initial trip to Russia in 1927, and then returned with him to TC as his secretary, this fits very closely the pattern of the KGB's use of translator/guides for developing, assessing and running espionage agents. After assignment in Russia, if the translators establish a strong enough relationship with their targets, they can manipulate that relationship for operational purposes.

The years 1924 to 1927 are still unaccounted for in Nucia's life. From the time she graduated Clark, to her first meeting with Counts, was she in America, or in training in Russia, or was she serving elsewhere?

Her later smooth transition to using various names would seem to indicate that she was skilled in tradecraft. Could she have been operational elsewhere during those missing years? In her letters to the Cossack general, she called herself "Anna Osipovna," Joseph's daughter Anna, the traditional Russian formal form of address.

She indicated on her resume that, in addition to speaking "Russian and English equally well," she also could "speak French and German," and that she could "understand Polish and Ukranian." She appeared to have cleansed the old Hebrew-speaking Anna Perlmutter from her mind, if not from history. It's likely that Nucia was able to slip into and out of a variety of identities, with little difficulty.

Nucia in Russia

In Tenenbaum's story of TC Professor Kilpatrick's academic career, in 1929, when Kilpatrick went to Russia, he discovered that he was well known. His books had been translated into Russian and were being used in all the teacher-training institutions.

Professor Pinkevich, president of a Moscow university, and later Counts' source for his first book on Russian education, greeted him warmly. Kilpatrick had met the Russian as a visiting professor in the United States.

Kilpatrick's greeting at the Russian Educational Bureau was also warm. Revealing both his awareness of restrictions on free movement, followed by naiveté in believing the answer, Kilpatrick asked, "Am I free to go anywhere I wish?" He credulously accepted the answer, "Yes," he was told, "you are free to go into any school at any time without asking anybody anything."

Using an operational ploy to attach a handler to a visiting American, the KGB assigned Nucia to Kilpatrick. As Tenebaum told it, "At the time, Professor Counts of Teachers College was visiting Russia. He was away from Moscow, traveling somewhere, and he placed at Kilpatrick's disposal his secretary, Miss Nucia Perlmutter, who spoke and read Russian."

Playing along with Kilpatrick, Nucia arranged a bit of Potemkin Village theater. Tenebaum wrote, "Early one morning Kilpatrick and Miss Perlmutter went up to the first policeman they met and asked him to direct them to the nearest school. Kilpatrick thought that this provided the best way of locating a typical Moscow school."

The NY Times quoted Nucia at an educational exposition in Leningrad in August 1930. The exposition was organized to celebrate the Soviet advances in education in the second year of their Five Year Plan.

The American exhibit of American Progressive education was presented to the Russian attendees, in their native language by two Teachers College staff, one of whom was Nucia Perlmutter. As reported in an August 24, 1930 article, Nucia wrote to the NY Times in glowing terms about the exhibit, extolling the visits of "the workers" as the most interesting element" of the exhibit.

Later Life

She was naturalized as an American citizen, in Chicago, on January 6, 1927. She continued to work as Counts' secretary/assistant/translator until he retired from Columbia in 1956. She then moved to the Hoover Institution at Stanford University, where she worked from 1956 until her death in 1983, at the age of 96.

Publications

Nucia was a scholar in her own right. In 1934, she published an article in the Educational Yearbook of the International Institute of Teachers College entitled: *The University And A Student Of Yesterday – The Birth Of The Russian University*. Also in 1934 Nucia published *Higher Education And The Student Of Today: The New World In The Making Of The New Man.*

Both of these articles, especially the latter, are fairly gushing in their description of the changes brought about by the Bolshevik October Revolution. These two articles appear to be graduate level research done in conjunction with Dr. Counts at TC.

Her thesis at Clark University, completed in 1924, was an exhaustive historical review of the several centuries of Russian education systems. Her research ended with the then-new destruction of Russian education and society by the "Bolshevikis."

Nucia's academic articles echo Counts' own publications of the same time period. As Counts was enthusing about the death of individualism and the emergence of collectivism as the new way for America, Nucia wrote: "The...difference between the old and the new student is that the former was an individualist, whereas the latter is a collectivist."

Nucia listed her publications on her resume. She included the 1929 first work she translated and Counts "edited," *The New Education in the Soviet Republic*, as well as 1930's best-seller, *New Russia's Primer*. These two books both credited Counts as co-translator.

After she and Counts rejected their Muenzenberg Creed covert influence operations, they attempted to build their credentials as anti-communists. In this vein, she and Counts published three more books, as co-translators or co-authors, 1948, *I Want to be Like Stalin;* 1952, *The Country of the Blind*; and 1956, *The Challenge of Soviet Education.*

Princeton, New Jersey
June, 2010

From the maze of interstates and the Jersey Turnpike, to the tree-lined drive into Princeton, I negotiated a jumble of construction and detours on a June morning. Eighty-five degrees and sticky, cicadas screamed at each other as I drove into the New Jersey suburb of Philadelphia, with the windows down.

The Firestone library was on the left just before the main drag. With just a few short hours to spend in the Special Collections room, I looked for a parking spot near the library. A couple blocks away, the town offered free parking on the street until 4pm.

Quick walking pace through the college downtown, a trickle of sweat dripping down my back, I crossed Nassau Street onto the campus. The place reeked of America's elite. The Dulles brothers, one Eisenhower's Secretary of State, and another the first Director of Central Intelligence, were both Princeton graduates.

Coming around the corner from Washington Road, a hexagonal addition on the ancient stone library has a plaque affixed. The dedication notes the building is the Dulles Library of Diplomatic History, named after the diplomat, not the CIA brother.

Wending my way through the lobby to the Special Collections Department, I begin the bureaucratic process of signing up for a pass to gain access to the Special Collections, which hold the archives of the John Day Publishing Company.

John Day published books by George S. Counts and Nucia Perlmutter Lodge. The archives index showed extensive correspondence between Counts and Nucia, and their John Day editor, Richard Walsh, who later became Mr. Pearl S. Buck. The correspondence started in 1929, and ended in the early-1950s.

Following the bored librarian's monotone instructions, I got a photo ID card, washed my hands in a 1920s bathroom, and deposited all my possessions but one pencil and my laptop in a locker. I've used up 45 minutes of precious time. The short and stocky librarian escorted me to the Special Collections reading room, which coincidentally is in the Dulles hexagon.

Finally, the reading room librarian wheeled up a cart with boxes of archive folders, and let me have them one at a time. I had to fill out a permission form to take a digital photo of any document. She had to take the form for approval to another librarian, hidden away in another room. All this sucked up precious minutes.

The discoveries in the John Day archives make all the aggravations worthwhile. Handwritten and typewritten letters from both Counts and Nucia are in the archives, dozens of them. The letters reveal details of their relationship. But correspondence between Walsh and Counts provided the most interesting new information.

A letter from Counts to Walsh, March 20, 1933. "My dear Dick," Counts began. Typing the letter himself, on his office letterhead, "International Institute, Teachers College, Columbia University, Office of the Associate Director."

Counts, by mid-1933 was deeply involved in KGB covert influence. He launched directly into his pitch, "Do you know General Victor A. Yakhontoff? He was assistant secretary of war under the Kerensky regime and is the author of Russia and the Soviet Union in the Far East. *He is an extremely able and interesting man."*

The dapper little professor, attempting to gain access to the American publishing industry for another KGB influence agent, proposed that Yakhontoff come by the publisher's office because, "you might like to see him and get acquainted."

Walsh's secretary annotated the letter with the date and time of the John Day executive's planned meeting with Yakhontoff—Monday, April 3, 1933 at 11 o'clock.

Then again, in 1936, a Walsh letter to Counts reveals that Yakhontoff had continued to play a role in their relationship, exactly what role is not clear. On July 2, 1936 Walsh wrote, "General Yakhontoff tells me that you are leaving soon for nine months in Russia. Congratulations! I think it is fine that you are going back."

As the Special Collections lady hustles me out at closing time, I'm lost in thought, imagining the extensive network of agents that the KGB had created 80 years ago. Their professionalism, expertise and efficiency are amazing.

Now I have to find out just who Yakhontoff was. Later research reveals him to be an influence agent for the Soviets—he traveled around America lecturing on the need for recognition of the Soviet Union throughout the 1920s. After their op paid off in 1933, with Roosevelt's formal diplomatic acknowledgement of the communist enemy that was striving to destroy his country, it appears that Yakhontoff continued his influence work and then disappeared.

Another solid link from the KGB to Counts.

Where the hell did I park? I retrace my steps, through a quaint row of offices and shops. A walkway through the back alley comes out on Madison Ave. Two blocks up, across Paul Robeson Place, named in honor of the black American communist singer, a tool of the Soviets, there's my car.

Damn! Another ticket. Research costs more in parking tickets than it does in library fees.

Post-Script

Counts and Nucia both rejected their influence work, sometime during, or shortly after World War II. Nucia must have admitted to Counts the truth of the many years of their relationship, pouring out her heart and soul, revealing the methods and techniques the KGB used to control her, and to control him. Maybe Nucia's defection was the catalyst that drove Counts to reject his former influence work.

They went on to write several anti-communist/Soviet books together, always with Counts as the main author, and Nucia as his unsung co-author. The details of KGB methods and the darkness of the totalitarian society, written in the first person, could only have come from Nucia's first-hand experience of the brutal intelligence agency of her motherland.

Yet Counts and Lodge never recanted their opinions or writing in public, nor did they withdraw their previous work from the public domain. They never publicly admitted the reasons behind their 180 degree turnaround. Counts continued to be a professor until his death at age 84, becoming an eminence grise at SIU.

Counts renewed the copyrights on his books written as covert influence, extolling the virtues of collectivism. His daughter Martha has continued to renew them after his death.

Unfortunately, PC-Progressive educators of today, nearly 100 years after the peak years of Counts' communist covert influence work, still view Counts as a prophet. Education journals constantly cite the fruits of the KGB's Counts operation. A recent (July 2009) Google Scholar search revealed 329 citations of Counts' 1934 work, *Dare the School Build a New Social Order*, evidence of the KGB's continuing influence on our academic/education elite today.

Counts and Nucia continued their work together into the 1950s, with a strong anti-communist theme. Yet, they never admitted, at least publicly, that they were wrong, misled, duped, or just stupid. They simply changed their point of view in mid-stream, abandoning their collectivism for anti-communism.

And yet, Counts railed against the McCarthy investigations, all the while knowing that McCarthy was right. Self-satisfied, smug, and arrogant to the end, Counts' donated his body for medical study at his death.

Nucia lived out the end of her life far from Counts, dying in California in 1983. She did translation work for the Hoover Institute at Stanford University, where she had followed another Russian revolutionary, Aleksandr Kerensky, helping to translate his memoirs.

CI Analysis of George S. Counts—3-Question Screening

Visited the USSR?

Success not consistent with recent past?

Content of work consistent with Muenzenberg creed?

Question 1—Visited the USSR?

Yes. Counts made multiple trips to the USSR, from 1929 to 1936. He spent months at a time in Russia. On his first visit, not speaking Russian, he met Nucia Perlmutter. Nucia became his constant companion for the next twenty-seven years.

Nucia provided Counts with contacts to high-level Russians, accompanying him on visits to Stalin, Lenin's wife, Krupskaya, and others. She was his translator/assistant for the rest of his career at TC.

Counts, in 1929, did a Potemkin Village-style "self-guided" 6,000 mile automobile trip around Russia. He was accompanied by Russian handlers for at least 5,000 miles of the trip.

Question 2—Success not Consistent with Recent Past?

Yes.

Counts had toiled in relative obscurity, working in a series of universities in the ten years prior to his achieving national prominence in 1929, with the publication of *New Russia's Primer*.

In a matter of months, Counts' name was regularly mentioned in the pages of the New York Times, and national news magazines.

By February 1930, Counts was confident enough of his own national prestige to issue a press release to newspapers on issues relating to the Soviet Union. The New York Times printed his words, with little commentary.

For the rest of his life, Counts milked his fame and notoriety, publishing books that were usually translations of Russian sources, or if his own words, run-on philosophic ramblings. The peak of his string of inconsistent success came in 1952 when he was the Liberal Party candidate the U.S. Senate in New York.

Question 3—Content of Work Consistent with Muenzenberg Creed?

Yes.

From the time he visited Russia for the first time in 1927, until he turned against the communists in the early 1940s, the gist of Counts' message was a virtual carbon copy of the Muenzenberg creed.

Soon after returning to American from his 1929 automobile tour of Russia, in February 1930, Counts got in touch with the press. The New York Times noted that he was just back from "a seven-months tour of Russia as official representative of the International Institute."

The Times article, seemingly based on Counts' press release, quoted the professor of education on issues totally outside his realm of expertise.

The article headlined Counts' warning to the American religious community. Channeling the KGB, his words were a thinly veiled threat to annihilate Russian believers,

> Any effort on [the part of the American religious community] to effect an alleviation of conditions within Soviet Russia will be regarded as attacks of avowed enemies and will tend to harden the attitude of the revolutionary leaders toward the [Russian] church. Of course, if these protests were designed to consolidate the opposition of the Western peoples toward the revolutionary experiment in Russia, they will probably succeed admirably.

This is Muenzenberg's "Russia is trying a grand experiment. You hope they succeed." Right out of the covert influence workbook.

In the same statement, Counts took up the issue of the day for the KGB—the "Peace" movement. Muenzenberg was, at the same time, convening international congresses for peace, co-opting the liberals and recruiting Willing Accomplices to implant Moscow's message in America.

Counts, promulgated the Muenzenberg Creed Peace message, "If we as a people think that we can move toward ultimate world peace and at the same time ignore the existence of Soviet Russia I fear that we are practicing the most extreme type of self-deception."

Following the Muenzenberg Creed, Counts passed on the message to Americans that their country was the real threat to peace and the Russian's noble experiment.

The article ended with Counts' observation that the most likely threat to world peace was "the danger of a struggle between Soviet

Russia and certain of the Western countries." Read "America" for certain of the Western countries, of course.

Again the Muenzenberg Creed rings out, loud and clear: "You believe in peace. You yearn for international understanding. You are shocked, frightened by what is going on right here in our own country."

In a Times article published on August 6, 1930, Counts addressed a captive audience of Summer session students at TC.

After Russian cargo was seized by the Treasury Department because it was suspected of being produced by convict labor, Counts said, "it would be difficult to prove that convict labor exists to any extent in Russia. I observed no evidences of it. I believe investigation will prove it to be a tempest in a teapot."

Muenzenberg payload, "You think the Russians are trying a great human experiment, and you hope it works."

In the same lecture at TC's Summer session, Counts told the students, "Much depends on this season's harvest, which...promises to be abundant. Collectivization went forward much more rapidly than had been expected."

Muenzenberg Creed, "You think the Russians are trying a great human experiment, and you hope it works."

Counts next returned to another Muenzenberg Creed point, war-mongering America threatened peace-loving Russia, "Those people who are expecting the present regime to fall are doomed to disappointment. If they are building policies on that assumption they are likely to endanger the peace of the world through antagonism and misunderstanding."

Muenzenberg Creed reference: "You believe in peace. You yearn for international understanding."

In Count's 1932 *Dare the School Build a New Social Order*, he may have tread as close to the covert influence line as possible, without crossing into propaganda. But he always stayed on the covert side of the line, allowing deniability.

He hewed straight down the Muenzenberg methodology, never violating the first part of the Creed, "You do not endorse Stalin. You do not call yourself a Communist. You do not declare your love for the regime. You do not call on people to support the Soviets. Ever. Under any circumstances."

With those limitations in mind, speaking about capitalism, Counts declared,

> With its deification of the principle of selfishness, its exaltation of the profit motive, its reliance upon the forces of competition, and its placing of property above human rights, it will either have to be displaced altogether or changed so radically in form and *spirit that its identity will be completely lost*.

You can almost hear Muenzenberg reciting his point from the Creed: "You think the capitalist system is corrupt."

In his 1931 *The Soviet Challenge to America*, published by his friend Richard Walsh at the John Day Company, Counts declared:

> Soviet Russia is endeavoring with all the resources at her command to bring the economic order under a measure of rational control. She may fail in the attempt, but in the meantime every student of human affairs should follow the effort with breathless interest. She issues to the Western nations and particularly to the United States a challenge--perhaps one of the greatest challenges of history. But she issues it not through the Communist International, nor through the Red Army, nor through the Gay-Pay-OO (political police), as most of our citizens naïvely and timorously believe, but through her State Planning Commission and her system of public education."

Again, and again, and again, Muenzenberg's Creed: "You think the Russians are trying a great human experiment, and you hope it works."

Tracing the Muenzenberg Creed DNA in Counts' writing is fruitful. These examples will stand to support the resounding "Yes" answer to the last CI screening question. Try it yourself. Read any of Counts' work from his Muenzenberg period. Try to find the Creed.

Conclusion: George S. Counts—KGB Willing Accomplice in the Destruction of American Culture

I believe that the 3-Question CI screening of Counts' life and work provides clear evidence that he was a Willing Accomplice in the Muenzenberg covert influence operations to destroy American culture.

Specifically, Counts targeted both higher education, Academia, and the kindergarten to 12th grade system, Education. His unique position as a professor of Education provided access to both of these important transmission belts of American culture.

Counts was able to insert the Muenzenberg Creed into American academia and Education for more than 10 years.

Counts' continuing influence in American Schools of Education, even today in 2011, demonstrates the enormous efficiency of covert influence operations. Long after the Rosenbergs fried in the electric chair; long after Muenzenberg's neck was snapped by a rope; long after Counts himself had passed on to that faculty lounge in the sky, his anti-American, anti-individualism, pro-collectivist influence messages are injected into young American skulls every semester throughout the country.

The cost of the Counts operation was negligible to the KGB. Maintaining Nucia Lodge probably required no money, just manpower to meet and motivate her. Counts' motivation was recognition and approval. They provided him access to high level personalities, research material, and books and other resources that no one else was able to access, all of which was virtually cost-free. Once he had been primed with the Muenzenberg protocol, he was on auto-pilot; albeit with a handler just outside his office door every day.

Willing not Necessarily Witting

It's important to note one of the little-understood nuances of the psychology of covert espionage agents here.

The fact that Counts was Willing to carry out the influence operation against his country does not necessarily mean that he was witting of exactly who he worked for, or what the KGB's and Comintern's ultimate goal was.

To be willing to go along with an operation, an agent must be convinced that his actions are parallel with his own best interests. A case officer simply needs to help an agent see how his own best interests are served by the operation.

The case officer does not necessarily have to make the agent completely witting of who he works for, or the goals of the operation.

That said, Counts surely understood that the KGB controlled Russia completely. In more than one of his books, he mentioned the "Gay-Pay-Oo" (Russian pronunciation of the intelligence service's contemporary initials, GPU) and its pervasiveness in Russian society.

In Counts' case, it's possible that he was not witting of his contacts', or his handlers', true affiliation with the KGB. He may not have been witting of the true overall objective of the KGB's covert influence operation.

But, in the end, it does not matter whether he was fully witting of a KGB operation to destroy American culture in order to rebuild the country under communism or not.

The case officer provides an agent what that particular agent needs in order to survive psychologically. If the agent needs a "fig leaf," a philosophical justification for helping to destroy his country, then the case officer can provide that.

Willing suspension of disbelief is required on the part of the unwitting agent, but the human psyche is amazingly flexible, and able to do tricks that most people wouldn't believe.

Witting or un-witting, George S. Counts was Willing to use the material provided by the KGB, to follow the Muenzenberg Creed, to the detriment of his country. Willing Accomplice in the destruction of American culture—George S. Counts.

Chapter 2

Willing Accomplice in the Media: Walter Duranty

Duranty is an avowed proponent of American recognition of the U.S.S.R. since he is aware that recognition would greatly enhance his reputation in the Soviet Union and give him a cheap triumph in the United States.

M. Vyvyan, British diplomat in Moscow, 1933

For a covert influence operation against America in the early 20th century, there was no better target than the *New York Times*. The editors and publisher of the country's "newspaper of record," prided their publicatoin as being somehow above the fray, superior to the pack of also-ran yellow-pseudo-journalists.

Its un-self-conscious motto, *All the News that's Fit to Print* says it all. The world of American information, intelligence, who's who, what's what, where's where, when's when, begins and ends with "The Old Gray Lady."

From the less easily swayed by pretentious boasts point of view of the 21st century, the *Times'* self-important posing as a somehow above petty politics and possession of some sort of secret access to the well-spring of truth and righteousness is preposterous.

The *New York Times* is today one of the most biased and untruthful organs of PC-Progressivism. Its faithful adherence to the party line as dictated by the PC-Progressive cabal is almost *Pravda*-like.

The enemies of PC-Progressives are regularly dealt with via the old covert action response—Andemca. Without admitting the truth of exposures of their PC-Progressive brethren, the Times responds with attacks. Wave after wave of counter-accusations fill the pages of the party organ. See coverage of Sarah Palin, Ronald Reagan, George W. Bush, for examples.

When did the *Times* become the organ of PC-Progressivism? That's for another research project. In this chapter, we will conduct the 3-Question CI Screening of a *Times* super-star, Walter Duranty.

Although many have researched and analyzed Duranty's writing for the *Times*, and many have branded him, for example, *Stalin's Apologist*, the title of the best biography of Duranty, no one has provided a CI analysis that allows us to definitively identify him as a Willing Accomplice and KGB covert influence agent.

S.J. Taylor wrote the definitive biography of Duranty, *Stalin's Apologist,* in 1990. She dug up original sources, waded through the tangle of lies her subject left in his wake, and produced a solid piece of scholarship. She revealed virtually all the details required to perform a CI analysis of Duranty, which leads to the conclusion that he was a KGB agent. Yet, without understanding the import of her revelations, and without a background in espionage, Taylor was unable to bring herself to the obvious conclusion that her own writing revealed. She was content to let her conclusion be that of her title—Duranty was just an apologist for the communists.

Taylor's mis-analysis of the facts is not due to a lack of intellect or energy. She simply was unequipped to make sense of the details she uncovered. Like a Martian listening to broadcasts from the Earth, Taylor did not have the experience, expertise, or knowledge required to decipher what she recorded.

This chapter will apply CI expertise to Taylor's research.

Background

Walter Duranty enjoyed the trappings of success. Feted as a "Russian expert" across America. Rewarded with a Pulitzer Prize. Hailed for his wise, practical view of communism, Stalin, and the Soviet Union.

Yet he was no real expert on Russia. He arrived in the Soviet Union around 1921, with no background in, or special understanding of Russia, the recent Revolution, the civil war, or anything in the country. In other words, he was a perfectly blank slate.

He was also nearly perfectly vulnerable to recruitment as an intelligence agent. To an experienced case officer, Duranty represents a case study in clear and exploitable motivations. He represented an amalgamation of the three requirements for recruitment: access, motivations, and suitability.

Duranty had access to the mainline artery of American public opinion. For the case officers responsible for carrying out the Comintern's Muenzenberg covert influence operations, the *New York Times* was probably the mother lode, the direct route to American public opinion, the most trusted, revered, and read organ of the American media. Duranty's eventual status as the *Times'* correspondent in Moscow represented the best access that the KGB could hope for in a candidate to be a covert access agent.

Duranty's motivations would have been easy for the skilled KGB case officers to discover. An opium addict; an inveterate late-night partier; a drinker; a lover of fine wine, fine food, and good song; a lover of young women; a vain and arrogant man with a need to demonstrate his superiority. Each of these facets of Duranty's personality was a motivation that a good case officer could manipulate to effect a solid recruitment.

Duranty was probably uniquely suitable for his eventual role as a covert influence agent because of his ability to compartmentalize and lie fluently. He developed a persona that was a blend of fact and fiction. He killed off his family in his autobiography, creating an orphan, only child, Duranty at age 10, when in fact his parents lived well into his adulthood, and he also had a sister. His strange dallying with the demonic Aleister Crowley, involving drugs and perverted sex, gave him experience in living a double life.

So, when he applied for a visa to report from Moscow, as a New York Times correspondent, in 1921, he was ripe for development as an influence source.

Clearly the KGB chose well. For the next 19 years, Duranty built a career as the premier authority in the American media, and maybe all western media, on all things Russian. The Soviets provided Duranty with stories, access, insight, and, as we'll see, the Muenzenberg Creed.

The main objective of the KGB's Duranty covert influence op was to maintain the Muenzenberg Creed line in America of "You think the Russians are trying a great human experiment, and you hope it works." The main goal was to achieve American diplomatic recognition of the Soviet Union. In this specific goal, they were fantastically successful.

The KGB's tactics in the Duranty op finally resulted in his true status becoming public. Other journalists who reported on the Ukrainian famine, for example, exposed Duranty's covert influence lies and distortions.

Although these journalists were solidly supported by actual truth, other Willing Accomplices in the media practiced typical Active Measures reaction to exposure—Andemca.

Duranty's critics were attacked and demonized by Willing Accomplices. It took decades before the tissue of lies spun by the KGB through Duranty began to fall away and the truth to emerge. Even now, however, Willing Accomplices seem unable to deal with the truth.

The Pulitzer Prize committee refused to take back Duranty's Pulitzer, in 2003. He had won the prize in 1932, the year of the famine in the Soviet Union. Although the *Times'* publisher suggested that Duranty might not have deserved the honor, the Pulitzer committee demurred, and left Duranty's name on the list.

Willing Accomplices of today observed, took note, and pressed on with their continued operations.

Early Life

Walter Duranty was born into a prosperous Liverpool merchant family in May 1884. His father was a pillar of the Presbyterian community in Liverpool. His grandfather died wealthy and made Walter a bequest which allowed him to waste away his 20s unproductively.

Until he was 15, when some unknown event took away his father's ability to live a productive life, Duranty was an upper class British boy. He attended private schools, wearing the uniforms, as Taylor put it, "complete with top hat on Sunday, straw hat during the week."

Duranty excelled at languages, Latin, Greek and French. In the meantime, as British private boys schools tend to do to their students, he was toughened up. Duranty did not take well to this life. When his father's mysterious "drop out of sight" occurred, Duranty returned home and attended public schools until his graduation in early summer 1903.

Walter earned the top award in Classics, which qualified him for a scholarship to the prestigious British university, and later fertile communist recruiting ground, Cambridge.

Duranty participated on the rowing team, and excelled in his classes. While Taylor does not make clear if Duranty finished his studies at Cambridge, he stayed for at least three years. It appears that the Duranty trail went cold for Taylor.

New York Times in Paris

The next sure piece of the Duranty story, based on sources other than Duranty's own untrustworthy writing, has the British citizen appearing at the *New York Times'* office in Paris, where he badgered the bureau chief for months until he was finally offered a job. He began full-time work for his chosen journalistic target organization on December 1, 1913.

In between leaving Cambridge and beginning work with the *Times* in Paris, there are hints that Duranty dabbled with Satanist pervert Aleister Crowley, and traveled extensively, including to the U.S. It appears that he lived on his grandfather's bequest. But it's just as likely that he developed other sources of income.

He did, during those years develop a singularly effective method of cultivating friendships; in effect he learned the skills of an intelligence officer. In addition to his remarkable presence and charm ("He had a kind of magic. An evening with him was like an evening with no one else."), Duranty cultivated his listening skills, "always allowing the other person to talk as well."

He also cultivated what became a life-long addiction to women, who were as attracted to him as he was to them. A colleague journalist said that Duranty was "one of the great lady's men of his generation."

Duranty did journeyman reporter duties in Paris, up to and through WW1. He was a small fish in a large pond, learning the craft of journalism, and establishing himself in the foreign correspondent pecking order. Just how a Brit in France working for an American newspaper fit is not clear. But it does seem likely that his expatriate status allowed him to slip between the cracks, making the most of his status as an outsider, both at his paper and in France.

Finding his Niche

After the Russian revolution, Duranty's reporting for the *Times* from Paris had a decidedly anti-Bolshevik spin. Interestingly, this may have been what brought him to the attention of the KGB.

In the late summer of 1921, when he applied for a visa to enter Russia from Riga, Latvia to report on the American anti-famine missions, headed by Herbert Hoover, Duranty claims he came to the attention of the Russians.

According to Taylor, Duranty was able to "ingratiate himself with the Soviet press officer...by the name of Markov, who... had been educated in England." In Taylor's recitation of the story, based on Duranty's later recounting of the incident, Markov took a liking to Duranty, and fed him a pro-Moscow leak about Lenin's New Economic Policy.

Markov's exclusive leak to Duranty allowed him to simultaneously scoop the rest of the foreign press, and ingratiate himself to the KGB's influence operators.

It is likely that this story was the cover story Duranty and his handlers concocted to explain his "stroke of luck" in receiving a visa. More likely is that he had been spotted and was under assessment and development, potentially even already recruited, when he arrived in Riga. Or Markov may have been his first contact with the KGB apparatus.

Regardless, Duranty was now on the KGB's scope, and they clearly liked what they saw.

Arrival in Moscow

Duranty's first arrival in Moscow, according to him, was without fanfare. No welcoming committee, just a truck ride to a fleabag hotel, escorted by KGB soldiers. No sooner had he settled in than the *Times* demanded some work for their investment.

He traveled to the famine-struck regions and filed emotionless reports about dying children and towns. Other *Times* reporters were more affected. Their stories were full of the emotional turmoil they had experienced when they encountered scores of dying and dead peasants.

A week later, Duranty was filing stories from Moscow. He delighted in informing his readers that, "if only you knew where to go and if you had the right money," you could feast on "fresh Astrakhan caviar, with pre-war vodka; white bread and butter, delicious borsht soup, with old sherry; grilled salmon and roast partridge, with vintage burgundy or champagne; cakes of every kind, cream, sugar, custard, fine Russian cheese, hothouse grapes, old port and older cognac."

Duranty had arrived in Moscow with no Russian language skills at all. He had no background of experience, study, or interest in the culture, the people, the history, or anything else having to do with Russia. Now, less than a month after his arrival in the communist capital, after his visa was expedited by "the Foreign Office," Duranty had found the good life.

Russian Expert

Within a matter of months, Duranty was writing from Moscow as if he had been there all his life. As Lenin's health deteriorated, in January 1923, Duranty, speculating about the potential change in leaders, gave a verbal hug to Josef Stalin, crediting the Georgian strongman with creating "the new Russian Union, which history may regard as one of the most remarkable Constitutions in human history. Trotsky helped him in drawing it up, but Stalin's brain guided the pen."

Duranty seemed at home in the communist workers paradise. The New Economic Plan opened up Moscow's pleasure industry. Gambling, alcohol, brothels, and drugs were all freely available to those "in the know." The Bolsheviks made divorces easy and affordable, and Lenin seemed to encourage freedom in sexual relations.

Within less than a year of his arrival, in the spring of 1922, Duranty claimed that "he and another correspondent threw in a thousand or so dollars" to renovate a small house. He claimed that such renovations then allowed them to live rent free. Another correspondent remembered differently. He remembered Duranty living in the house with his wife, Jane Cheron Duranty.

According to an American correspondent who visited the Durantys regularly, the household included a Russian girl who was both the cook, and Walter's mistress.

Still less than a year in Russia, the British *Times* employee on the make was surprisingly well-kept. According to Duranty himself, at that time in Moscow he also had "a little T-model Ford and a chauffeur...a comfortable apartment and an excellent cook."

The future guru of all things Soviet and Russian had made a quick start of finding the good life in the communist capital.

Success and Comfort

Duranty settled into the good life. His housed became a meeting spot for expatriate Americans, radicals passing through or in exile. Duranty would listen and commiserate, into the night if needed.

He established a relationship with the radical dancer Isadora Duncan. He ran with the artistic crowd in Moscow.

Duranty had hit the big time. World famous people were his companions, Russian, American, and European. He was not the bitter boy from Liverpool. He was reinventing himself, creating a new Duranty.

In the next couple of years, Walter tried to get out of Moscow regularly. Taylor notes that these trips often turned into "extravagant holidays." Taylor never questions the source of Duranty's funds, for the trips, the extravagance, the drugs, the parties, the food, or anything else, whether in Moscow or in New York.

Taylor chronicles Duranty's mixing with the then-famous group of writers who formed the Algonquian Round Table. They included the writer and screenwriter, Dorothy Parker, and Alexander Woollcott, a Duranty friend from his time in Paris.

Two years into his Russian residence, Duranty took a trip to Europe. A train accident resulted in a severe injury to his left shin. Infection resulted in his foot being amputated, between the ankle and the knee.

Duranty, who had been smoking opium for years, now used the accident to justify his drug use. It also seems to have emboldened him to discuss opium more openly, which Taylor says "he apparently loved to do." In addition, Duranty claimed that the French government paid a substantial compensation, to explain extra money that "would give him a measure of independence."

The accident did provide him with his trademark cane, which he used as a conversational prop for the rest of his life. His convalescence kept him from Moscow for nearly a full year.

He returned in summer of 1925, claiming that he had "read everything he could lay his hands on." As the struggle for control of the Soviet Communist Party unveiled, Duranty had a front row seat. Not only was he in the front row, he was cheering on one of the contestants, and he seemed to have inside information.

Duranty consistently backed Stalin, and said that the Georgian was bound to defeat Trotsky. Between a trip to China and other distractions, Duranty covered the internal power struggles in the Soviet Union.

As the struggle came to a head in 1928, Duranty's personal situation did not include his wife. An American visitor to the Duranty house described how "an extremely pretty girl" greeted the guests, only to reappear later in the evening to tell Durant that "she has finished the *Izvestia* proofs. Then they go to bed together." Duranty clearly enjoyed flaunting his special status to impress his American friends.

In 1930, Duranty's reporting came under scrutiny in the business office of the *Times*. Some readers and employees complained about his clear bias towards the communists. Evidently the inquiry came up with no conclusion. Luckily for Duranty, for he was about to score his biggest scoop yet.

Interview with Stalin—Superstardom

In November 1930, an American socialist correspondent for the United Press, Eugene Lyons, was rewarded for his ideological purity by the Soviets. He was chosen to be the first Western foreign correspondent allowed to interview Stalin. Duranty was out of Russia at the time of the interview, but returned as soon as he heard the news.

He protested that as he was the "longest-serving Western correspondent in the country it was unfair not to give him an interview as well." One week later, Duranty scored his scoop; he too was invited to interview Stalin.

Duranty's article excused Stalin's hardness (the dictator of the Elite Vanguard warned that capitalism would cause another world war) as the result of Stalin suffering under "the repression of the priests during his years as a novitiate in the Russian Orthodox Church."

With this fawning portrayal of the brutal tyrant, Duranty had finally arrived on the world stage.

He enjoyed his time on the stage. In 1932, he won the Pulitzer Prize for his 1931 reporting on the New Economic Plan. This award gave him "the authority he needed to quell his critics."

As the new decade unfolded, with the Depression settling in on America's economy and spirit, Durant found that he had "somehow moved into position as the Western representative of things Soviet." In 1932, the *Times* published a Duranty poem, *Red Square*.

This doggerel was not memorable, except for the lines that live on, "Russian may be hungry and short of clothes and comfort, But you can't make an omelet without breaking eggs."

Famine in the Ukraine—Famine, What Famine?

From the spring of 1932 the terrible results of Stalin's attempts at forced collectivization of Russian farms and of his war against the kulaks, the upper-class peasants were evident. The bread basket region of the Soviet Union, the vast swath of "amber waves of grain," primarily in the Ukraine, was failing. The harvest had been poor and would be worse. Starvation stalked the land. The peasants were supposed to be the winners in the communist redistribution of property. The peasants were supposed to be enjoying the collectivist utopia dreamed of by the mad theorists and revolutionaries for the last 70 years. The peasants. The peasants. The peasants were starving. They were eating dirt. They were reduced to an animalistic existence.

The famine was Stalin's retribution for their resistance to his utopian, collectivist land redistribution schemes. Such an inhuman, inhumane plan, all in the name of bringing utopia to humanity. But in the meantime, the humans were suffering.

And the suffering, dying, starving, were not pretty. Nor was the famine convenient. The USSR was so close to achieving recognition from the U.S. The new President Roosevelt would be more amenable to the communists. If only they could manage the perceptions. If only they could influence the Americans.

Walter Duranty reported calmly on the famine. In August 1933, Duranty's article in the *Times* said, "The excellent harvest about to be gathered shows that any report of a famine in Russia is today an exaggeration or malignant propaganda."

At the same time, other Western reporters and diplomats saw reality. Malcolm Muggeridge, a British Socialist, came to Moscow in the fall of 1932, intending to join in the task of "building Socialism." Quickly discouraged by the reality of the communist dystopia, he instead chronicled the truth. He observed that "The famine is an organized one...a military occupation; worse, active war."

Shock troops dispatched from Moscow searched for kulaks hoarding grain, while the fields, choked with weeds, cattle dead, people starving and dispirited, no horses for plowing or for transport, not even adequate supplies of seed for spring planting." Muggeridge cataloged the crimes.

Gareth Jones, a young Welshman who was well-versed in the Russian language, spent three weeks walking through the Ukraine. After he left the country, he held a press conference in Berlin to report his observations of the horrible mass starvation.

Duranty, at the behest of the Soviet censors, responded to Jones' and Muggeridge's truthful accounts with a blast in the *Times*. It was "all too true that the novelty and mismanagement of collective farming...made a mess of Soviet food production. But—to put it brutally—you can't make an omelet without breaking eggs...There is no actual starvation but there is widespread mortality from diseases due to malnutrition, especially in the Ukraine, North Caucasus, and Lower Volga."

American Diplomatic Recognition of the USSR

Duranty did not reach his professional peak until November 1933. The moment he had been working for finally arrived. Duranty accompanied the Russian Minister of Foreign Affairs to Washington DC. President Franklin Roosevelt gave a press conference in the White House. Duranty was the only member of the foreign press corps from Moscow present at this historic event.

During Roosevelt's announcement that the U.S. and the USSR agreed to normalize relations, Duranty had a choice spot, standing close to the President's desk. The limping, one-legged Brit, who had spun the Soviet point of view for 12 years, "the intimate of presidents and dictators, the matchmaker for the marriage of convenience between two superpowers—this is how he viewed himself...At last he was reaping his reward."

In New York, a few days later, a grand dinner at the Waldorf-Astoria by the Russian-American Chamber of Commerce celebrated the new marriage of opposites—the capitalist engine of the world's economy and the communist engine dedicated to destroying everything America represented. Of the 1500 movers and shakers, Russian and American, Duranty was the most popular, and received the most applause upon introduction by the host.

Also in on the ceremonies and celebrations was Roosevelt's hand-picked first American ambassador to the Soviet Union—William Bullitt. The new ambassador had divorced Louise Bryant, John

Reed's widow, and one of Alexander Gumberg's journalist charges after several years of marriage.

Back in Moscow, Duranty was rewarded with his second, and final, interview with Stalin, in the Kremlin, on Christmas Day, 1933. According to Duranty, who seems to have used this quote for the rest of his life, Stalin told him, "you bet on our horse to win when others thought it had no chance and I am sure that you have not lost by it."

The Great Duranty

Duranty came to America in 1934. He had published one book the year before, *Duranty Reports Russia,* and put out an autobiography, *I Write as I Please*. He was in demand for speeches, appearances, guest columns. The press corps referred to him as "The Great Duranty."

In his autobiography, Duranty prattled about a scheme to solve the Depression. Taylor, Duranty's biographer, said, "Duranty now considered himself a world figure of sufficient importance to influence the outcome of major social and economic issues."

During the summer of 1936, Duranty, now spending less and less time in Russia, brought his mistress and their young son to England for a holiday. A simple peasant girl, she begged to return to Moscow, and did.

His writing for the *New York Times* began to taper off. Occasional "think pieces" for the Sunday supplements on Russian topics were his mainstay product.

Used up and Discarded

During WW2, Duranty made his way to Beverly Hills, where he rented "a nice little cottage for six months, complete with a car and a colored couple." In Hollywood, he was in the thick of the Muenzenberg Popular Front. Aldous Huxley, Dorothy Parker, Greta Garbo, Marlene Dietrich and others from the Hollywood Anti-Nazi League were his social circle. This front, facilitated by Otto Katz, provided cachet and style to the mostly expatriated European social circle.

Duranty drifted back and forth from California to New York, staying for a month or two here or there. He wrote books and book proposals, tried to write fiction. Taylor says, "When Duranty had money, he spent it. When he didn't have money, which was more often the case nowadays, he still spent it."

At sixty years old, on a lecture in the Midwest, Duranty came down with pneumonia. He spiraled into a slow decline, ending up an invalid in Orlando, Florida. When Stalin died in 1953, Duranty wrote an article for the Orlando paper. In 1957, Duranty begged the *New York Times* editor for a pension. He got a check for $2500. Less than a month later, in October 1957, the one-legged influencer died in a hospital of internal bleeding and emphysema.

CI Analysis of Walter Duranty—3-Question Screening

Visited the USSR?

Success not consistent with recent past?

Content of work consistent with Muenzenberg creed?

Keeping in mind the Muenzenberg covert influence operation, and the content of his payload, the truth behind Duranty's life and work should be nearly transparent now. While many people made the correct diagnosis, during his lifetime, and after, however, no one has laid out a CI analysis putting the puzzle together.

The following analysis should rectify that situation.

Question 1—Visited the USSR?

Yes.

Duranty first went to the Soviet Union in 1921. Upon arrival he had no specialized background in the history, culture, or language of Russia.

Once in Moscow, Duranty had constant and close contact with Konstantin Umansky, who worked for the Soviet press bureau as the censor for foreign correspondents. Umansky later worked for the Soviet press agency TASS, then for the Ministry of Foreign Affairs, finally becoming the Soviet ambassador to the U.S., and then to Mexico. This career trajectory and the close relationship he had with Duranty seem to indicate that he was likely a KGB officer.

Even if Umansky was not Duranty's handler, the potential for clandestine handling of Duranty, covert meetings, covert communications, and other tradecraft necessary for such a high level influence agent, would have been quite simple to arrange, since the operation took place in the Soviet capital. But using Umansky, to whom Duranty reported each time he filed a story, would be much more elegant. Hiding in plain sight is the best kind of cover.

Duranty lived more than 10 years in Moscow. During the first week he was in the country, the KGB would have understood all of his motivations and vulnerabilities. The speed and apparent ease that all of Duranty's physical and psychological needs were met is consistent with an intelligence service making a high quality developmental agent happy.

Duranty's ability to meet every one of his needs—nice housing, live-in mistress and multiple girlfriends, narcotics, fine food, good wine and liquor, a car and driver, servants, ease of travel into and out of Russia—indicates that he enjoyed the support of the KGB.

Duranty did visit Russia.

Question 2—Success not Consistent with Recent Past?

Yes.

When Duranty arrived in Moscow he was a mid-level foreigner just squeaking by on the foreign staff of the *New York Times*. His reporting was on a variety of subjects. He had worked during WW1 in Paris. He had no real expertise, and showed no special potential. It is really not quite clear where he spent nearly all of his 20s. He may have lived off an inheritance, but he had no money and no real background or expertise in anything.

Regardless, he was all but a nobody when he arrived in Moscow in 1921. In 1932, the *Reno Evening Gazette* reported that the Democrat candidate for President, New York governor Franklin Roosevelt met with Duranty for lunch in Albany, where Duranty "informed him of affairs in Soviet Russia."

And the next year, the one-legged Brit was in the White House, part of a select group in the President's office for the announcement of America's recognition of the USSR.

In 1944 a Nevada paper reported Duranty's views on Russia's potential plans for the end of WW2. He was described as the "famed correspondent considered the leading interpreter of Russian events for the English-speaking world."

He was hailed as "Duranty the Great" in press circles. He was sought after to speak about Russia. He wrote best-sellers. His newspaper articles were read around the world.

Duranty's success was totally inconsistent with anything he had done prior to his involvement in Russia.

Question 3—Content of Work Consistent with Muenzenberg Creed?

Yes.

The content of Duranty's influence writing on Russia is highly consistent with the Muenzenberg creed. Duranty tip-toed on the line between covert influence and propaganda. His brazen participation in the operation to hide first the existence, and then the extent of the Ukrainian famine in 1932-33 is probably the most egregious example. The wonder is that Duranty, at the time, was taken seriously at all.

In an article in the *Times* Duranty sneered that Gareth Jones' (truthful) reports were "greeted here with scorn and indignation," and that "the present crop is so abundant that...the national food supply is fully assured for the coming year." Duranty filed this article from Moscow in the middle of the Stalin-engineered famine that killed at least 10 million Soviet citizens. Duranty kept Muenzenberg's "great Russian experiment" safe.

During the winter in between the two growing seasons when Stalin's forced collectivization created the famine, January 1933, Duranty wrote glowingly of the plans for the coming season. He knowingly commented on the cultural character of the Ukrainians, who were even then dying by the thousands,

> The Russian peasants—especially in the North Caucasus, where there has always been a high percentage of more or less self-sufficient individualists—have found the agrarian revolution, otherwise known as collectivization, pretty much in accord with their own position. Whether foreigners realize it or not—and they are beginning to—that is the fact of the case.

As Muenzenberg's Creed had it, "You think the Russians are trying a great human experiment, and you hope it works." Duranty's fervent desire for the experiment to work is palpable. He cloaks his cheering for the success of the Russian experiment in journalistic jargon and style. It's clear that revealing the truth would be harmful to the success of the great experiment. So, Duranty carefully concealed the truth behind a thin façade of half-truths and a tissue of lies.

As the Duranty-assisted climax of the influence operation drew near, in 1933, the KGB and Duranty were forced to deal with overt accusations of Duranty's being "friendly" with the Soviets. In typical covert action fashion, Duranty's response was Andemca—dealing with the accusation head-on, he admitted nothing, denied everything, and in his best sneering, condescension, he implied that his accusers were dunces and morons.

Duranty went on, in his June 1933 article, to imply with his sighing acceptance of the burden of answering the fools that dealing with the questions of his being a Soviet "propagandist" were taking away from the serious business that he was about. He needed to be free of these time-wasters. Andemca. From the KGB's textbook.

The content of Duranty's work for the *New York Times* on the Soviet Union is so congruent with the Muenzenberg Creed, and so obviously written to influence rather than inform that no one can seriously doubt that he was following the Muenzenberg influence Creed.

Conclusion: Walter Duranty—KGB Willing Accomplice in the Destruction of American Culture

As we have seen above, analysis of Walter Duranty's life resulted in resounding "Yes" to each of the questions in the 3-Question CI Screening tool.

Duranty was in Russia for years, where he submitted himself to KGB control, reward and punishment. His lifestyle and life circumstances were significantly improved after he began working with the KGB. And finally, his writing was thoroughly imbued with the Muenzenberg Creed.

There can be no doubt. This analysis confirms that Walter Duranty was a Willing Accomplice to the covert influence operations designed to destroy American culture. He was the premier influence agent in American media. He set the standard for the media. He showed how influence could be worked into everything, or anything you wrote. He showed how to get away with it, and demonstrated the attitude of sneering condescension that the PC-Progressive media have perfected, 80 years later.

Duranty's legacy to journalists, and to PC-Progressives, is a lesson in brazen anti-American lying. He showed how to lie loud, lie often, lie everywhere. And he demonstrated that brazen lying could be honored, and could result in awards, rewards, recognition, and fame.

The results of Duranty's legacy to journalism are evident in American PC-Progressive media every day.

Chapter 3

Willing Accomplice in Hollywood: Dorothy Parker

Just remember, I don't take money from people I disapprove of. No rich people.

Dorothy Parker, quoted by John Keats.

Dorothy Rothschild was born in 1893, the daughter of a middle class New York City merchant, evidently not related to the wealthy banking family of the same name. Raised in comfortable circumstances, she attended private schools and a finishing school. Her mother died when she was four, and a step-mother died five years later. Her father, whom she did not like, died, probably as an invalid under Dorothy's care, when she was 19. Premature, sad, untimely, and mysterious deaths seem to follow her.

Magazine Career—Hateful Barbs Disguised as Wit

She sold a poem to a New York magazine at 21, beginning a career in magazines. She worked as an assistant at a couple of stylish New York publications, writing captions for advertisements. She worked her way up to writing reviews of plays. She was fired in 1920, maybe for being too critical of the plays she reviewed. After that she wrote poems and reviews for several liberal New York magazines.

A representative example of her "witty" commentary was her review of what is now a time-tested, beloved children's story that touches heart-strings and captures the tender emotions of childhood, Winnie the Pooh. The "witty" Parker, writing as "Constant Reader" in a trendy New York left-wing magazine, said that as she read the now-classic children's story, "Tonstant Weader fwowed up."

Acid-tongued? Sure. Witty? Maybe. Borderline insane? Clearly.

She was obviously at odds with the world, herself, society, America, business, men, women, the economy, and pretty much anything normal. In short, Dorothy Parker was a perfect target for recruitment as an anti-American KGB agent.

Married to a Reverend's Son—Suicides Begin

In 1917, she married the namesake son of a prominent Hartford, Connecticut pastor, the Reverend Edwin Pond Parker. Dorothy's relationship with Edwin Pond Parker II appears to have been tumultuous, as were all her relationships. Soon after her marriage to Parker II, his father died, in 1920. Within a year, her husband's younger brother, Burton, was arrested for mail fraud.

Dorothy tired of her husband, who reportedly went overseas to serve in WW1. She divorced him in 1928. In keeping with the pattern of intimates of Dorothy Parker, Edwin Parker killed himself with an overdose of "sleeping powders" in 1933.

Parker practiced her purported "wit" as a drama critic, an unusual position for a woman of those days. Always a heavy drinker during her adult life, she began lunching at the Algonquin Hotel restaurant with a group of literary drinkers. They began writing about their lunches, and each other, and soon built a reputation as a group of sparkling geniuses. One of Walter Duranty's best friends, Alexander Woollcott was also one of Parker's Algonquin group, and a lifelong friend.

Free Lance Writer—Unexplained Affluence

Her last regular job at a magazine ended with a firing. She "opened an office" with Robert Benchley, as free lance writers. The office seems to have been a joke, as it closed soon after.

Her biographer, John Keats, notes that "throughout 1920 and 1921 there is no record of any sale to any magazines...some of her friends wondered if she was really doing any writing. Yet she seemed to have money enough to go everywhere and do everything...perfume, handmade lingerie, and expensive dresses..."

Later, Parker published short stories and poems, and wrote criticism for trendy New York magazines. Her writing tended towards derisive and hateful, delivered with a smile. She derided men and women, the relationship between the sexes, other writers, life, and everything else in between.

Her special venomous hate was reserved for upper class Americans. Like many Willing Accomplices, she enjoyed the good life among her despised targets. Parker prospered among the upper class. She mixed and mingled, dallied and played, and built a prosperous lifestyle among the upper class Americans she so despised in her writing.

During this period, she established a close relationship with Donald Ogden Stewart, an Algonquinite, and later a staunch Muenzenberg Willing Accomplice.

Death, Suicide, Dying, Suffering

She published a book with suicide as its theme. One of her main literary subjects was death and killing—and her writing included many depressing details about her own numerous suicide attempts, presented in a "funny" way.

Her morbid attraction to death was sick. And her morbid love/hate relationship with wealth was too. Was she responsible for any of the multiple early deaths that seemed to trail in her wake? Would this explain her sick obsession with death? Or was she obsessed with death and suicide because she just happened to be unlucky and suffer multiple deaths of family members in untimely, suspicious circumstances?

Travel to Europe—Contact with Comintern Agents?

In 1926, with no apparent means of regular support, Parker went to Paris, probably after meeting Ernest Hemingway in New York. In her typical style, she fashioned a cover story that told the truth while hiding the truth. She would explain the trip later with a flip, "I ran off to the Riviera with a Trotskyite."

Seward Collins, an enigmatic wealthy publisher, later identified with Trotsky, and even later declared himself a fascist. Evidently, Collins paid her way to Europe, and accompanied her. That is, until she rejected him, and he slunk off back to America.

Reports of Parker's months in France, with the Americans in Paris, including Stewart and Hemingway, dwell on heavy drinking and personal rifts.

Willi Muenzenberg was working in Paris at the same time, as was the master KGB officer, Otto Katz, and multiple Comintern influence operators.

Parker's activities and contacts in Paris are murky, however, her actions and associations after the Paris trip reveal who she was likely involved with in Europe in 1926. Ten years later she worked with Katz again, establishing Muenzenberg fronts in Hollywood and across the U.S.

In one of the first American Muenzenberg operations, minor artistic types joined the usual suspects—communists, anarchists, and revolutionaries—to protest the death sentences of two anarchists sentenced for robbery and murder, Sacco and Vanzetti.

Parker showed up at the protests in Boston, in 1927, just after her return from Europe. She was arrested during the demonstration, and fined. This was her first public involvement with KGB-sponsored operations. It was the first of many. She also wrote for the Communist Party magazine, *New Masses*.

In 1930, Parker again spent time in Europe. She claimed that she was there to help a wealthy family with their invalid son, in Switzerland. This seems so out of character for Parker that it is likely a cover story.

She never used any of her European experiences as literary fodder. Why? Hemingway, Fitzgerald, all her friends and contemporaries mined their experiences in Europe, with many of the same friends as Parker, for their books and stories. Yet nowhere in Parker's writing is there a hint that she spent time in Europe. What was this exhibitionist author hiding?

Second Mr. Parker—Acting in Juvenile Roles

Dorothy remarried, in 1934. She mocked Alan Campbell, the new Mr. Parker (Dorothy used her first husband's name for the rest of her life) for being effeminate. Eleven years her junior, he was probably either homosexual or bisexual. In a new article announcing their marriage, the New York Times noted that the couple had set up house in Denver, where Campbell was acting "juvenile roles," in a local theater.

In a personal letter to a friend, Dorothy noted that at that moment Alan was "out buying lumber" with a male friend. "How vewy butch," she noted with characteristic venom. It appears she met him "in Europe," maybe in Paris, thus probably in the Comintern milieu that must have facilitated her development by Katz, or a colleague. Campbell was later not only her "writing partner," but also served the Comintern fronts that Dorothy set up in Hollywood.

Campbell seemed to be her cover, providing a male figure in her life for public consumption. They got contracts in Hollywood, where he was her partner in writing several screenplays. They divorced and remarried. He was found in their Beverly Hills home, dead in bed. His death was initially termed an accidental overdose of sleeping pills and alcohol. However, later investigation revealed that he, like the first Mr. Parker, had likely killed himself. The clue that tipped off detectives to suicide was the plastic bag tied over his head.

Hollywood with Katz

She appeared to live well beyond her means. For a young writer it must have been difficult to afford, during the Depression, lunches out every day, rounds of parties, and international travel. The New York Times, in a review of celebrity tax returns, in 1934, reported that Parker's income for 1932 was $15,000.

In the depths of the Depression, and the height of the Muenzenberg operations, Parker relocated to Hollywood, simultaneous with Otto Katz's arrival and organization of fronts. Her meeting and greeting activities have been very helpful in organizing a network of like-minded Accomplices. She was a near perfect social broker for a foreign case officer.

Parker, whose name appeared on several scripts, along with her husband, Campbell, couldn't have had much time for actual movie work. The Internet Movie Database lists twelve movies produced between 1936 and 1949 in which Parker was credited. It appears that most of her work was adding snappy dialog, or other patchwork writing.

She first wrote screenplays in 1929, and later returned to Hollywood, this time for nearly a decade, in 1934. It's not clear where her paycheck came from until she went to Hollywood, supposedly to write from Metro-Goldwyn-Mayer, in 1934. She may have received a good salary from her writing, but maybe not. She shared Oscar nominations for work on two screenplays, in 1937 for A Star is Born; and in 1948 for Smash-up: The Story of a Woman. Otherwise, her achievements in Hollywood were not impressive.

She was notoriously lazy as a writer, well-known for taking advances and not producing anything of value. This sort of non-production was not usually rewarded by the Hollywood moguls. Her friend and contemporary, F. Scott Fitzgerald found out the hard way. During his time in Hollywood, trying to write screenplays, he also drank heavily, made promises on which he did not deliver, and produced low quality work. He was fired.

Parker's experiences were the opposite of Fitzgerald's. She remained in Hollywood for nearly a decade. When she was employed as a writer, she even came with a toy-boy husband, a failed actor who she required to be billed as her "co-writer," and who received a salary too.

In 1935, she and Campbell bought a farm in the radical refuge of Bucks County, Pennsylvania. Her neighbors included George S. Counts, Willing Accomplice from Columbia Teachers College.

Spanish Civil War

In 1936, fighting began in the Spanish Civil War, the "Republican" side a front for Moscow controlled communists. The war provided the KGB with maximum international propaganda and covert influence opportunities. Parker showed up in communist-controlled Madrid. While there, she made a radio broadcast. She was involved with the American Muenzenberg fronts that supported the communists and the volunteer Americans, the Abraham Lincoln Brigade, for many years after the war.

She was extremely busy working on Muenzenberg fronts. Katz's efforts to recruit Hollywood bore fruit, and Parker was a juicy plum. She seemed to know everyone, and everyone knew her. She had an extensive network, and she put it to use for Muenzenberg front organizations.

Un-American Activities in California

In 1947, the California State Senate created a Fact-Finding Committee on Un-American Activities in California. It carried out extensive investigations, and heard testimony from many involved in the activities under investigation.

The committee findings, published in 1948, show that many Americans understood the threat that our country faced. The committee said that "Persons and groups, motivated by hatred of American

ideals, our republican form of government and democratic processes, some bound together by allegiance to foreign powers, are even now seeking to achieve by subversion what we have so valiantly fought to sustain from force."

Without understanding the operational methodology behind what they had found, and without understanding the exact operations in progress, they understood very clearly both the threat posed by the communists, and the extent of the communist success in their great State. For anyone who doubts the long-term efficiency of the anti-American covert influence operations run in California, just look at the state today. It is virtually bankrupt, virtually lawless, and held hostage by corrupt unions, anti-capitalist interests, and the heirs of Dorothy Parker and her KGB handlers.

The committee identified Dorothy Parker as an active member, a signatory, or an officer of the following front organizations:

Screenwriters Guild

Hollywood Anti-Nazi League, Alan Campbell—Secretary

Actors' Laboratory Theatre

American Committee for Yugoslav Relief

Artists' Front to Win the War

Voice of Freedom Committee

Friends of the Abraham Lincoln Brigade

History Today

Harry Bridges Defense Committee

Hollywood League for Democratic Action

League of Women Shoppers

Motion Picture Artists' Committee

People's Peace

Spanish Refugee Appeal (chairman)

Joint Anti-Fascist Refugee Committee

United Spanish Aid Committee

Writers Congress at the University Of California

People's Songs

Unwelcome Wit

In 1949, Parker, her cover as an influence agent blown by on-going investigations, finished her last major film project. Her "biting satire" was not appreciated by post-war America. The director said that the movie was "one of the few pictures I disliked" during production.

Fleeing the gathering storm as investigators of the House Un-American Activities Committee (HUAC) uncovered details of Willing Accomplices, including Parker, she asked for help from her New York set to find a refuge. The 1950s seem to have been a wasteland for Parker. The McCarthy and related Congressional investigations uncovered the web of Soviet and KGB operations throughout American society. The truth of the Muenzenberg front organizations was revealed by members and some of Parker's former friends. Her name was named.

HUAC Revelations

Parker never admitted her cooperation with the KGB or the Soviets. She was called to testify. Initial investigations included interviews with the FBI. During one such interview, Parker, who lived in a residential hotel in New York reportedly said, "My influence? Look at these two dogs of mine. I can't even influence them."

Trouble was that she had been up to her neck in dealings with foreigners who wanted to overthrow her country. From 1929 through the 1940s, Parker was involved in nearly 20 organizations that provided cover for KGB operations, and communist influence.

Her involvement in KGB-sponsored actions and organizations was not casual. Her involvement was deep, original, and secret. She went behind KGB lines in Spain, and broadcast propaganda.

Parker's FBI file included further details about her memberships and activities in other Muenzenberg front and related organizations. Some of those included: National Win the Peace Conference, 1946; American Committee for Yugoslav Relief,1945; Save the Voice of Freedom Committee, 1947; American Council on Soviet Relations, 1941; National Council of American Soviet Friendship, 1945; American Council for Democratic Greece, 1946; Signatory of "Statement of American Progressives on Moscow trials," during Stalin's purges, clear presumption of guilt of the defendants, 1938; Signatory of letter in Soviet Russia Today hailing Stalin's wonderful 5 year plan, 1937.

Used up and Discarded

Her fabled "wit" failed her. Her smart remarks no longer sounded smart, just cruel. She was unable to find real work in Hollywood again. She seems to have wobbled around in an alcoholic daze for the rest of the 1950s. She returned to Hollywood in 1961, reconciling with Campbell, who she had divorced and remarried. Unfortunately for Campbell. Their work was not interesting to paying customers. Within two years of their reconciliation, Campbell was dead in bed, a plastic bag tied around his head, his body full of drugs and alcohol. Caustic wit. Willing Accomplice. Angel of death?

Parker went back to New York, and filled the last four years of her life with booze-soaked days and nights, and a seemingly endless string of dogs. She died "of a heart attack," in a residential hotel. After a memorial service, she was quickly forgotten. Her ashes, unclaimed, sat for years in the funeral home, and then in a file cabinet in her lawyer's office. Parker left her entire estate, worth somewhere around $15,000 to the National Association for the Advancement of Colored People. Her fellow Willing Accomplice, Lillian Hellman, evidently misled about her inheritance, filed suit against the NAACP, and then withdrew. In 1988, the NAACP claimed Parker's ashes. They built a brick patio at their headquarters in memory of Parker.

CI Analysis of Dorothy Parker—3-Question Screening

Visited the USSR?

Success not consistent with recent past?

Content of work consistent with Muenzenberg creed?

Question 1—Visited the USSR?

There is no evidence that Parker ever visited the USSR.

Remember that we use this screening question to determine if we can be absolutely certain that the subject was assessed and developed by the KGB. Because the KGB had absolute control of foreigners inside Russia, a suspect foreigner's visiting the USSR is nearly certain proof of their KGB contact.

However, espionage operators are able to work outside their own countries, and the KGB was no exception. The KGB spotted, assessed, and recruited a large number of agents who never visited Russia.

Thus, in Parker's case, we need to expand the screening question a bit, in order to consider the potential for her having been met, assessed, developed, and possibly recruited outside Russia. The question we must ask of Parker is: Visited the USSR, or other venue totally under KGB control?

And the answer is a resounding yes.

We know that Parker visited Paris in 1926, supposedly in the company of Ernest Hemingway. We know that Willi Muenzenberg's operation used Paris as a headquarters. We know that many other American Willing Accomplices and agents of Russia were in Paris, in Hemingway's circle at that time. John Hermann and Josephine Herbst, close friends of Otto Katz, and close friends of Parker were hanging out in Paris in 1926. They were later tightly woven into Muenzenberg's and other KGB operations.

Parker moved in the same hard-drinking, arrogant social circle as Hemingway, Herbst, and Hermann. They all ended up serving as KGB accomplices, in both the Spanish Civil War, ten years later, and in Hollywood and Washington, for the next forty years, or as long as they survived. Hermann was involved in the Alger Hiss espionage ring, run by Harold Ware. Herbst, much like Walter Duranty, worked in covert influence operations as a journalist.

Parker was likely under Comintern agent's development during her time in Paris, if not before. It is likely that the Paris trip was designed by her KGB case officers as a chance for intensive time-on-target, time in which the case officer could deepen the relationship, and probably make her a fully witting agent of the KGB.

Other periods in which we know that Parker was in close, intimate, and continuing contact with KGB case officers include her time in communist Spain, and setting up Comintern fronts in Hollywood, under Otto Katz's control.

Her visit to the Spanish Civil War, in 1937, is almost undistinguishable from a visit to Moscow at the same time. The Spanish "Republicans" were a wholly-owned subsidiary of Stalin's Soviet Union. The same elements of total control of those in Russia were in place in communist Spain. The KGB acted with impunity. The Russian intelligence organization arrested ideologically unsound suspects, conducted purges, and conducted summary executions, just like they did across Russia. At the same time, they compiled dossiers of assessment and motivations on all the Americans who passed through the war-torn country.

Parker, in addition to being subject to the KGB's absolute control in Spain, regardless of her mission there, was completely under control of the KGB's propaganda arm when she made a speech broadcast on radio in October 1937. This speech is evidence of her complete subservience to the KGB. Witting or not, she was serving the KGB's propaganda efforts, in a covert and subtle way, but under the KGB's control nonetheless.

Our analysis must therefore conclude that, in Parker's case, we can positively prove that she was under the control of the KGB, during at least two formative periods of her life, although not inside the borders of Russia. In Paris, in 1926, she was in a social circle of American literary figures. In the coming years, nearly all of the members of that circle would be revealed as Soviet agents, covert or overt, witting or unwitting.

Parker herself later alluded to her conversion to the KGB's side during this trip, telling a probably apocryphal tale of visiting the steerage class passengers during the steamship voyage across the Atlantic. There she met the aged mother of American communist icon Tom Mooney, on her way to Russia with other American communists. Deep discussions with Mrs. Mooney, according to Parker's cover story, affected her deeply. This cover story is likely a concoction of truth and fiction, typical of cover stories dreamed up by case officers. It does however, point to Parker's clear connection to the Russian communists during this trip.

In Spain, as discussed above, Parker was a tool of the KGB. She performed at least one covert influence job for them. She was also writing for American publications during her visit to the communist side of the civil war. In Spain, in 1937, she would have been totally under KGB control. If they did not yet have full assessment data on her, this would have been developed in the first few days she was in the country. By the time she left, she would have been fully developed by her KGB handlers.

Thus, although we have no evidence that Parker ever visited Russia, we can conclusively answer that she was under absolute KGB control at least once in her life.

Question 2—Success not Consistent with Recent Past?

Yes. Parker suddenly and inexplicably rose to fame and prominence.

Parker was a gag-writer and editorial assistant for magazines from 1917 to the late 1920s. Around then, she fell in with the Algonquin group. At least one, Alexander Woollcott, was closely tied to Walter Duranty, a KGB covert influence agent.

The other members of the group were highly intelligent, educated literary notables. Maybe Parker was actually talented. She very quickly vaulted into national prominence, which she clearly relished, with little actual achievement. She published a collection of her magazine ditties, and then a book of short stories. A few years later, she followed up with another book of poems, and another book of short stories.

Her move to Hollywood marked her abrupt arrival as a national name. Her deep involvement in Otto Katz's Muenzenberg influence fronts rocketed her name to coast-to-coast prominence. From the mid-1930s until the HUAC and McCarthy exposure of Parker's communist ties, and the withdrawal of KGB operations officers from America, Parker was at the top of the social whirl.

In company with other Willing Accomplices of the high-point of the Muenzenberg era, Parker scaled the summit of American success. In 1934, her reported income of $16,000 would likely not have covered her lifestyle.

Soon after, Parker and Campbell bought a farm in Pennsylvania, rented a suite at a fashionable New York address, traveled far and wide, all while producing sporadic scripts under short-term contracts in Hollywood.

Dorothy Parker could be the poster girl for success inconsistent with her past, or her capabilities.

Question 3—Content of Work Consistent with Muenzenberg Creed?

Parker's early work can be characterized as mean and cruel. She reveled in criticism and hateful insults disguised as witticisms. It does not take much analysis to reveal her thinly disguised contempt for her country.

Her most famous poems can be parsed to a common essence. Parker was shocked and disgusted with American society. She was so shocked and frightened by her country that she seemed to be constantly prepared to commit suicide. And she constantly let her readers know how shocked and disgusted she was by the society, economy, the people and everything else about her country. One of her poems spewed hatred for the corrupt women she competed with for men.

> Not a man you meet that doesn't fall for you;
> Lady, pretty lady, how I hope you choke!

One of her other main themes was the corruption of the capitalist system. She mocked the businessmen of New York. She badgered and mocked her first husband, the stock broker son of a staid Protestant minister until he killed himself.

Besides her poetry, she was famous for her "wisecracks." Many reflect the Muenzenberg creed:

> If you want to know what God thinks of money, just look at the people he gave it to.

In Hollywood, she worked on a script for an Alfred Hitchcock movie. As quoted earlier, a speech she wrote was right out of the Muenzenberg creed, mocking the moron millions of normal Americans, she was "shocked, frightened by what is going on here in our own country:"

> You're one of the ardent believers, a good American. All the millions like you, people that plod along without asking questions. I hate to use the word stupid, but it seems to be the only one that applies. The great masses, the moron millions. Well, there a few of us who are unwilling to troop along. A few of us who are clever enough to see that there is much more to be done than just live small complacent lives. A few of us in America desire a more profitable type government. When you think about it Mr. Kane, the

> competence of totalitarian nations is much higher than ours. They get things done.

Her public following of the Muenzenberg covert influence line began in earnest almost immediately after she returned from her first trip to Europe. In 1927, she became publicly involved in one of Muenzenberg's first American influence operations, the Sacco and Vanzetti protests. Parker went to Boston, protested publicly, and was arrested.

It was during this period, roughly parallel to Stalin's push for international support for the Soviet Union, when Muenzenberg was pushing the anti-fascist line, that Parker had a hand in creating or marketing a multitude of covert influence fronts, disguised to be palatable for average Americans to support. She set up the Hollywood Anti-Nazi League, under Otto Katz's tutelage.

In this effort she found her true calling. From a cocktail party to raise money for the Joint Anti-Fascist Refugee Committee, to a speech in support of the Hollywood League for Democratic Action, Parker's work was, in effect, influence by action.

Her broadcast from Madrid, under the control of the KGB bordered on propaganda. Yet she never crossed the line from influence to propaganda. The line was in the most important part of the Muenzenberg Creed, the preamble, if you will:

> You do not endorse Stalin.
>
> You do not call yourself a Communist.
>
> You do not declare your love for the regime.
>
> You do not call on people to support the Soviets.
>
> Ever. Under any circumstances.
>
> You claim to be an independent-minded idealist.

Parker was careful to always follow this precept. She never publicly praised Stalin; nor did she call herself a communist; nor did she declare her love for the regime. She did hew carefully to the Muenzenberg creed though.

Especially broadcasting from KGB-controlled Madrid, she followed Muenzenberg's covert influence principles.

In her speech her theme was the creed points: "You hate fascism. You think the capitalist system is corrupt."

> It is knowing that nothing devised by fat, rich, frightened men can ever stamp out truth and courage, and determination for a decent life.

Emoting about a school she had visited in communist Spain, the cynical, Hollywood-dwelling, uneducated Parker gushed about the Soviets' great human experiment, which she clearly hoped would work:

> In the schools for young children, there is none of the dread thing you have heard so much about–depersonalization. Each child has, at the government's expense, an education as modern and personal as a privileged American school child has at an accredited progressive school.

As the Congressional House Committee on Un-American Activities hearings run by Congressman Martin Dies, of Texas zeroed its sights on Hollywood, in early 1940, investigators found former Willing Accomplices who were now willing to tell the truth about the subversive effects of communist influence in Hollywood. Humphrey Bogart, Lionel Stander, and Frederic March indicated their willingness to provide details about activities against America in Hollywood.

Spooked, Parker went on the attack. Writing in the April 1940, "Hollywood Number" of *Direction* magazine, Parker toed the Muenzenberg line with an attack, following the Creed's requirement, "You're shocked, frightened by what is going on right here in your own country." And finally she trumpeted, for one of the first times, the soon-to-be-timeworn-PC-Progressive epithet, "Fascist!"

> The people want democracy - real democracy, Mr. Dies, and they look toward Hollywood to give it to them because they don't get it any more in their newspapers. And that's why you're out here, Mr. Dies - that's why you want to destroy the Hollywood Progressive organizations - because you've got to control this medium if you want to bring fascism to this country.

Conclusion: Dorothy Parker—KGB Willing Accomplice in the Destruction of American Culture

This CI analysis of Dorothy Parker's life reveals that she was a Willing Accomplice working to destroy America from within. Her activities were mostly in the domain of Hollywood, where she actively recruited and proselytized for the anti-American PC-Progressive point of view.

It is almost certain that she was also witting that she was involved in a KGB influence operation. Her participation in the Popular Fronts supported by Muenzenberg was too great, too deep, and too extensive for her to have been unwitting.

She was in the first wave of organizers of Muenzenberg front organizations in Hollywood. Otto Katz was in Hollywood to help set these up. Parker had been in France, in the company of other Willing Accomplices and KGB officers and agents ten years previously.

Later Parker traveled to wartime Spain, into KGB-controlled territory, where she made influence radio broadcasts touting the Muenzenberg influence Creed.

The effects of Parker's influence operations are felt today. Generations of Americans, especially adolescent girls, seem to admire Parker's point of view and attitude. She seems to be some sort of role model for many young Americans.

In the extensive literature review I carried out for this CI study of Parker, the adoring fan point of view accounts for the bulk of writing on her life. A standard explanation of her covert influence work for the KGB's operations to destroy America may be found by Binging her name. The same line appears in dozens of websites: "Politically liberal, she was investigated by the FBI for suspected involvement in Communism during the McCarthy era."

PC-Progressives clearly believe that this is explanation enough. Their talismanic invocation of McCarthy is like a Catholic's receiving absolution by saying a Hail Mary. If McCarthy was involved, Parker was a victim.

Unfortunately for those who put her on a pedestal as a sainted victim of vicious Red-baiters, the truth is that Dorothy Parker was a drunken, vicious, witting Willing Accomplice in the KGB's covert influence operations to destroy American culture and society.

PART 5

21ST CENTURY AMERICA

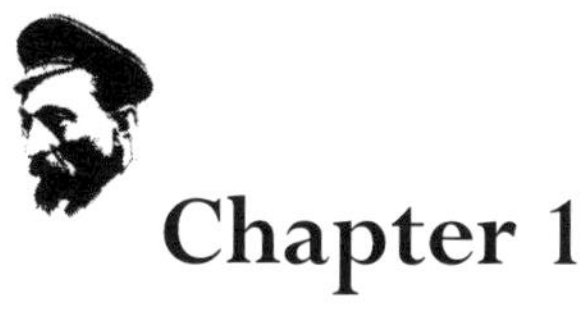

Chapter 1

Muenzenberg's results

The ideological force-feeding of undergraduate students that characterized the University of Delaware's residential life program had numerous components: radical environmentalism, an attempt to stigmatize traditional moral sentiments, foregrounding questions of sexual orientation, efforts to promote deep distrust of American society, promotion of identity politics, and an aggressive focus on racial grievance.

Thomas Wood, PC in Academia, 2008

As we have seen in the earlier historical review of the KGB's covert influence operations against the U.S., the effort to destroy America from within began soon after the Bolsheviks seized power in Russia. As soon as they were able to consolidate their power in the Russian civil war, around 1920, Lenin turned his attention to the Main Adversary. The Marxist theory of an inevitable evolution of all societies to communism proved to be either totally false or totally over-optimistic. Real human nature turned out to be much different from the German philosopher's naïve theories.

Lenin adjusted the theory with his addition of the Elite Vanguard, which of course included himself, which would guide the uncooperative proletariat through the process of reaching communist nirvana. In Russia this required force, and a lot of it. Lenin realistically realized that he could not muster the force necessary to bring the proletariat of the Great Adversary around to communism.

So, Lenin turned to his strong suit, covert operations. He laid out the guidelines of a plan to destroy the Main Adversary from within. Although he delegated the operation to his espionage agency, what later became the KGB, Lenin kept a close eye on the operations. He met with several American influence agents, and their handlers—Alexander Gumberg, handler, and his American agent, Raymond Robins; Gumberg and his agent, Bess Beatty among others.

Lenin entrusted his close associate from his time in exile, Willi Muenzenberg, with the operation. Muenzenberg planned the methods and payloads. The KGB supported and monitored Muenzenberg himself, as well as his agents.

Stalin inherited Lenin's covert influence operations, and allowed them to continue for a time. However, it appears that he began to modify the objectives and some of the payload. He became obsessed with obtaining American diplomatic recognition for the Soviet Union. It appears that this became Stalin's main objective for the influence ops.

This goal was reached in 1934, thanks largely to one of Muenzenberg's most successful penetrations of the American press, Walter Duranty. Stalin met privately with this covert influence agent, providing his handlers with a reward for the success of the mission. But there were many other Willing Accomplices in the American press.

All the while, one of Lenin's main targets, the American education and academic system was under a constant barrage of influence operations. As we saw, the George S. Counts operation was probably the most successful and influential of these operations. But there were many others.

Stalin and his espionage operators, inherited from Lenin, realized the power of America's Dream Factory, Hollywood. After Stalin consolidated his power, Muenzenberg's operations against Hollywood picked up speed. He sent one of his most capable case officers, Otto Katz, to Hollywood to set in motion the textbook covert influence operation that infiltrated the KGB's influence payload throughout the movie industry.

Dorothy Parker was probably the most influential and effective of the Hollywood Willing Accomplices, but there were many others.

We now have identified the components of the massive covert influence operation designed to destroy American culture, including the brains, some operators, the methodology, the payload, and some agents.

The question remains—what happened to the operation? What happened to the operators? What happened to the payload? What happened to the agents?

The brains of the covert influence operation, Willi Muenzenberg, along with most of the case officers who spotted, assessed, developed and recruited the influence agents, died in Stalin's purges.

A large percentage of KGB officers died during the years of Stalin's power. In order to consolidate his power, he made false accusations, created imaginary coup attempts, created imaginary conspiracies against him, and manufactured other reasons to accuse loyal communist espionage officers of treason. His purges hit the KGB and the Comintern hard.

Muenzenberg was one of the tricky ones. He avoided responding to Stalin's call to return to Moscow, where he would have died. He was able to eke out a couple of extra years on the run, before he was finally eliminated, as the Nazis overran France.

Otto Katz survived into the 1950s, succumbing to Stalin's purges during a show trial, an abject confession of absurd crimes, and finally the same fate as his colleague, Muenzenberg, a rope around the neck, and a communist death.

Alexander Gumberg escaped the Stalin purges, maybe. It appears that he never went back to Russia alone and always traveling with his targets and recruited agents, providing them with translation and guidance during their trips to Russia. He did die young, struck down by a heart attack as he "walked on the grounds of his Summer home" in Norwalk, Connecticut. He was an executive without portfolio for an American investment conglomerate, the Atlas Corporation.

Gumberg's extensive influence operations, and his true status as a KGB handler, revealed publicly in this book for the first time, deserve much closer scrutiny and analysis. His masterful use of capitalist cover for his operations could very well have set the template for later KGB operators.

The influence agents, those Americans who lent their talents to their communist masters, like Dorothy Parker, Walter Duranty, and George Counts, lived out their natural lives. Each, in their own way, was more or less pitiful after their KGB operational use was over.

Parker dived into a bottle, and drank herself to a slow death. She played on her Andemca response to her exposure by the HUAC and other investigations, never admitting the truth of her operational involvement. She died alone, with a dog or two, in a residential hotel in New York.

George Counts evidently rejected his operational use, around the time of WW2. Yet he never admitted the truth of his covert influence work, or who his co-conspirators where. He publicly morphed into an "anti-communist liberal," yet he never denounced publicly, or privately, the content of the payload he inserted into American education and academia. As a result, his influence operations continue to bear anti-American fruit till today.

Counts destroyed the evidence of his covert operations when he left his Teachers College office for the last time, upon his unceremonious forced retirement. His papers, at SIU-Carbondale, contain only a few hints of his work in Russia.

Nucia Lodge, Counts' handler, may have been the most skillful and the luckiest of all the handlers and agents uncovered in this research. She lived well into her 90s, working as a Russian researcher and translator at the Hoover Institute of Stanford University.

It appears that Nucia must have let Counts in on the details of the operation she ran against him. They must have agreed to make a coordinated turn against the KGB, calculated for the best effect for both of them. This was likely Nucia's plan.

The results of her plan were spectacular. She was able to reinvent herself as a plain Russian researcher, hiding all traces of her connections with the KGB, and the Bolsheviks. Counts was less successful, and came up in HUAC and other investigations. Counts used the Andemca strategy, portraying himself as the victim of an out of control, semi-fascist government.

Walter Duranty died a pitiful, sick drunk with all his support systems, including financial support, collapsed. He never admitted the truth of his cooperation with the KGB, and also played the Andemca card when accused of being an "Apologist for Stalin."

It is important to note that the break in the Muenzenberg operation occurred about the time of Muenzenberg's own death. The near-absolute cleansing of the KGB in Stalin's purges created a vacuum in which the KGB lost its institutional memory.

KGB case officers who followed the heroes of the Cheka, most of whom were purged, as one of them told me, knew better than to delve into the history of specific KGB operations. Instead, they only learned the generalities of each type of op, collection or covert influence, for example, and then went out and reinvented the wheel.

There was never another effective, efficient, powerful, focused influence operation like Muenzenberg's. Later KGB attempts to influence American politics were mildly successful, but were hampered by the post-McCarthy counter-intelligence focus. Never again would the KGB have such free reign in American institutions as they did during the height of the Muenzenberg operations.

So, even though the KGB attempted influence operations after WW2 and the exposure of their massive operations against America during the 1950s, they were never again effective.

The results of the operations, therefore, spring almost entirely from the early KGB operations, carried out between 1920 and 1940, for the most part.

What was the Effect on America?

The question that needs to be explored further, however, now that the KGB's handling case officers, their covert influence agents, and the leaders who conceived of the ops are all dead and gone is: What was the effect of the Muenzenberg operations on America?

We need to keep in mind the point introduced in an earlier chapter—the effects of influence operations, unlike collection operations, can go on forever.

The ideas, the payload, that Muenzenberg created, were inserted into American culture by his operators. The attitude that Muenzenberg created, the elite, more-caring-than-thou, above-the-moron-millions point of view was lovingly nurtured by the influence agents, and passed on by the multitude of cover organizations.

The result of inserting the payload in the transmission belts of American culture was to create a new point of view, unseen before in American society, that echoed Muenzenberg's Creed. This point of view held that America was a racist, sexist, foreigner-hating, unfair, unjust, imperialistic, war-mongering nation that needed to be taken down a notch.

Those who adopted this point of view also adopted the attitude that they composed an elite, intelligent, enlightened, more-caring-than-thou clique that would be the saving grace of the disgraced U.S.

This point of view, and this new attitude, was reinforced by the influence agents' Andemca attacks during the McCarthy era. The Andemca response, picked up and echoed through all three cultural transmission belts, created a new pantheon of victimized heroes for the new political class.

Their point of view grew in power throughout the 1960s and 1970s. They message and attitude infiltrated education and academia first. The anti-war, hippie, yippie, counter-culture movements were direct outgrowths of the KGB's payload from the 1920s, 30s and 40s.

As older, traditional Americans left positions of influence in academia, Hollywood and the media, they were replaced by younger people who grew up with the anti-American point of view their whole lives.

The 1980s was two or three generations removed from the Muenzenberg operations. Yet this is when the full effect of that influence genius's plans was finally evident in American society. Political correctness gained strength and consolidated its power in institutions of the cultural transmission belts.

First universities fell to the PC-Progressive commissars. Next education organizations became PC-Progressive. Media institutions followed closely. By the end of the 1980s, PC-Progressives controlled all three of Muenzenberg's targeted domains.

Only after PC-Progressives, parroting Muenzenberg's Creed, controlled all three elements of cultural transmission did normal America really notice. By then, the PC-Progressive clique had its boot on our neck, and was planning the demise of traditional America.

21st Century "Bigots, Racists, Deniers"

We have come to see in the 21st century that those who "hunger for righteousness" have seized upon the ploy of defining who is guilty in society. PC and its practitioners today provide the descendants of Muenzenberg's Innocents with clearly defined groups of "bigots, racists, sexists, homophobes, and global warming deniers" and other undesirables. To be against this rogue's gallery of sinners is to be on the side of the angels, even if you're an atheist (which, of course is the only possible PC religious preference).

Because of the penetration of our educational system by the covert influence payload, Americans are ignorant of history. The seeds of anti-Americanism were planted. Innocents denied any communist influence. If anyone observed the seeds being planted, they were castigated for their lowly hatreds. A more efficient and effective influence operation has yet to be conceived or carried out.

Has the PC Creed dictated by Muenzenberg actually thrived through the decades, long after his rotting corpse was found swinging from the low hanging limbs of a French tree? Is it possible that the Soviet covert influence payloads were so potent?

Let's trace Muenzenberg's DNA. Pick a line of Muenzenberg's creed at random, any line. How about, "You think the capitalist system is corrupt." Now, Google "capitalist system is corrupt." Up pops an interview from yesterday with R. Victoria Arana, who teaches in the English department of Howard University. R. Victoria says, "Oh, yes. Contemporary black British writers take up all sorts of social issues, and a newish sort of "green" critique of capitalist excesses pops up fairly regularly these days."

Whoa! Has she been talking to Willi? Once you've been sensitized to Muenzenberg's operational creed, you begin to realize its prevalence in America today. How about, "You're frightened by the racism, by the oppression of the workingman."

Google "oppression of the workingman" and we find an American high school social studies lesson plan that calls for students to "discover the depth and breadth of capital's oppression of the working man."

The lesson claims to answer the question, "Who really deserves to enjoy and savor the greater share of the fruits of the working man's labor?" I'll bet I can guess the answer. And it's not the big fat capitalist pig who owns the factory.

Uncanny! Did Willi's ghost whisper in the ear of the University of Pittsburgh's Center for American Music, which produced this curriculum? Maybe he did. For in the Resources list of this lesson, we find a film, *Salt of the Earth* (1953), which was the result of the collaboration of several Hollywood communists, all of whom were in direct contact with Muenzenberg's KGB operators.

Further on in the resource section we see books by the Foner brothers, both Communists, one a history professor, and one a labor organizer from the 1930s. Once you are aware of the threads, it is not hard to trace them back to their source.

The Muenzenberg covert line played out in an American high school lesson plan in 2008, posted on the Internet. Conspiracy? Well, yes. Conspiracy and espionage, achieving their greatest heights in covert influence, were the strengths of the KGB.

Presidential Politics – 2008—Willi, Is That You?

Let's look at another example, ripped from the headlines in 2008, and see how the results of Muenzenberg's covert influence operations played out in the American presidential election of 2008. The news of then-candidate Barack Obama's former pastor's decidedly anti-American messages from the pulpit hit the news.

In Muenzenberg's Creed, one of the rules begins, "You're frightened by the racism." So what was the gist of the Reverend Jeremiah Wright's damnation of the USA? In his PC-Progressive view of America, the country has "failed its citizens of color." And his rant against his country continued, "The government lied about inventing the HIV virus as a means of genocide against people of color."

Wright's toxic babbling provides an example of an unusual double whammy. He echoed the Muenzenberg Creed of fright at American racism. But the big covert influence payoff is Wright's insertion of a KGB disinformation payload: "AIDS was a United States government creation."

Planting the story of the American government's role in creating the AIDS virus was a KGB operation that was, "probably the most successful [KGB] anti-American [disinformation campaign] of the Gorbachev era..." The KGB's role in this disinformation operation has been known publicly for more than 10 years.

Obama's Philadelphia response speech made use of Andemca. He admitted nothing, denied wrongdoing, and made counter-accusations, including against his own grandmother. At the same time, he managed to weave in several of Muenzenberg's other anti-American themes.

Analyze the theme of the statements of virtually any PC-Progressive today, and you'll see the one of the tenets of Muenzenberg's Creed. The messages are all around us. Willi

Muenzenberg's covert influence operations are more vibrant today than when they were first inserted into our culture.

The kudzu seeds were planted nearly a century ago. The vines dove underground for a time, but continued growing. PC is their name. Its omnipresent vines wrap tightly around the throats of Americans today. Are you tired of it yet?

Chapter 2

Our dilemma—what must be done?

I'm not a politician or a social worker. It's not my place to solve the problems that PC has created. My contribution is to identify where PC came from, and those who were responsible for it. So I'll leave specific prescriptions for actions to others. But, I will offer these observations.

The Muenzenberg influence operation stripped away traditional American values. Willing Accomplices created an elitist attitude that became PC-Progressivism.

We trusted Willing Accomplices—academics, educators, reporters, writers, editors, screenwriters, directors—with our culture. These Willing Accomplices destroyed America.

What can we do? We can restore traditional American values. We can reject PC-Progressive "Change."

Since the Reagan era, normal Americans have been fighting back against the PC-Progressives, by fits and starts. However, the PC clique maintained absolute control over all three cultural transmitters, until the rise of the Fox television network, and the internet.

The "culture war" that arose in the late 1980s and early 1990s continues today. It is, in effect, a political struggle for the soul of America. The real American soul was replaced by a communist covert influence operation, over the course of decades.

The only way to win back the American soul is to first identify the operation that took our soul—the communist covert influence operations planned by Muenzenberg. Then we must identify the payloads that Muenzenberg inserted via that operation. Then we must identify each time that payload is repeated in our cultural transmission belts, and ask if that message is appropriate.

If we recognize the payload inserted in our children's schools, we must aggressively reject it, and demand instead that our children be taught the wonder of the greatest country in the history of the world. We must regain control of our children's education from the PC-Progressive education mafia.

E.D. Hirsch created an exceptional curriculum and series of books, *Cultural Literacy,* designed to pass on our unique, traditional American culture. He created a book for each year of school. The first is called *What Your 1st Grader Needs to Know.* He covers all aspects of a solid American education in this series. It would be a solid foundation for a traditional American curriculum.

At the very least, you should pay attention to your local school board, and vote in elections. Pay attention to your State school organizations. And pay attention to the Federal Department of Education. Vote.

If we recognize the PC payload in universities, we must insist that the professors and institutions be responsible for their views. We must identify the individual professors and the institutions that insert the PC-Progressive, hate America messages. Then we must withdraw our support from those individuals and institutions—financially and morally.

If we recognize the payload inserted in the media, TV, radio, newspapers, websites, or others, we must withdraw our support from those individuals, stations, networks, or organizations that propagate the anti-American PC-Progressive point of view.

If we recognize the payload inserted into Hollywood movies, we must withdraw our support. Don't go to PC-Progressive movies.

We must reject the carriers of the foul PC-Progressivism. Stay strong. Do not despair. We will win back our country.

Epilogue

The human toll of espionage

But your influence operation lives on. And your agents' families live on. And the terrible secrets they carried with them corroded the lives around them.

From the tone of her voice, it was obvious that the 85 year old lady was proud of her long-dead father. She spoke lovingly of the trans-Atlantic trips she had taken with him and her family. Her accounts of his scholarship were glowing. When the conversation turned to his political views, and how they had evolved from 1927 to 1957, she adamantly denied that her father had ever been anything but a patriotic American.

He was *not* a communist, nor was he sympathetic to the communists. That had been concocted by Hearst and the American Legion.

A daughter's love for her father, her need to protect his memory, all are understandable. However, in this case, the proof is there for all to see. George S. Counts had glowingly spoken of the need for collectivism in the USA, well after the founding of the first communist state, the USSR, had shown the true results of collectivist government.

Any literate person could have read reports in the U.S. press about the results of the collectivization of Russian farms. But Counts was not just any literate person. He spent long periods of time in the USSR, at least three different times, for up to 7 months at a time. One of those trips involved driving 6,000 miles across the USSR, in an American automobile.

Counts had been there. Counts had seen it. He had to know what Russian communism was all about. And yet, he still bemoaned American individualism, and lauded Russia's advances in education, science, and industry.

Counts was not just an apologist for Stalin, he was a cheerleader who was actually playing in the game. His influential university, his work with the International institute, his leading students to study in Moscow, his authoring of popular, *NY Times* best-selling books, scholarly books, academic articles, popular articles in newspapers and magazines provided an ideal channel for the communist covert influence message to penetrate deep into American culture.

Counts' "collectivist" writings are still, to this day, in 2011, cited and quoted by American students of Education. His profound influence on American education, rhapsodizing the collectivist and denigrating the proto-typical "rugged individualism" of the American spirit, assisted in creating wave after wave of negative changes in American schools. The ultimate effect of his KGB covert influence operation was PC in academia and the American school system.

However, the effects of the espionage operations that provided Counts with the messages that he fed into American culture, were far deeper than just the macro-changes in American culture.

These espionage operations also created individual victims, friends and relations of those involved. Whole families were torn asunder, thanks to the KGB's manipulation of its agents.

Counts' daughter Martha, a PhD herself, fondly recalls her family's trips to Europe, which culminated, for her, in a year in an international school in Switzerland in 1936. Her father never allowed his daughters into Russia with him, telling them that it was "too dangerous." His wife remained in Vienna or Switzerland with the girls, occasionally visiting Counts in Russia.

But the European idylls came with a price. Counts' performance of his influence duties focused negative attention on him. He became a target for those contemporaries who saw through his subtle, and not so subtle, cheerleading for the brutal Communists.

Implementing the standard covert action response to confrontation, Counts admitted nothing, and made counter-accusations. This acrimony must have been hard for the family to bear. In Counts' case, as in so many others, he was elevated as a martyr to "red-baiting," or "McCarthyism."

Martha Counts chokes up when she tries to explain how she was subjected to negative consequences as a result of her father's association with Communists and the Soviets.

The younger Dr. Counts, cannot continue past "I've felt the sting of McCarthyism." She believes that her father was one of the victims of an unjust witch-hunt. And yet, as we have seen with our analysis of the actions of Dr. Counts, the elder, he was a Willing Accomplice, spreading the virus of communist covert influence in American culture, planting the invasive seeds that grew into PC and destroyed our traditional point of view.

Regardless of his motives, or his level of knowledge of the identity of his co-conspirators, he played the game, he benefited greatly in fame and fortune. He also suffered the consequences.

The mental gymnastics that are required to ignore the reality of a situation, and to blame others for actions they take in response to your own (or your father's) actions, must take a huge emotional toll. What was the effect on the lives of Counts' family? George Counts and his KGB handlers dropped a pebble into a pond, hoping to create a tidal wave. They were successful; however, the wave also swamped the lives of many others.

Nucia Perlmutter Lodge's family settled in Chicago. Her two sisters married Russian-Americans and raised families. Nucia traveled the world, bouncing between Russia and the U.S., hiding her tracks well.

At some point, Nucia fell under the sway of the Soviet espionage system. Was she recruited in Russia, before she left, or in New York City during the 1920's, a hotbed of communist espionage?

Whenever it was, she hit her stride after the operation became successful. Not leaving Counts' side for years, she stayed with him through the denials and counter-accusations. Ultimately, both she and Counts decided to tell a little bit of the truth, without actually revealing their own relationships with the Russian intelligence apparatus. Their last collaborations were anti-Soviet translations and books, or at least their attempts to be anti-Soviet.

What of Nucia's family while she was manipulating and being manipulated: Her elder sister, Rayousha married and had a daughter, Lola Jean. Lola Jean idolized Nucia. Intelligent and curious, just like her aunt, Lola Jean was accepted into the University of Chicago at only 16 years of age.

On her registration forms, she listed her aunt Nucia as her "closest relative," even though Nucia was nowhere near Chicago, and her own mother was within 10 miles of the university, as was her father.

The sensitive, intelligent girl worshipped Nucia, who could not respond. Nucia was doing the bidding of the KGB. She could not settle down in Chicago and help her precocious niece mature. The family issues that Lola Jean was experiencing might have melted away with long heart-to-hearts with her favorite aunt. But Nucia was in Moscow, or New York, or Washington, not Chicago.

Lola Jean threw herself into her schoolwork and unhealthy relationships. Marrying early to a classmate, she was soon divorced, giving up her young son to the father, both of whom she never saw again. Lola Jean grew up in a household that dared not reveal even her mother's own maiden name.

Not even their place of origin was admitted. It was "Russia," and nothing more. Moscow? St Petersburg? Siberia? Not even a hint was passed on. Hushed whispers of the origins of the family silver, or their previous lives as servants to the tsar.

Rayousha's wonderfully elaborate and skillful banquets could have only come from someone with training in the service of the royal family. Maybe, maybe not. The atmosphere was one of secrets and secret shame. What were they hiding?

Another marriage and a slow deterioration into mental illness. break-downs, hospitalizations, talk of surgeries, apparent remissions, a treadmill of mental anguish led to Lola's involuntary commitment to a mental institution.

Lola Jean needed her role model, an American success story who she longed to emulate, but Nucia was paralyzed, and unable to respond to the young girl's needs; too busy with the whirlwind of activity required to run the op against Counts and to write, translate, and be Counts' secretary, her cover job.

The ultimate effects on human lives was more than the KGB case officers had ever anticipated, more than they could have anticipated, and clearly of absolutely no concern to the communist monolith that ate its own young.

Collateral damage from the explosion of an artillery shell can include property and lives. Collateral damage of an intelligence operation is less tangible, more emotional.

Martha Counts' denials and counter-attacks, her clinging to the purity of her father's reputation, to the notion that he had been one of the many victims of a mindless, hateful, baseless attack. Nucia's family's secrets. Lola Jean's insanity.

You're the KGB case officer, working under cover with the Comintern in 1927. You're under great pressure to destroy the capitalist enemy from within through covert influence operations.

Do you consider the effects of your operations 80 years from today? Or do you simply do your best to move a promising operation down the road, maintaining operational security today, with the goal of getting Counts' anti-American book published as soon as possible?

Of course, you do what is expedient and helps your career. But you only live another three years, because you are caught up in a Stalinist counter-revolutionary purge.

You were too close to your American targets. You die with a Tokarev TT30 7.62mm pistol slug in the base of your brain, your precious memories and operational savvy nothing but bloody muck sloshed into the drain in Lubyanka's basement.

But your influence operation lives on. And your agents' families live on. And the terrible secrets they carried with them corrode the lives around them.

Bet that wasn't in your last cable to the Center.

Note

On the KGB and terminology

In this work I take a wide view of Soviet intelligence operations against the United States. The Soviet intelligence personalities and organizations involved, considering espionage operations within the United States across a period stretching the better part of half a century, were numerous and ever-changing, as were their targets and recruited agents. The name by which the KGB itself has been known has changed numerous times from the Russian Revolution until today.

Without going into laborious details, the use of KGB throughout this work is a simplification in order to focus on the operations and the results, not the bureaucratic history of the organizations.

While this simplified way of referring to Soviet intelligence agencies will likely grate on the nerves of some old-timers, I'd like to point out that the American intelligence community is dealing with the same issue today. With multiple reorganizations, and the addition of more layers of bureaucracy, the CIA itself has been known by many names. Specifically the Directorate of Operations (DO) is now officially known as the Clandestine Service (CS). And yet many still refer to the DO as the DO, because it is less confusing.

Soviet Intelligence Agencies—Nomenclature

This is not a chronicle of the history of Soviet intelligence. That history is intricate and complicated, and the subject of many other studies. In this work, I've simplified the terminology used to refer to Soviet intelligence. Also, since the majority of my readers are not bilingual Russian-English speakers, I'll use the standardized terminology of American intelligence. For example, even though the Russians call their intelligence office working out of foreign locations a "residency," and they call the head of their residency the "resident," the American terminology for these two terms are "station," and "station chief," and that's what I'll use here.

In the same spirit, I'll use KGB to mean Russian intelligence here. You are welcome to look further into this issue, and to further clarify the name of specific Communist intelligence agencies in other sources, if it is important to you. I believe that this simplified nomenclature will open up this subject to many who may have been put off by the extremely complicated history of the KGB, and confused by the multitude of names used by the KGB through its history. See the bibliography for references that explore the Soviet nomenclature in great detail.

Calling all Soviet intelligence organizations, "the KGB" does not mean that I am ignorant of the various bureaucratic reorganizations throughout the history of the Soviet Union, which resulted in renaming the KGB numerous times. It also does not mean that I am unaware of the Soviets' military intelligence organization, the GRU, or other intelligence agencies.

Alger Hiss, the US State Department official who worked as a Soviet espionage agent for many years, was originally recruited by the GRU. It appears that his handling many have been taken over by the KGB at some point. But for the purposes of this work, it doesn't matter which Soviet service ran him when. What matters is that he was working for Soviet intelligence. The use of KGB throughout this work is a simplification in order to focus on the operations and the results, not the bureaucratic history of the organizations.

This work, while focusing on covert influence operations, mainly during the between the World Wars era, takes a wide view of Soviet intelligence operations against the United States. The Soviet intelligence personalities and organizations involved, over a period stretching the better part of half a century, were numerous and ever-changing, as were their targets and recruited agents.

For reference, here is a chronological list of the acronyms by which the KGB has been known, and the year the name was first used: **Cheka** (1917); **NKVD/GPU** (1922); **OGPU** (1923); **NKVD/GUGB** (1934); **NKGB** (1941); **NKVD/GUGB** (1941); **NKGB** (1943); **MGB** (1946); **KI** (1947); **MVD** (1953); **KGB** (1954).

It is likely that the covert influence operations I examine in this series were run by a secretive and compartmented branch of Soviet intelligence, which seems to not even have been identified by name. These operations were run under the cover of the Communist International (Comintern), probably under the International Liaison Service (Russian acronym—OMS). OMS files have not been available to researchers, even when access to KGB files was opened in the couple of years following the collapse of the USSR.

The Comintern's international work was taken over by the Communist Party of the Soviet Union (CPSU) in 1943. The International Information Department (IID) was established in the CPSU to handle the overt work of the Comintern. It is very likely that the Comintern's international intelligence operations were subsumed into the KGB at that time. However, there have been no files revealed that shed light on this assumption.

Intelligence Terminology

The terminology of espionage, although seemingly straightforward and intuitive, in many cases is confused and jumbled by those who are not practitioners of the art. Popular fiction and film have made this situation even more confusing. Therefore, before we launch into this story, let me provide a brief overview of a couple of terms of art. While this glossary is not all-inclusive, it may assist the reader in making sense of this story

Access agent—a covert agent who provides introductions to people or organizations who might assist operations. Some access agents simply provide names and contact information for potential targets. A case officer may ask an agent to actually make personal introductions to potential targets. An access agent could also be involved in the initial meetings and assessments of new targets.

Active Measures—intelligence operations in support of foreign policy, using covert methods or deception. Also known, in American terminology, as Covert Action. Covert actions are intended to influence opinion and actions of targeted governments or individuals. KGB stations were responsible for generating ideas for, and implementing, covert action operations.

Agent – [also—Asset] a person outside an intelligence agency, not a government employee, who has been recruited by the intelligence agency to provide services to the organization. These services may be stealing secrets, providing a safe house, or communicating covert influence messages. The agent is, in effect, a contractor, providing his services in exchange for compensation. The compensation may be a monthly salary, deposits in a secret bank account, bottles of rare Scotch, a medal from KGB headquarters, a pat on the back from his case officer, or the satisfaction of doing his part for the struggle against fascism. Note: An "agent" in espionage terminology is not the same as an FBI agent. An FBI agent would be called an officer in the terminology used by intelligence services.

Case officer—[also—Operations officer] an employee of an intelligence service trained in the art of human intelligence. The case officer's job is to run covert operations. A case officer is a bureaucrat, a government employee, subject to the direct control and discipline, as well as enjoying the benefits (regular salary, benefits, travel, housing, children's schooling) that come with that position. The case officer is not a "spy," in the usual sense of the word. A better description of a case officer's job is "spy manager." A typical KGB case officer may have been responsible for managing a dozen or more spies ("agents"), or operations, or developmental operations. This American terminology derived from the legal backgrounds of the early Office of Special Services (OSS) officers. They were recruited mainly from Wall Street law offices, most with ties to the Ivy League law and professional schools. "Case" refers to a court action. Thus all of the elements involved in that court action are the "case." Since the recruiting agents and running espionage operations is similar to a legal action—resources are identified and allocated, legal justifications are prepared, people are recruited and assigned—the "case" moniker has stuck. While this terminology has probably helped to institutionalize the profession of espionage, it is likely that the law-profession mindset has also crippled the profession, in the U.S. Intelligence Community, in many ways.

Chief of Station—[also, COS] the senior intelligence officer in a foreign country. The COS is authorized from the highest levels of the intelligence bureaucracy to make operational, personnel, and resource allocation decisions in his country. The COS's decisions are subject to review from his headquarters.

Comintern—Communist International. Founded in 1919, after the Bolsheviks seized power in Russia. An organization devoted to spreading the communist revolution throughout the world, conceived and initially guided by Vladimir Lenin. Its overt reason for being was to act as a democratic body for communist parties throughout the world. Its semi-overt mission was to spread the Soviet Revolution throughout the world. The Comintern had offices and branches worldwide. It provided cover for communist intelligence gathering, and covert action operations around the world. The Comintern's operations seem to have been kept separate from the newly formed KGB. Thus, it seems that the Comintern intelligence apparatus operational records were not merged with those of the KGB. For example, no records have yet been uncovered to document the extensive operations of Willi Muenzenberg and Otto Katz under Comintern cover. Observers and espionage specialists believe that the Comintern's intelligence operations were run out of the International Liaison Department of the Comintern. This group was known by its Russian acronym: OMS.

Counter-intelligence (CI)—the process of investigating and taking action against actual and attempted operations by hostile intelligence services to penetrate our society, government, agency, operations, or other friendly resources. Also, the process of ensuring the validity of operations run by our own espionage services by vetting contacts, agents (old and new) and other individuals, and organizations of interest .

Cover—Official—in order to protect their true identity and affiliation, intelligence officers may be deployed in target countries posing as an employee of a non-threatening organization or affiliation. For example, a KGB officer under official cover may appear to be a member of the Soviet embassy's consular staff, or as a Pravda journalist.

Cover—NOC [Soviet terminology is **Illegal]**—Non-officially covered operations officer. An operations officer who operates in foreign countries under the guise of a businessman, student, tourist, or other non-government cover. The KGB made extensive use of NOCs, and their Russian successor, as evidenced by the ring of officers and agents uncovered in 2010, continues to do so.

The Soviets called their intelligence officers working in another country under non-official cover "illegals." An example of a KGB NOC was the officer known as "Rudolf Abel," who operated in America. Arrested by the FBI in 1957, Abel was eventually traded for the American U2 pilot, Francis Gary Powers. Abel's cover was a self-employed artist in New York City. He was actually the KGB's NOC COS for America, managing NOC operations, probably including the Rosenberg's courier network.

Covert Influence—a form of covert action intended to influence targeted governments, individuals, organizations, or cultures. Covert influence is similar to brand advertising. A subtle message (the payload) is introduced into a target via a carrier. In advertising, for example, the Nike swoosh symbol is placed prominently on Tiger Woods' hat. Every time his image on the golf course appears in media, the Nike swoosh is there, quietly, but persistently pushing its payload—"Buy Nike products." An example of a covert influence intelligence operation is the British operation to bring the United States into World War I. They used covert influence agents to insert payloads in the press. They used covert influence agents in Congress, and the Executive office. This type of covert operation, unnoticed by the uninitiated, is extremely powerful and extremely difficult to detect.

Fellow Travelers—Americans who were not overt members of the communist party, but whose political and social stances mirrored the communists. Many Fellow Travelers were also Willing Accomplices, participating directly in covert influence operations.

Innocents—Willi Muenzenberg's term for the Americans who bought into his fake anti-fascist appeals. The KGB handlers who designed and ran the covert influence operations were disdainful of the Innocents. The term was an insult and indicated the contempt with which the communists held the Americans. The Innocents were very close to being Willing Accomplices.

Marxism-Leninism—Lenin's attempt to rationalize the irrational Marxist system of beliefs. The core tweak that Lenin introduced actually destroyed the fundamental belief of Marxism. In a tacit acknowledgement that Marx's theory of human behavior and motivation was totally wrong, Lenin threw out Marx's utopia—

the Dictatorship of the Proletariat—and inserted in its place an Elite Communist Vanguard. This Vanguard, according to Lenin, would help the masses understand how lucky they were to be under the thumb of the communists, and would give way to the Proletariat, at some undetermined point in the future. Reality has destroyed Lenin's lies as thoroughly as Marx's.

Payload—the message of a covert influence operations. It is the thought, idea, philosophy, or information that the covert operator wishes to communicate. The payload is usually conveyed in subtle terms in covert influence operations. Instead of printing a poster that says, "America is racist," a covert influence campaign would insert that payload, with at least some basis in truth, into movies, news stories, and academic discussions, articles and texts. In this way, the payload is communicated to the targeted population without an obvious fingerprint of the originator. This method is very much like the time-tested technique of story-tellers: "Show, don't tell." Once covert influence agents understand the technique, and the payload, and are motivated, the operation can continue to run with no participation of case officers or the sponsoring espionage organization. Also, once the payload is inserted in the carrier—book, movie, article, work of art, or other medium—it has a virtually unlimited lifespan. Movies made in the 1930s continue to influence people in the 21st century. Academics who wrote and taught in the 1920s continue to influence students today. The first draft of history, written by journalists in the early 20th century, has permeated American culture, and still is influential today.

PC-Progressive—the modern American political point of view which in general supports: economic socialism, anti-nationalism, internationalism, and reform of traditional social practices (no-fault divorce, abortion, death penalty, homosexual acceptance, global warming). After the communists took over Russia, political terminology became malleable, and morphed, in an attempt to create uncertainty among opponents. The same set of political views has regularly been known by different labels over the last 100 years, as normal Americans figure out the beliefs that are actually behind the labels: Socialist, Liberal, Progressive, and Democrat. In 2011, there are 75 Congressmen and one Senator in the Congressional Progressive Caucus. In the 21st century, Politically Correct Progressives (PC-Progressives) is the most accurate term for this group of Willing Accomplices. They are monolithically PC, and seem to prefer to be called Progressive. Because PC-Progressives must lie about their real beliefs, in order to win votes from normal Americans, they also must lie about the foundation of their political parties (Democrats, Greens, Liberals, and Socialists). An indication of what results when Americans figure out the basis for PC-Progressives is the fate of the political label "Liberal." Liberalism is so toxic now, after it was exposed in the 1990s, that the PC-Progressive media will only mention it with a euphemism: "the L-word."

Recruit—a person who has agreed to work for an intelligence service. The person may not realize that he is working for an intelligence service, or he may not know which intelligence service recruited him (false flag), but he knows that he has agreed to perform a service for an organization or individual.

Station—the bureaucratic office of an intelligence agency in a foreign country. Most officially covered stations are declared to the host government, and the identities of the station managers are known to the host government. Unofficially covered stations use a variety of commercial or non-governmental covers. The first KGB station in America was covered as the Soviet official trade office, Amtorg. One KGB commercial station used a commercial cover of a travel agency specializing in travel between the USSR and the USA.

Willing Accomplice—a person who cooperates with a hostile espionage service to subvert his own country's social, political, or economic foundations. The Willing Accomplice may not know that he is working with an intelligence service, but he does know, or it is obvious to him, that the tasks he undertakes are against the best interests of his country. Thus, he is *Willing* to take on the tasks, and he is an *Accomplice* with the hostile espionage service, even if he is unwitting of the actual identities of the service or his handlers.

Witting/Unwitting—the mental state of a recruit's being aware of the identity of the espionage service for which he performs services. An unwitting recruit is unaware of the true identity of those for whom he is performing services. He may believe he is working for a commercial entity, or he may believe he is helping an international anti-fascist organization. Sometimes, recruits need the comfort of being unwitting so that they can avoid the necessity of dealing with the mental strain involved in performing tasks that damage or destroy their country.

Acknowledgements

Without the help, advice, and guidance of numerous people and institutions, this project would have been impossible. That said, this is a project that will likely never end. There are too many resources that are difficult to access, and too many stories that are unpublished, to ever be sure that we have a full view of this issue.

I owe huge debts to many people for assistance in this work. While there is not enough space to mention everyone who helped along the way, I'd like to acknowledge my gratitude to all individuals and institutions that provided guidance, ideas, corrections, support and other acts of kindness, research, and scholarship. Lack of mention here is not meant to indicate lack of gratitude on my part. And mention here in no way indicates agreement with all, or part, of the analysis or views in this work. The analysis and views, unless credited to others, are strictly my own.

Just a few deserving of note, in random order, are: Joe Goulden, James Earl Haynes, the Institute of International Studies, Princeton University Rare Books and Special Collections Archive,

Southern Illinois University Archives, John Talbot, John Falk, John Footen, Pete Bagley, Jim DeFelice, Jim Newman, J.R. Dunn, Brett Joshpe, Chris Ruddy, John Tierny, Institute of World Politics library, Bernie Reeves, Jim Simpson, Jayson Blair, Tom Fields, Amy Russell, Pat Mahoney, Stanford University's Hoover Institution Archives, Jonathan Chaves, Gerald Gutek, Arthur Aikman, John Tierney, John Fox, Andrey Suvorov, Juliana Pilon, Tom West, Alda Harrison Smith, Ken Wood, Michael Del Rosso, Jamie Glazov, Jeff Gardner, FrontPageMag, BigPeace, BigJournalism, Dan Gifford, Peter Schweizer, Alexander Marlow, Michael Walsh, Jim Newman, David Patten, Guy Benson, Larry Andersen, American Thinker, Elise Cooper, PJTV, Matt Bruce, Russ Morley, A.J. Rice, Al Simon, Howard Hart, Jim Senner, Chris Schotts, CIA Publication Review Board, Mark Bowden, Cristy Li, Otto Marasco, Paul Jackson, Stale Fagerland, Bill Tew, Tengiz Tkebuchava, Jose Garcia, Webb Cook, Robert Bruton, Alan Simon, Rev. Raymond Cannata, Richard Spence, Elias Clizbe, Isaac Clizbe, and the Rock of Ashburn, Norliyah Clizbe.

Of special note is Stephen Koch, the author of *Double Lives: Stalin, Willi Muenzenberg and the Seduction of the Intellectuals.* This excellent, stream of consciousness, tightly woven tapestry is the gun that has been quietly smoking since first published in 1994. Koch's interview with Babette Gross, Willi Muenzenberg's widow was the final link in my CI analysis. Her explanation of the credo of Muenzenberg's operators could have been written by an anti-American, Politically Correct activist in 2010. What Koch did not understand, because he has no background in espionage, and what Babette either did not share, or also did not understand, was that this credo was a carefully planned covert influence payload, intended to devastate American culture. What Koch does understand, and Gross likely did too, was that Muenzenberg's operations were amazingly effective. Koch simply missed making the final link from his Muenzenberg's ops to PC today.

Other authors whose work was crucial in helping me understand the USSR, the KGB, communism, and their intersection in the United States were Robert Conquest, Herb Romerstein, Stan Evans, Christopher Andrew, Tim Tzouliadis, Andrew Meier, Harvey Klehr, and Richard Pipes.

See the Bibliography for a full listing of resources used in this research.

The internet makes available resources that previously would have been nearly impossible to access. A great resource online is Questia (www.questia.com) , which provides access to ancient sources—books and periodicals—in an easily searchable interface, with note-taking, bibliography producing, and citation generating capabilities. Also, the genealogy website Ancestry.com, provided access to travel records, birth and death records, and other valuable resources normally inaccessible at best.

Sources

George S. Counts Sources

Personal Interviews

Aikman, Arthur L. Personal interview. July 7, 2009.
Counts, Martha L. Personal interview. July 9, 2009.
Gutek, Gerald L. Interview via email. July 18, 2009.

Manuscripts and Archives

George S. Counts papers (unpublished letters, notebooks, notecards, miscellany), 1907-1974. Southern Illinois University Special Collections Research Center. Carbondale, Illinois. Boxes 1, 6, 12.

Manuscripts (unpublished). Gerald Gutek Collection of George S. Counts. Southern Illinois University Special Collections Research Center. Carbondale, Illinois. Box 1.

Letters (unpublished). Counts, George S. Archives of John Day Company, Inc., 1926-1969. Princeton University Library. Department of Rare Books and Special Collections. Manuscripts Division. Princeton, New Jersey. Boxes 23, 64, 80, 94, 113, 121, 128, 134, 142, 150, 160, 180, 190, 214, 232, 247, 262, 299.

S.S. President Jefferson. Ship Manifest, List of United States Citizens, p. 8. Sailing from Manila: May 5, 1925; Arriving at Port of Seattle, May 28, 1925.

US Census, New York City, 1930, Counts, George S. college professor, Wife, Lois B., 2 daughters, 9 and 6, rent $165 per month. www.ancestry.com

SS St Louis Ship Manifest. Sailed from Southampton on Jan 18, 1930, arrived in NYC, Jan 27, 1930; George S. Counts and daughter, Esther Counts, 9 years old. www.ancestry.com

SS Berengaria Ship Manifest. Sailed from Southampton on Jan 28, 1937, arrived in NYC Feb 3, 1937, George S. Counts, Address: New Hope, PA. www.ancestry.com

SS Albert Ballin Ship Manifest. Sailed from Hamburg on 9 Sept 1927; arrived NYC 19 Sept 1927, George S. Counts, wife, Lois, and daughters, 6 and 3. Passport #: 373781, issued 2 May 1927, Wife's PP#: 371256, issued 29 April 1927, Address: Teacher's College, Columbia, NYC. www.ancestry.com

Counts as Author

1915

A study of the colleges and high schools in the North central association. Washington, Govt. print. off., 1915.

1922

The Selective Character of American Secondary Education. Chicago: University of Chicago Press, 1922.

1925

Education in the Philippines, *The Elementary School Journal*, Vol. 26, No. 2 (Oct., 1925), pp. 94-106. http://www.jstor.org/stable/995649

1927

The Social Composition of Boards of Education: A Study in the Social Control of Public Education. Chicago: University of Chicago Press, 1927.

1928

School and Society in Chicago. New York: Harcourt, Brace, 1928.

1929

Secondary Education and Industrialism. Cambridge: Harvard University Press, 1929.

1930

A Ford Crosses Soviet Russia. Boston: Stratford Company, 1930.

The American Road to Culture: A Social Interpretation of Education in the United States. New York: John Day, 1930.

1931

New Russia's Primer: *The Story of the Five-Year Plan*, M. Ilin, Nucia P. Lodge, George S. Counts. Houghton Mifflin Company: Boston, 1931. http://www.execulink.com/~mdavids/counts.htm

The Soviet Challenge to America. New York: John Day, 1931.

"Dare Progressive Education Be Progressive?" *Progressive Education*, Vol. IX, No. 4, April 1931

The Soviet Challenge to America. New York: John Day Company, 1931.

1932

Dare the School Build a New Social Order? John Day: New York, 1932.

1933

A Call to the Teachers of the Nation. New York: John Day, 1933.

1934

The Social Foundations of American Education. New York: Scribner's, 1934.

1938

The Prospects of American Democracy. New York: John Day, 1938.

"Relations of public education and private enterprise". New York: Advanced school of education, Teachers College, Columbia University, 1938.

1946

Education and the Promise of America, Macmillan: New York, 1946.

1947

"I Want to Be Like Stalin," from the Russian text on Pedagogy by B.P. Yesipov and N.K. Goncharov, translated by George S. Counts and Nucia P. Lodge, John Day: New York, 1947.

1949

with Nucia Lodge. The Country of the Blind: The Soviet System of Mind Control. Boston: Houghton Mifflin, 1949. Questia. 9 July 2009 <http://www.questia.com/PM.qst?a=o&d=6513369>.

1951

American education through the Soviet looking glass. New York: Bureau of Publications, Teachers College, Columbia University, 1951.

1952

Education and American Civilization. New York: Teachers College, Columbia University Press, 1952. *Questia.* Web.

1969

Khruschev and the Central Committee Speak on Education, University of Pittsburgh Press: Pittsburgh, 1969.

New York Times—Counts Subject and Author

1924, April 23. New Faculty Members Appointed at Yale.
1924, December 20. Experts to Survey Filipino Schools.
1924, October 22. 3rd Party Endorsed by 200 Educators.
1925, November 17. Yale to Honor Professor Chapman.
1925, November 21. Hits at Filipino Schools.
1928, July 20. Study Education in Europe.
1928, October 7. See School as Step in Social Order.
1930, April 20. Books and Authors.
1930, August 6. Counts Assails Russian Embargo.
1930, December 7. Heckled by Socialist.
1930, February 23. Plea to Soviet Vain, Dr. Counts Advises.
1930, February 26. Urges Radio's Use in Rural Schools.
1930, March 9. Reds Use Schools to Aid 5-Year Plan.
1930, July 6. How Education has Changed in Three Ex-Monarchies.

1930, July 27. A Gulliver Looks at Our Schools; Dr. George S. Counts Criticizes Their Lack of Social Vision.

1930, September 28. Sees no Soviet Danger.

1931, May 17. Making Little Robots in Soviet Russia.

1931, July 19. Russians Educate Through Activities.

1934, August 19. Where Red Flags Wave in China; General Yakhontoff's Survey of the Chinese Soviets is a Useful, If Not Completely Reliable Guide to the Situation.

1934, November 12. Dr. Counts Sees New Social Era.

1935, June 3. 350 U.S. Educators to Study in Russia.

1934, July 20. Foreign Students Balked in Moscow; More than 200 Bewildered on Learning of Dissolution of Summer Institute.

1936, February 24. Dr. Counts Assails 'Liberty's Enemies'; Teachers Cheer Attack on Smith, Hearst, Coughlin, D.A.R. and Liberty League.

1938, October 2. American Democracy.

1947, March 22. Plan Urged to Aid U.S.-Soviet Accord; Prof. Counts Tells Teachers Ignorance of Russia Is One Obstacle to Agreement.

1947, November 23. Stalin's Myth Man.

1951, March 12. Lies on Education Charged to Soviet; Official Article's Distortions of Our Practices Likened by Dr. Counts to Nazi Tactics.

1956, March 27. William Russell, Educator, 65, Dies; Head of Teachers College at Columbia, 1927-54, Served as an Official at I.C.A.

1974, November 11. George Counts, Educator, Dies; Ex-Head of State Liberal Party.

Counts as Subject

Keenan, Claudia J. The Education of an Intellectual: George S. Counts and Turn-of-the-Century Kansas, Kansas History, Winter 2002/2003, pp. 258-271.

Time, July 20, 1936. Education: Unmentionable Counts.

Federal Bureau of Investigation. *George S. Counts File; [censored];* FBI Archives, 2009.

Education: One Wonders, *Time*, Feb. 20, 1939.

Education: Legionnaire's Thesis, *Time*, Monday, Jul. 11, 1938.

Walter Duranty Sources

Duranty as Author

The Kremlin and the People, Reynal & Hitchcock: New York, 1941.

I Write as I Please, Simon and Schuster: New York, 1935.

New York Times

1933, June 11. Foreign Press Free of Soviet Pressure.

1933, January 30. 50,000 Soviet Reds Will Direct Drive to Socialize Farms.

1933, February 28. Soviet Peasants Resist by Inaction.

1933, January 1. Soviet Reds Face Purging Uneasily; Fear it May Rival 1921 in Severity.

1933, August 24. Famine Toll Heavy in Southern Russia.

1933, August 21. Famine Report Scorned.

1933, November 18. President Reveals Pact; Reads to Press Letters in Which He and Litvinoff Bind Nations.

Duranty as Subject

Duranty's Deception; Walter Duranty Won a Pulitzer Prize While Covering Up the Atrocities of Josef Stalin. Is the Reluctance of the New York Times to Return the Prize a Result of the Newspaper's Own Failure to Come to Grips with Its Guilt? *Insight on*

the News 22 July 2003: 18. Questia. 9 July 2009 <http://www.questia.com/PM.qst?a=o&d=5001967483>.
Mccollam, Douglas. "Should This Pulitzer Be Pulled? Seventy Years after a Government-Engineered Famine Killed Millions in Ukraine, a New York Times Correspondent Who Failed to Sound the Alarm Is under Attack." *Columbia Journalism Review* Nov.-Dec. 2003: 43+. *Questia*. Web.
Paluch, Peter. "Spiking the Ukrainian Famine, Again." *National Review* 11 Apr. 1986: 33+. Questia. Web.
Taylor, S.J. *Stalin's Apologist: Walter Duranty: The New York Times's Man in Moscow*. New York and Oxford: Oxford University Press, 1990.

Alexander Gumberg Sources

Archives and Manuscripts

Letters (unpublished). Between Esther Seibel and family, and Alexander Gumberg. 1909-1917. Private collection of Raymond Cannata.

Gumberg as Subject

Johnson, Claudius O. *Borah of Idaho*. New York: Longmans, Green and Co., 1936. *Questia*. Web.
Libbey, James K. *Alexander Gumberg& Soviet American Relations 1917-1933,* University Press of Kentucky: Lexington, 1977.
Sisson, Edgar. *One Hundred Red Days: A Personal Chronicle of the Bolshevik Revolution*. New Haven, CT: Yale University Press, 1931. Questia. Web.
Salzman, Neil V. *Reform and Revolution: The Life and Times of Raymond Robins*. Kent, OH: Kent State University Press, 1991. Questia. Web.

Paxton Hibben Sources

New York Times

1922, March 21. Duranty in Russia--Letter to the Editor--Paxton Hibbens.
1924, August 30. Paxton Hibben Called Before Army Inquiry.
1928, December 6. Paxton Hibben Dies on 48th Birthday .
1910, May 16. Paxton Hibben Joins Roosevelt in Holland.
1920, September 12. The French in Greece--Letter to the Editor, Paxton Hibben.
1922, April 15. Russian Transportation--Letter to the Editor--Paxton Hibben.
1917, June 2. Dollar Diplomacy Divides Publicists.
1924, August 30. Paxton Hibben Called Before Army Inquiry.
1928, December 6. Paxton Hibben Dies on 48th Birthday.
1910, May 16. Paxton Hibben Joins Roosevelt in Holland.
1920, September 12. The French in Greece--Letter to the Editor, Paxton Hibben.

Willi Muenzenberg Sources

New York Times

1934, July 7. Red Leader Sees German Revolt; Muenzenberg, Former German Deputy, Predicts Overthrow of Hitler Soon.
1952, October 8. Shift in Soviet Line Deemed Harbinger of Popular Front; Communists in West are Already Starting Efforts to Revive Device of 1930s.

1934, July 8. Hitler Debacle Seen by Ex-Reich Leaders; Dr. Rosenfeld and Muenzenberg Predict a Free Socialist State in Few Years.
1934, August 23. Radical Gain Here Forecast in Reich; Strikes are Regarded as Beginning of Huge Leftist Labor Movement; German Red's Hand Seen; Muenzenberg is Believed to be Active—Five Communists Sentenced in Berlin.
1948, September 5. Communism's First Years of Power.

Muenzenberg as Subject

Gruber, Helmut, "Willi Muenzenberg. Propagandist For and Against the Comintern," *International Review of Social History* 10 (1965), pp. 278-297
Gruber, Helmut. "Willi Muenzenberg's German Communist Propaganda Empire 1921-1933." *The Journal of Modern History*, Vol. 38, No. 3: pp. 278, September 1966.
Koch, Stephen. *Double Lives: Stalin, Willi Muenzenberg and the Seduction of the Intellectuals*. New York: Enigma Books, 1994.
McMeekin, Sean. *The Red Millionaire: A Political Biography of Willi Muenzenberg, Moscow's Secret Propaganda Tsar in the West,* Yale University Press: New Haven, 2003.
Schleimann, Jürgen, "The Life and Work of Willi Muenzenberg," *Survey* 55 (April 1965), pp. 64-91.

Dorothy Parker Sources

New York Times

1925, February 16. A New Weekly Coming.
1927, August 11. Arrests Check Picketing; New York Writers are in Group of 39 Jailed in Boston.
1927, August 12. Sacco Plea to be Heard by High Court on Tuesday; Men Leave Deathhouse.
1928, April 9. Writer Wins Divorce.
1928, May 1. Speakers 'Blacklisted' to Defy D.A.R.; To Join 'Honor Roll' Party Here on May 9.
1928, November 25. Left New York for the Coast.
1933, October 25. Roosevelt a Topic in Moley's Weekly.
1934, August 11. Dorothy Parker a Scenarist.
1934, February 7. 'Guests' Aiding Strike Beaten at the Waldorf; Fists, Bon Mots Fly in Empire Room Fracas.
1934, June 16. Dorothy Parker Wed in October.
1934, September 16. Hollywood Solves Some Problems.
1935, August 11. Hollywood Gets the Lyricists.
1935, May 26. The Satirical Stories of Tess Slesinger.
1936, August 24. Dorothy Parker, Farmer.
1936, December 12. News of the Screen.
1936, December 13. The Rueful, Frostbitten Laughter of Dorothy Parker.
1936, January 8. Salaries of 18,000 over $15,000 in 1934.
1936, July 31. Apartment Rentals.
1936, November 24. News from Hollywood.
1936, October 19. Authors Aid Roosevelt.
1937, January 8. Apartment Rentals.
1937, July 25. Down to Earth in Spain.
1937, March 1. 98 Writers Score Spanish, Rebels.
1937, May 24. Screen News.
1937, October 17. Footnotes on Headliners.
1938, June 29. Aids Spanish Children.
1938, November 22. 20,000 Jam Garden in Reich Protest.
1939, April 23. Magazine Fights Racism.

1939, August 17. Ocean Travelers.
1939, January 17. Hunger Sit-downs Protest WPA Cuts.
1939, January 27. Appeal is Made for Spanish Needy.
1939, January 8. Miss Parker Never Poses.
1939, June 13. Celebrities Open Fair in Village.
1939, June 27. Writers Assailed by Federal Judge.
1939, March 16. $488 Party No Joke to Dorothy Parker.
1939, March 17. $1,000,000 Campaign for Refugees Planned.
1939, March 9. Authors Aid Loyalists.
1939, November 15. Milk Fund Benefit Dec. 10.
1939, November 27. Protests Alien Registry.
1939, September 26. Spellman Warned on Christian Front.
1940, December 15. Artists to be Guests.
1940, September 1. Party Aids Spanish Youth.
1941, November 16. Hoover Food Plan Scored.
1941, September 8. Henderson, Aides Accused by Dies.
1942, March 14. Dinner for Paul Robeson.
1943, October 10. Obituaries, Rothschild, Bertram.
1943, October 11. Dorothy Parker's Brother Dies.
1944, June 11. Speaking of Books.
1944, October 10. PAC Women Hold Meeting.
1944, October 19. Park Avenue Suite Leased by Executive.
1944, September 29. Women Form PAC Group.
1945, March 24. National PAC Votes to Continue Work.
1947, November 3. 19 Movie Figures to Fight Charges.
1947, May 23. Dorothy Parker is Sued; Alan Campbell Asks a Divorce Based on Separation in War.
1947, June 12. 2,500 at Leftist Rally; Robeson Says Liberals Accept Challenge of Fascists.
1949, June 9. Film 'Communists' Listed in FBI File in Coplon Spy Case.
1949, June 9. Hundreds Named as Red Appeasers; California's Tenney Committee Lists Actors, Musicians and Others as 'Line' Followers.
1949, September 11. 382 Aid Film Men in Contempt Plea.
1950, August 15. Dorothy Parker to Rewed Writer.
1950, August 18. Dorothy Parker Rewed.
1953, June 28. McCarthy Calls 23 for Book Enquiry.
1955, February 16. Anti-Franco Body Votes to Disband.
1955, February 26. Red Fronts Face Fund Appeal Ban.
1958, December 10. Inquiry on Spain Asked.
1959, April 18. Soviet Prints Dorothy Parker.
1960, December 30. 18 in Hollywood Sue on Blacklist.
1961, January 8. Hollywood Trial; Suit by Blacklisted Writers, Actors Puts Controversy in Spotlight.
1962, May 6. Dorothy Parker Discusses TV.
1963, June 15. Dorothy Parker's Husband is Found Dead on Coast.
1966, January 30. Knights-errant in Error?
1967, June 8. Examples of Saucy Wit.
1967, June 10. Dorothy Parker Recalled as Wit.
1967, June 8. Dorothy Parker, 73, Literary Wit Dies.
1967, June 27. Dorothy Parker's Will Leaves Estate of $10,000 to Dr. King.
1970, October 11. Writing was Torture, but not Writing was Worse Torture.

Parker as Subject

Federal Bureau of Investigation. *Dorothy Parker File; [censored];* FBI Archives, 2009.
Keats, John, *You Might as Well Live: The Life and Times of Dorothy Parker*, Simon and Schuster: New York, 1970.

Nucia Perlmutter Lodge Sources

Personal Interviews

Russell, Amy K. Personal interview. July 11, 2009.

Manuscripts and Archives

Education in Russia (unpublished). Perlmutter, Nucia. June, 1924. Master of Arts Thesis. Clark University Archives and Special Collections.

Resume and letters (unpublished) 1966-1967. Lodge, Anna NuciaOsipovna. Ivan Alekseevich Poliakov Papers. Hoover Institution Archives. Stanford University. Stanford, California. Box/Folder: 13:21.

Letters (unpublished). Lodge, Nucia Perlmutter. Archives of John Day Company, Inc., 1926-1969. Princeton University Library. Department of Rare Books and Special Collections. Manuscripts Division. Princeton, New Jersey. Boxes 30, 51, 71, 85.

New York Times

1930, August 24. Exhibit of Schools Stirs the Russians.

1930, April 13. Radio Programs Scheduled for the Current Week.

General Sources

Personal Interviews

Aksilenko, Val. Personal interview. July 3, 2008.

Bagley, Tennet. Personal interview. March 28, 2008.

S., Andrey. Personal interview. March 27, 2008.

Books, Articles, Websites, Other

Alston, Joshua. "Diversity Training." *Newsweek*, Feb 11, 2008.

Andrew, Christopher and Vasili Mitrokhin. *The Sword and the Shield: The Mitrokhin Archive and the Secret History of the KGB*. New York: Basic Books, 1999.

Andrew, Christopher and Vasili Mitrokhin. *The World Was Going Our Way: The KGB and the Battle for the Third World*. New York: Basic Books, 2005.

Applebaum, Barbara. Is Teaching for Social Justice a "Liberal Bias"? *Teachers College Record*, Volume 111: Number 2, 2009, p. 376-408, http://www.tcrecord.org ID Number: 15200, Date Accessed: 10/19/2010.

Bailey, Herbert. Root Mission More Hopeful, New York Times, June 29, 1917.

Barker, Hannah, and Simon Burrows, eds. *Press, Politics and the Public Sphere in Europe and North America, 1760-1820*. Cambridge, England: Cambridge University Press, 2002. *Questia*. Web.

Batsell, Walter Russell. *Soviet Rule in Russia*. New York: Macmillan, 1929. *Questia*. Web.

Behreandt, Dennis. "Duranty's Lethal Lies: Using Terror and Famine, Josef Stalin Murdered Millions in the Ukraine. Walter Duranty, the Pulitzer Prize-Winning Journalist, and the New York Times Covered Up the Massacre." *The New American* 8 Sept. 2003: 14+. Questia. 9 July 2009 <http://www.questia.com/PM.qst?a=o&d=5002554355>.

Beichman, Arnold. "A Life That's Fit to Print." *The Washington Times* 10 Mar. 1999: 17. Questia. 9 July 2009 <http://www.questia.com/PM.qst?a=o&d=5001872804>.

Bell, Fraser. "Dead Man on Furlough: Willi Muenzenberg's Wars." *Queen's Quarterly* Winter 2004: 536+. Questia. Web.

Bledsoe, Jerry. *Death by Journalism: One Teacher's Fateful Encounter with Political Correctness*. Winston-Salem, NC: Down Home Press, 2001.

Bloom, Allan. *The Closing of the American Mind*. New York. Simon & Schuster, 1987.

Bork, Robert H. *Slouching Toward Gomorrah: Modern Liberalism and American Decline.* New York: Regan books, 1996.

Brooks, C. E. P. *Climate through the Ages: A Study of the Climatic Factors and Their Variations*. London: Ernest Benn, 1926. Questia. Web.

Brown, John. *The Anti-Propaganda Tradition in the United States*, Bulletin Board for Peace, 29 June 2003.

Budenz, Louis F. *The Techniques of Communism*. Chicago: Henry Regnery, 1954.

Bullert, Gary. "Franz Boas as Citizen-scientist: Gramscian-Marxist Influence on American Anthropology." *The Journal of Social, Political, and Economic Studies* 34.2 (2009): 208+. Questia. Web.

Bullert, Gary. *The Politics of John Dewey*. Buffalo, NY: Prometheus Books, 1983. Questia. Web.

Burchett, Bessie R. *Education for Destruction*, Philadelphia, 1941.

California Legislature. *Fourth Report of the Senate Fact- Finding Committee On Un-American Activities. Communist Front Organizations.* 1948

Campbell, Andrew. Double lives: three Australian fellow-travellers in the Cold War.(Brian Fitzpatrick, Manning Clark, Clement Byrne Christesen), *National Observer—Australia and World Affairs*, June 22, 2006.

Campbell, Kenneth J. *Moscow's Words, Western Voices*. Washington, DC: Accuracy in Media, 1995.

Cashill, Jack. *Hoodwinked: How Intellectual Hucksters Have Hijacked American Culture,* Nelson Current: Nashville, 2005.

Chamberlin, William Henry. *The Confessions of an Individualist*. New York: The Macmillan Company, 1940. Questia. Web.

Chambers, Whittaker. *Witness*. Washington, DC: Regnery Publishing, Inc, 1952

Choi, Jung Min and John W. Murphy, *Politics and Philosophy of Political Correctness*, Praeger, 1993.

Collins, Edward M. *Myth, Manifesto, Meltdown: Communist Strategy, 1848-1991.* Westport, Connecticut and London: Praeger, 1998.

Colvin, Richard Lee. "What Hath 9/11 Wrought? In the Aftermath, School Leaders See Shifts in Thinking, Priorities and Curricular Emphases." *School Administrator* Feb. 2002: 42+. Questia. 9 July 2009 <http://www.questia.com/PM.qst?a=o&d=5000694757>.

Connor, R.D.W. *The Story of the United States for Young Americans*. Raleigh. The Thompson Publishing Company, 1918.

Conquest, Robert. *Stalin: Breaker of Nations,*Penguin Books: New York, 1991.

Conquest, Robert. *The Harvest of Sorrow: Soviet Collectivization and the Terror Famine,*Oxford University Press: New York, 1986.

Conquest, Robert. *The Great Terror: A Reassessment,* Oxford University Press: New York, 1990.

Coulter, Ann. *Godless: The Church of Liberalism*. New York: Crown Forum, 2006.

Creel Work Broadened; Edgar Sisson to Head Foreign Section of Committee. Jul 25, 1918, New *York Times*.

Creel, George. *How we advertised America: the first telling of the amazing story of the Committee on public information that carried the gospel of Americanism to every corner of the globe*. Harper & Brothers: New York, 1920.

Cull, Nicholas John and David Holbrook, David Welch. *Propaganda and Mass Persuasion*, ABC-CLIO: July 2003.

Cyberalert, April 2, 2008. "Turner: Iraqi Insurgents 'Patriots,' http://www.mrc.org/cyberalerts/2008/cyb20080402.asp#1

D'Souza, Dinesh. *Illiberal Education: The Politics of Race and Sex on Campus*, Praeger, 1992.

Davis, Donald E., and Eugene P. Trani. *The First Cold War: The Legacy of Woodrow Wilson in U.S.-Soviet Relations*. Columbia, MO: University of Missouri Press, 2002. Questia. Web.

Davis, Jerome. T*he Russian Immigran*t. New York: The Macmillan Company, 1922. Questia. Web.

Dennis, Lawrence J. From *Prayer to Pragmatism: A Biography of John L.* Childs. Carbondale, IL: Southern Illinois University Press, 1992. Questia. Web.
Deriabin, Peter and T.H. Bagley. *The KGB: Masters of the Soviet Union,* Hippocrene Books: New York, 1990.
Deriabin, Peter, and Frank Gibney. *The Secret World.* 1st ed. Garden City, NY: Doubleday, 1959. Questia. Web.
Dewey, John. *Impressions of Soviet Russia and the revolutionary world,* New Republic: New York, 1929.
Dies, Martin. *Martin Dies' Story.* New York: Bookmailer, 1963.
Dietrich, John. *The Morgenthau Plan: Soviet Influence on American Post-War Policy.* New York: Algora Publishing, 2002.
Dolgun, Alexander with Patrick Watson. *Alexander Dolgun's Story: An American in the Gulag,* Alfred A. Knopf: New York, 1975.
Dollar Diplomacy Divides Publicists. (1917, June 2). *New York Times* .
Dos Passos, John. *U.S.A.: A. The 42nd Parallel; B. Nineteen Nineteen; C. The Big Money.* New York: Modern Library, 1937. Questia. Web.
Draper, Theodore. *The Roots of American Communism.* New York: Viking Press, 1957. Questia. Web.
Dukes, Paul. *The USA in the Making of the USSR*: The Washington Conference, 1921-1922, and "Uninvited Russia". New York: Routledge, 2004. Questia. Web.
Dunant, Sara, ed. *War of the Words: The Political Correctness Debate* (1994);
Ebon, Martin. *The Soviet Propaganda Machine.* New York: McGraw-Hill, 1987.
Ebon, Martin. *The Soviet Propaganda Machine.* New York: McGraw-Hill, 1987.
Education: Father & Son, *Time,* 1946, Nov. 4.
Elleman, Bruce A. *The Secret History of Sino-Soviet Diplomatic Relations, 1917-1927.* Armonk, NY: M. E. Sharpe, 1997. Questia. Web.
Ellis, Frank. "Political Correctness and the Ideological Struggle: from Lenin and Mao to Marcuse and Foucault." *The Journal of Social, Political, and Economic Studies* 27.4 (2002): 409+. Questia. Web.
Ellis, Frank. "Political Correctness and the Ideological Struggle: from Lenin and Mao to Marcuse and Foucault." *The Journal of Social, Political, and Economic Studies.* Volume: 27. Issue: 4, 2002. p. 409.
Evans, Frank Bowen. *Worldwide Communist Propaganda Activities.* New York: McMillan, 1955.
Evans, M. Stanton. *Blacklisted by History—The Untold Story of Senator Joe McCarthy and His Fight Against America's Enemies.* New York: Crown Forum, 2007.
Filene, Peter G. *Americans and the Soviet Experiment, 1917-1933.* Cambridge, MA: Harvard University Press, 1967. Questia. Web.
Fischer, Louis. *Men and Politics: An Autobiography.* New York: Duell, Sloan and Pearce, 1941. Questia. Web.
Flynn, John T. "Who Owns Your Child's Mind?" in *Public Education Under Criticism,* ed: C. Winfield Scott, and Clyde M. Hill, books for libraries: Freeport, New York, 1954
Foglesong, David S. *America's Secret War against Bolshevism: U.S. Intervention in the Russian Civil War, 1917-1920.* Chapel Hill, NC: University of North Carolina Press, 1995. Questia. Web.
Footman, David, ed. *International Communism.* Carbondale, IL: Southern Illinois University Press, 1960. Questia. Web.
Fox, John F. Jr. *What the Spiders Did: U.S. and Soviet Counterintelligence before the Cold War,* Journal of Cold War Studies - Volume 11, Number 3, Summer 2009, pp. 206-224.
Frazier, Ian. "John Reed's Unblinking Stare." *American Scholar* Summer 2002: 29+. Questia. Web.
Friedman, Marilyn and Jan Narveson, *Political Correctness: For and Against,* Rowman & LIttlefield, (1995)
From a Russian Diary: 1917-1920 by An Englishwoman. John Murray: London, 1921.
Gates, John. *The Story of an American Communist.* New York: Nelson, 1958.

Goldberg, Bernard. *Bias: A CBS insider Exposes How the Media Distort the News*. Regnery: Washington DC, 2002.
Goldberg, Jonah. *Liberal Fascism*, Doubleday: New York, 2008.
Gupton, Carole, Mary Beth Kelley, Tim Lensmire, Bic Ngo, & Michael Goh (Chair), *Teacher Education Redesign Initiative*, Race, Culture, Class, and Gender Task Group, University of Minnesota, Teacher Education Redesign Initiative Blog, July 16, 2009, http://blog.lib.umn.edu/cehd/teri/
Hadden, Sally. "Review of *Amistad* (film by Stephen Spielberg)." 1998. http://www.tntech.edu/history/amistadr.html (April 16, 2008).
Hale, William Harlan. "American and Russia: Part VII, When the Red Storm Broke: To a Russian revolution, America sent rival groups of amateur diplomats. The calamitous results of their indecision still afflict us." *American Heritage Magazine*, Volume 12, Issue 2, February 1961.
Hapgood, Norman, ed. *Professional Patriots*. New York: Boni, 1927. Questia. Web.
Haslam, Jonathan, "The Comintern and the Origins of the Popular Front," *Historical Journal* 22 (1979), pp. 673-691.
Haynes, John Earl and Harvey Klehr. *Early Cold War Spies: The Espionage Trials that Shaped American Politics*, Cambridge University Press: New York, 2006.
Haynes, John Earl and Harvey Klehr. *In Denial: Historians, Communism and Espionage*, Encounter Books: San Francisco, 2003.
Haynes, John Earl and Harvery Klerh, and Alexander Vassiliev. *Spies: The Rise and Fall of the KGB in America*.Yale University Press: New Haven, 2009.
Haynes, John Earl and Harvey Klehr. *Venona: Decoding Soviet Espionage in America*, Yale Nota Bene: New Haven, 1999.
Healey, Dorothy and Maurice Isserman. *Dorothy Healy Remembers: A Life in the American Communist Party*. New York: Oxford University Press, 1990.
Heilbrunn, Otto. *The Soviet Secret Services*. New York: Frederick A. Praeger, 1956. Questia. Web.
Hicks, Granville, and John Stuart. *John Reed: The Making of a Revolutionary*. New York: Macmillan, 1936. Questia. Web.
Hook, Sidney. *Marx and the Marxists: The Ambiguous Legacy*. Ed. Louis L. Snyder. Princeton: Van Nostrand, 1955. Questia. 9 July 2009 <http://www.questia.com/PM.qst?a=o&d=54044667>.
Howe, Irving, Lewis A. Coser. The American Communist Party: A Critical History, 1919-1957. Boston: Beacon Press, 1957. http://www.gutenberg-e.org/kod01/kod03.html
Isserman, Maurice. *Which Side Were You On?: The American Communist Party During the Second World War*. Middletown, CT: Wesleyan University Press, 1982.
Jasper, William F. "The Dogs That Don't Bark: A Watchdog Will Not Bark at a Burglar If It Recognizes Him as a Friend. the Mainstream Media's Failure to "Bark" at Communism's Crimes Speaks Volumes about Its Loyalty." *The New American* 10 Feb. 2003: 17+. Questia. Web.
Johnpoll, Bernard K., ed. *A Documentary History of the Communist Party of the United States*. Vol. 2. Westport, CT: Greenwood Press, 1994. Questia. Web.
Kalugin, Oleg. *The First Directorate: My 32 Years in Intelligence and Espionage Against the West*. St. Martin's Press: New York, 1994.
Kaminsky, James S. *A New History of Educational Philosophy*. Westport, CT: Greenwood Press, 1993. Questia. Web.
Kenez, Peter. *The Birth of the Propaganda State: Soviet Methods of Mass Mobilization 1917-1929*. University of Cambridge: New York, 1985.
Kirkpatrick, Evron M. *Years of Crisis: Communist Propaganda Activities in 1956*. New York: McMillan, 1957.
Klehr, Harvey, John Earl Haynes and Fridrikh Igorevich Firsov. *The Secret World of American Communism*. New Haven and London: Yale University Press, 1995.
Knight, Amy. *How the Cold War Began: The Igor Gouzenko Affair and the Hunt for Soviet Spies*,Carroll & Graf Publishers: New York, 2005.
Koestler, Arthur. "A Note on 'Darkness at Noon'." *New Statesman* 29 Oct. 2007: 62. Questia. Web.

Kowalsky, Daniel. Stalin and the Spanish Civil War. 0-231-50217-6. Gutenberg<e>, Columbia University Press. 2004.
Kronenwetter, Michael. *Covert Action*. New York: Franklin Watts, 1991.
Kupelian, David. *The Marketing of Evil: How Radicals, Elitists, and Pseudo-experts Sell Us Corruption Disguised as Freedom*. Cumberland House Publishing: Nashville, 2005.
Kurzweil, Edith (Editor) and William Phillips (Editor) *Our Country, Our Culture: The Politics of Political Correctness*. Partisan Review Press, 1995.
Labin, Suzanne, Subcommittee to Investigate the Administration of the Internal Security Act and other Internal Security Laws of the Committee on the Judiciary United States Senate 90th Congress First Session. *The Techniques of Soviet Propaganda*. Washington DC: U.S. Government Printing Office, 1967.
Labin, Suzanne. *The Unrelenting War: A Study of the Strategy and Techniques of Communist Propaganda and Infiltration*. New York: American-Asian Educational Exchange, 1960.
Lasch, Christopher. *The American Liberals and the Russian Revolution*. New York: Columbia University Press, 1962. Questia. Web.
Lasswell, Harold Dwight, Dorothy Blumenstock. *World Revolutionary Propaganda: A Chicago Study*. Freeport, NY: Books for Libraries Press, 1970.
Latham, Earl. *The Meaning of McCarthyism,* D.C. Heath and Company: Boston, 1965.
Leighton, Marian Kirsch. *Soviet Propaganda as a Foreign Policy Tool*. New York, NY: Freedom House, 1991.
Lenin, V.I. "What is to be done?" *Lenin: Collected Works* Vol. V. http://www.marxists.org/archive/lenin/works/1901/witbd/index.htm
Leo, John, "Identity Group Commencements." *Minding the American Campus*, June 14, 2007, http://www.mindingthecampus.com/originals/2007/06/identity_group_commencements.html.
Leonard, Raymond W. Secret Soldiers of the Revolution: Soviet Military Intelligence, 1918-1933. Westport, CT: Greenwood Press, 1999. Questia. Web.
Levchenko, Stanislav, *On the Wrong Side: My Life in the KGB*. Washington: Pergamon-Brassey, 1988.
Lincoln, W. Bruce. *Red Victory: A History of the Russian Civil War,* Simon and Schuster: New York, 1989.
Lind, Bill. *The Origins of Political Correctness*. 2000, http://www.academia.org/lectures.html.
Louisiana Legislature Joint Committee on Un-American Activities. *Communist Propaganda Infiltration in Louisiana*. Baton Rouge, 1962.
Lumley, Frederick E. The Propaganda Menace. New York: Century, 1933. Questia. Web.
Lunev, Stanislav with Ira Winkler. *Through the Eyes of the Enemy,* Regnery: Washington D.C., 1998.
Lyons, Eugene. The Red Decade: The Stalinist Penetration of America. 1st ed. Indianapolis: Bobbs-Merrill, 1941. Questia. Web.
MacDonnell, Francis. *Insidious Foes: The Axis Fifth Column and the American Home Front*. New York: Oxford University Press, 1995. *Questia*. Web.
Malkin, Morris L. *Return to My Father's House: A Charter Member of the American Communist Party Tells Why He Joined, and Why He Later Left to Fight Communism*. New Rochelle, NY: Arlington House, 1972.
Mamet, David. "Why I Am No Longer a 'Brain-Dead Liberal': An election-season essay", *The Village Voice*, March 11, 2008.
May, Ernest R. and Philip D. Zelikow. The *Kennedy Tapes: Inside the White House During the Cuban Missile Crisis*, Cambridge: Harvard University Press, 1997.
May, Gary. Un-American Activities: The Trials of William Remington. New York: Oxford University Press, 1994. Questia. Web.
McConnell, Malcolm. *Inside Hanoi's Secret Archives: Solving the MIA Mystery,* Simon and Schuster: New York, 1995.

Mccollam, Douglas. "Should This Pulitzer Be Pulled? Seventy Years after a Government-Engineered Famine Killed Millions in Ukraine, a New York Times Correspondent Who Failed to Sound the Alarm Is under Attack." *Columbia Journalism Review* Nov.-Dec. 2003: 43+. Questia. 9 July 2009 <http://www.questia.com/PM.qst?a=o&d=5002060137>.

McDonnel, Sharon. In from the Cold, American Journalism Review. June, 1995.

McKnight, David. *Espionage and the Roots of the Cold War: The Conspiratorial Heritage.* Portland, Oregon and London: Frank Cass Publishers, 2002.

Media Research Center. "The Dan Rather File." http://www.mrc.org/profiles/rather/crisis.asp

Meier, Andrew. *The Lost Spy: An American in Stalin's Secret Service,*W.W. Norton & Company: New York, 2008.

Miller, Donald Lane. *Strategy for Conquest: A Study of Communist Propaganda Techniques.* Washington: Public Affairs Press, 1966.

Miller, E. Ethelbert, "Interview with R. Victoria Arana. " *Foreign Policy in Focus*,. http://www.fpif.org/fpiftxt/5145 (April 15, 2008).

Mishler, Paul C. *Raising Reds: The Young Pioneers, Radical Summer Camps, and Communist Political Culture in the United States.* New York: Columbia University Press, 1999. Questia. Web.

Moley, Raymond. After Seven Years. New York; London: Harper & Brothers Publishers, 1939. Questia. Web.

Moynihan, Daniel Patrick. "Defining Deviancy Down." American Scholar; Winter 1993, Vol. 62 Issue 1, p17, 14p

Nelson Aldrich Rockefeller: A Biographical Chronology, Rockefeller Foundation Archives. http://www.rockarch.org/bio/narchron.pdf

Nelson, Richard Alan. *A Chronology and Glossary of Propaganda in the United States.* Westport, CT: Greenwood Press, 1996. Questia. Web.

Niblo, Peter. *Influence*, Elderberry Press: United States, 2001.

Nollau, Günther. *International Communism and World Revolution: History & Methods.* New York: Frederick A. Praeger, 1961. Questia. Web.

Obama's Pastor's Sermon: 'God Damn America',FOXNews.com, March 14, 2008, http://elections.foxnews.com/2008/03/14/obamas-spiritual-adviser-questioned-us-role-in-spread-of-hiv-sept-11-attacks/

Padover, Saul Kussiel, Harold Dwight Laswell, and Foreign Policy Association. *Psychological Warfare: The Strategy of Soviet Propaganda.* New York: Foreign Policy Association, 1951.

Parks, Ward. *Political Correctness and the Assault on Individuality*, Heritage Lectures, 1993.

Perry, Roland. *Last of the Cold War Spies: The Life of Michael Straight, the Only American in Britain's Cambridge Spy Ring,* Da Capo Press: Cambridge, 2005.

Peterson, Trudy Huskamp. "Access Matters: Four Documents," Conference on the Power of Free Inquiry and Cold War International History, Cold War History Conference, September 25, 1998.

Pfannestiel, Todd J. *Rethinking the Red Scare: The Lusk Committee and New York's Crusade against Radicalism, 1919-1923.* New York: Routledge, 2003. Questia. Web.

Philby, Kim. *My Silent War,* Grove Press: New York, 1968.

Pincher, Chapman. *The Secret Offensive: An Expose of the Soviet Disinformation Campaign*, St. Martin's Press: New York, 1985.

Pinkleton, Bruce. "The Campaign of the Committee on Public Information: Its Contributions to the History and Evolution of Public Relations." *Journal of Public Relations Research* 6.4 (1994): 229-240. Questia. Web.

Pipes, Richard. *The Russian Revolution,* Knopf: New York, 1990.

Poole, Dewitt and C. Humphrey Milford. *The Conduct of Foreign Relations under Modern Democratic Conditions.* New Haven, CT: 1924. Questia. Web.

Prados, John. *Safe for Democracy: The Secret Wars of the CIA,* Ivan R. Dee: Chicago, 2006.

Provost Responds to Faculty Letter Regarding Lacrosse, April 3, 2006, Duke News & Communications (April 21, 2008).
Pryce-Jones, David. "A Man Who Knew His Century: Arthur Koestler, Born 100 Years Ago." *National Review* 12 Sept. 2005: 42. Questia. Web.
Radosh, Ronald, and Allis Radosh. *Red Star over Hollywood: The Film Colony's Long Romance with the Left,* 2006, New York: Encounter Books.
Rauch, Jonathan. *Kindly Inquisitors: The New Attacks on Free Thought,* University of Chicago Press: Chicago, 1993.
Ravitch, Diane. *Left Back: A Century of Battles Over School Reform,* 2001.
Reed, Sally D. *NEA: Propaganda Front of the Radical Left,* 1984.
Remnek, Miranda Beaven. "Russia, 1790–1830." *Press, Politics and the Public Sphere in Europe and North America, 1760-1820.* Ed. Hannah Barker andSimon Burrows. Cambridge, England: Cambridge University Press, 2002. 224-241. Questia. Web.
Revoking Duranty's Pulitzer. *The New American* 17 Nov. 2003: 5. Questia. 9 July 2009 <http://www.questia.com/PM.qst?a=o&d=5002564102>.
Rhodes, Bejamin D. *James P. Goodrich, Indiana's 'Governor Strangelove': A Republican's Infatuation with Soviet Russia,* Associated University Press: Cranbury, NJ, 1996.
Ridenour, Ron. *Backfire: the CIA's Biggest Burn,* Jose Marti Publishing House: Havana, Cuba, 1991.
Riley, Naomi Schaefer. "The Ivory Tower Leans Left, but Why?" *The Wall Street Journal,* February 29, 2008, page W11.
Romerstein, Herbert and Stanislav Levchenko. *The KGB Against the Main Enemy: How the Soviet Intelligence Service Operates Against the United States.* Lexington, MA: Lexington Books, 1989.
Romerstein, Herbert. *Soviet Agents of Influence.* Alexandria, VA: Center for Intelligence Studies, 1991.
Romerstein, Herbert and Eric Breindel. *The Venona Secrets: Exposing Soviet Espionage and America's Traitors,* Regnery Publishing: Washington D.C., 2000.
Rose, Clive. *The Soviet Propaganda Network: A Directory of Organizations Serving Soviet Foreign Policy.* London: Pinter in Association with John Spiers; New York: St Martins Press, 1988.
Russell, William F. "Address at New York Department Convention of the American Legion, Endicott, N. Y., August 12, 1938." *Teachers College Record* Volume 40 Number 2, 1938, p. 89-98. http://www.tcrecord.org. ID Number: 8680, Date Accessed: 7/9/2009 10:15:40 PM
Russell , William F. Teachers College Record Volume 31 Number 5, 1929, p. 395-409 http://www.tcrecord.org. ID Number: 6402, Date Accessed: 7/9/2009 10:36:51 PM
Rutgers University, New Brunswick, NJ Department of Sociology. United States Information Agency Research and Intelligence. *The "Vigilance Drive" and the Cold War: A Case Study in the Technique of Propaganda,* Prepared for the Office of Research and Intelligence, U.S. Information Agency. New Brunswick, NJ: 1954.
Saari, Dawn J. Bixby. " Whose Fruits and Just Desserts?" *American History Through Music, Unit 6: Emergence of Modern America.* http://www.voicesacrosstime.org/come-all-ye/ti/2006/Lesson%20Plans/06SaariFruits.html (April 15, 2008).
Saboteur, Screenplay by Dorothy Parker, Peter Vierter, and Joan Harrison., Directed by Alfred Hitchcock, 1940.
Schlesinger, Arthur M. Jr. *The Disuniting of America,* W.W. Norton & Company: New York, 1992.
Schuman, Frederick Lewis. "American Policy toward Russia since 1917: A Study of Diplomatic History," *International Law & Public Opinion.* London: Martin Lawrence, 1928. Questia. Web.
Shearman, David and Joseph Wayne Smith. *The Climate Change Challenge and the Failure of Democracy,* Praeger, 2007.
Shirave, Eric, Vladislav N. Zubok. *Anti-Americanism in Russia: From Stalin to Putin.* New York: Paul Grave, 2000.

Sibley, Katherine A.S. *Red Spies in America: Stolen Secrets and the Dawn of the Cold War*, University Press of Kansas: Lawrence, Kansas, 2004.
Sims Jr, Robert J, editor. *The Rise of Communism*. San Diego: Greenhaven Press, 2004.
Snyder, Alvin A. *Warriors of Disinformation: American Propaganda, Soviet Lies, and the Winning for the Cold War: An Insider's Account*. New York: Arcade Publishing, 1995.
Solzhenitsyn, Alexander. *One Day in the Life of Ivan Denisovich,* Lancer Books: New York, 1963.
Soviet Union Information Bureau. *Facts, Descriptions, Statistics Facts, Descriptions, Statistics*. Washington, DC: Soviet Union Information Bureau, 1929. Questia. Web.
Spence, Richard B. "Senator William E. Borah: Target of Soviet and Anti-Soviet Intrigue, 1922-1929," *International Journal of Intelligence and CounterIntelligence*, Volume 19, Issue 1, 2005, Pages 134 – 155.
Steinberg, Peter L. *The Great "Red Menace": United States Prosecution of American Communists, 1947-1952*. Westport, CT: Greenwood Press, 1984. Questia. Web.
Strakhovsky, Leonid I. *American Opinion about Russia, 1917-1920*. Toronto: University of Toronto Press, 1961. Questia. Web.
Sudoplatov, Pavel and Anatoli Sudoplatov. *Special Tasks: The Memoirs of an Unwanted Witness,* Little Brown and Company: New York, 1994.
Sykes, Charles J. *Dumbing Down Our Kids: Why American Children Feel Good About Themselves But Can't Read, Write, or Add*, St. Martin's Griffin: 1996.
The Nature of Soviet Propaganda. London: K-H Services, 1952.
Thompson, Ronald, and Paul V. Harper, eds. *The Russia I Believe in: The Memoirs of Samuel N. Harper, 1902-1941*. Chicago: University of Chicago Press, 1945. Questia. Web.
To Close Foreign Bureau; Creel Cables Order to Local Service Under Ernest Poole. Dec 25, 1918, Wednesday Page 17, *New York Times*.
Toppo, Greg. "Teens losing touch with common cultural and historical references," *USA Today*, Feb. 26, 2008.
Trento, Joseph J. *The Secret History of the CIA*. New York: MJF Books, 2001.
Trotsky, Leon. *My Life: An Attempt at an Autobiography*. New York: Charles Scribner's Sons, 1930. Questia. Web.
Tyson, James L. *Target America: The Influence of Communist Propaganda on U.S. Media*. Chicago: Regnery Gateway, 1981.
Varadarajan, Tunku. The Fallout from WikiLeaks' Latest Exposure, *The Daily Beast*, http://www.thedailybeast.com/blogs-and-stories/2010-11-29/wikileaks-documents-fallout-from-diplomatic-cables-exposure/
Wade, Martin J. , and William F. Russell. *The Short Constitution: Elementary Americanism Series, Being a Consideration of the Constitution of the United States, With Particular Reference to the Guaranties of Life, Liberty, and Property Contained Therein, Sometimes Designated The Bill Of Rights*, American Citizen Publishing: Iowa City, 1921. http://www.gutenberg.org/files/34839/34839-h/34839-h.html
Walter, Edward. *The Rise and Fall of Leftist Radicalism in America*. Westport, CT: Praeger, 1992. Questia. Web.
Walters, Cathy Darlene. *Naval Postgraduate School Perceptions Management: Soviet Deception and Its Implications for National Security*. Monterey, CA: National Postgraduate School, 1988.
Warming Inaction: Cannibalism. http://www.mediaresearch.org/cyberalerts/2008/cyb20080402.asp
Weinstein, Allen and Alexander Vassiliev. *The Haunted Wood: Soviet Espionage in America- The Stalin Era*. New York: The Modern Library, 2000.
West, Tom. *Marx and Lenin*. http://www.claremont.org/publications/pubid.4/pub_detail.asp.
Whitney, R. M. *Reds in America: The Present Status of the Revolutionary Movement in the U. S. Based on Documents Seized by the Authorities in the Raid upon the*

Convention of the Communist Party at Bridgman, Mich., Aug. 22, 1922. Boston: Western Islands, 1970. Questia. Web.
Weinstein, Allen and Alexander Vassiliev. *The Haunted Wood: Soviet Espionage in America—the Stalin Era,* The Modern Library: New York, 1999.
Wienir, David, and Marc Berley, eds. *The Diversity Hoax: Law Students Report from Berkeley*. New York: Foundation for Academic Standards & Tradition, 1999.
Wight, Theodore M., Letter to the Editor, re: "Share the Wealth (But Don't Touch My iPod!), *Wall Street Journal*. Thursday, March 20, 2008.
Wilbur, C. Martin, and Julie Lien-Ying How. *Documents on Communism, Nationalism, and Soviet Advisers in China, 1918-1927: Papers Seized in the 1927 Peking Raid*. New York: Columbia University Press, 1956. Questia. Web.
Williams, Albert Rhys. *Through the Russian Revolution*. New York: Boni and Liveright, 1921. Questia. Web.
Wilson, John K. *The Myth of Political Correctness: The Conservative Attack on Higher Education*. Durham, NC: Duke University Press, 1995. Questia. Web.
Wolin, Simon, and Robert M. Slusser, eds. *The Soviet Secret Police*. New York: Frederick A. Praeger, 1957. Questia. Web.
Wynne, Greville. *The Man from Odessa: The Secret Career of a British Agent,* Granada Publishing: New York, 1981.
Zinn, Howard. "America's Blinders." *The Progressive* Apr. 2006: 22+. Questia. Web.

U.S. Government Sources

Boghardt, Thomas. "Operation INFEKTION, Soviet Bloc Intelligence and Its AIDS Disinformation Campaign," *Studies in Intelligence* Vol. 53, No. 4 (December 2009)
Campbell, Major Edward J. Soviet Strategic Intelligence Deception Organizations, DIA, 1991. http://www.globalsecurity.org/intell/library/reports/1991/CEJ.htm. Possible fake.
Committee on Un-American Activities, U.S. House of Representatives. (1951). *The Shameful Years: Thirty Years of Soviet Espionage in the United States*. Washington, D.C.
Communist Activities among Aliens and National Groups: Hearings before the Subcommittee on Immigration and Naturalization of the Committee on the Judiciary, United States Senate, Eighty-First Congress, First Session, on S. 1832, a Bill to Amend the Immigration Act of October 16, 1918, as Amended. Washington, DC: U.S. Govt. Print. Off., 1950. Questia. Web.
Department of State. *The Soviet Union, 1933-1939*. Washington, DC: U.S. Govt. Print. Off., 1952. Questia. Web.
Langbart, David A. "No Little Historic Value: The Records of Department of State Posts in Revolutionary Russia," Prologue (a magazine—of the National archives), Vol. 40, No. 1Spring 2008.
Langbart, David A. Five Months in Petrograd in 1918: Robert W. Imbrie and the US Search for Information in Russia. *Studies in Intelligence*, Vol. 52, No. 1 (March 2008), Web Supplement, https://www.cia.gov/library/center-for-the-study-of-intelligence/csi-publications/csi-studies/studies/vol-52-no-1/pdf-files/(U)%20Langbart-Petrograd-Web%20Supplement.pdf
NARA Record Number: 104-10219-10099
Ricci, Maria L. Affidavit for a Criminal Complaint, Vicky Pelaez and 8 co-conspirators. Southern District of New York, June 25, 2010.
Soviet Active Measures in the "Post-Cold War" Era 1988-1991: A Report Prepared at the Request of the United States House of Representatives Committee on Appropriations by the United States Information Agency; June 1992
Startt, James D. "American Film Propaganda in Revolutionary Russia" *Prologue*, Vol. 30, No. 3, Fall 1998.
U.S. Department of State, *Soviet Influence Activities: A Report on Active Measures and Propaganda*. Washington DC: The Department: Supt. Of Docs., USGPO, 1987.

United States Information Agency Research and Reference Service. *Communist Propaganda Activities*. Washington, DC: 1962.
United States Information Agency. *Communist Propaganda, A Factbook 1957-1958*. Washington DC: The Agency, 1958.
United States Subversive Activities Control Board. *Annual Report of the Subversive Activities Control Board*. Washington DC: USGPO, 1951.
Whaley, Barton. *Biographical Index of Soviet Intelligence Personnel*, Appendix C, Soviet Clandestine Communications Nets. Behavioral Sciences Division, AFOSR, SLRB, 1970. http://www.dtic.mil/cgi-bin/GetTRDoc?Location=U2&doc=GetTRDoc.pdf&AD=AD0705665
William H. Martin, A Former US Citizen and Member of the National Security Agency, Openly Identified Himself as One of the Two Americans who Defected to the USSR in July 1960. CIA memorandum on William Martin, http://www.maryferrell.org/mffweb/archive/viewer/showDoc.do?docId=48404&relPageId=2 viewed 8 feb 2011.

13789964R00222

Printed in Poland
by Amazon Fulfillment
Poland Sp. z o.o., Wrocław